KONRAD ADENAUER

TERENCE PRITTIE

KONRAD ADENAUER

1876-1967

COWLES BOOK COMPANY
A subsidiary of Henry Regnery Company

Library of Congress Catalog Card Number: 70-163245

Cowles Book Company, Inc.
A subsidiary of Henry Regnery Company
114 West Illinois Street, Chicago, Illinois 60610

Printed and manufactured in Great Britain by
Richard Clay (The Chaucer Press), Ltd.,
Bungay, Suffolk

Contents

List of Illustrations

*For permission to reproduce photographs, the
publishers wish to thank the following:
Bavaria-Verlag, Munich; Black Star Publishing
Co. Ltd, London; Camera Press Ltd, London;
"The Daily Express", London; Foliac, Bonn;
Imperial War Museum, London; IN-BILD, Bonn;
Keystone GmbH, Munich; Landesbildstelle,
Berlin; Presse und Informationsamt der
Bundesregierung, Bonn; Süddeutscher Verlag,
Munich; Ullstein Bilderdienst, Berlin.*

In writing this life of Konrad Adenauer, Chancellor of the Federal German Republic from 1949 to 1963, I am seeking only to meet a temporary need. The Chancellor's private papers are the property of the State, in so far as they relate to the business of state, and are not likely to be released for publication for years – probably many years – to come. In writing this book I have been much helped by the Federal Press Office (*Bundespresseamt*), the Cologne City Archives (*Stadt-Archiv*), the Press Office of the Christian Democratic Union, the Library of the Federal Parliament (*Bundestag*), the German Embassy in London and the German Institute in London.

I would like to thank four members of Konrad Adenauer's family for their help. They are Dr. Max Adenauer, Dr. Paul Adenauer, Frau Ria Reiners and Frau Libeth Werhahn. In addition, the following have given me valuable help in greater or lesser degree:

H. G. Alexander, Lord Annan, Herr Felix von Eckardt, Professor Dr. Ludwig Erhard, Hans-Werner Graf Finck von Finckenstein, Dr. Hans Globke, Professor Dr. Walter Hallstein, Dr. Heinrich Krone, Herr Ernst Lemmer, Prinz Hubertus zu Loewenstein, The Earl of Longford, Mr. John McCloy, Dr. Erich Mende, Mr. James O'Donnell, Mr. John Paice, Mr. Lance Pope, Dr. Hermann Pünder, Herr Will Rasner, Lord Robertson, Herr Georg Schröder, Dr. Gerhard Schröder, Dr. Leo Schwering, Sir Christopher Steel, Herr Herbert Sulzbach, Herr Weber (Dr. Adenauer's interpreter) and Dr. Erwin Wickert.

I have drawn, but I hope not unduly, on my own reports for the *Manchester Guardian*. As this newspaper's correspondent in Germany from October 1946 to June 1963, I covered all but the last four months of what has come to be known conventionally as the 'Adenauer Era'.

Finally, I would like to add my special thanks to Lord and Lady St. Oswald, whose generous hospitality has made it possible for me to finish this book in ideal surroundings.

T. C. F. PRITTIE

Pelayo, Provincia de Cadiz November 1970

Foreword

Despite the outward changes in Germany and in Europe we are still too close to the Adenauer era to expect 'the' definitive biography. There are many archives to be opened and not a few personal accounts to be written. More light will be thrown on various aspects of his astonishing career-in-old-age and that career and his achievements may look different from a farther distance.

Still, it is high time that we had a balanced and documented account and one, moreover, which has the benefit of a great mass of firsthand news and views from the already shrinking company of people who knew the Chancellor well and were directly concerned in the same events as he. This is a fund which will be inaccessible to the historian of say 2000, or even 1990. You cannot put questions to memoirs and there are not many that would stand up well to cross-examination.

Terence Prittie must have asked a number of pertinent questions, for he has obviously received some frank answers – not least because in the years of his final decline the grand old man forfeited a good deal of the loyalty with which his collaborators in the great period surrounded him.

Naturally it is Adenauer's relations with the British which have principally interested me. The question will always be asked whether he found us fundamentally unsympathetic from the start, whether he was permanently alienated by Brigadier Barraclough, when dismissed from his post of Mayor of Cologne, or whether, as I believe, and I saw him repeatedly over the whole period of his chancellorship, he only settled into petrified hostility to us when he had lost his touch and was blindly trailing de Gaulle.

The argument about his dismissal by the Brigadier will probably never be completely settled. The really regrettable part of the incident was the denial of visits to his wife and that was unpardonable. The rest was the rough of military government and who can say that ours in those early months compared too badly with other occupations – notably German? On the other hand, the corollary which Adenauer drew from the Military Government's action, namely that it was an 'instrument of the Labour party in sponsoring the German Social Democrats' requires some comment. I am quite sure in my own mind that the Control Commission which, as Col. Noel Annan's intervention showed, was beginning to exert authority in these matters, received no instructions of this kind whatsoever. Indeed we received very little guidance of *any* kind. Politics under the SHAEF direction were to be put to sleep for an indefinite period and London was interested in, if anything, administration affairs such as 'breaking up the Junker's Estates'.

In fact there were no Junkers in the British Zone and the Russians had already done the job in the east.

Nevertheless there is an interesting background to Adenauer's belief. While politics could be ignored for a while in the British Zone, in Berlin they were already on the boil. The Russians had been there nearly three months before we occupied our sector and when we did so we found that they had fathered fully-fledged political parties including KPD (Communist), SPD (Socialist) and CDU (Christian Democratic). By early in 1946 it was clear that under heavy Soviet pressure the SPD would be swallowed by the KPD in the *Sozialistische Einheitspartei*, 'SED', unless something was done.

The Political Division of which I was the Chief was closely in touch with the Intelligence unit in Berlin which contained a number of active and enterprising young officers. All of us felt that this takeover would be a disaster not only in Berlin but for the Western Zones as well; but we were precluded by our Whitehall direction from intervening. In the event we used our young Intelligence friends (who would soon be demobilized and could be disowned) to encourage the rank and file of the SPD and instruct them in the, to them, mysterious technique of forming a breakaway party.

SPD feeling was strong and as always in Berlin remarkably courageous. At the Congress called *in the Soviet Sector* to consummate the union of the two parties, Franz Neumann stood up among bristling Soviet bayonets and refused. He received overwhelming support and the project was dead. I should say here that I did not feel able to tell General Robertson about our part in this until many years later. On the other hand General Ray Barker, the U.S. Commandant in Berlin, took advantage of General Clay's absence to issue a statement soundly condemning the party union in evangelical terms. This had a powerful effect on the issue. As far as I know Schumacher had nothing to do with this early but crucial development.

Nevertheless the relevance of all this to him and to Adenauer is not far to seek. As soon as we could, the Political Division began to take such steps as were open to us in the British Zone to build up the SPD, and in particular Schumacher, against the Communists who were very strong in the Ruhr – *not* against the CDU. There was not a great deal we could do. We had no funds to give them but we were allowed to help with transport and so on. In this respect the CDU, which had already begun to gather support from Industry, could much more easily look after itself. On the other hand when we began to handle party newspapers we were as scrupulously fair as we could be. Where the Military Government could not intervene was in regard to fraternal contacts between the SPD and the Labour Party. There were quite a few of these but they were a party matter beyond our control. I think Adenauer would have had a case if he had blamed the Conservative Party for their total disinterest in the CDU.

Adenauer's attitude to the British British Occupying Power was not, I think, as negative during the period of Military Government as it may have seemed to Adenauer when he came to write his memoirs. Certainly, as Terence Prittie says, he came to have real trust in General Robertson. Even I was myself considerably in his confidence because he was a friend of my father-in-law, who was Military Governor of Cologne after the First World War. Our personal relations remained good all through the tedious debates over the Basic Law and we were in a sense allies over the siting of the Federal Capital. By totally evacuating Bonn we gave it a crucial advantage over Frankfurt where the Americans clung to the I.G. Farben complex of buildings. Thus when the Federal Government really began to function in September 1949 we were on good terms with the new Chancellor, who had been a passionate advocate of Bonn, and this state of affairs was maintained all through the first year at Bonn.

Almost immediately we were confronted by the dismantling problem. Terence Prittie rightly points to the importance of the Petersberg Protocol. It would be going too far to ascribe the American intervention as an important factor in this, but it was we, the British, who bore the brunt of the trouble this caused because it all happened in one Zone; but both we and the Americans had been hamstrung by our reparation obligations to the Russians. The Blockade of Berlin morally cancelled those obligations but the German agitation had been so bitter and wrongheaded that simply to call off the work of dismantling would have been an unacceptable abdication.

It fell to us therefore to get ourselves out of our dilemma, and the Protocol with its contractual basis, which obliged the Chancellor to join the highly unpopular Ruhr Control Authority, was our answer. Though Adenauer has drawn a rather opaque veil over this negotiation it was in fact a straight British–German deal on equal terms – a package. But it was also a turning point and for years afterwards Adenauer used to say with appreciation that he had made his first 'treaty' with us. It is regrettable that his memory of the actual circumstances was afterwards clouded by other considerations.

Next came rearmament. Adenauer played with this crucial question for several months before he made up his mind. When he did so, as Terence Prittie records, he came to General Robertson with his proposal for 100,000 militarized police. But later he went further and asked us to recommend a German general to be his defence adviser! The fact that our nominee soon fell from grace and was dismissed does not alter the fact that Adenauer seems then to have had more confidence in British advice and discretion than any other.

I left Germany at the end of 1950 and went to Washington but in mid-1953 I became British Permanent Representative on the NATO Council in Paris and was thus again involved at once in the German rearmament question. There is no doubt that Adenauer was sold on the European Army, but no genuine military experts thought it would work.

All the same, when the crash came in 1954 it was only the British who had a plan ready and a plan moreover which enhanced German status far beyond the previous prospect. Had the European Army plan gone through, Germany would not have been a member of NATO. She would have been represented on the Council by France as President of the EDC. As it was, she attained, thanks to our pledge to keep four divisions permanently in Europe, her present effectively independent status. Adenauer fully appreciated this and used to describe with relish Eden's dramatic foiling of Mendès-France at the Nine Power Conference in Lancaster House. Not long afterwards in the Suez Crisis he showed his appreciation. When the NATO Council under American leadership looked like condemning the Anglo-French action it was his representative, Herbert Blankenhorn, who said: 'The Chancellor does not understand. He thought this was an alliance in which we gave each other wanted support.'

I returned to Bonn in 1957 and received a warm welcome, but I think it was our self-exclusion in that year from the Treaty of Rome which opened the Chancellor's mind to de Gaulle's insinuations a year later that we did not belong to Europe. He had attained in only eight years the once seemingly inaccessible goal of independence – not to speak of prosperity – and it was natural that he should set his sights on some other ideal. That ideal was of course a Europe in which Germany could sublimate all the things that he regretted about her past. Europe now meant, more than ever before, his long-sought *rapprochement* with France and here the prospects were at last a little brighter. The Saar was out of the way and French fears of German rearmament had been stilled by our commitment to the Brussels Treaty. At the same time France was in ferment and was tearing herself to pieces over Algeria.

Adenauer's careful contacts with the MRP and even his successful negotiations with Mendès-France hardly looked like bearing long-term fruit. In the summer of 1958 however the General arrived and in September Adenauer went to see him at Colombey. I saw Adenauer immediately on his return and found him deeply depressed. 'This is a military dictatorship,' he said, 'it is terrible.' I did my best to comfort him, pointing out that it could have been much worse, but he was really inconsolable.

Yet, two months later at Bad Kreuznach the picture was totally reversed. We may never know the full story unless Herbert Blankenhorn has some light to shed, which is probable. My own opinion is that initially it was de Gaulle who changed. Perhaps in September, confronting for the first time this redoubtable old man who now represented the hereditary Germany, he played it as cool as he most certainly could and gave nothing away. In the interval to November he had evolved his policy – not to fight Europe and Germany but use them to attain his own objectives.

Perhaps he turned on the charm and opened up visions of a Catholic traditional world cleared of Anglo-Saxons and Prussians. But whatever else he did he certainly began his campaign to undermine Adenauer's confidence in the British Government by warnings of our breakdowns and unreliability in face of Khrushchev's threat to Berlin. Macmillan's Moscow visit, the success of which he never understood or admitted, confirmed his suspicions for good. Thereafter, despite the warnings of some who had been his closest supporters, he fell increasingly under the General's influence and in the process seemed to lose more and more the sure touch in home affairs as well. Though he survived and laughed off the astonishing affair of his candidature for the Presidency he was not the same. Who can imagine him in his prime sacrificing the faithful Brentano for a mess of pottage or backing Strauss (whom he despised) in the 'Spiegel' Affair?

De Gaulle's mysterious ascendancy, for it was no less, was I think the central factor in Adenauer's life from the date of that second meeting until his death. It is not too difficult to explain: only the degree of Adenauer's subservience – he who was so independent and steadfast in all things – is surprising. Of course there was a natural affinity. Two elderly, austere, dominating characters, each deeply conscious of a similar religious and historical background, were bound to feel closer to each other in many ways than to the far younger men by whom they were surrounded. In lofty calm they pursued their apparently common ideal yet they did not mean the same thing. Adenauer hoped he was burying German nationalism for ever. The General was just building France on a grander scale.

This said, there is no doubt of the great things that Adenauer achieved in the process. The Treaty with its youth exchanges and so on is consolidating a vastly improved Franco-German relationship. When one thinks of the years of French foot-dragging on Germany after the war and, more personally, of François Poncet's studied asperities at High Commission meetings while British and Americans fidgeted with embarrassment, this is indeed a monument. But it was achieved at the price of excluding Britain from Europe. Less than a week, if I remember, after Mr. Heath and Gerhard Schröder had been over the entire negotiation at Chequers and concluded that the prize was there for the taking, de Gaulle launched his veto. The *Bundestag* had voted unanimously for British entry and he could not have done it except with the assurance of Adenauer's support. In fact the Chancellor honoured his bond and signed the Franco-German Treaty, but as Terence Prittie's chronicle shows he was now far on the way downhill.

It is sad that he who stood so firmly on the side of the Western Allies during the crucial Fifties should have parted company with our contingent, one of the most faithful, at the last. But it must not obscure our gratitude for his main contribution. If anyone had been granted in 1945 a vision of West Germany as she is today he would have been incredulous. No one then could have hoped for the half of what has been attained not only economically but morally and politically. It happened under Adenauer, and that, I think, will always be the last word about him.

Sir Christopher Steel, GCMG, MVO

Political adviser to Commander-in-Chief, Germany, 1947
Deputy High Commissioner, 1949
HM *Ambassador to Bonn, 1957–63*

1 Four Germanies

Konrad Adenauer was born on January 5, 1876, in the Rhineland city of Cologne. He died on April 19, 1967, at his home in Rhöndorf, only a relatively few miles from his birthplace. His life spanned almost a century, a century as tumultuous and tragic as any in German history.

His life spanned, also, four distinct eras of German history. He was born into the *Kaiserreich*, the German Empire created after the tremendous military victories of the 1870 Franco-Prussian War. He was already middle-aged when the last Emperor, William II, fled to Holland at the end of the First World War. The second era of German history, that of the Weimar Republic, lasted only fourteen years, from 1919 to 1933. The third, Nazi Era, was even shorter, twelve years up to the end of the Second World War in 1945. Finally, there were the first two post-war decades of a Germany divided into two Republics, of the West and Bonn and the East and Berlin. When this fourth era began, Adenauer was already an old man.

These four eras are so strikingly different from one another that one can talk of 'four Germanies'. Each of them had totally different primary characteristics. Living through the lot, Adenauer had to adapt himself to three cycles of revolutionary change. Three times the world in which he lived was swept out of existence. The third time that this happened he emerged as the one great German statesman of this century, beginning a new career at the age of over seventy. He became West Germany's Chancellor at 73. He was then less than two years younger than the only great German statesman of the nineteenth century, Bismarck, when the latter's political career ended. Here is an authentic element of romance.

What were the salient characteristics of the four Germanies in which Adenauer passed his long life? First, the *Kaiserreich*.

The Germany into which Adenauer was born was powerful, prosperous and disciplined. It was dominated by 'the cold but living hand of Prussia, the kingdom which dips one wing of the eagle in the Niemen and the other in the Rhine.'[1] Prussia, the 'state of soldiers and officials', had unified Germany in 1871, five years before Adenauer was born, by successive military victories over Denmark, Austria and France. States like Bavaria and Wurtemberg became valuable component parts of the new, unified

1 ....*Evolution of Prussia*, J. A. R. Marriott, p. 435.

Germany, but they could not balance the dominant power of Prussia, with nearly two-thirds of Germany's total population, a military machine of matchless efficiency and, in the Ruhr, the industrial heart of Western Europe.

The Hohenzollern dynasty had by then held the throne of Prussia for two centuries, but the newly-united German State was something of a parvenu in Western Europe. Prussia had been traditionally regarded as an East European power, a land of swamps and forests which had gained the Rhineland and a foothold in Western Europe largely as a result of Marshal Gebhardt Blücher's providential appearance on the battlefield of Waterloo. Like her political unification, Germany's industrialization came late in the day. Not until the beginning of this century did Germany become a maritime power.

But the *Kaiserreich* must have been in many ways a wonderful place in which to live. It was a hive of enthusiasm and energy, backed, at least on the surface, by tremendous self-confidence and optimism. The late but well-ordered industrial revolution led to a huge explosion of economic activity, which sent Germany surging past her rivals in a sustained sprint. Overseas trade began to flourish, after the old Hanseatic ports of Hamburg and Bremen joined the Reich. In the 1880s, when Adenauer was still not 10 years old, a German colonial empire began to come into being.

Bismarck was building up a system of alliances – the Triple Alliance of 1882 with Austria and Italy and the Reinsurance Treaty with Russia of 1884 – which seemed to guarantee what was already the strongest military power in Europe from any danger of attack from east or south and from the gnawing, traditional dread of encirclement in the heart of Europe. In 1878 Bismarck won his greatest prestige victory by acting as 'honest broker' to secure European peace at the Congress of Berlin. The *Kaiserreich* became then what the Germans call *hoffähig* – accepted at court, by the older European powers.

'Prussia,' according to one historian, 'imposed her institutions, her civil service, her standard of values and of work, her ideals on non-Prussian Germany.'[2] Prussia stood for the strength and authority of the State – as early as 1801 Georg Friedrich Wilhelm Hegel defined his theory of the 'State as power'. But the State was itself founded on traditional 'Prussian virtues' – self-discipline, devotion to duty, piety, thrift, courage and absolute and undeviating loyalty. It was these qualities, as much as military expertise, which made Prussia's armies the most formidable since the legions of Rome. It was these qualities which, in theory, were to be transmitted to the rest of the German nation. It was these qualities, too, which

2............*Evolution of Prussia*, J. A. R. Marriott, p. 411.

inspired the average German of that era with boundless pride in the Reich, and with an immense sense of solidarity. Wilhelm Kleefeld was right when he wrote,

> 'Wir alle stehen wie ein Mann
> Für Kaiser und für Reich.'
> ('We stand together, as one man, for Emperor and Reich.')

During the *Kaiserreich*, up to the outbreak of the First World War, Germans lived in increasing material comfort and in a mood of national pride which sometimes bordered on arrogance. Arrogance was best exemplified in the posturings of Kaiser Wilhelm II, imagining himself as the all-powerful 'All-Highest' but likened by one of his advisers, Count Alfred von Waldersee, to 'a child who screams to keep up his courage'. National arrogance was supplemented by national myopia; the German nation dealt in day-dreams, in misty but grandiose concepts like *Schicksal* and *Verhängnis* – barely translatable as 'fate' and 'destiny'. This made the experience of military defeat and revolution in 1918 all the more shattering and traumatic. In retrospect it is easy to see why the 1918–33 Weimar Republic failed. It was saddled with what seemed the monstrously unjust (and *was* the undeniably tough) Treaty of Versailles, and with the odium of war-guilt which the great bulk of the German people honestly could not accept. It was asked to pay unrealistically large sums as war-debts and to surrender a colonial empire which had scarcely been a factor in the European war. The fall of the House of Hohenzollern[3] contributed to the failure of Germany's first experiment in truly democratic government; the aristocracy and a considerable section of the middle class never accepted the Republic. To them, it was never 'our' Germany but a régime recognizing defeat and betraying the national heritage. In reality, it was the House of Hohenzollern which betrayed Germany. The Kaiser deserted his country and people, and three of his sons later joined the Nazi Party.

The outstanding characteristic of the era of the Weimar Republic was the political and economic anarchy with which it tried to compete. It may be that the European industrial revolution brought a 'spiritual nihilism'[4] in its wake. Certainly, military defeat and a degree of degradation in the eyes of the civilized world flung the Germans back on themselves and developed a searing xenophobia. German intellectuals offered no crumb of comfort, and it is painful to find such a man as Thomas Mann writing in 1918, 'Away with the foreign and repulsive slogan "democratic". The mechanical democratic institutions of the West will never take root here.'

In the event, the first five years of the Weimar Republic produced

3............*The Soldier Kings*, Walter Henry Nelson, Chapter 18.
4............*The Secret War against Hitler*, Fabian von Schlabrendorff, p. 26.

serious internal disturbances, which aroused very little interest in the outside world. There was a separatist movement in the Rhineland, Communist risings in various parts of the country, right-wing *Putsches* – all of them resulting in bitterness and bloodshed. There was hunger and unemployment, followed by the major monetary crisis of the inflation of the currency, and the collapse of the Mark. When the currency crisis was mastered, there was only a sadly short 'springtime' of the Republic, before it was sent reeling under the impact of the World Financial Crisis. From then, 1929, until the Nazi seizure of power four years later, democratic government was slowly dying. The multiplication of political parties led to the disintegration of the political centre, and to the growth of the extremist Nazi and Communist parties. Sectionalism helped to undermine the parties of the centre, with Bavarians and Rhinelanders concerned with local interests and the Prussian landed class relying on the German Nationalist Party. Leading democratic politicians were assassinated for being *Erfüllungspolitiker* who tried to implement and fulfil the unpopular Treaty of Versailles. Street fighting became endemic in the last years of the Republic. Law and order, as well as government, was breaking down.

The last democratic Chancellor of the Weimar Republic, Heinrich Brüning, claimed ever afterwards that when his Government fell in 1932, it was only 'one hundred metres away from its goal'. Measures were being taken to combat unemployment. Debts agreements were mitigating the severity of the reparations clauses of the Treaty of Versailles. Admission into the League of Nations meant that Germany was being re-accepted into the comity of civilized peoples. All this progress failed to keep pace with the disintegration of the democratic political parties. Whereas a socialist ex-saddler, Friedrich Ebert, had as President from 1919 to 1925 tried to breathe life into the Republic, Paul August von Hindenburg, a dyed-in-the-wool Conservative without a single constructive political thought in his head, presided inanimately over its death-throes. The Presidency had too much power, the Government too little.

The Weimar Republic was created out of revolution, which was bloody in many parts of Germany. The Nazi Revolution of 1933 was almost bloodless, for the seizure of total power by Adolf Hitler brought street-fighting to an end and for the next ten years there was no sign of open resistance to the régime. The secret of Hitler's success lay in his exploitation of the German people's sense of injustice following the settlement after the First World War and its resulting frustrations, fears and latent xenophobia. The Weimar régime had been utterly lacking in popular appeal and magnetism. Hitler set out to give his Government *Glanz*, the glitter and display which Germans had known under the *Kaiserreich* and which they continued to crave. Back came the flags, the military bands with their stirring marches, the uniforms, the torchlight processions. Back came the jingoistic slogans and cracker-mottoes, the rabble-rousing war-cries. Germany's enemies were restored to a people who needed scape-goats – the Jews, the Marxists, the 'decadent' Western democracies, the Bolshevik Soviet Union. If one had to pick out a single characteristic of the Nazi 'New Order', it would not be efficiency, military strength or even physical repression, but the deliberate exploitation and canalization of human hatred.

The end of the Nazi Era happened so recently that it requires no description here. What Fabian von Schlabrendorff described as 'a combination of terror and habit' led to the German people accepting Nazism with such docility.[5] All those Germans who have condemned the Allied decision to enforce unconditional surrender on their country ignore the vice-like grip which the Nazis applied. It took total defeat and total occupation to uproot and destroy Nazism. More efficacious than revolution was the cold compress of Allied post-1945 administration. It was the very completeness of the German catastrophe which produced the first seeds of hope for the Germany of the future.

Yet its completeness must have seemed horrific to a man like Adenauer, already in his seventieth year, who had seen democracy fail once before and whose innate distrust of his fellow-Germans had been born out of bitter experience. Germany's cities were in ruins and German citizens in a state of stupor. The outstanding feature of the nation's life was its very real impotence. For the first time for nearly a hundred years Germany was no longer a Great Power. Its kernel, Prussia, had ceased to exist altogether, and the German people was rent asunder by the Iron Curtain frontier running between the power-blocs of East and West and through the middle of their land. Had one been asked to hazard a guess during the first two to three years after the Second World War, one would have said that full-scale Allied military occupation would have to go on for at least twenty years, that democratic government would have to be introduced by carefully measured-out stages, and that a real new start would only be possible when a whole generation of Germans – who had surrendered to Nazism even when they did not actively support it – had died out.

The contrast between the pre-1914 Germany in which Adenauer grew up, and the post-1945 Germany in which it devolved upon him to lead the German nation, or the larger part of it, could scarcely have been greater. He grew up in an aura of stability and strength; in 1945 he found himself in a community which no longer knew what to believe, or even what it wanted to believe. It took a man of Adenauer's balanced and incisive

5............*The Secret War against Hitler*, Fabian von Schlabrendorff, p. 29.

intellect to realize that the post-1945 Germany was fertile ground for a completely new political start. Democracy was helped to grow roots under the protection of the democratic Western Powers; had they not been in absolute control of the country, it would have been terribly difficult for a second democratic experiment to succeed. All the odds are that it would have fallen prey to a new resentment and frustration, a sickly infant doomed to a premature death.

Writing in 1930, the novelist Ernst von Salomon had this to say: 'If there is a power whose destruction it is our task to accomplish by any means, it is the West and the German class that has allowed itself to be alienated by it.'[6] There was nothing new about this streak of nihilism. Sixty years earlier the philosopher Friedrich Nietzsche described the need to destroy anything that is 'toppling' and claimed that 'everything', in his own day, was 'toppling and decaying'; while Hitler, in the splenetic fury caused by knowledge that the war was lost, called down total destruction on his country and people. Would a significant proportion of the German nation – without the unavoidable necessity of conforming to Allied ruling and planning – have capitulated once again to this lemming-like urge towards self-destruction? There was, at least, a strong possibility of this happening. For the elite of the German opposition to Hitler had been systematically put to death. What was left was mainly an adult population of ex-Nazis and non-Nazis, who had settled down to survive. All too many myths have been propagated in twentieth-century Germany. The myth that German 'democrats' should have been allowed, after the Second World War, to take over such tasks as adjudicating war-crimes, eliminating Nazism and creating a democratic German community from scratch, is one which should not be encouraged. Allied administration of post-1945 Germany was often muddled and inept; but it gave Germans time to think.

What has been achieved in post-1945 Western Germany, comprising more than three-quarters of the divided German nation, will be an integral part of the story of Konrad Adenauer. That part, the most important part, of this story will show that Adenauer rejected nihilism and such nonsense with all his heart. From the beginning of this century until 1945 experiences crowded in on the German people, a nightmare procession of circumstances which moved faster and faster, applauded only by those disciples of the creeds of historical inevitability and immutable force. Somewhere, at some time, a halt had to be called and reason had to be invoked. This is where Adenauer comes into the picture.

6............*The Mind of Germany*, Hans Kohn, p. 341.

2 The Making of a Mayor

The circumstances of Konrad Adenauer's early life were simple, even humble. His family lived in a small, inelegant house in the Balduinstrasse in Cologne. If not poverty-stricken, the family was certainly poor. His parents were Roman Catholic, and it was perhaps fortunate that there were no more than four children, with two elder brothers and a younger sister. Even so, life was both hard and earnest.

It was also undocumented, and the only authentic account of it came from Konrad Adenauer himself, when Paul Weymar wrote his 'official' biography in 1956.[1] According to his account, a part of the house which had a ground floor and two storeys above, was let to sub-tenants. The three Adenauer sons slept in a single room, and Konrad had to share a bed with his brother Hans up to the age of 17. The house's sole asset from the children's point of view was a small garden at the back, where they were given tiny plots of their own. Konrad recalled planting flowers and radishes, but the radishes died when he pulled them out of the ground to see how they were doing.[2]

His father, also Konrad, seems to have been a man of few words and even fewer ideas. One of the two remarks of his recorded by his son was when his radishes died – 'One must be patient and give things time to grow.' The other was when Konrad junior tried to cross pansies and geraniums, and so create a 'creeping pansy'. This was, 'One must never try to interfere with the work of God.' Konrad senior had been brought up in his father's bakery in Bonn, had worked hard but unremuneratively as a farmhand and in a brick works and had finally joined the Prussian Army. Curiously, this was regarded at the time as a 'back-door' to the civil service, but he joined a short time before the outbreak of the Austro-Prussian War of 1866. He found himself – and this was no part of his plans – on the bloody battlefield of Koeniggrätz (Sadowa) on July 3, 1866.

Thirty thousand men died before the Prussian army won what turned out to be the decisive victory of the 'Six Weeks War'. Konrad senior, according to his son's version, was literally buried beneath a heap of corpses in the bitter defensive action which took place in the early stages of the battle, before the Crown Prince's forces arrived to reinforce the out-

1 ....*Konrad Adenauer*, Paul Weymar (English Edition), London, 1957.
2............*Konrad Adenauer*, Paul Weymar (English Edition), London, 1957, p. 17.

numbered Prussians. According, once again, to his son, he was awarded a commission as an officer on the same day, as a reward for his gallantry – a most unusual proceeding in the caste-conscious Prussian Army.[3] But he was not to enjoy his commission for long. Back from the wars, he met the daughter of a bank-clerk, Helene Scharfenberg. He wanted to marry her. Prussian regulations, which must have been severely stretched to allow him a commission at all, laid down that the parents of the bride of an officer had to provide an 'adequate' dowry. For the officer and his wife would have to live in suitable state, entertain a little, wear the right clothes. Adenauer senior left the army of his own accord, married and became a clerk of the District Court, first for a short time in the town of Kleve, then in Cologne. At least he had found his back-door into state service.

His taciturnity may have been partly the result of his gory experience at Koeniggrätz and of the premature ending of his military career. Pictures of him show a man with a hard, level gaze, a neat beard and a flowing moustache which does not conceal the fact that his mouth was full and surprisingly sensual. One writes 'surprisingly', because he preached the virtues of an almost monastic discipline – honesty, duty, industry, thrift and self-control. If there were any sensuality in his make-up, his family were not intended to know about it. He was a man of short temper, who did not welcome questions of any kind.

His wife Helene may well have had much more character. The pity of it is that nobody will ever know. She kept no diary, and her children never committed any interesting thought about her to paper. She had a fine, high forehead and the high cheekbones which were perhaps the most distinctive feature of the face of her third son, Konrad.[4] He, Konrad, recalled only that she worked very hard, took in needlework and sewed oil-cloth kitchen-aprons to help make both ends meet. Konrad Adenauer was, at the age of five, pulling out tacking threads and earning his very first pocket-money – one pfennig per apron. From the few pictures which have survived, one can guess that Helene Adenauer transmitted one tremendously important characteristic to her children. This was what the Germans call *Ausdauer*, staying-power. She had it; her husband, although of peasant-stock, did not.

Konrad senior's salary, in the 1880s and 1890s, was around 300 Marks a month. It was not a bad salary by any means. In 1970 terms it may have been worth up to £200 or $500. But Konrad senior must have had an ingrained ambition, for his family if no longer for himself. He wanted its members to 'better' themselves. He sent all his four children to secondary school, after they had completed the statutory eight to nine years primary

3............*Konrad Adenauer*, Paul Weymar (English Edition), London, 1957, p. 9.
4............*Konrad Adenauer*, Georg Schröder, p. 50.

Konrad Adenauer at his first Communion

The young law graduate, 1900

With members of his

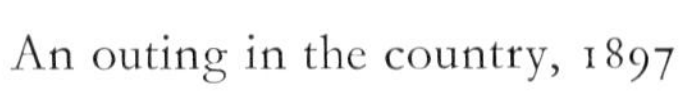

An outing in the country, 1897

The junior barrister

Adenauer and his fiancée Emma Weyer, later his first wife.

education. He sent all his three sons to a university. He planned this in advance. This meant sacrifices for everyone. The children did odd jobs, to earn pocket-money, and went without meat on Sunday – eating, at their own request, only potatoes and salt. The sacrifice of their meat-course enabled their small savings to be channelled into a 'Christmas pool' of money used to buy candles and a Christmas tree.

Konrad was sent to the 'Apostel Gymnasium' in Cologne, a secondary school where he was chiefly noted for his great height. Pictures of the early teenage Adenauer show a child with an invariably serious face, and sometimes a haughty expression. But then he was posing for the camera. At the Apostel Gymnasium one classmate – his name was Lohmer – remembered Konrad as having as much sense of mischief as the others, and his work as being 'not nearly as brilliant as I had been led to believe'.[5] He was, apparently, always ready to help classmates with their work, and let them 'look-over' his exercise-book. He was a very fast reader. In his own view, he was a good pupil, who enjoyed the business of learning. He probably was; little Lohmer's father, who happened to be the Adenauers' family doctor, remembered years later that he was really good at Latin and German.[6] A parent of a boy's friend does not usually remember anything like that.

When Konrad junior reached the age of 18 there was too little money for him to be sent to a university. One senses the hideous embarrassment of his father, and his own disappointment. But there seemed nothing for it but to earn a living, and on April 1, 1894, he started work with the Cologne banking firm of Seligmann. It was dreary work into the bargain – most of his time was spent locking and unlocking strong-boxes, carrying ledgers, running errands and pouring out cups of coffee for the senior clerks. He himself later recalled that he wrote to a Cologne newspaper, asking how long it took to work one's way up in a bank, and received an answer which was 'not encouraging'. The answer was that for a young man without money or influence it probably took a lifetime.

His father sensed his depression, although even at this early age Konrad Adenauer was not a person to complain of hardship. Konrad senior applied to a Cologne scholarship foundation, the Krämer Fund, for a grant for his son. He got it, managed to scrape a little together from his slender resources, and sent his son to Freiburg University. It was the beginning of six years at different universities – Germans habitually spent, and still spend longer at the university than their American, British or French counterparts. Konrad junior studied the law, then as now an over-crowded profession, but one which was a convenient stepping-stone to a

5............*Konrad Adenauer*, Paul Weymar, p. 21.
6............*Konrad Adenauer*, Paul Weymar, p. 22.

career in government service. Konrad's own ambition, at this stage of his life, was to pass his examinations and open a practice in a small country town. He had a hankering for fields and forests, and had retained his early love of flowers. The Eifel hills in the Southern Rhineland may have held a vague sentimental attraction for him; in the middle of them is the village of Adenau, and it is quite possible that it was the origin of his family's name.

His years at the university seem to have been uneventful. One of his biographers [7] thinks this was because he was a prig and introvert, making no real friends and showing no signs of personality. He probably was a late developer. But his run-of-the-mill existence as a student was almost certainly due to two other factors. He was very poor, managing on 90 Marks a month, out of which he had to pay university fees and save something for holidays. He was also not very strong physically. When he reached the age of 20 his university studies should have been interrupted by military service; but the army refused him because of a weak chest and weak lungs.[8]

At Freiburg he did make one close friend. This was Raimund Schlüter, like him a Roman Catholic, sharing his poverty and the rigid self-discipline which both of them had to impose on themselves in order to manage financially. Their favourite recreation cost nothing but shoe-leather; they went for long walks together. But Schlüter was more sociable and introduced him into the Catholic students association, *Brisgovia.* Schlüter went on from Freiburg University to Munich University with him, where they both stayed for a year and a half, or three full terms. This was a happy interlude for both; in term-time they spent their few spare pfennigs on the cheapest seats at the Opera, and during the long summer holiday they went abroad, to Northern Italy and Switzerland, living rough, but looking at pictures, churches and the countryside. These journeys must have given the young Adenauer his first clear concept of 'his' Europe, the Western Europe for which the Rhinelanders felt a real sense of kinship, and to which they 'belonged' much more than to Prussia. Only a few years earlier Heinrich von Treitschke had written scathingly of Adenauer's countrymen – 'They remembered only the blessings of the French administration. They raved about the glorious ideas of 1789, they preferred to read French or Belgian newspapers, and were convinced that the sun over Europe would rise in the West.' Adenauer remained a Western European all his life.

From Munich Adenauer went to Bonn University, and settled down to the best part of three years of hard, slogging work for his examinations.

7............*Adenauer. Democratic Dictator*, Charles Wighton.
8............*Konrad Adenauer*, Georg Schröder, p. 5.

They can hardly have been exciting years, although he was close to his family in Cologne, where one elder brother was studying the law and the other preparing to enter the Church. He was still a somewhat lonely figure, although not shy. Certainly, there was never a hint of a love affair in these early years. He took his final law examinations at the age of 23, and then passed into the state judicial service a year later. According to an unfriendly biographer,[9] 'he only just managed to scrape a pass in his examination for the state judicial service, in which second-class honours are considered the indispensable minimum for success.' Once again, one suspects late development of his mental capacities. He worked hard enough, and his own vivid memory of this period was of staying up half the night at his books, and putting his feet in a pail of ice-cold water in order to keep awake.

Adenauer applied for a job in the State Prosecutor's office in Cologne, as good a training as any for a young lawyer. Meanwhile his one great friend Raimund Schlüter took a post at the district court in Gmünd, in the Eifel hills, where he quickly became engaged to be married but almost at once died, of tuberculosis. Adenauer attended the funeral, a tall, serious, silent young man. According to one of Schlüter's school friends, 'He was utterly composed. He stood at the grave, stiff and erect, without a tear.'[10]

What sort of man was being launched into the world at this stage? He was obviously very reticent, the result of being brought up in a highly disciplined and devout family. He was a stoic, determined to show no sign of weakness, never to complain or grumble for personal reasons. This quality would stay with him all his life. There was, too, something about him suggestive of a mundane and matter-of-fact version of Don Quixote. He had impeccable manners, and showed particular courtesy to women.

From earliest childhood onwards he displayed no sign of fear, and pictures of him as a child show a singular, almost comical haughtiness and self-assurance, in contrast with the pensive, unprecocious faces of his brothers. In his play *Camino Real*, Tennessee Williams has Don Quixote entering the derelict, sleepy village on the road to nowhere, bringing out his toothbrush at the fountain in the main square and then going serenely to sleep. One feels about Adenauer that he could have accepted any equally uncomfortable situation without a murmur, and automatically make the best of it.

He was not a dandy, but scrupulously neat in his dress. Clothes hung well on his lean but not gaunt frame. Very early in his life he developed a taste for dark suits, with long, tubular jackets. For his work he wore shirts with stick-up collar and bow tie. Even as a small boy he was scrupulously

9............*Konrad Adenauer*, Rudolf Augstein, p. 9.
10..........*Konrad Adenauer*, Paul Weymar, p. 28.

tidy. One problem appears to have been difficult to settle. As a student at Munich University he affected a pawky moustache, and there is one picture of that period which shows him wearing a billycock hat set squarely on his head, peering over what appears to have been a bale of straw, with two girls on either side of him. All of the girls are laughing, but his own face remains preternaturally serious. He may well have been displaying the studied waggishness which later blossomed into a keen and trenchant wit. A couple of years later his moustache had gone, but it returned in more flowing form sometime in 1901 or the very beginning of 1902. He retained it for the next thirty years, but its upturned points disappeared when the Kaiser abdicated in 1918.

Was there, outside the family and his immediate environment, a formative influence in Konrad Adenauer's early years? Events sometimes leave a deeper imprint on the human mind than people. As it happened, there was an event – or rather development – of considerable importance in the Rhineland just before Adenauer was born. In the early 1870s a struggle began between Bismarck's Reich Government and the Roman Catholic Church, which left an indelible mark on German history.

This struggle, the so-called *Kulturkampf*, reached its height a year or two before Adenauer was born, but it rumbled on until around 1886, when he was already 10 years old. In his deeply religious family it was bound to be the main political subject of conversation. And the strongly Roman Catholic Rhineland as a whole found itself aligned against 'heathen', Protestant Prussia and the highly authoritarian Reich Chancellor. Here was the germ of the ingrained distrust of Prussia which stayed with Adenauer for the rest of his life.

The facts of the *Kulturkampf* are simpler than the rights of it. Bismarck regarded the Roman Catholic Church as a state within the State. He wanted to limit the numbers of the priesthood, to force the Church to abandon its 'confessional' schools and surrender all share in education, and to ban some religious orders. Between 1872 and 1876 the Jesuit Order was banned, and its members expelled. Priests were forbidden to interfere in political matters, and priests in Germany had to be German. The Catholic Bureau in the Ministry of Education was abolished, and Catholic seminaries were placed under state control. Civil marriage was made compulsory.

Most of these steps were incorporated in the May Laws of 1873. The Roman Catholic Church, backed by the Vatican, resisted. On March 31, 1874, Cardinal Paulus Melchers, Archbishop of Cologne, was arrested in his Palace. Bismarck rushed in where, sixty years later, even Hitler hesitated to tread. A huge crowd assembled outside the Palace and in spite of a menacing display of military force, sang *Wir sind in wahren Christentum.*

But the Archbishop was hustled off to the gaol of Klingelputz. Six of his Bishops were imprisoned too, and 1,300 parishes deprived of priests who refused to obey the May Laws.

The immediate consequence of Bismarck's display of the mailed fist was that, in the 1874 elections, the Clerical Party which had its main strength in the Rhineland, increased its representation in the *Reichstag* (the German Parliament in Berlin) from 63 to 91. Bismarck gave way only gradually and with reluctance. In 1881 penal legislation applying to violation of the 'May Laws' was replaced by the exercise of the discretionary powers of the law-courts. In 1886 the State examination for priests was dropped, and a whole series of compromise arrangements even enabled the Clerical (now Centre) Party to give grudging support in Parliament to Bismarck. But in their hearts the Rhinelanders remained unreconciled. They remembered the words of the Trier lawyer, Ludwig Simon, in 1848 – 'If you allow yourselves to be conquered by Prussia, you will preserve in Germany the peace of the grave and the order of the churchyard.'[11] Adenauer, too, proved in later years that he had a long memory. Certainly, his childhood memories of what Prussia meant to his family were never forgotten.

Adenauer was only a very short time in the State Prosecutor's office. Early in 1902 he was offered a job in the private firm of a Herr Kausen, the Chairman of the Centre Party in the Cologne City Council and one of the best civil lawyers in the district. Kausen found plenty of work for this steady, sensible young man. He impressed on him the need for absolute precision and clarity of thinking – Kausen obviously owed much to the Roman heritage of Cologne. Another Cologne lawyer has been quoted[12] as saying of Adenauer – 'He had no brilliant oratory but, instead, an enormously effective way of convincing people with the sheer weight of his sober and factual arguments. This peculiar eloquence of his worked upon the judge's bench like quiet and persistent rain which gently and stubbornly soaked every objection and counter-argument until they simply disintegrated.'[13]

In the early summer of 1902 Adenauer became engaged to be married. This was a more important event than is often the case in a man's life. For Adenauer contrived to marry for both love and gain. Emma Weyer came from a decidedly well-to-do Cologne family (Adenauer's existence was so parochial that one can hardly imagine him marrying 'outside' Cologne). She was pretty into the bargain, but could not afford to be gay. Her father had died some years before, and her mother had made the mistaken decision of believing that she could best serve his memory by remaining in perpetual semi-mourning, purposefully grieving for her dear one and

11..........*The Mind of Germany*, Hans Kohn, p. 130.
12, 13.....*Konrad Adenauer*, Paul Weymar, p. 28.

confidently awaiting the time when she would be reunited with him. This made for anything but a merry life for Emma and her sister Mia, but by great good luck for them, they were allowed to join a Cologne tennis-club, with the strange name of Pudelnasz. There Emma met Adenauer, already a devotee of physical exercise but decidedly not one of the local Lotharios. He must have appealed to her precisely because he was so much more serious and understanding than his contemporaries, perhaps too because of his unusual sensitivity. Adenauer carried out his love-making in the style of the day; he called on Emma's mother sprucely and correctly dressed and promised her that he would be in a position to support her daughter, on a prospective income of 6,000 Marks a year. This was the rough equivalent, in 1970 terms, of about $8,000 (£3,200), not great riches but a competence. Mrs Weyer 'accepted' him, on behalf of her daughter. That was how things were done in those Wilhelminian–Victorian times. They were married in January 1904.

Adenauer's father had been in the personal sense an unambitious man, but he had nursed ambitions for his sons. That was why he sent them to secondary school and university. Now, his youngest son had most emphatically 'bettered himself'. Emma's mother was a Wallraf, and a Wallraf cousin was shortly to become Lord Mayor of Cologne. One grandfather was a Berghaus, a family which had produced plenty of local dignitaries. Another was Peter Weyer, who owned a sizeable art collection. These were all excellent 'connexions' for a young and ambitious newly-wed. He moved with his wife into a flat in the respectable suburb of Lindenthal. Their first son was born in September, 1906.

By then Adenauer had taken the first crucial step in his career. At the beginning of 1906 a place on the Cologne City Council fell vacant. Kausen, a man of standing in the Catholic Centre Party, wanted a judge from Saarbrücken appointed. Adenauer went to his employer and argued the case for his own candidature with quiet but complete assurance. He was already a member of the Centre Party. Through the Wallraf family he had useful connexions with the Liberal Party, the only other important middle of the road group in the City Council. He was close to Kausen, saw eye-to-eye with him and could be relied upon to represent Centre Party interests. Centre Party and Liberal support for Adenauer was mobilized and on March 7, 1906, he was elected *Adjunct*, or Member of the Council, by 35 out of 37 votes cast. This marked the beginning of a municipal career which lasted 27 years, until the Nazi seizure of power.

His salary was 6000 Marks. It was no more than a coincidence that this was the exact amount which Adenauer told his future mother-in-law that he would expect to earn, when courting Emma. The young couple moved at once to a larger house, in a residential area just off the road to Aachen.

This was where Konrad (Koko) was born. There was a second son, Max, in 1910, and a daughter, Ria, in 1912.[14]

The entirely happy start to Adenauer's married life was clouded by two events. The first was the death of his father, after a stroke, only three days after he became a City Councillor. The second was the state of Emma's health. Bearing the first child disclosed the fact that she suffered from curvature of the spine; in addition she developed a kidney disease. Adenauer called in a specialist, then sent her to a sanatorium. Nothing helped, and the bearing of each child was a terrible strain on her back, which in turn brought pressure on her kidneys. From 1912 onwards she was a chronic invalid. There were plenty of periods of sadness in Adenauer's life, then and later.

In his full-length biography of Adenauer, Paul Weymar has given an interesting picture of his home life. He was a light, and later on a bad sleeper, and always rose early. He was at work by 8.30 in the morning and after he was promoted in 1909 to First Adjunct, or Deputy to the Lord Mayor, stayed in his office up to 8 in the evening. He took a two hour break for lunch. He was invariably punctual, and did not suffer the unpunctual gladly. In 1909 Max Wallraf, his relation by marriage, became Lord Mayor; he was often away in Berlin on other business and Adenauer spent much time deputizing for him. He was in charge of the Finance and Personnel departments of the municipality, and this meant a great deal of extra work when the Municipal Council was in session; then, he often worked until after midnight.

In the home he was a disciplinarian. With too little time for his children at this stage of his career, he expected them to be ultra-tidy and obedient. He seems to have had strong views on hygiene; later, he commandeered the services of a municipal employee who had once been a hairdresser and who came to the Adenauer home once a fortnight to give him and his two sons a skin-head 'Prussian shave' with the clippers. It was a curious concession to the Prussia which Adenauer disliked; he told his children it was 'hygienic and cheap'. They did not argue about it – arguing by members of the family was something which Adenauer would not tolerate.

Immersed in his work and family affairs, Adenauer had no time at all for national politics and world affairs. The Germans of his day had a fixed belief in minding their own business, in leaving government to those who governed and in playing the part of cogs, large and small, in the machine of State. As it happened, Adenauer was, from the time that he became a City Councillor to the outbreak of war in 1914, living through very stirring times indeed. In 1907 the signing of the Anglo-Russian Alliance

14..........Later married a businessman and became Frau Ria Reiners.

brought the Triple Entente with France into being, as a counter-weight to the much older Triple Alliance of Germany, Austria and Italy. There was constant talk of the *Einkreisung* or 'encirclement' of Germany by her potential enemies, and of France's suspected desire to wage a 'war of revenge' for the recovery of Alsace-Lorraine, lost after the Franco-Prussian War of 1870.

In 1908 Kaiser Wilhelm II did one of his many disservices to the German people by giving an interview to the London *Daily Telegraph*. He alleged that he had worked out a military plan for ending the Boer War and sent it to his grandmother, Queen Victoria; and also accused the British people of chronic hostility towards Germany. In 1911 the German cruiser, the *Panther*, was sent to Agadir, and a crisis in Franco-German relations developed over Morocco. In the following year a feeble effort to get productive Anglo-German talks going failed, and record naval expenditure took Germany into second place to Britain as a sea power. Ten years earlier, Germany had been a bad fourth, but the German Government showed no recognition of the fact that the British Empire was absolutely dependent on its naval supremacy.

A peculiarly revealing incident took place in 1913 at the little town of Zabern (Saverne) in Alsace. An arrogant young officer chased some of the townsfolk off the streets and proclaimed martial law when they protested. In Berlin, the Social Democratic Party called for a vote of no confidence in the Government. But although the garrison was removed from Zabern, the offending officer was given a decoration. One can see why it was not only abroad that Prussian militarism had become a bogey. Rhinelanders like Adenauer probably felt more sympathy for the citizens of Zabern, around half of whom had been French, than for the soldiers of the German garrison.

Equally revealing but with a pleasant element of comedy was the incident of the so-called 'Captain from Koepenick'. The 'Captain', an unemployed workman, dressed himself up in uniform, collected a party of soldiers whom he met in the street of this Berlin suburb and seized the Town Hall, putting the Mayor and members of his staff under arrest. Their protestations were swept aside with the statement that a Prussian officer had 'total authority'.

If Adenauer had any thoughts about these happenings, he did not communicate them later on either to his biographer or to his children. The First World War probably came as much a shock to him as to most people in Europe. With a population of 68 million, Germany was strong as well as being prosperous and proud. Cologne was expanding fast, and there was a great deal of work for the City Council. Adenauer himself was prosperous now; his salary had been raised to 15,000 Marks a year, really good money for those days, and he had built his family a new home in the Max Bruch Strasse. He had his troubles too. In 1914 he developed a thrombosis in one leg, and told his elder son, Koko, 'If the blood-clot in my leg begins to move, I shall fall down dead,'[15] an untypically dramatic statement for him. Far more worrying was Emma's condition. By this time she was desperately ill. Adenauer's performance as a husband was epic. He spent his midday break with her, and in the evening sat for hours at her bedside, reading to her, telling her stories and seeing her safely to sleep. Afterwards, as often as not, he sat up over his own work until the small hours of the morning. This was probably the period when he began to sleep badly – a habit which remained with him for the rest of his life.

On Sundays he took his children eastwards across the Rhine for excursions in the *Siebengebirge*, the hills opposite Bonn. For the first time that they could remember, he had time to talk to them, although they were too small to make it more than a monologue. On October 16, 1916, Emma died and the whole family went into deep mourning. There were no more excursions to the Siebengebirge for more than a year. Adenauer later on in life spoke of this period as being 'absolute Hell'. The only relieving feature was the ceaseless activity of his mother in looking after the children. But she was an old lady by now and unable to cope with the housekeeping. There were troubles with the servants, and an unpleasant amount of stealing after war had broken out and food and other goods began to be in short supply.

On June 28, 1914, the Archduke Franz Ferdinand of Austria was murdered at Sarajevo. On July 5 the Kaiser told the Austrian emissary, Count Hoyos, that Serbia, as the assumed instigator of the outrage, should be disciplined. On July 23 came the Austrian ultimatum to Serbia, and on July 28 the Austrian declaration of war. The Austrian ultimatum demanded that the Serbian Government should suppress all anti-Austrian publications, remove all officers and functionaries who were judged by Austria to be anti-Austrian and to accept the collaboration of Austrian officials in suppressing 'subversive' movements and societies in Serbia. The ultimatum called, in effect, on Serbia to surrender her national sovereignty. Russia began general mobilization of her armed forces on the next day, and the German ultimatum to Russia followed on July 31. France mobilized on August 1, and the very next day the 'Schlieffen Plan' – entailing an immediate strike through the Low Countries against France – was put into action. The violation of Belgian neutrality brought Britain into the war on August 4.

It was a popular war in Germany, even in the unwarlike Rhineland. On

15..........*Konrad Adenauer*, Paul Weymar, p. 37.

the day that Britain entered the war the German Social Democratic Party – theoretically committed to the cause of peace and supported by one third of the voters in the country – gave a unanimous vote in favour of the proposed war-credits. *Es war ein grosses Halali* (the word used for the blowing of the mort on the hunting-horn) was a phrase used by Rhinelanders in later years. The Kaiser announced: 'I know no more parties; I know only Germans,' and the Social Democrats took refuge in the argument that the war had to be fought against reactionary Tsarist autocracy and French national revanchism.

Cologne marched with the rest of Germany to the wars. A citizen of Cologne, Carl Erwin Bruchheuser, produced a 'Hymn to our German Kaiser'.[16] It referred to him as 'God's anointed' and ended on a note of solidarity – 'Germany's *Furst* (Prince) and People are one!' In Cologne a certain Max Bewer was producing stirring musical tributes to Hindenburg and Ludendorff, the victors of the first big battles on the Eastern Front, and the scores preserved in the city archives show how appropriate they were for the slap and stomp of the military bands and the marching regiments.

Ernst Lissauer (surprisingly, a German Jew) was later to write his 'Hymn of Hate,' to the motif of *Gott strafe England!* (May God punish England). A forerunner of this sort of 'poetry' came from an inhabitant of Cologne's neighbouring, traditionally rival city of Düsseldorf – a Johannes Wintgen offered up his own hymn of hate under the horrific title of 'The Youth of Germany's Hate'. More comical, even if unintentionally so, was this contribution from a Cologne poet, Wilhelm Speiser. It was entitled 'Song to a cannon', and its recurring verse went:

> 'Der Krupp in Essen ist nicht dumm;
> Er machte uns das Bum-Bum-Bum,
> Vor dem die Feinde, voll Respekt,
> Gleich fallen, mit der Naes im Dreck.'[17]

(a rough translation could be:

> *'Our Krupp in Essen isn't dumb;
> He made for us a great big gun,
> To which our enemies in terror
> Go noses-in-the-dirt together.'*)

The Kaiser, predictably, had his own contribution to make towards maintaining the patriotic fervour of Cologne. In January 1915 he sent a message of fulsome congratulations to the men of the 28th (Cologne)

16, 17.....Cologne City Archives.

Infantry Regiment of the Reserve and their Colonel, Bonsack, for gallantry on the field of battle. In his message the Kaiser expressed the somewhat bloodthirsty hope that, when the 'war of movement' was resumed (it never was), the *Kölner Jungs* (Cologne youngsters) would inflict the maximum casualties on the enemy, and would return from battle proud victors. The Kaiser's letter ended, melodramatically and inappropriately, *Adieu, Musketière!*, written in purple ink – inappropriately, since the French word *Adieu* implies farewell-for-ever. In answer, Colonel Bonsack assured his liege of the readiness of every one of his men to die 'an honourable, fine, soldier's death'.[18] This kind of frenzied patriotism was not peculiar to Germany at the time; but it took its extreme form in front of a German audience.

Jingoism in any shape was always foreign to Adenauer's level temperament. Quite apart from his domestic worries, he had too much on his mind to take part in histrionic displays. Shortly after the outbreak of war he was transferred to the Food Department of the City Council. Very quickly it became the key municipal department, for Germany was successively faced with food shortages, real hunger and, finally, near-starvation. Adenauer had to procure food for nearly 600,000 people. It was a grinding task which became steadily more difficult. He personally invented a 'Cologne soya-sausage', which he pronounced to be 'eatable', and a 'Cologne maize bread', for which he took out a patent. (He had always been interested in inventions, and two others of his were magnetic hair-pins, and light metal sheets for car-bodies.) More importantly, Adenauer entered into agreements with wartime farmers' co-operatives, under which he paid in kind for their produce, with seed, fertilizers and farm machinery. He operated quite simply, on the principle of 'first come, first served'. His primary object was to ensure that his own citizens of Cologne stayed alive.

In the summer of 1917 drama entered into his personal life with brutal suddenness. Driving him one morning from the Max Bruch Strasse to the Town Hall, his chauffeur fell asleep at the wheel. This most un-Germanic performance was the consequence of overlong working hours and too little food. The official City Council car swerved into the path of an oncoming tram. The car was totally wrecked, but the chauffeur was flung clear and suffered only minor bruising. Adenauer crawled out of the wreckage pouring blood, but with typical dignity and determination managed to get to his feet and insisted on walking to the nearby Trinity Hospital. His cheekbones and nose were broken, his lower jaw was crushed and dislocated, several teeth were knocked out, his eyesight was

18..........Cologne City Archives.

affected and he had deep gashes on his head. The lesser mortal, the chauffeur, was carried off on a stretcher.

Adenauer had to be stitched up without an anaesthetic – the German doctors may have been worried by his weak lungs or his recent thrombosis, or perhaps anaesthetics were being kept as far as possible for soldiers at the front. After it was over, he fainted. Later his cheekbones, nose and jaw were re-set, his cheekbones so badly that when members of the family came to visit him in hospital they could not at first recognize him. He had always had high cheekbones, but after the accident they gave him a look of a Red Indian chief or a Chinese Mandarin. The accident left him with double vision, temporarily, and with recurrent headaches, from which he suffered ever afterwards.

Almost as soon as he was reasonably well again, the post of Lord Mayor fell vacant. Max Wallraf was appointed Under Secretary of State in the Ministry of the Interior in Berlin. While Adenauer was still convalescing in September 1917 in a sanatorium in the Black Forest village of St. Blasien two city councillors visited him. They wanted to test his mental reflexes and went about this in a most ham-handed manner. After a totally aimless conversation Adenauer remarked with dry humour that it was only the exterior of his cranium which had suffered.[19] He stood for election and was elected by 52 votes to none against, with two ballot papers left blank. It was a remarkable tribute to a man who, only a few years earlier, had been criticized for youthful hastiness and inexperience. At the same time as being elected Mayor, he was given a seat in the Prussian State Council, or second House of Parliament, an honour which he had neither sought nor expected.

On October 18, 1917, he was installed as Lord Mayor of Cologne. His eldest son has left this description:[20]

'My father mounted the rostrum. As he stood there, tall, slim, clad in solemn black, reading his speech in a clear ringing voice, I felt very proud of him. I still remember one passage of his speech:

'"There is nothing better life can offer than to allow a man to expend himself fully with all the strength of his mind and soul, and to devote his entire being to creative ability. This field you have opened up for me by electing me Lord Mayor of the City of Cologne, and for this I thank you from the bottom of my heart."'

Konrad Adenauer was 41 years old. He had, he must have supposed at the time, reached the pinnacle of his career.

19, 20.....*Konrad Adenauer*, Paul Weymar, p. 40.

3 Rhineland Republic

The wild enthusiasm with which the German people greeted the outbreak of the First World War ebbed away soon enough. For the first year of the war a huge wooden statue of the Cologne 'Boor', the clumsy and bucolic clod-hopper who is a traditional figure of the annual Carnival, was set up in the Guerzenich square. The people paid for nails to stick in it, and the money raised in this way was spent on food and tobacco for the troops at the front. Whole school-classes made pilgrimages to the Gürzenich square and even tiny children were held up in order to take a perfunctory initial smack at a nail bought with their pocket-money.[1]

The schools had half holidays each time a victory was announced, and early in 1915 one finds the Lord Mayor's office being firmly reminded by the military authorities that there had been cases of secondary schools not being informed of the 'victory news' and going on working.[2]

But after this there were fewer victories to celebrate. Instead, the newspapers were filled with an unending stream of obituary notices and with lists of war-wounded arriving at Cologne railway station, with accounts of their injuries. Worst of all were the lists of the 'missing'; plenty of 'unknown soldiers' were dying at the front. One sad letter from the Lord Mayor's office admitted, unwillingly, the need to start burying citizens of Cologne in the German military cemetery at Maubeuge, three hundred miles from home.[3] The City Fathers were worried, too, by the flippancy of Cologne's youth in singing a popular jingle in the streets, which went:

> 'Im Osten kaempft das tap'fre Heer,
> Im Westen steht die Feuerwehr.'
> (*In the East our gallant Army is fighting,*
> *in the West we have the fire-brigade.*)

And, typifying the unpredictability of the human race, the Town Hall was bombarded with letters from the *Deutscher Abwehr-Bund gegen die Ausschreitungen der Abstinenzbewegung* (the German defence association against the excesses of the Abstainers' movement). The writers argued that

1............*Kleine Illustrierte Geschichte der Stadt Köln*, Hans Welters and Helmut Lobeck, p. 159.

2, 3.........Cologne City Archives.

soldiers at the front could not do without alcohol – which proved that alcohol was good for the rest of humanity too.

The food situation continued to deteriorate after Adenauer became Lord Mayor in 1917. Ration cards for bread had been introduced two years earlier. Now, even bread and potatoes were running short, and for long periods turnips were the only vegetable available. Mobile communal kitchens were introduced, serving one warm meal a day to all and sundry. In the summer of 1917 children were coming to get their meal barefoot; in the winter that followed they were wearing clogs. The Kaiser, as usual, had something crazily inappropriate to say on the matter. He announced that, in spite of the Allied plot to keep milk out of Germany and kill German children, he would never allow his own children and grandchildren to starve but would first blow up Windsor Castle, with the British Royal Family inside it.[4]

Writing in 1880 to the Swiss jurist, Johann Kaspar Bluntschli, the German Field-Marshal Helmuth Count von Moltke maintained that: 'Eternal peace is a dream, and not even a beautiful one. War is a link in God's order of the world. In war, the noblest virtues of man develop; courage and renunciation, devotion to duty and readiness for sacrifice, even at the risk of one's life. Without war, the world would sink into materialism.' The German people had been brought up to regard war, if not as welcome, at any rate as logical, useful and inevitable. But by the end of 1917 it was getting very tired indeed of this particular war. On July 6 one of Adenauer's colleagues of the Centre Party, Matthias Erzberger, called for a 'just' peace, without territorial annexations. In 1914 Erzberger had demanded the annexation by Germany of the whole of Belgium, much of North-West France, of the French and Belgian Congo; the creation of Polish, Baltic and Ukrainian satellite states; and the payment of the entire German national debt by Germany's enemies.[5]

On July 12, 1917, the majority of the Centre Party gave its formal backing to Erzberger's peace-proposal. But in March 1918 Germany imposed a brutally tough peace on Russia at the Treaty of Brest-Litovsk, forcing the new Bolshevik Government to cede Poland, Finland and the Baltic States, while leaving White Russia and the Ukraine under German military occupation. Only a few months earlier the Social Democrats and parties of the centre had secured a two to one vote in favour of their peace resolution of 'no annexations, no indemnities!'

Early in 1918 Adenauer told Max Wallraf that the war was going to be lost.[6] This, at all events, was his subsequent recollection. Unconcealably,

4............*My Four Years in Germany*, James Gerard, p. 243.
5............*The Mind of Germany*, Hans Kohn, p. 301.
6............*Konrad Adenauer*, Paul Weymar, p. 41.

1918 was a terrible year, of mutinies in the Navy, growing hunger at home and increasing and inexorable pressure on the German armies on the Western Front. The great German spring offensive petered out by the end of June and the last real hope of a German victory vanished – 'Our men had learnt to their bitter experience, in the desperate offensive at Rheims and on the Marne, only too well that the enemy commanded an increasing superiority in men and materials.'[7] In September the vaunted 'Hindenburg Line' was breached. On November 3, 1918, the Kiel sailors mutinied. Three days later Adenauer learned that a large detachment of them were on their way to the Rhineland. Their intention was to set up soldiers', sailors' and workers' councils all over Germany and to seize all administrative power. At Spa, eighty miles west of Cologne, the Kaiser was with his General Staff, trying to decide whether to resist the Revolution. Cologne still had a small garrison, but the morale of its population, undernourished, depressed by their country's defeat and confronted by possible anarchy, was terribly low.

Adenauer made an effort to prevent or at least delay the arrival of the Kiel sailors. He warned the Military Governor, who refused to take emergency action by cordoning off the railway station. He next asked the Reichsbahn railway management to have the train bringing the sailors diverted to a siding somewhere in the countryside. This proposal was rejected on the grounds that the train would probably be wrecked – an epic of bureaucracy. The police, at least, co-operated, but only half-heartedly. They placed a cordon round the railway station square, and instructed the hundreds of mutineers on arrival that they could not go into the town wearing their red rosettes. The sailors merely pocketed their rosettes, spread out through the town and stuck them back in their button-holes.

Next day the Republic was proclaimed by loud-speaker in the town's squares. Mobs milled through the streets, demanding the surrender of the officers of the garrison. Adenauer suggested to the Military Governor that a display of force – he was presumably thinking of fire being opened by the military over the heads of the mob – might restore a situation which was now very obviously out of hand. There was a battery of field artillery with adequate ammunition standing in the courtyard of the Apostel Gymnasium, Adenauer's old school. But the Military Governor refused to use it.

In the afternoon Adenauer accordingly went to the Town Hall and agreed to talk to nominated representatives of the hastily-formed 'Workers' and Soldiers' Council.' They conferred all afternoon, and

7............*Schuld und Verhängnis*, Karl-Heinz Abshagen, p. 15.

reached what amounted to a reasonable compromise. The Red Flag was not to be hoisted on the Town Hall. The Military Governor was allowed to leave Cologne without hindrance, and so was the officer commanding the Cologne Fortress. Agreement was not reached a moment too soon. On the next day a large part of the garrison mutinied[8] and joined the mob. The garrison had constituted one of only two cards in Adenauer's hand; the other was the certain impending return of the front-line units.

A graphic account was given to Paul Weymar of the situation at the time by Captain Otto Schwink, appointed by the Kaiser's headquarters at Spa to replace the Military Governor.[9] Schwink left Spa on November 8, the day that the Kaiser fled into neutral Holland. In his account, he paid handsome tribute to Adenauer, whom he described as 'one of the bravest men I've come across'. He needed to be. For long weeks Cologne was in a state of incipient anarchy. Mobs wandered the streets, waving red flags and chanting slogans. They laid almost permanent siege to the Town Hall, clamouring for food and fuel. There was widespread looting.

Adenauer, according to Schwink, worked 18 to 20 hours a day. He procured food from the surrounding countryside and set up field kitchens which worked round the clock. He ordered police into action against looters, and on one occasion had them pour three hundred litres of alcohol into the Rhine at night, in order to prevent it falling into the hands of an already excitable mob. He requisitioned all army property, sold it for ready cash and used the money for further relief measures. He managed, most important of all, to induce soldiers to surrender their arms, by making this a condition for the receipt of discharge papers, railway warrants, pay and rations. Amid all the excitement, according to Schwink, 'Adenauer remained absolutely calm and unruffled ... This man, I felt, was a true Commander-in-Chief.'[10]

Adenauer's remarkable composure and invariable common sense paid off. He restored a fair measure of order out of a chaotic situation, and spared Cologne the violence which took place in Berlin and other German cities. He carried the people of Cologne through the initial period of near-despair when the terms were announced of the Armistice signed on November 11, 1918. Under these terms, Germany was to be almost totally disarmed and to surrender her fleet. She was to evacuate all occupied territory, including Alsace-Lorraine, the spoils of the Franco-Prussian War of 1870. In addition, all territory west of the Rhine and a six-mile-wide strip to the east of the river were to be militarily evacuated. Cologne was to be under British military occupation.

8............*Kleine Illustrierte Geschichte der Stadt Köln*, p. 169.
9............*Konrad Adenauer*, Paul Weymar, pp. 43–45.
10..........*Konrad Adenauer*, Paul Weymar, p. 44.

Adenauer dealt faithfully with the long, seemingly endless columns of soldiers returning from the front, who had to be temporarily housed, fed and sent on their way. On December 3 the last returning contingent crossed the Rhine at Cologne, still marching with superb discipline but so weary that they allowed the Cologne school-children to tug their gun-carriages across the bridges. It was this impeccable discipline which induced the newly elected President Friedrich Ebert to announce: 'I salute you, who return unvanquished from the field of battle' – a remark which helped to foster the destructive legend that Germany lost the war only because her army had been 'stabbed in the back'.

On December 6, hard on the heels of the last German stragglers from the front came the main British forces of occupation, an infantry brigade and the 3rd Cavalry Regiment (Hussars), under the command of General Algernon Lawson. According to the official records,[11] Adenauer and the General had an amicable discussion. Adenauer put three empty barracks at the disposal of the British troops. He suggested that they should march through the city to these barracks, so that the populace would know that they were there. Lawson said his men were tired but agreed to have a march on the next day. Adenauer said he hoped the General would not mind if children ran behind the troops – Cologne children were naturally inquisitive. The General's answer was that he hoped that his men and the children of Cologne would soon be the best of friends.

But there were some unwelcome provisions in the proclamation which Lawson had brought. All citizens had to carry passes, all residents had to be registered. No traffic was to be on the roads after 8 p.m. and the use of light in homes after 9.30 p.m. was restricted. Non-military weapons, like shot-guns, were to be handed in to the military authorities. Nobody was to ride on horseback in the streets. Finally, male citizens were to 'salute' British officers by raising or touching their hats to them. Adenauer objected vigorously to this last provision; allegedly he told Lawson that he could 'not imagine that an English gentleman would wish to humiliate a vanquished people in this way'.[12] Lawson was no martinet; the proclamation was never posted up and the city authorities were allowed to implement its provisions in their own way.[13]

In the event, relations between Adenauer and the British authorities worked fairly smoothly. When a British Commissioner, Mr. J. L. Piggott, took over control from the British Army, he became a personal friend of the Adenauer family. Even before that, Adenauer was evidently able to talk freely to the military authorities – only a few days after the British

11..........Cologne City Archives.
12..........*Konrad Adenauer*, Paul Weymar, p. 46.
13..........Cologne City Archives.

occupation began, one finds him declaring that the people of Cologne were different from 'other German tribes', being of mixed blood and descent and priding themselves on their ready sense of humour.[14] His complaints about regulations got a fair hearing, and sometimes secured requisite action. Requisitioning of foodstuffs by the British forces was ended at his request. The British garrison was soon on good terms with the people of Cologne, and there were few complaints about their behaviour. On the other hand, one finds a German café proprietor being sent to prison for setting his dog on to a British Captain![15]

Adenauer had been confronted by terribly difficult problems when he became Mayor in 1917: it is a moot point whether his problems were not even more difficult when war ended. The end of the monarchy solved nothing. In the opinion of one historian: 'The change of régime did not come as a result of any long-planned revolutionary movement. It did not represent any basic change of heart on the part of the German people themselves. It was brought about without any great deep-seated conviction or willingness on the part of its progenitors, who would certainly at the time have preferred to retain the Monarchy. It occurred, in very great measure, because those in power believed that by this means alone could Germany comply with President Wilson's preliminary prerequisite for peace, and partly because of the fear of Bolshevism; both courses being the result of pressure from outside rather than from within Germany.'[16]

The Revolution, in fact, had been no true revolution. It was the product of disillusionment and resentment, of war-weariness and of the end of the tradition of an invincible army. Behind it was little idealism and no real ideology. A constitution was drawn up which could be regarded as 'liberal-bourgeois'. Half-hearted plans for the socialization of heavy industry were dropped. A solitary and supposedly 'popular' concession was the lowering of the voting age to 20 and the granting of female suffrage. Very few Germans felt that anything substantial had been done in the way of constitutional change. For the Centre Party the new constitution was too secular, and power remained too much centred on Berlin. For the Social Democrats, it symbolized the defeat of democracy, and for the Nationalists the defeat of the nation. A decent, honest but uninspiring President was found in Friedrich Ebert, whom Theodor Heuss (later to become President of the post-1949 Federal Republic) called, with a singular lack of perspicacity, 'the Abraham Lincoln of German history'.[17] Ebert was popularly, and more appropriately known as *Friedrich der Vorläufige* – Frederick the Provisional.

14, 15.....Cologne City Archives.
16...........*The Nemesis of Power*, Sir John Wheeler-Bennett, p. 19.
17...........*Würdingungen*, Theodor Heuss, p. 220.

In Berlin the extreme left wing 'Spartacists' were on the march, and pitched battles were fought between them and the 'Free Corps' formed by disbanded officers. A similar state of civil war developed in Bavaria and Saxony. And the 'Foreign Minister' of the Bolshevik 'Republic of Bavaria', a Dr. Libh, 'declared war' on Wurtemberg and Switzerland for refusing to loan his government 60 railway locomotives.[18] The Reich looked, in these early months, like disintegrating.

Adenauer, in Cologne, was well aware of this very real danger. He had for that matter, plenty of troubles of his own. In the last year of the war the citizens of Cologne, as ungrateful as the rest of the human race, had demonstrated in the streets with the warcry of *Nieder mit dem Graupenauer!*, a reference to the barley, or *Graupen*, which had become their staple diet and which they regarded as cattle-fodder. The newly-formed Communist Party attacked him as a 'Catholic reactionary' and his City Council as a *Saustall und Adenauer-Zirkus* (pigsty and circus).[19] One Sunday, Adenauer and Captain Schwink, walking through a park, found a grave with a wooden cross above it bearing the inscription 'Here lies Konrad Adenauer'.[20] A small crowd had gathered round it; Adenauer took a look at the inscription, then walked on without any change of expression. But personal popularity counted far less with him than the fate of Cologne and the Rhineland. This became his main preoccupation once the war ended. Indeed, the fate of the whole Rhineland remained in some doubt for the next six years.

Even before the war ended, Adenauer had confidential talks with other Centre Party leaders about the Rhineland's political future. Most of them agreed that some measure of local autonomy, in a state with a federal system of government, would be preferable to 'Berlin rule'. This preference was reinforced by the fact that the Rhineland was Roman Catholic, and Berlin and Prussia Protestant. With the end of the war, the men of the Centre Party were further influenced by the state of chaos in Berlin and by the appointment of a Social Democratic atheist, Adolf Hoffman, as Minister responsible for education.

On December 4, 1918, a meeting was called in Cologne's Gürzenich assembly hall to discuss the establishment of a separate Rhineland state and, possibly, to present the British occupation authorities with a *fait accompli*. Adenauer, allegedly, was invited to this meeting but cried off at the last moment, after learning that the Reich Government in Berlin was totally opposed to the creation even of a 'federal' Rhineland within the German Reich. A Catholic priest, Bertram Kastert, presided at the meeting

18..........*Schuld und Verhängnis*, Karl-Heinz Abshagen, p. 56.
19..........Cologne City Archives.
20..........*Konrad Adenauer*, Paul Weymar, p. 45.

but was prevented from proclaiming the Rhineland State – although there was considerable approval of the idea.[21]

Adenauer had already discreetly sounded both the Social Democrats and the Liberals.[22] Whatever it was that he wanted to achieve, he certainly did not want to move too fast or uncircumspectly. On December 10 he was airing the idea of a Reichstag meeting in nearby Coblenz, or Limburg-on-the-Lahn. This would have done two things; it would have encouraged a serious discussion, on a nation-wide basis, of the possibility of creating a Federal Germany, and it would have taken the wind out of the sails of the extreme separatists. Nothing came of this thought. But on December 13 Adenauer clarified his own position, in a talk with the Minister of the Interior, Breitscheid. He said that, prior to the December 4 meeting in the Gürzenich, he had been approached by a hothead and asked to put himself at the head of the separatist movement.[23] His answer had been that he had no intention of 'appearing on Cologne's Neumarkt' (one of the main squares) in order to proclaim a Rhineland Republic.

This statement should have made – indeed, at the time, it did make – absolutely clear that Adenauer opposed the detachment of the Rhineland from the German Reich. But the question of the status of the Rhineland, within the structure of a federal Germany, remained unresolved. Clearly, Adenauer had strong views about this. He was all for federalism. In addition, he wanted a 'Greater Rhineland' to be an influential component in a Federal German State. This 'Greater Rhineland' would include the industrial Ruhr and a substantial part of the old province of Westphalia, to the east of the Rhine. It seems that he discussed his ideas about this in mid-December, 1918, with a certain Josef Dorten, who became an extreme separatist (if he was not one already). Adenauer had further meetings with Dorten on January 23 and 31, 1919, and again on March 5.[24] But he made it clear that a new Rhineland–Westphalia state would have to remain part of Germany.

Apparently to further this idea, Adenauer became Chairman, on January 7, 1919, of a 'Committee for a Rhineland–Westphalian Republic'.[25] The Committee had ten members, and was to collaborate with a political sub-committee of nine. Here was assembled the 'cream' of the Centre Party in its stronghold of the Rhineland, with a few outsiders. At

21, 22.....*Adenauer in der Rhein and politik nach dem ersten Weltkrieg*, Karl Dieter Erdmann, p. 29.

23..........*Adenauer in der Rhein and politik nach dem ersten Weltkrieg*, Karl Dieter Erdmann, p. 33.

24..........*Adenauer und der rheinische Separatismus*, Günther Meinhardt. Has references to these meetings.

25..........Cologne City Archives.

this inaugural meeting, it was decided that the new Republic should have its own armed forces and should, if necessary, have the approval of the Entente Powers (*dass eine militaerische Macht notwendig sei*[26]). The meeting took place at the house of a Cologne banker, Baron von Stein; afterwards a memorandum was produced, which was never dated or signed, but which again reiterated that the 'Rhineland–Westphalian Republic' should remain within the Reich.

Ever since that date, Adenauer was subjected to periodic accusations of having wanted to detach the Rhineland – *his* Rhineland – from the German Reich. The fact that the January 7 memorandum was undated and unsigned did not help him. But on January 23 von Stein, who may well have been having second thoughts about the matter, wrote to Adenauer on the eve of a separatist meeting in Aachen, urging the need to oppose all plans for separation from the Reich. Adenauer wrote a soothing letter back on January 25.[27] On January 27 his correspondence with the firm of Oppenheim referred to the French as 'our enemies'.[28] The separatists believed in some kind of association of their 'free state' with France; clearly, Adenauer never believed in *that*.

But on February 1, 1919, Adenauer's attitude was explained beyond any further doubt. Members of the German and Prussian national assemblies met in Cologne's *Hansasaal*. This was a representative if unofficial gathering of all Parliamentarians from the left bank of the Rhine. Adenauer made the principal speech to this assembly.[29] It was a long and full speech, lasting three hours, and its main points were the following:

Prussia, with 42 million out of Germany's 65 million inhabitants had a 'hegemony' position in the past. The dynasty which had kept Prussia intact, and had expanded its power, had gone. Other parts of Germany had the right to their own, chosen form of existence – 'East Prussia and the Rhineland are as different as East Prussia and Bavaria.' Any rearrangement within Germany should take account of France's real fear of German might, but should avoid the detachment of the left bank of the Rhine from Germany. Adenauer stressed that such a rearrangement could perhaps be organized. He underlined the word 'perhaps'. He also insisted that a French annexation of the left bank of the Rhine, 'in any sort of manner', would bring another war 'as surely as the sun rises tomorrow'. At the same time, he made it clear that the creation of a 'Rhineland–Westphalian' state, within the Reich, would not weaken the Reich and would certainly not leave Prussia, as had been suggested in some quarters, 'defenceless' against Poland.

The *Hansasaal* meeting ended with a resolution. It rejected any separation of the Rhineland from the rest of Germany, and claimed the right of

26, 27, 28, 29. Cologne City Archives.

self-determination so that 'we should remain united with our fellow nationals in the Reich'. It laid down that a committee should be set up to prepare plans for the establishment of a West German Republic within the framework of the Reich; and Adenauer was unanimously elected chairman of this committee. The delegates who had attended the meeting had been particularly impressed by Adenauer's grasp of European politics. He had argued essentially for an understanding with France, and for steps to prevent France from pursuing policies so hostile to German interests that yet another Franco-German war would be inevitable.

Adenauer's admirers and critics have produced diametrically opposite explanations of his behaviour at the meeting of February 1, 1919. His admirers have suggested that he 'disarmed' the separatist movement, and have cited in favour of this explanation the fact that he never convened his Rhineland committee once. His critics consider that he wanted a separate Rhineland state, because he knew that his Centre Party would control it, and he believed that he personally would control the Centre Party. The truth probably lay somewhere between these two explanations. Adenauer wanted an administrative separation from Prussia. He wanted to make a friendly gesture towards France. But he did not want his Rhineland annexed by France or turned into a French satellite state. He had read plenty of European history; French satrapies on German soil had a uniformly bad record.

As it happened, he won a breathing space for the Rhineland. The London *Times* speculated on the objectives of the German federalists and came to the conclusion that there was a far-flung movement favouring the creating of four large republics out of Germany and Austria. They were to comprise, apparently, a South German State based on Austria and Bavaria, a North German State centred on Hanover, Prussia within her pre-1815 frontiers and Adenauer's expanded Rhineland.[30] Patriotic associations were formed in the Rhineland and elsewhere, demanding that not one square mile of German territory should be lost to the Reich, and a 'patriotic' poet, Hermann Haase, wrote a rousing 'hymn', whose last verse read:

> 'Laszt die Feinde jubeln, lachen
> Spotten uns'rer groszen Not.
> Deutschland ist nicht totzumachen –
> Macht es sich nicht selber tot.'
> (*Enemies may jibe and jeer,*
> *And our deep distress deride.*
> *Germany won't disappear –*
> *Save through her own suicide.*)

30..........The London *Times*, March 21, 1919.

The respite which Adenauer won for the Rhineland was of very short duration. The general commanding French troops in Germany was Charles Mangin, known to the men under his command as 'the butcher', or the 'eater of men'. An arresting picture of him has been painted by Alistair Horne, in his book on the Battle of Verdun, *The Price of Glory*.[31] Here, it is enough to say that he was ruthless, highly patriotic and possessed of considerable charm. Mangin quickly got into touch with leading separatists. He invited them to his headquarters at Mainz and informed them, insinuatingly, that the Rhineland was in any event going to be detached from the German Reich. It would therefore be best for the Rhinelanders to build up their own buffer-state; this could even ease the peace-terms still to be imposed on Germany as a whole (this was in May, 1919, and peace negotiations were going on in Versailles).

Allegedly, Mangin told two of the separatists, Froberger and Dahlen, that the creation of an independent Rhineland would mean that France, in return, would give up her claim to the Saar, and Belgium would not insist on annexing Eupen and Malmédy[32] (in the event, these places were assigned to Belgium only a few weeks later under the terms of the Treaty of Versailles, and the Saar was put under League of Nations administration and detached from Germany for the next sixteen years). This kind of refined, yet ruthless, blackmail brought other separatists to Mainz, and a meeting on May 17 lasted three hours. Adenauer got wind of what was going on, and himself went to Berlin to report and to discuss the situation with the Reich Government.[33] On May 30 he told his City Councillors that the visits of prominent Rhinelanders to General Mangin in Mainz should be strongly discouraged.

By a curious coincidence two officers from General Mangin's headquarters called on that very day at the office in Cologne of the commanding British officer, General George Sidney Clive. The account of what happened as a result is that of the British General:[34]

General Mangin's spokesman, a Colonel André, told Clive that a movement to create an independent Rhineland was under way, and indicated that it was a serious matter. General Mangin wanted to know what General Clive's attitude, and the British attitude in general, would be.

Clive answered that these were political matters about which he knew nothing. As a British officer commanding troops in Cologne his duty was to maintain order there. But when the two Frenchmen had gone, Clive convinced himself that he should report this curious visitation. A man of

31..........*The Price of Glory*, Alistair Horne, p. 232.
32, 33.....Cologne City Archives.
34 ....Memorandum of General Clive. In the possession of his son-in-law Sir Christopher Steel.

action, he set off by car, motored through the entire night and arrived in Paris at 8 a.m. the next morning. He asked to see the British Prime Minister, Mr. Lloyd George, who was taking part in the peace negotiations. Mr. Lloyd George was setting out for an early morning walk in the Bois de Boulogne and took Clive with him.

On this lovely early summer morning the Prime Minister, who had not breakfasted, was in a poor humour. According to Clive, he 'upbraided me' for getting mixed up in politics. But he did at least make clear that Britain would not be in favour of the creation of an independent Rhineland. For Britain's interest, as Lloyd George told Clive, lay in maintaining a viable Germany as a buffer against Russian Bolshevism. There seems little doubt that Clive's message left its mark, both at the time and on future British policy.

The indefatigable Clive motored the whole way back to Cologne on that same day, May 31. It was a Saturday; if ever a man had earned a weekend in Paris, he had. But there was work to be done. On Sunday morning Colonel André rang him up from Wiesbaden; the independent Rhineland movement was 'moving north from Wiesbaden and going very well', he said. It was being led by 'a man who wore an eye-glass', a Dr. Dorten.[35]

Clive at once sent for Adenauer and one of his leading officials, a Dr. von Starck. According to his account, both were very agitated, and Adenauer told him that feeling in Cologne was absolutely against separatism. He suggested a ban on separatist meetings. Clive had a better idea; he sent for several newspaper editors the next day, June 2, and told them the Wiesbaden story. Clive, in a memorandum on the episode, maintained that Cologne was duly 'roaring with laughter' at the idea of a movement to separate the Rhineland from Germany being launched from an obscure place like Wiesbaden.[36]

Separatism, however, was no laughing matter. On June 2, Dr. Josef Adam Dorten, under the protective wing of the redoubtable General Mangin in Mainz, announced that the 'Rhineland Republic' was now in existence, with Mainz as its temporary 'capital' and with the 'seat of government' to be moved to Wiesbaden. On the same day, he informed the Prussian Minister President that the Rhineland was no longer a part of Prussia and that his government was sending a delegation to the peace talks at Versailles. This telephoned message resulted in the Reich Government at once declaring that Dorten and his henchmen were guilty of treason. On June 4, 1919, Dorten's followers, with French arms and a French escort across the Rhine, 'marched' on Wiesbaden and tried to seize its government build-

35...........Dorten was goodlooking, 39 years old at the time. His nickname was 'Pretty Addi'.

36...........*Adenauer und der rheinische Separatismus*, Günther Meinhardt.

ings. They were repelled by a hastily collected volunteer 'defence force', composed of railway and factory workers, who drove them back to the banks of the Rhine and beat up two of them so badly that they landed up in a Mainz hospital.[37]

In Cologne the Centre Party met and drafted a statement sharply condemning separatism which was sent to all leading newspapers in the Rhineland. But something more was needed, and on June 5 Adenauer, accompanied by leading members of the Centre and Social Democratic Parties, travelled to Versailles for talks with the head of the German delegation there, Count Ulrich von Brockdorff-Rantzau. The Count took note of their determination to combat separatism, and at the same time argued strongly against the creation even of a Rhineland state within the Reich. He told Adenauer that there was not the slightest chance of the Allies making concessions in return – one which had been aired in the Rhineland was the possible creation of a semi-autonomous Alsace-Lorraine, rather than its re-annexation by France.

This meeting may well have convinced Adenauer that even the Rhineland state which he had envisaged was not a practical proposition. The danger of revolution, directed from Berlin, had passed. Prussia was consolidating itself and would certainly oppose a federalist experiment in the Rhineland. Nor was there sufficient local enthusiasm for his proposals. Indeed, a German General Staff memorandum made available at this time to the City Council pointed out that interest was restricted to half a dozen large towns, whereas in the countryside there was complete apathy.[38] What is sure is that Adenauer, at least for the next four years, did nothing to promote his original plan of a Rhineland state within the Reich.

All talk of this plan being instrumental in securing concessions from France ended on June 28, 1919, when Count von Brockdorff-Rantzau signed the Treaty of Versailles in the Palace's famous Hall of Mirrors. The Count had actually received the peace terms on May 17 and had been given fifteen days to obtain his government's signature. From then on he fought a hopeless rearguard action by letter – he was not allowed to argue Germany's case in person at the Peace Conference. In Berlin the Social Democratic government led by Gustav Bauer was forced to accept the Treaty's harsh terms by June 23, but still argued feebly in favour of deleting clauses which charged Germany and individual Germans with war-crimes. Not a word of the Treaty was altered. Under its terms Germany was committed to paying massive reparations, beginning with a

37..........*Adenauer in der Rheinland Politik nach dem ersten Weltkrieg*, Karl Dieter Erdmann, p. 63.

38..........Cologne City Archives.

down-payment of $5 billion in gold (approximately £208 million); her army was to be reduced to 100,000 men, with no more than 4,000 officers; Alsace-Lorraine was to be returned to France. Posen, Upper Silesia and the so-called Danzig Corridor were to be ceded to Poland, and much smaller pieces of territory went to Belgium and Denmark; no kind of union with Austria was to be permitted.

Adenauer's Rhineland was particularly affected by the clauses governing Allied military occupation. The whole Rhineland, west of the river, was to be occupied for fifteen years, and was divided up into zones held by the French, British, Belgians and Americans. When the fifteen years were up, the previously occupied area would remain demilitarized, as would a 50 kilometre (32 mile) wide strip of territory to the east of the Rhine. Where Allied occupation was concerned, the Rhineland was to pay the whole bill for Germany's alleged and assumed war-guilt.

Cologne remained in the British zone, and the very fact of British and American participation in the Occupation meant that it was going to be more difficult for the separatists to create their independent state. Separatism, however, smouldered on. In Düsseldorf, on July 23, Adenauer spoke publicly against it, and at his request, the British Military Government banned separatist activity in its zone from August 22, 1919. For his part in this, Adenauer was given a 'death sentence' by a 'Revolutionary Tribunal' convened under French military protection in Coblenz. Adenauer's dry comment was that 'this verdict is worth more to me than any decoration'.[39]

Dorten had by now been joined by a different group of separatists, led by a Josef Smeets, a former member of the Social Democratic Party. Smeets brought with him his *Rheinische Republikanische Partei*, a weekly paper and a number of very rough characters who seemed to be more interested in looting than in politics. Smeets was responsible for the proclamation of a separatist 'republic' in Birkenfeld, close to the borders of the Saar, on September 15, 1919. In January 1920, Dorten and Smeets formally founded a *Rheinische Volksvereinigung*, which was intended to be an umbrella organization for all separatists in the Rhineland and neighbouring districts. A month later the two men formed a para-military force, the *Rheinwehr*. Its arms clearly came from the French forces of occupation – although the separatists' chief protector, General Mangin, had by now been recalled to France; and it had interesting links with the Communist Party. Smeets was almost certainly implicated in Communist risings which took place in the Ruhr and southern Rhineland in March, 1921.

39..........*Konrad Adenauer*, Paul Weymar, p. 54.

Adenauer's view at this time was that the separatist danger had passed, and that the preachings of its hard core could be 'killed' by ridicule. He made one determined attempt to convince the French authorities that separatism was doomed to failure when he visited Berlin in November, 1920, for talks with the French Ambassador, Charles Laurent.[40] Adenauer told Laurent that Dorten was 'an absurd figure' (*eine lächerliche Figur*) and that the people of the Rhineland treated him as an object of scorn. He complained of French support for Dorten and contrasted French interference in civil affairs with the absolutely fair behaviour of the British authorities in Cologne. He was also irritated by the excessive number of French officers in inter-Allied reparations and disarmament commissions. Adenauer put very strongly to Laurent his view that Franco-German relations would be immensely helped by large-scale and imaginative economic co-operation.

Rhineland separatism looked like dying a comparatively peaceful death throughout 1922. But early in 1923 an event occurred which brought it back to life with a violent jolt. On January 11, 1923, French troops, followed by Belgian, marched into the industrial area of the Ruhr, to the east of the Rhine. France and Belgium decided on this step because of persistent shortfalls in German reparations deliveries of coal and pit-props. Their action was opposed by both Britain and the United States. It was opposed by the Ruhr railwaymen, coal-miners and other workers, who resorted to a policy of passive resistance. Trains ceased to run and the miners stayed at home. The French, in a popular phrase of the times, 'had to dig coal with their bayonets'.

The Ruhr's misfortune was the separatists' opportunity. They could be useful to the French and so could count on increased French support. The deteriorating situation actually helped them. In February the French instituted punitive measures in the Ruhr; they deported striking railwaymen from their areas of occupation, imposed prison sentences and huge fines on Germans who refused to carry out their orders, mobilized forced labour, requisitioned housing and property, and put in 3,000 French officials and railwaymen to supervise over 3,000 miles of railway-line. Passive resistance was now supplemented by a German sabotage campaign; track was torn up, bridges dynamited and trains derailed. The French countered by arresting saboteurs and shooting them after summary court-martial.

All this very much suited the separatists' book, but they suffered some early reverses. On the night of January 25–26 the offices of Dorten's paper, the *Rheinländer*, were destroyed by indignant patriots. On the night

40..........Cologne City Archives.

of March 9–10 the same thing happened to the Gutenberg printing works at Coblenz, which worked for Dorten. On March 17 a series of brawls culminated with several of Smeets' men being killed and Smeets himself being wounded by the 'patriotic commando' led by Leo Schlageter (later to be executed by the French). In April Dorten was in Paris, asking the French Government for increased military support and for final steps to be taken to create an autonomous Rhineland State.

A new factor now entered the situation. The Communists decided to take a hand, either because of their links with Smeets or because of increased Communist activity in other parts of Germany and a serious attempt to create a three-state Communist Republic in Saxony, Thuringia and Brunswick (Walter Ulbricht, later to be head of the post-1945 Communist East German State, took an active part in this). By May, 1923, Communist-provoked strikes and demonstrations were endemic, particularly in the industrial Ruhr. The French authorities made little effort to control them. In one particularly disgraceful incident, members of the German civil 'Green Police' were murdered under the eyes of the French Army by a separatist mob in Düsseldorf.[41] This mob appears to have mobilized, under French protection, in the middle of a major Communist demonstration.

Adenauer's attitude towards these developments was at first clear-cut but became slightly blurred, as the situation grew steadily more serious in the Ruhr and the whole of Germany suffered from the consequences of the Ruhr's industrial paralysis. The German economy had already been seriously weakened by Allied occupation, industrial unrest and the huge burden of reparations. By mid-summer a catastrophic inflation of the Mark had reduced paper-money to less than the value of the paper on which it was printed. Adenauer foresaw this development when he wrote to the Government in Berlin shortly after the French marched into the Ruhr. He asked for a major diplomatic effort to get the French out again, and warned of the irreparable damage which would be done to international relations as well as to the German economy. His letter was subsequently published in the *Kölner Tageblatt*.[42]

He was getting plenty of advice, some of it unsolicited. The British military authorities made their attitude plain; they thoroughly disapproved of the French action in the Ruhr, and they supported Adenauer when the French authorities complained that he was encouraging German 'national-

41...........A graphic account of the incident was given in Geoffrey Moss' novel *Defeat* (Constable: London, 1944). There is also a reference to it in *The Revolver Republic*, a book written by *The Times* correspondent, G. E. R. Gedye.

42...........Cologne City Archives.

ist' propaganda and acts of sabotage.[43] And Adenauer was urged to stand firm, even against the provisions of the Treaty of Versailles and the 'sadistic crimes' of the *grande nation*, France, in a series of letters written by a Mr. Arthur Turnbull, of 208 Upper Clapton Road, in London's East End. Letters from citizens of Cologne poured in, for they regarded their Mayor as perhaps the only public figure on whom they could depend. One of these letters contained some somewhat repetitive poetry; its last verse went:

'Kein prahlend Nein! Kein Nein mit Reden!
Ein Nein dem Eid gleich soll es sein.
Ein bindend Nein fuer einen Leden,
Ein echtes, wahres, deutsches Nein!'
(*No boastful No! Nor yet with speeches!*
Our No must be as a pledge.
A No that binds as a thong,
A true, authentic, German No!)

In July, 1923, Adenauer appealed, in a letter, to a member of the British House of Commons, Sir Philip Dawson, for the same sort of help for the occupied Rhineland as had been so readily given by Britain to occupied Belgium during the war. In the same month a deputation of the British Transport and General Workers Union, led by Mr. Ben Tillett, M.P., visited the Ruhr. Their report made sombre reading. Industry was working at about 25 per cent of capacity and coal-pits were closing down every week. The Mark had lost any semblance of real value and a three-room working-class flat was costing 80–100 million Marks to build. The cost of living was 685 times higher than pre-war, and strikes were endemic. The report concluded by calling the Ruhr 'the hell-cauldron of a new and terrible war', accused the French of a deliberate plan to destroy German industry, and stated that 'Unless France clears out of the Ruhr within a few weeks, it would have been better for the world in general and Europe in particular if the Germans had won the war.' A copy of the report was sent to Adenauer.[44]

The French were not prepared to content themselves with their military occupation of the key industrial area in Germany. Their old plan for creating an independent Rhineland state had never been abandoned, but only put on ice. They had evolved a new technique for its implementation; law and order were to be undermined, even in areas under British

43..........Adenauer wrote to the head of the British section of the Inter-Allied Rhineland Commission, Major J. L. Piggott, denying this and asking for a guarantee of tenure of his post of Mayor. Cologne City Archives.

44..........Cologne City Archives.

occupation, and the Ruhr could be held until the right conditions had been created for the seizure of power in the Rhineland by the separatists. A useful line of argument suggested itself to the French; their withdrawal from the Ruhr could be part of a tacit agreement that they would be left free to organize favourable political conditions on the left bank of the Rhine.

Adenauer undoubtedly had forewarning of their aims. From September 4–6 he was in Berlin, for talks with the Reich Government. He took with him Louis Hagen, a Jew who was a member of the City Council and the Chairman of the German Economic Committee for the occupied areas. Since August 12, Gustav Stresemann had been Reich Chancellor, having taken over from Wilhelm Cuno at the precise moment that Germany suspended all further reparations payments to the Allies. Stresemann wanted to end the struggle over the Ruhr, which was costing Germany large sums in relief payments and was digging a bottomless pit of international ill-will. Adenauer distrusted Stresemann, personally and politically. He believed that Stresemann was prepared to save the Reich further financial and political embarrassment, at the expense of the Rhineland.

He believed, in fact, that Stresemann might give the French a free hand in the Rhineland. He and Louis Hagen argued in favour of an agreement under which the French allowed political deportees to return, released political prisoners and recognized the restoration of the authority of the Reich in the Ruhr. A curious and still unexplained episode in history followed, in which Stresemann made an approach to the French Government, was apparently rebuffed, and the French asked to negotiate with local, Rhineland authorities – other than Adenauer. The Government in Berlin at the same time 'leaked' the news about Adenauer's confidential talks with Stresemann, and the *Berliner Tageblatt* of September 7, 1923, published an account of the talks in which its correspondent stated that Adenauer and Hagen had guaranteed to frustrate French schemes to support a separatist movement and the creation of a separate currency in the Rhineland.[45] One can make what one will of this episode; Adenauer's reaction was understandable – he wrote to Stresemann reminding him that their talks had been confidential, that he was only a Lord Mayor and Hagen a City Councillor, and that they could 'guarantee' nothing.

In the event, Stresemann did exactly what Adenauer had expected; he announced the end of the Ruhr 'confrontation'.[46] He called off all forms of resistance. He was, of course, after much bigger game – political and

45...........Cologne City Archives (and Meinhardt).

46...........The exact date of his decision is not clear. Sir John Wheeler-Bennett (*Nemesis of Power*, p. 106) says the decision was taken in August. Günther Meinhardt (*Adenauer und der rheinische Separatismus*) dates the announcement September 24,1923.

financial agreements with the Western Allies, entry of Germany into the League of Nations and the termination of the Allied occupation of the Rhineland. But there is more than a suspicion that he explained neither his motives nor his methods to Adenauer and Hagen, whose advice he had sought and whom he used as mere sounding-boards.

Stresemann may have been proved right in the long run. But the immediate consequences were unpleasant. 'Pretty Addi', Dr. Dorten, at once announced the separatist aims. There was to be an independent Rhineland state, running from Frankfurt to Essen and including all of Germany west of the Rhine, as well as important areas to the east of the river. This state was to have its own currency, railways and postal service, issuing its own stamps. The announcement was backed up by the organization of armed 'commandos' of hired thugs, some of them ex-convicts. The first commandos were used in Düsseldorf and Mülheim, and on September 30, 1923, a pitched battle was fought in the streets of Düsseldorf, in which the police routed the separatists. French tanks moved into the middle of town in order to protect the separatists, and cover their retreat.

Early in October there were food riots in most of the cities of the Rhineland, fomented by both Communists and separatists. There was also mass unemployment, and just that atmosphere of despair which the French and their separatist stooges hoped to exploit. The French occupation authorities in the Rhineland were doing everything in their power to promote anarchy; two members of the Rhineland Commission, a Colonel d'Arbonneau and a M. Roussellier, produced reports in which Adenauer was declared to be 'hostile to France' and to have been one of the organizers of passive resistance in the Rühr.[47] The French authorities suspected Adenauer of trying to invoke British aid, or at least mediation, and made it plain that he would not be the right person to preside at talks between the Reich Government and the Allied Rhineland Commission. The thought of Adenauer, in the light of his post-1945 career, being pro-British is an intriguing one. It is a remarkable tribute to his strength of character that he remained, in fact, solidly and consistently in favour of Franco-German understanding.

The separatists struck on October 21, 1923. On that day they seized Aachen and proclaimed, not for the first time, the inauguration of their 'Rhineland Republic'. Aachen had a symbolic importance; it had been the nominal capital of the domains of the Emperor Charlemagne. And on the next day, October 22, the separatists attacked another 'historic' city, Trier, which had even longer ago been Roman headquarters in Germany. In Mainz and Coblenz the separatists could maintain themselves under French

47..........Cologne City Archives.

protection; they were now able, if only temporarily, to seize Wiesbaden, Trier, Duisburg and Krefeld. But they could not hold them, and their commandos went over to a 'war of movement' in which motorized columns terrorized the countryside and lived off plunder.

On October 31, 1923, the London newspaper, the *Daily Chronicle*, published this account from their Special Correspondent in Cologne:

'I have spent a couple of days visiting the "Rhineland Republic" and I find it very hard to believe that the whole thing is not a hideous nightmare ... This "republic" is a republic of hunger and terror; a republic run by convicts, and "policed" by imported ruffians of the most aggressive type. With the "Rhineland Republic" the Rhinelanders have absolutely nothing to do.'

The observations of the *Daily Chronicle* were strictly accurate. In Bonn the 'Republican' chief was a naturalized American, who had fled to Germany to escape criminal charges.[48] In München-Gladbach the two 'Republican' commissioners were ex-convicts; the same was true of the two commissioners in Düren, who shared 43 convictions between them. It was perhaps significant that the first action of the separatist commando which seized Krefeld was to destroy all the criminal records kept at police headquarters.

The situation in the Rhineland was desperate, and it was at this stage that Adenauer decided or was induced to have a talk with M. Henri Tirard, the French President of the Inter-Allied Commission in Coblenz. The talk took place on November 14, 1923. On the day before, Adenauer had a meeting with Reich Chancellor Stresemann in Berlin. His subsequent version of this meeting was that Stresemann urged the creation of a 'provisional' independent Rhineland, stated that the Reich could not give the Rhineland any further financial aid, and advised a meeting with Tirard.[49] This was, predictably, inconclusive. Tirard at once reported that Adenauer 'agreed' that the Rhineland should be detached from the rest of Germany, and should have its own currency, defence forces and diplomatic representation abroad. France has produced many single-minded, dedicated men who have served her interests, without regard to moral considerations. No more need be said of M. Tirard.

As it happened, Tirard corrected his first report of his talk with Adenauer. On November 27 he informed the French Prime Minister, M. Poincaré, that Adenauer was being obstructive. On November 29 Adenauer supplied his reasoned objections to Tirard's various proposals. He sent him a letter in which he wrote that a Rhineland state would have

48..........Cologne City Archives.
49..........*Konrad Adenauer*, Paul Weymar, p. 56–58.

to remain in the Reich, although it could stay demilitarized and could be given some sort of international 'gendarmerie'. A Rhineland state of this kind would act as a valuable link between France and Germany, and could be the vehicle for close economic co-operation. Stresemann's Government had fallen in the meantime, and Adenauer's views were endorsed – albeit most hesitantly – by the new Reich Chancellor, Wilhelm Marx. On December 12, Tirard answered Adenauer's letter, rejecting his ideas. This was the end of a correspondence which Adenauer had never sought and which could never have led anywhere.

The separatist movement had, by this time, already reached and passed its climax. In the autumn of 1923 a series of bitter battles took place in widely scattered places in the Rhineland. The separatists were ejected from the towns by a concerted drive on the part of the police. They retreated into the countryside, and preyed on it. In November there were pitched battles in the hilly *Siebengebirge* area east of Bonn, and the separatists were routed by a 'farmers' militia' armed mainly with shotguns and pitchforks and ready to use their weapons without hesitation. In December there were isolated engagements, which continued into 1924. The hated separatists – more loathsome parasites had never been produced by any nation – were hunted down, shot, scythed asunder and beaten to death. The last of them to die on German soil were flung into the flames of government offices in Pirmasens which they had themselves set on fire. The separatists who survived fled to Alsace-Lorraine or found service in the French Foreign Legion.

All fighting ended by February 1924. 'Pretty Addi', Dr. Dorten, fled to France, settled in Nice and became a French citizen. The President of the 'Autonomous Government of the Palatinate', a Herr Heinz, was assassinated in his self-designated capital of Speyer in January, 1924. At about the same time the Poincaré Government was replaced in Paris by a Socialist, non-annexationist administration led by Edouard Herriot. This, then, really was the end of the French effort to detach the Rhineland from Germany.

This French effort constitutes a highly confusing episode in history. For Adenauer it was a crucial period, for he was ever afterwards accused of complicity with France's dark designs. In the late 1920s and the early 1930s, he found himself obliged to take legal action on a number of occasions. The Nazis labelled him a separatist, an easy way of 'smearing' a political opponent. Even after the Second World War, Adenauer's part in the five troubled and tumultuous years after the First World War was the subject of much uninformed, misguided or partisan comment.

In the light of the evidence available, his attitude during those five years, 1919–24, can be summed up as follows:

He disliked centralism under Prussia, and favoured a federal structure for the post-1919 German Reich. It followed that an enlarged Rhineland could be an important component in such a Federal State, and its enlargement was necessary if it were to act as a counterweight to the power of Prussia. Both in 1919 and again, if with less conviction, in 1923, Adenauer thought that a federal solution for Germany was still on the cards.

He opposed separatism. His dealings with General Clive and other British officials in the Rhineland reveal this most clearly of all. So do the contemporary comments of French officials and the French Press. France's leaders were entirely aware that Adenauer was an obstacle to their plans either for annexing the left bank of the Rhine or for creating a completely independent Rhineland State. Yet, although it fell to Adenauer to play a key role in frustrating these plans, he never lost sight of the need for Franco-German reconciliation and co-operation. Within a few months of the end of the First World War, he was advocating industrial collaboration and the investment of foreign capital in the Ruhr.

Finally, Adenauer never lost his head, even in situations which looked almost hopeless. He had to compete with vigorous French pressure, with a lack of sympathy on the part of the Government in Berlin, and with periods of anarchy caused by the destructive activities of the separatists and Communists. When Stresemann began to give up hope of keeping the Rhineland in Germany, Adenauer remained calm and determined. So much space has been given to this tortuous and troubled period because, prior to 1945, it was the most formative in a political sense of Konrad Adenauer's life.

4 King of Cologne

Adenauer married for a second time on September 25, 1919. His bride Auguste (Gussi) Zinsser, was 25 years old; he was a mature 43. The disparity in age caused some minor complications. The Zinssers had been friends of the Adenauer family for the best part of ten years. Adenauer's three children by his first wife found it difficult to start calling 'the Zinsser girls' (Gussi had an elder sister, Lotte) 'Mummy' and 'Auntie'. His elder son, Konrad (Koko), complained indignantly, 'How can I call her Mummy, when I've seen her going to school with her satchel!'[1]

Courting Gussi Zinsser involved some problems too. Her father was a doctor, a skin specialist, attached to Cologne University. He was fond of children and had treated the little Adenauers as almost his own after their mother died in 1916. He thought Adenauer too old. In addition, he and his family were Protestants and he did not like the idea of his daughter marrying a Roman Catholic. Nor did he want her to marry a widower with a family; he was well aware of complications which arose in such cases. Then, his daughter was old enough to know her own mind, but she would have heavy responsibilities as the 'First Lady' of Cologne.

Gussi was 'sent away' to stay with relatives in Wiesbaden and have time to make up her mind for sure. The plan was for her to stay six months away, but she returned after a few weeks. She told her parents that she was determined to marry Adenauer, and one of her first actions was to join the Roman Catholic Church. Pictures of Adenauer's first wife, Emma, show an intelligent, reserved and sensitive face. Gussi was simpler, gayer, easier perhaps, fond of children and flowers, very ready to laugh, full of enthusiasm in a way which must have touched Adenauer's heart. The sad, lonely years were over; Gussi set to work to make a real home once more out of the house in the Max Bruch Strasse. There was one early shock in their married life; her first child, Ferdinand, was born weak and sickly. His mother was found to be suffering from a kidney complaint, eclampsia.[2] Ferdinand was born prematurely and lived for only three days. He died at dawn on June 7, 1920; from midnight onwards Adenauer held him,

1............*Konrad Adenauer*, Paul Weymar, p. 64.
2............*Konrad Adenauer*, Paul Weymar, p. 65. Eclampsia is the result of retention of sodium by sluggishly functioning kidneys.

warmly wrapped, in his arms. The doctors had told him there was no hope of the child living.

His older children have happy memories of the years that followed. Gussi's health improved, and four more children were born, Paul, Lotte, Libeth (Elizabeth) and 'Schorsch' (George). This made a big household and it was a happy one. Adenauer was tremendously busy, and perhaps his only regret was that he had too little time for his children. They remember his being, at this time, very strict and exacting.[3] Evidently he believed in the same sort of family discipline which had been his own experience as a child. He was a 'perfectionist',[4] and some of the family later on in life were of the opinion that he had 'read up' about how one should bring up a family, possibly when his first wife died. He was particularly keen that his children should work hard and understand that knowledge was worth while for its own sake; and he expected something extra from his oldest son, Koko.[5]

But the atmosphere in the home was not 'stiff'.[6] Gussi had love to spare for the older children as well as her own, and both parents were determined that the family should be a united one. This meant that the three older children were encouraged to take an interest in the younger ones, and interest and affection seem to have been reciprocated all round. When he had the time to spare, Adenauer showed plenty of affection for his children, and there was always much talk about what he was doing as Mayor and what was happening to Cologne. In these early days there was no mention of politics; but Adenauer wanted all of his children to know what was going on directly around them. He wanted Cologne to be 'their' city, as well as his own.

Adenauer had, in effect, three different 'lives' between 1919 and 1934. The first of these three lives has already been dealt with; it had to do with the chequered story of Rhineland separatism. The second was, of course, his role as Lord Mayor of the city which regarded itself as the 'capital' of Catholic Germany. The third centred on Berlin; in 1920 Adenauer became the Chairman of the Prussian State Council, the second house of Parliament in Prussia. This brought him into periodic touch with national policies and, on two occasions in the 1920s, looked like turning him into a political figure of national importance.

First, then, his work for Cologne. Obviously there was a tremendous amount to do for a city which had looked, in 1914, like growing quickly into a *Millionenstadt* (a town with more than a million inhabitants), and whose development had then been halted by the war. In 1919 Cologne was

3............Frau Ria Reiners, in private conversation with the author.
4, 5.........Dr. Max Adenauer, in private conversation with the author.
6............Frau Ria Reiners, in private conversation with the author.

a city with over half a million inhabitants, which had expanded, in a physical sense, without any coherent planning. Cologne proper was on the left or west bank of the Rhine. It had for centuries been enclosed by a line of fortifications, stretching in an almost perfect crescent from north, to west, to south. Suburbs had grown up, higgledy-piggledy, outside the old fortifications, and on the right or east bank of the Rhine as well. As an important garrison town, Cologne had retained fortifications which had been wildly out-of-date since the 1870 war.

It was unluckier – in parentheses – than neighbouring Düsseldorf. Napoleon's nominee, Marshal Murat, made Düsseldorf his capital of the short-lived 'Grand Duchy of Berg' and razed its fortifications to the ground. He turned them into parks and water-gardens, and gave Düsseldorf an 'ambiance' which resulted in Düsseldorfers claiming ever since the title of 'Little Paris' for their city – without understanding why.

Adenauer's first task, after the First World War ended, did not have to do with the intricacies of city planning. It was concerned with the creation of a university. Cologne badly needed one.

There had been a Cologne University in the past. Indeed, it was the fourth which had been created in the Holy Roman Empire, in 1388 (the only older universities were those of Prague, Vienna and Heidelberg).[7] Cologne University was closed down by the French military authorities in April, 1798, when its Professors refused to swear an oath of loyalty to the French Republic. One is amazed by the effrontery of French military authorities who tried to enforce such an oath.

After the defeat of Napoleon, an impoverished Prussia had to content itself with re-opening one university in the Rhineland. The French had closed down Trier, Bonn and Mainz, in addition to Cologne. The Prussian Government picked Bonn, possibly because it had a handy princely castle. Bonn, then, remained for the next century the only seat of university learning in the Rhineland.

In 1913 agitation began for re-founding the University of Cologne. Plans were drawn up, largely as a result of Adenauer's personal initiative. There was immediate opposition from Bonn University and, much more important, from its 'old boys', the *Alte Herren*, many of whom were influential members of the Prussian administrative hierarchy. They were abetted by the liberal parties, which argued that Bonn University would lose its status as the 'second university' in Prussia, if a rival institution opened in Catholic Cologne.

Adenauer went to Berlin to argue his case. He made two points: the

7............The historical details are set out in *Die Universitaet Köln* (Verlag Oskar Mueller.)

Rhine would lose Strasbourg University to France and so needed a second university, and the Allied occupation of the Rhineland made it imperative to promote centres of learning there and so stiffen the German national spirit.[8] Adenauer had his way; on January 4, 1919, the Government of Prussia approved his plans for re-establishing the university. On May 29 a detailed agreement on ways and means was drawn up. Temporary courses were arranged for the summer, with a staff of 91 teachers which was doubled in the autumn. By the end of the year, 4,000 students had enrolled themselves. Thereafter there were around 7,000 enrolled students, and 25,000 matriculated in the ten years, 1919–29. Cologne University was decisively launched.

Adenauer was to make a habit of getting his way in the management of Cologne's affairs. Speaking at Cologne University in July, 1920, he said that there were three main problems to be solved. The first was to remove the old fortifications and put the ground on which they stood to good use. The second was to dispose of the 'empty zones' on the left bank of the Rhine, by using them for housing, industry or other purposes. The third was to adjust Cologne's economy to the situation created by the Treaty of Versailles. The Mayor had two immediate pieces of information to give: he had already secured ownership rights over the terrain occupied by the fortifications, and he proposed to create a girdle of woods and meadows round the perimeter of the city.[9]

The remnants of the old forts were swept away without too much trouble. This work had the full approval of the British occupation authorities. In no sense a military man, Adenauer had no false sentimentality about this. But the forts built by Prussia in the 1880s and 1890s were only the very last of the long series of bastions and earthworks which had stood in roughly the same place for two thousand years. A Celtic tribe, the Ubii, had founded Cologne in 38 B.C. and had defended these same outworks against the legions of the Roman Emperor Claudius, who renamed their primitive encampment Colonia Agrippinensis. Cologne had maintained its outer fortifications ever since.

The landscaping and planting of the girdle of meadow and forest was carried out without any objection from the British authorities and without legal difficulty.[10] But difficulties arose later on, and self-designated 'Belt Owners' formed an association and demanded compensation for the loss of tenuous grazing and squatting rights. Their claims took some years to

8.............*Aus Kölnischer und Rheinischer Geschichte*, Ed. Hans Blum, p. 208–9.
9.............Cologne City Archives.
10...........*Konrad Adenauer*, Paul Weymar, p. 70. The author states Adenauer had difficulty in securing the city's ownership rights at this time. In fact, the rights were secured on December 3, 1918. Cologne City Archives.

iron out by due process of law. Long before then the whole area had been reorganized. The parks and forests which were created then survived the Second World War and have remained virtually untouched ever since. In 1945 Adenauer remarked to his brother-in-law, Dr. Willi Suth (he married Adenauer's sister Lilli), 'The churches have gone, but my Green Belt has remained.'[11]

To help him with plans to fill the 'empty zones' on the left bank of the Rhine Adenauer secured the services of a distinguished architect and town-planner from Hamburg, Fritz Schumacher. He came early in 1920 on a three-year contract but has himself described how, soon after his arrival, Adenauer took him for an all-day ramble in the *Siebengebirge* and did his damndest to convince him that he should stay in Cologne for good.[12] When he had arrived, Schumacher was told by nearly everyone he met that it was hopeless to make a start on coherent town-planning under the British military occupation. The one optimist was Adenauer, and Schumacher has paid two handsome tributes to his tremendous energy and his obstinate determination in getting his own way. In his experience, Adenauer 'had no idea of the limits of human endurance'.[13] Again, he required a real challenge – 'That awoke in him the imagination of the real tactician and the determination of the chess-player.'[14]

Schumacher has one revealing story about him. Adenauer favoured the construction of a *Hochhaus* – nominally, a 'skyscraper', but in fact a building of a modest dozen storeys – about half a mile to the north-west of the Cathedral. There were immediate objections in the City Council, that it would be 'inappropriate' to have an office-block of this kind within 'plain view' of the Cathedral, which was the pride of Catholic Cologne.[15]

Adenauer let all his critics have their say; the feeling of the Council was plainly against his project. Then he told its members a story. Once upon a time, there had been a pious and respectable old spinster who objected to a Public Bath being built near her home. It was an offence to her sense of propriety. A commission was sent to her home to examine the facts, and discovered that the offending building was out of sight from every window in the house. The old lady had an answer; she took them to an upstairs room – 'If you stand on this table' she said, 'you will then see the full horror of it.'

Adenauer did not need to argue his case any further. The *Hochhaus* was built and, like the Green Belt, it survived the Second World War, when

11..........*Konrad Adenauer*, Paul Weymar, p. 72.
12..........*Stufen des Lebens*, Fritz Schumacher, p. 344.
13..........*Stufen des Lebens*, Fritz Schumacher, p. 365.
14..........*Stufen des Lebens*, Fritz Schumacher, p. 369.
15..........*Stufen des Lebens*, Fritz Schumacher, p. 366.

nearly 80 per cent of Cologne's buildings were either destroyed or damaged.

Another revealing story concerned Cologne's electricity supply. The *Rheinische Braunkohlenwerke*, which mined its 'soft' or surface coal to the west of the city, and which supplied Cologne with much of its electricity, announced increases in price. Adenauer believed that the price increases were unjustified. He thereupon collaborated with the Mayor of Frankfurt in buying the Rossenray coalfields near Duisburg (later the property of the Krupp family) and announced that Cologne would soon have its own electric power plant. The *Rheinische Braunkohlenwerke* gave in at once and signed a new agreement, at Adenauer's terms, for supplying Cologne. And Adenauer resold the Rossenray coalfields at a profit.[16] Nor was Adenauer in the least impressed when so-called progressives in the City Council tabled a plan for converting an area between the Cathedral and the river into a car-park. The *Altstadt*, or old city, was something which he intended to preserve. With patrician contempt he announced that the 'be-all' of Cologne was not that of a freeway for motorists. The car-park plan was dropped.

During the 1920s a whole series of improvements were carried out in Cologne. A sports stadium was built in the Green Belt, along with over fifty sports grounds. The Cologne *Messe* or 'Fair' buildings were planned, and were duly built in the suburb of Deutz, on the right bank of the Rhine. In May 1922 the small township of Worringen was incorporated into Cologne, for use as an industrial area. The incorporation of other outlying townships followed, each time with the permission of the Prussian *Land* Parliament. By 1924 Cologne was, after Berlin, the largest German city in area. A crescent of railway line was built round the western side of the City, the so-called *Gürtelbahn*, and major extensions were made to the city's harbours.

Before the First World War, goods traffic from the harbour had amounted to around only two million tons a year, against ten million tons carried by rail. The existing harbour in the middle of the city was now extended and modernized, and a new harbour of four parallel basins built to the north. This river frontage was a mile and a half long and backed on to a new 'Industrial Zone' in which factories and workers' housing began to go up. Thanks to his influence in the Prussian Parliament, Adenauer was able to link these developments with the national plan to expand canal traffic. Up to 1914 the Rhine had not been linked with any other waterways. After 1919 the Rhein–Herne Canal was built, joining the Dortmund–Ems and Ems–Weser canals. These were later linked with the Mittelland canal, enabling barges to travel all the way from the Rhine to the Elbe and its tributaries. The Main–Danube canal linked the Rhine with Bavaria.

16..........*Konrad Adenauer*, Paul Weymar, p. 73.

Of course there was plenty of opposition to what was done. Adenauer and Fritz Schumacher were criticized for placing too much emphasis on water transport, for 'over-industrializing' a city of cultural and commercial traditions, for building too many big blocks of flats – above all for being too grandiose. Schumacher made no secret of the fact that Cologne was intended to become a city of a million inhabitants in the next two decades, and of even two million in the more distant future. Yet he and Adenauer were careful to preserve the contours and even the narrow streets of the central 'Old City' – Adenauer had a distaste for motor traffic, which he claimed should be the servant and not the master of the people of Cologne.[17] The newspaper, *der Kunstwart*, may have been overgenerous when it wrote in June, 1925, that Cologne would soon be one of the most beautiful cities in Germany. It was, at least, being planned with great commonsense. Town-planners came from a score of countries, and from as far as Japan, to see what was being done there.[18]

On March 23, 1926, a historic ceremony took place in Cologne, the visit of the Reich President, ex Field-Marshal Paul von Hindenburg. This was to celebrate the evacuation of Cologne by the British armed forces. The evacuation was, in fact, completed on January 31. On the evening of the same day Adenauer spoke to a huge crowd in front of the Cathedral. He told them, 'We are once more free and united with our Fatherland, after seven years of separation;' asked them to join in the hope that 'our sufferings have not been in vain, and that a truly new spirit will enter into the peoples of Europe'; sent greetings to Germans in areas still under foreign occupation; and concluded with an appeal for total loyalty to the Fatherland, '*Deutschland, geliebtes Vaterland – Hoch! Hoch! Hoch!*'[19]

There had been some doubt up to the last moment as to when the British troops would leave. A reasonable interval was therefore allowed for, before Hindenburg's visit. He was greeted at the railway-station by the Adenauer family, and Adenauer's daughter Ria presented him with a bouquet of flowers. There were speeches in the *Rheinpark* – Adenauer's was surprisingly emotional, Hindenburg's more sober – a banquet for 400 guests in the Gürzenich Hall, and a torchlight procession in the evening. Adenauer maintained that the celebrations had gone off like clockwork (he used the phrase *in muestergueltiger Weise*). The State Porcelain Works in Meissen in Saxony struck a 5 Mark silver coin in honour of the occasion, bearing the words *Koln Befreit. 1926* ('Cologne liberated'), and in Cologne itself a number of special coins were minted – a 6 Mark piece in bronze, a 35 Marks in silver and a 500 Marks in fourteen carat gold.

17..........Cologne City Archives.
18..........*Neubau*, a journal, March 24, 1924.
19..........Cologne City Archives.

There had been some annoyances. Right-wing organizations took part in the torchlight procession, and there was some ostentatious displaying of the old, royalist black, white and red colours. The Social Democratic *Reichsbanner* organization, on the other hand, did not take part and claimed that it had not been invited. There was a street battle between uniformed rightwingers and Social Democrats in plain clothes, and a member of the *Reichsbanner* was shot and wounded. A six year-old boy dressed in a miniature Prussian Guards uniform, with a papier-maché Pickelhaube steel-pointed helmet was presented to the aged President who was himself wearing a black tail coat and stove-pipe hat. Hindenburg was taken aback by this militaristic dwarf, and must have been even less favourably impressed by the appearance of a Dr. Krummacher, who was a scout-leader and old enough to know better, in a resplendent Hussars' uniform. It was, after all, unwillingly accepted in the Weimar Republic that uniforms were for the battlefield, and that there were to be no more wars.

There were other annoyances in the life of a Lord Mayor. A year earlier there had been a ludicrous incident. The French newspaper, *Cyrano*, published a story on January 23, 1925, that Adenauer had committed a singularly cold-blooded act by marrying off his daughter to the 'Chief of Staff' (*chef d'État Major*) of the British General in Cologne. *Cyrano* castigated equally the General for enlisting a 'collaborator' in this manner, and Adenauer for 'trading' his daughter in order to curry favour.

Adenauer's grave, ironical answer came on January 30. He expressed surprise at the news of his only daughter's marriage. He had at once taken her aside and asked her to tell him the truth. She had denied being married to any British officer. Adenauer's letter concluded: 'As she is only 12 years old and still at school, I decided that I had to believe her, in spite of what you had published.'[20]

Smears have a way of sticking. In December, 1928, Guy de Traversay, writing in *La Revue de Paris*, repeated the myth that Adenauer had married off his daughter to a British officer. This time, Adenauer paid no attention. But in November 1930, the *Hamburger Neueste Nachrichten* published the story more circumstantially. Adenauer wrote at once, pointing out that this story was now nearly seven years old, that his oldest daughter was even now only just over 18, and that his younger daughters were 5 and 2. The Hamburg paper published an apology.[21]

The period of really frantic monetary inflation, from the beginning of 1923 to the middle of 1924, produced a major problem of accountancy. Adenauer was never, as Mayor, going to be poor, but the settlement of his children's school fees became a nuisance in its own right. In July, 1923, Adenauer was writing to the city savings' bank, the *Sparkasse* telling them

20, 21.....Cologne City Archives.

to pay 75,000 Marks for two months schooling for his sons, Konrad and Max. In October a bill for a single month at school for the two boys came to 192 million Marks. In November the situation was even crazier; the month at school for Konrad and Max had cost 12,000 million Marks!

At his office Adenauer received the daily paper, the *Kölnische Volkszeitung*, which insisted on payment for one month in advance. For November, 1923, Adenauer's office had to pay 707,364,000 paper Marks, but was given the option of settling for 4·7 Gold Marks. In January, 1924, the price had risen to 6,500,000,000 paper Marks.[22] In April it had come down to something like the November price. This sort of nonsense was bad enough when there was an office staff to deal with it; the average German housewife must have gone through unmitigated misery when she dealt with the weekly bills for bread, milk and potatoes.

A couple of years later Adenauer was invited to join the 'German Committee for Palestine', which had been formed to assist Jewish settlement in Israel. This had been one of the rare occasions when a particular cause transcended even the bitter hatred engendered by a major war. Britain formally sponsored the creation of a 'Jewish National Home' in 1917, through the 'Balfour Declaration' which took its title from the British Foreign Secretary of the day. The German committee was formed in 1918, while the war was still going on.

Adenauer may have been asked to join for purely 'representational' reasons. In his usual careful way he scanned the list of sponsors and found on it the name of Dr. Ludwig Kaas, an official of the administration of Cologne Cathedral. He wrote to him, and Kaas replied that he had joined in order to promote Jewish settlement in the Holy Land. Adenauer joined the Committee on January 20, 1927.

In February the Committee chose its 'Praesidium' or governing body. It included some exceptionally gifted Germans who were Jews (Einstein was one) and others who were not Jews. On November 22, 1927, the Committee held its first public rally (*Kundgebung*) in Cologne. Adenauer was invited to be a principal speaker at it. He demurred at first, then agreed to speak, then withdrew. But he sent a letter, to be read at the meeting, in which he praised the Jewish sense of history and spirit of self-sacrifice, stressed the human aspects of Jewish settlement of Palestine and reminded his unseen audience that Moses Hess, who had propagated the Zionist message in the middle of the previous century, was buried in the cemetery of Cologne-Deutz.[23] This discreet diplomacy earned him some unpleasant letters, full of abuse which remained somewhat opaque. Later on, anti-Semites were very ready to pick on Adenauer as a German who had tried to show a genuine sympathy with Jewish aspirations.

22, 23.....Cologne City Archives.

There were attacks on him by the Social Democrats for his 'luxurious' style of living – rather naïvely they cited as examples of this the fact that he lived in a 'two-storey villa' and his donation of crucifixes to an orphanage. The Communist Party (KPD) maintained a running fire of diatribe, and Adenauer paid the Communists the compliment of keeping them under constant surveillance. His police evidently succeeded in infiltrating the Communist Party organization, as the city archives became choked with information about its activities – the 'cells' which were being created in factories and the trade unions, the particular attention paid to communications as being vulnerable to disruption, the strong-arm squads mobilized for demonstrations and counter-demonstrations, and the names of Communist 'agents' in the civil service. Every now and then, a nasty libel would be published against Adenauer, on account of his supposed support of the separatist movement.

One curious story which was to be raked up again much later on concerned the 'misbehaviour' of the Director of a city museum. He was believed to be having a love-affair with a secretary, and was watched from the window of a house facing his office. Whether the watch on him was instituted by Adenauer or not was never made clear, but the Mayor of Cologne had much more important things to worry about. At all events, Adenauer received in due course a report that the Director had been 'observed' kissing and cuddling his secretary. He then paid a visit to the 'observation post' – not, as his enemies were to maintain, in order to watch a repeat performance but to satisfy himself that there was in fact a clear view of the Director's office. The reputation of a 'Peeping Tom' is not an enviable one; a word, in time, to the Director might have paid off better than the climb up the stairs of the building opposite the Museum.

In 1929 there was a final instalment of the old controversy over ownership rights in the Green Belt, and the farmers association of the *Landkreis* or country borough of Cologne threatened to suspend deliveries of milk. Adenauer shamed them into withdrawing their threat, by pointing out that the main sufferers would be unoffending infants. More serious was an inquiry into Cologne's finances, demanded by Adenauer's opponents in the City Council. It revealed that Cologne had debts totalling 301 million Marks. Once again, Adenauer silenced his critics by pointing out that the City's assets amounted to 926 million Marks. Money which had been borrowed had been well spent.

In 1929, too, Adenauer's leadership was challenged over the question of building a new bridge across the Rhine to the suburb of Mülheim. This led to an interesting trial of strength, which has been described at some length in Paul Weymar's biography.[24] The alternatives under discussion in

24..........*Konrad Adenauer*, Paul Weymar, p. 74–5.

the City Council were an arched bridge for which the Essen firm of Krupp had put in a tender, and a plainer suspension bridge. Adenauer had decided in advance for the latter, and he did his best to convince the City Council that there were ethical objections to the arched bridge, which would block the view towards the hills of the Sauerland and Bergischland to the east. The City Council had appointed a committee of experts to give a ruling on the best design, and seven out of nine members of the committee were in favour of an arched bridge – and primarily on ethical grounds!

Adenauer set out to convince both the experts and the Councillors that he was right, even expatiating on the beauties of the suspension-bridge in Leningrad (which he had never seen!). Finally, he produced a surprise argument, that the sandy soil of the river-bed was not able to support the greater weight of an arched bridge built in stone. A City Councillor, Dr. Heinrich Billstein, acted as his spokesman in this, and Adenauer capped this improbable argument (there was already one arched bridge over the Rhine at Cologne) by producing estimates which purported to show that the arched bridge would be vastly the more expensive. On April 28, 1927, the City Council approved the building of the suspension bridge by 43 votes to 36. Once again, Adenauer had demonstrated his talent for 'out-staying' opponents in order to get his way.

In December, 1929, Adenauer was due to stand for re-election as Mayor. He was at the height of his power at this time. According to one authority,[25] he was the highest paid official in the whole of Germany, with a bigger salary even than the Reich President. In 1926, according to the city records, he was drawing 33,000 Marks a year in salary and getting another 4,800 Marks a year for personal expenses.[26] The City paid, in addition, mortgages on his house and a handsome maintenance allowance for it which included water, light, heat and general upkeep. What this all amounted to is a matter for conjecture. Adenauer's biographer, Weymar, suggests that around 43,000 Marks a year were paid for the expenses connected with the house in Max Bruch Strasse alone,[27] and that his total emoluments were around 84,500 Marks a year. (In 1970 terms this money would have had a purchasing power of perhaps $30,000 or £12,000.) These were the sort of figures which were bandied about in the debates of the City Council, where he was fiercely criticized for extravagance and where a motion to cut his total spending to 35,000 Marks a year was narrowly defeated.

Some of his political opponents rejected this motion on the grounds that Adenauer could have earned four or five times as much in industry.

25..........*Ruin and Resurgence*, R. C. Mowat, p. 359.
26..........Cologne City Archives.
27..........*Konrad Adenauer*, Paul Weymar, p. 78.

He was, in fact, earning plenty on the side already. In 1928, for instance, he was Chairman of four companies – the Cologne–Bonn Railway Co., the Cologne Building Corporation, the Cologne Fairgrounds Co. and the Rhine–Westphalia Air-Transport Co. It could be argued that none of these companies was of real financial consequence, but in addition Adenauer sat on the boards of the Rhine–Westphalia Electricity Works, the *Deutsche Bank*, the Rhine Brown Coal Co. and the embryonic national airways *Lufthansa*.[28]

Adenauer liked having money, not because he was avaricious but because it gave him a sense of achievement and authority. He was in no way mean, but he did not throw money about ostentatiously. Brought up very simply, he had always had simple tastes, but it was probably in the mid-1920s that he developed an interest in good food – which he ate with appreciation but always sparingly – and good wine. He dressed quietly but with real elegance, and he looked at his best in overcoat and top-hat, with highly polished shoes and perfectly rolled umbrella. The top-hat would, for that matter, conceal his shaven skull – it was at this period that he developed what amounted to a fetish about having his own head and those of his boys unattractively shaved. His moustache seems to have been discarded around 1926, possibly when it began to turn grey. Pictures of him at the end of his first term as Mayor show a commanding figure, tall, straight-backed, with his face wearing that hint of aloofness which had been comically present when he was a child.

This expression of reserved 'hauteur' may have been misleading. One of his Social Democratic opponents in local politics, Robert Görlinger, had this to say of him at a later date[29] – 'The man is generally considered cold, reserved, unfeeling. This notion is quite wrong. Rather, he possesses the remarkable gift of generating warmth and friendliness in precisely the direction where he senses his own advantage. This is, I think, his real secret. He feels genuinely sympathetic towards people whom he can use, and as soon as they have fulfilled their function, this sympathy dies away.'

Not, perhaps, an attractive picture. Adenauer kept his warmer feelings and moods for his family and his friends. Out of his family he was creating something of a dynastic body. One brother, Hans, was a Canon of Cologne Cathedral, the other, August, a leading lawyer. His brother-in-law Willi Suth sat on the City Council, and the families of both wives continued to provide useful connexions, including rich and influential American cousins of Gussi's. He had ambitions for his sons to carry on his work in the municipality, and one of them, Max, was later to become *Oberstadtdirektor* or Town Clerk.

28..........Cologne City Archives.
29..........*Konrad Adenauer*, Paul Weymar, p. 77–8.

His friends included some of the leading businessmen of Cologne, members of a group which was sometimes derogatively referred to as the *Kölner Klüngel* – the 'clique'. Two of them, Louis Hagen and Paul Silverberg, were Jewish financiers. Three others were businessmen of some standing: Baron von Stein, who first became a friend of Adenauer's when they were both opposing the extreme separatists, Otto Wolff and Robert Pferdemenges. Only the last-named became a close confidant. Robert Pferdemenges was the son of a wealthy mill-owner of München-Gladbach, a Conservative, a cosmopolitan and a Protestant (although an entirely loyal, although not over-fervent Roman Catholic, Adenauer was in no sense a bigot; some of his best friends were Protestants and Jews). Pferdemenges was of particular use to Adenauer in that he was much-travelled and, as a highly successful banker, had a considerable grasp of economic problems. Adenauer himself was apt to remark caustically that he had 'enjoyed the good luck' to have had to study economics only for two terms at the university.

An interesting member of a circle of friends which never became large was an American Jew, Daniel Heinemann. It was 'Danny' Heinemann who had arranged Adenauer's meeting in 1920 with the French Ambassador, Charles Laurent. Heinemann, then the head of the Sofina Corporation in Brussels, was probably introduced to Adenauer by one of Gussi's American relatives. In 1924 he brought Adenauer together with a French industrialist, Ernest Weyl, so that Adenauer could give him a clear idea of the economic situation in the Rhineland resulting from France's military occupation of the Ruhr. Heinemann was twice later to play an important role in Adenauer's life – in the early 1920s, when he tried unsuccessfully to float a major loan for the city of Cologne, and during the Nazi era, when he came to Adenauer's aid when he most needed help.

Why did a man of Adenauer's undoubted authority and talents choose to remain only a municipal politician and administrator, albeit probably the most powerful in Germany? Possibly the main reason was his instinctive caution. The era of the Weimar Republic was not one in which a stable political career could be made in Berlin. Reich Chancellors came and went with depressing frequency. Governments fell generally because of the multiplicity of parties, and the extreme difficulty of holding a coalition together. For the first years after the War, Reich governments struggled with internal anarchy and disillusionment, with the mounting burden of war-debts, with the unrest caused by the French seizure of the Ruhr and with the plots of the French-inspired and financed separatists. The right-wing parties rejected all policy of co-operation with the Western Powers by fulfilling the clauses of the hated Treaty of Versailles. Right-wing elements formed the 'Free Corps' which fought quite sizeable battles on the Polish frontier, and young right-wingers carried out a whole series of 'political murders', after 'sentencing' their victims to death in secret tribunal. In November, 1923, Adolf Hitler attempted to seize power in Munich for his still infant Nazi Party, although, at the time and for years afterwards the Nazis seemed to pose a much less potent threat than the Communists.

Admittedly, the Weimar Republic enjoyed a short, if illusory 'springtime' from mid-1924 to 1929. Hjalmar Schacht, acting for the Reich Chancellor Hans Luther, introduced the *Rentenmark* and ended inflation. The 'Rentenmark' was a completely new currency, theoretically based on the old gold mark and worth about three trillion of the virtually worthless paper marks. It was backed by a Government-sponsored 'mortgage' of all German land and industry, which in theory gave the Government the right to sequestrate in order to support the new currency. It amounted, in fact, to the withdrawal of worthless currency and the issue of a new one, based on public confidence. The American-sponsored 'Dawes Plan' eased the burden of reparations. The Plan provided for the evacuation of the Ruhr, a sliding scale of reparation payments and a large loan to Germany to finance the first year's payments. The Ruhr was evacuated and the separatist threat dissipated. There was an upsurge of industrial development, and unemployment was almost eliminated by 1928. And the Locarno Pact of October 1925 brought agreement with the Western Powers, developed a useful personal relationship between Gustav Stresemann and the French and British Foreign Ministers, Aristide Briand and Austen Chamberlain, and paved the way for the acceptance of Germany in the following year into the League of Nations. The Locarno Pact guaranteed the borders between France and Germany, and between Belgium and Germany, fixed under the Treaty of Versailles. As a codicil to the Pact, Germany signed agreements with Poland and Czechoslovakia calling for arbitration of any further dispute. In June, 1929, came the 'Young Plan', under which reparations payments were spread over a period of 59 years, and in August 1929 the Western Powers undertook, at The Hague, to complete the evacuation of the Rhineland by June, 1930. The Wall Street crash and the world economic crisis were then only a few months away.

German governments continued to be short-lived, for the perennial complaint against them was that they were achieving 'too little, too late'. Blame was apportioned equally between them and Allied governments. The striking advances made between 1924 and 1929 were barely noticed, and Germany's political leaders were given no credit for them. Adenauer may at this stage of history have developed his peculiar sensitivity for political atmosphere, almost a sense of 'smell'. One of his maxims always was to build without haste and build securely; he was building up a solid inheritance for his family, and his first duty was always to its members. As President of the Prussian second house, the State Council, from May, 1921, onwards, he had every chance of turning himself into a 'national' politician. Still, he did not do so. But he was twice sounded with a view towards forming a Reich Government, and he was considered as a candidate for the Chancellorship on at least one other occasion.

In May 1921 Adenauer was approached, in the restaurant of the Prussian *Land* Parliament in Berlin, by the Prussian Minister President, Otto Braun, and the Prussian Minister of Labour, Adam Stegerwald. They asked him if he were ready to form a new Reich (not Prussian) Government.[30] They were men who wielded considerable influence in the capital; Otto Braun was a 'moderate' Social Democrat, and Stegerwald a Christian Trade Unionist; both in fact were middle of the road politicians who wanted to strengthen the centre at all costs.

Adenauer said that he was not opposed to the idea but that he would have to await the meeting of the executive of his own Centre Party, which took place on May 10. At this meeting, Adenauer announced that an offer had been made to him, and said that he was prepared to be the Centre Party's candidate, on four conditions. These were: the new coalition must accept his taxation programme, with a shift from income-tax to taxes on consumption; there would be no 'socialization' of heavy industry, at any rate for the present; an extra hour would have to be added to the eight hour working day (for Adenauer understood very well that the German people could only live better by working harder); finally, he would choose his own Ministers.

These demands had a mixed reception from the Centre Party executive. It decided to give further thought to the matter, and its choice of a candidate lay between Adenauer and Joseph Wirth, a less tough and uncompromising character. But within a few days it became known that the Social Democrats wanted the post of Chancellor for themselves and would take the lead in forming the new government. That was the end, then, of Adenauer's candidature.

In November, 1922, there was another government crisis in Berlin and the names of Adenauer and another Centre Party colleague, Andreas Hermes, were mentioned as candidates. It got no further than that. Again, in May 1925, one finds Gustav Stresemann noting Adenauer's name as a candidate for high office, but expressing doubts whether he did not put Cologne first and Germany only a poor second. Then on May 5, 1926, the government of Dr. Hans Luther was brought down over the so-called *Flaggenstreit*, the dispute over the German national colours. Dr. Luther

30.......... *Aus Kölnischer und Rheinischer Geschichte*, Ed. Hans Blum. Details from the chapter by Hugo Stehkämper.

had given instructions that the German merchant navy could fly the old Imperial black, white and red flag, with a small jack in the Republic's black red and gold in the top left-hand corner. The Social Democrats refused to serve any longer under him.

This time Adenauer was approached by Adam Stegerwald and Theodor von Guérard of the Centre Party and asked to be their candidate for the Chancellorship. He was not at all keen. The 1921 episode had left a bad taste in his mouth.[31] He travelled to Berlin for the negotiations with some misgivings.

According to his own account,[32] the proposal made to him was that he should form a broadly-based coalition, embracing almost all important parties save the Communists on the left and the Nationalists on the right. This was not because of current parliamentary problems which, like the *Flaggenstreit*, were negligible. It was, in Adenauer's view, necessary to present a firm front to Allied demands for the fulfilment of the Dawes Plan on reparations – he believed that it should never have been accepted by a German Government. It was necessary, too, to revise a foreign policy which Adenauer described as having 'an unsteady, see-saw character'. He regarded the Locarno Pact as much less than the sort of alliance with the Western Powers which he would have wanted, and he distrusted Stresemann's policy of 'facing both ways' – in effect, playing off East against West. He would have preferred a strictly neutral attitude based on non-involvement with foreign countries. This offers a striking contrast to his views on the dangers of a foreign policy vacuum in Central Europe, when he became Chancellor over twenty years later.

In Berlin, Adenauer entered at once into talks with leading members of the Social Democratic, Centre and People's Parties. He made it plain that he would only take the post of Chancellor, if he were assured of a stable majority in the Reichstag. His talks with party representatives soon revealed how difficult it would be to get such a majority. The Social Democrats had objections to the People's Party, and the latter grave doubts about the Democratic Party. Some of the middle of the road politicians wanted to bring the Nationalists into the coalition – especially as this was the party of President Hindenburg – while others pointed out that this would alienate the Social Democrats and keep them out. The Social Democrats, for their part, showed a strong preference for keeping several parties out of power and for forming a minority government. And all and sundry made it plain that the parliamentary problems, which Adenauer had imagined were negligible, still caused rancour and distrust.

31..........Among a number of wild recriminations was an article in the *Rheinischer Volkswacht*, which referred to him as a 'vampire'! Cologne City Archives.

32..........*Konrad Adenauer*, Paul Weymar, p. 82–95.

Adenauer found himself spinning in the vortex of Berlin politics, and getting nowhere. His talks began on the morning of May 14 and by the evening of May 16 he had had enough. By then he had convinced himself that he did not wish to work with Stresemann, who wanted to remain Foreign Minister. As he subsequently made clear, he suspected that Stresemann was from behind the scenes sabotaging his efforts to form the broadly-based coalition which was needed.[33] On May 17 Adenauer returned to Cologne and later on the same day Dr. Wilhelm Marx was appointed Chancellor of the thirteenth Government formed since 1919. The Cologne press, and a part of the Berlin press, regretted the end of Adenauer's efforts, and the *Vossische Zeitung* remarked that it was 'a pity that an Adenauer Cabinet could not be successfully created. The Cologne Lord Mayor is certainly a difficult character, but he is a character all the same.'[34]

Adenauer seems to have had no regrets. Nor had Stresemann. Less than a year later he told the central committee of his People's Party that there was a trend in the country towards violation of constitutional order and towards the establishment of dictatorship in its place, and he added with barbed sarcasm that it was well-known that the Mayor of Cologne had excellent (*herzlich*) relations with Fascist regimes abroad (this was a reference to a friendly letter which Adenauer once wrote to Mussolini). Adenauer and Stresemann would not have worked well together. Both were too much individualists; both were too fond of getting their own way. Even purely physically, they were inimical to one another – Adenauer enjoying the well-co-ordinated big man's ease of manner, Stresemann small, porcine, prickly.

Could Adenauer have saved the Weimar Republic? In 1926, certainly, there was still time. The world economic crisis was still three years away. Adenauer, moreover, had the necessary toughness and resilience of character, the necessary belief in himself and the necessary persistence, determination and staying-power.

Ernst Lemmer, who was to serve many years afterwards as Adenauer's Minister for all-German Affairs, believed that he would never have been able to form a government of the Reich – 'He was an unknown quantity even to his own Centre Party, and he stood too far towards the right in it.'[35] Another man who served under Adenauer after the Second World War and who was his colleague in the Centre Party before it, Heinrich Krone, put it differently:

'Adenauer did not become Reich Chancellor in 1926 because he didn't

33..........*Konrad Adenauer*, Paul Weymar, p. 96.

34.. ....*Vossische Zeitung*, newspaper, May 16, 1926. Adenauer was still trying at the time.

35..........Ernst Lemmer, in private conversation with the author.

really want the job. He had ingrained doubts about it. He knew that the Weimar constitution made it all too easy for the Chancellor to be overthrown. He guessed that he could never win over the Prussian Junkers or prevent the alliance which was forming between them and the reactionaries of the right wing. He knew that President Hindenburg was a weak man and had the wrong kind of advisers. He knew that there were just too many political parties. Why should he have risked his career?'[36]

Many years later Adenauer undoubtedly told his version of events to his biographer, Paul Weymar, but with his tongue in his cheek.[37] He suggested that his friends in the Centre Party had not proposed him sooner for the Chancellorship, 'because they felt that I was too good and valuable a man to be wasted in a temporary capacity'. Then, again, 'I had to ask myself seriously whether in such circumstances it was not my duty to make a great personal sacrifice and take over the post of Reich Chancellor.' More truthfully, Adenauer complained that he might be forsaking his beloved Cologne, 'in order to use myself up in Berlin within a relatively short period'. But the example which he gave of a man doing this, Dr. Hans Luther, was not a good one; Luther was alive and well more than twenty years after being Chancellor.

There can be little question that Adenauer returned to Cologne on May 17, 1926, with a feeling of profound relief. He did not want the job of Chancellor because, with his invariable prescience, he saw that he would not be able to form a stable government. That nobody else could do so was beside the point. Back in Cologne, he fought off recurring bronchial trouble – one notes in the city archives the number of times he had to refuse invitations because of 'overwork'. But he was as indefatigable as ever in discharging his duties, and as punctilious in dealing with his massive correspondence. (His invariable rule was to answer letters without delay, unless they required no answer. In that case, he noted the fact in his own handwriting, signing the note with the single letter 'A').

In 1928 one finds him launching, at Wilhelmshaven, the third warship to be named after the city of Cologne (the first was sunk by the British Royal Navy, and the second was scuppered by its crew in Scapa Flo at the end of the First World War). A Cologne cigar merchant named his newest 'slim-Jim' product after the Mayor, and an unknown admirer wrote to the City Council that the Mayor was 'a very strong personality, perhaps the strongest personality in Germany at the present time'.[38] He may well have been right. Meanwhile Adenauer awaited his re-election, due to take place in December, 1929, with complete and understandable confidence.

36..........Heinrich Krone, in private conversation with the author.
37..........*Konrad Adenauer*, Paul Weymar, p. 84–5.
38..........Cologne City Archives.

5 The Shadow of the Swastika

Just after Adenauer's re-election as Mayor of Cologne in December, 1929, a graceful tribute was paid to him by the Brazilian Consul, Don Manuel Ochoa. Writing in the *Journal do Brasil*, he described Adenauer's re-election as a political event of the first importance. He added a sentence from Voltaire – 'Les âmes priviligées rangent à l'égal des souverains.'[1] Shortly before the election the Centre Party had suggested that he should remain in office until the summer, since a strong hand was needed at the helm while the world economic crisis was raging. The thought that the crisis would be over when the more clement weather came along, is in retrospect, an endearing one. In reality, the economic crisis in Germany was to persist, and worsen, until the Nazis came into power a little over three years later.

In reality, too, the manner of Adenauer's re-election was a shock for him. Whereas, in 1917, he had been elected Mayor by unanimous acclaim, in 1929 he scraped in with the smallest possible majority on the City Council, a single vote. It is difficult to find a single conclusive reason for this loss of popularity. The contributory causes were the economic depression, the widespread feeling of uncertainty, the growth of right-wing and left-wing radicalism, revived accusations of his luxurious living and resentment over his habit of getting his own way. Still, he was in; and, in theory, for another twelve year term. Under normal circumstances, he could have expected to retire from public life at the end of it.

The increasingly serious economic situation overshadowed everything else. It brought Adenauer into close touch with the new Chancellor, Heinrich Brüning, who took office in March, 1930. Like Adenauer, Brüning belonged to the Catholic Centre Party. Like him, too, he was a man of great courage and pertinacity, a patriot to the core who was prepared to work himself to death in Germany's service. Here, the resemblance ended. Brüning was an intellectual; Adenauer was not. The 1920s and early 1930s produced a great many divergent intellectual trends – the pacifism of Erich Maria Remarque and Fritz von Unruh, the romanticism of Stefan George and Rainer Maria Rilke, the 'conservative

1............Cologne City Archives.

revolutionism' of the right-wingers of the *Tat-Kreis*[2] and Oswald Spengler's gloomy prophecies of Western decline. All this, admittedly confusing and sometimes confused thought seems to have passed Adenauer by; he remained practical to the point of the mundane, bound up in day-to-day administrative problems, and uninterested in what the nation was thinking.

Brüning, unlike Adenauer, was unmarried. Unlike Adenauer, again, he had served with distinction in the First World War, and as a machine-gun company-commander had been decorated for gallantry. And, unlike Adenauer, he believed that it was his duty to enter the national political arena, which he first did in 1924.

With his considerable administrative experience, Adenauer would have been an admirable 'aide' for Brüning. But he liked him as little as he had liked Stresemann, and one is left with the afterthought that he found anyone hard to tolerate whom he regarded as being in any sense a rival. Adenauer might well have wished, in the long run, to gain control of the Centre Party. By 1929 Brüning, a younger man and already with a nationwide following, was blocking his way. According to Dr. Hermann Pünder, who worked as the head of Brüning's Cabinet Office, there were additional, more obscure reasons, for Adenauer's antipathy.[3] Brüning knew much about economics, which Adenauer affected to despise. He was much travelled and spoke several languages – Adenauer spoke none, although Pünder was wrong in supposing that he had only once been abroad. He had, in fact, been to France, Italy, Switzerland and Holland – but this was not an imposing list. Brüning was moody, and showed his feelings; Adenauer believed in hiding his. Brüning came from Münster, north of the Rhineland; the Münsterlanders had the reputation of dull dogs, of unpredictable temper.

Finally, there was the minor matter of answering letters. In this Adenauer was meticulous. But Brüning was even more dilatory than Stresemann and, unfortunately, Adenauer was to have a great deal of correspondence with him. Thus, one finds a letter of Adenauer's to Brüning of July 9, 1930, in which he complains of 'too many delays' in Berlin, an oblique reference to late answers to his requests for more energetic regional planning to combat unemployment.[4] In November, 1930,

2............The *Tat Kreis* was named after the Berlin paper, *Die Tat* (The Deed), which followed an anti-Western line of thought. Its main contributors were Hans Zehrer, Giselher Wirsing and Friedrich Zimmermann, all of whom survived the Nazi Era and became once again active in journalism. Hans Zehrer became Editor of the daily paper *Die Welt*. Adenauer referred to him contemptuously as 'that muddlehead'.

3............Dr. Hermann Pünder, in private conversation with the author.

4............Cologne City Archives.

Adenauer had a fresh grievance; out of 250 million Marks promised for a public works programme, only 6·4 million had been made available. The answer to this letter took weeks to come; Adenauer restrained his anger. But his letter of December 22 on the tax situation was still unanswered when Brüning paid a visit to Cologne at the end of January, 1931, and the latter's answer only arrived on March 13.[5] Adenauer regarded this as bad manners, and to him bad manners were criminal.

Brüning could well have pointed out that he had to deal with the affairs of the whole Reich, and had too little time to spare for the importunate Mayor of Cologne. The employment situation steadily worsened. By 1931 one worker in every four in Cologne was out of a job, and Adenauer was toying with the idea of an *Arbeitsdienst*, a system of 'labour service' for men and women up to the age of 25, who would work a seven-hour day for a twenty-week 'course', receiving communal feeding, recreational facilities, insurance and pocket-money amounting to around two Marks a day.[6] Brüning prepared plans for a nation-wide public works programme, which would give employment to 600,000 people and would cost an estimated 2,000 million Marks. But this sort of money could not be raised; the first government-sponsored loan was floated at 100, paying 7 per cent interest, and in no time the stock had dropped to 60–65. Brüning could have devalued the Mark – as British economists were advising – but this would have increased the sum, in gold Marks, of reparations.[7] Brüning was of course trying to get the burden of reparations lightened at the same time, and was succeeding too late. One can perfectly see why he could not find the time to answer Adenauer's letters!

The Nazis were to make much use of the slogan *Brot und Arbeit* (Bread and Work) in advancing to power. In the 1930 elections they suddenly emerged as a major political force, increasing their seats in the Reichstag from 12 to 107. The Communist Party representation rose from 54 to 77 at the same time. The increase in right- and left-wing radicalism threatened to destroy middle-of-the-road government. The German electorate, deeply worried, averagely fickle and mildly frivolous, was losing all faith in coalitions which failed to produce a government which lasted. Brüning's was the nineteenth since 1919. The Weimar Republic, like pre-Gaullist France thirty years later, was losing all popular appeal. Brüning, as one

5............Cologne City Archives.

6............Cologne City Archives. A small labour-service was, finally, launched in Cologne in 1932. Of 2,323 people who joined it, 2,013 were set to work. Adenauer may, unwittingly, have supplied the pilot scheme for the Nazis' subsequent nation-wide Labour Service (*Arbeitsdienst*).

7............*Vierteljahrsheft*, 3rd number, July, 1969. Article by Henning Koehler.

young man saw it at the time, was 'altogether too harmless'.[8] Only the fact that he had served as an officer with distinction in the war encouraged young people to stick up his election posters, at ten pfennigs an evening. (They spent five pfennigs on a stick of liquorice and put the other five in their money-boxes.) But Brüning had no charisma, and when he introduced his emergency legislation, early in 1932, the children started singing:

> 'Haut den Brüning auf die Glatze, dass die Notverordnung platze.'
> (*Give old Brüning's pate a clout, so his special law flakes out.*)

Adenauer was having his own troubles. He was being attacked in the press for 'boycotting' Brüning's meetings, for his 'high-handedness' in sending for Ministers of State from his hotel bedroom when staying in Berlin, for alleged speculation with city funds and, yet again, for supposedly favouring the separation of the Rhineland from the Reich.[9] According to one widely believed tale, he had lost a million and a half Marks, lent to him by the Dedi Bank, in speculations over artificial silk. One paper, the *Düsseldorfer Lokal-Zeitung*, pursued this story relentlessly and wanted to know why Adenauer did not deny it.

Another accusation was that he had organized a 'hide-out' for himself in Switzerland. The Communist paper, *Socialist Republic*, even 'discovered' that he had 'fled' to Switzerland, where he had allegedly bought a property on Lake Thun for one million Marks.[10] A rude 'ode' was written to him, entitled *Konrad Adenauer, der lustige schweitzer Bua* (literally, 'the merry Swiss yokel'). Any accusation of cowardice maddened Adenauer, and he appeared as a prosecution witness in September, 1931 when a Communist Party member, Karl Sattler, was sent to prison for four months for the statement about his non-existent 'Thun property'.

The Nazi Party attacked him for being pro-French. The Nationalists assailed him because he allegedly failed to pay 'due honour' to two German airmen, Köhl and Hünefeld, who crossed the Atlantic. The story was that Adenauer stayed away from a civic reception, because the two airmen had visited the ex-Kaiser in exile at Doorn.[11] The Social Democrats were once again castigating him for spending too much money, and the socialist Press in Belgium took up the refrain – asserting that he was not receiving, as his accusers said, 120,000 Marks a year, but 'only' 108,250. One newspaper, the *Westdeutscher Beobachter*, depicted Adenauer with

8............*Handelsblatt*, newspaper, April 2, 1970. Article by Antonius John.
9............Cologne City Archives.
10...........*Sozialistische Republik*, journal, October, 1930.
11...........Cologne City Archives.

caricatured 'Semitic' features.[12] What was remarkable about all these attacks was their sheer viciousness. It was a reflection on the mood of the German people, at that time ready to blame anybody for anything. Recrimination was becoming universal. This mood, more than any other factor, opened the way for the Nazis to seize power in 1933.

Did Adenauer recognize the real menace of the Nazis? Certainly, up to 1932 he was much more aware of the Communist threat.[13] This was, to him, more definable and more obviously directed against national interests. At one stage he made some fragmentary notes about the need to organize a *Sammlung der Mitte*[14] (a middle-of-the-road 'front'). It was to be a counterweight to the Communists, the Nazis and – the Social Democrats. The idea was not new, and the appropriate time to implement it had already passed. By 1932 Adenauer was toying with the thought of 'drawing the Nazis' teeth' by bringing them into the Reich Government. On August 6, 1932, he wrote a letter to Graf Wolff-Metternich, telling him in the strictest confidence that the Centre Party would support this course.[15] In later years Adenauer was to insist that the Centre Party's conduct in opposing Nazism up to the last was in direct contrast with the ambivalent attitude of the Allied Powers. The view which he expressed with hindsight was that the Allies were criminally foolish in ever supposing that the Nazis would modify their policies once they were in office.[16]

Adenauer's own attitude was ambivalent when a positive effort was made to 'contain' the Nazis. This was towards the end of 1931 and early in 1932. By this time uniformed Nazi strong-arm squads were continually on the move in the streets of every large city. Street fighting was becoming endemic, with the brown-shirted SA (*Sturm-Abteilungen*) Nazis usually emerging victorious against the Communist 'Red Front', while the Social Democratic *Reichsbanner*, intervening to restore order, almost always came off worst of all when both Nazis and Communists turned on them. In a single year, 1931, 182 people were killed in the street-fighting and over 15,000 wounded – 'a total of around 5,000,000 men in Germany organized in one way or another for the purposes of civil war, or, as some of them express it, to prevent civil war'.[17] To maintain order there were 10,000

12..........It is interesting to note that the same thing was done, in the 1950s, to the leader of the Social Democratic Party, Erich Ollenhauer. Surprisingly, he sued for libel. When subjected to much more vicious attack in 1930, Adenauer merely ignored the implied 'insult'.

13..........It is significant that in 1931 Adenauer warned the City Council against concentrating their attentions on the Nazis and forgetting about the Communists. Cologne City Archives.

14, 15.....Cologne City Archives.

16..........See, for instance, footnote on page 191.

17..........*Germany – Fascist or Soviet*, H. R. Knickerbocker, p. 139.

police; the 100,000 men of the *Reichswehr* (Army) were kept away from the warring factions. In December, 1931, the Prussian Ministry of the Interior proposed banning the use of all public buildings and sportsfields by 'parties hostile to the State.' By this was meant, plainly, the Nazi and Communist Parties.

On December 21, 1931, Adenauer wrote to the Prussian Ministry of the Interior on this subject.[18] His view was that the Prussian Ministry should not arrogate to itself the right, on the advice of the police, to decide which parties should, or should not use public buildings. This should be a matter for local authorities, and they should take whatever action they saw fit, in conjunction with the local police. This attitude was surprising, and Adenauer was to regret it bitterly two years later. But local authorities were incredibly, even insanely jealous of their rights. In February, 1932, the German *Städtetag* or 'diet of municipalities' rejected the claim of the Prussian Ministry of the Interior to limit the use of public buildings, sportsfields or gymnasia. The members of the *Städtetag*, to which Adenauer belonged, held that such questions came within the sole competence of local authorities. They supported Adenauer's view that organizations which had not themselves been legally banned could not be termed 'hostile to the State'. The *Städtetag* thereupon returned to what it considered more pressing business – such as a grant in aid for the publishing house of Baedeker in Leipzig, and moral support for the 'League to maintain German script'.[19]

In Adenauer's favour one must point out that he argued against repressive action because he believed that the Prussian Government was confusing cause with effect. The cause of civil unrest, Adenauer believed, was the deteriorating economic situation. In the big cities, theatres, public baths, swimming-pools and even hospitals and schools were closing down because of lack of funds. Cologne had to cut expenditure on street lighting and public parks drastically. Adenauer believed that local authorities should be given increased autonomy and responsibility for dealing with unemployment, and in January 1933 one finds him – in the middle of the controversy over banning Nazi and Communist meetings – complaining that 'the needs of the municipalities no longer make any impression on the Government of the Reich or on public opinion'.[20]

But, as the signs of lawlessness and massive intimidation increased, Adenauer began to appreciate the real menace of Nazism.

On July 22, 1932, he warned a German youth rally in Dortmund that 'terrible years' lay ahead. Battle had already been joined between Chris-

18, 19.....Cologne City Archives.
20..........Letter of January 25, 1932, to Dr. Mulert, President of the *Städttetag*.

tianity and the forces of materialism. On July 30 Adenauer repeated his warning of the dangers ahead in a speech at Cologne's *Reit und Fahrturnier*.[21] In August he and Gussi were holidaying at Chandolin in the Swiss Valais. There he learnt that some of his mail was being tampered with in Germany, and a friend, Wilhelm Elfes of Krefeld, wrote to him quoting Schopenhauer, that one should be prepared for the very worst – for then, the very worst may not happen at once and may not happen at all.[22]

Much later, on February 17, 1933, he told a Centre Party meeting in the Lindenthal borough of Cologne that there was a desperate need to shore-up the ethical foundations of the State – what was needed was solid support for the ideals of probity, truthfulness and freedom, and for the rule of law.[23] He repeated the phrase: 'Just itiaest fundamentum rei publicae.'[24]

Before he made this last statement Adenauer made two coherent efforts to oppose the Nazis, one in Cologne, and one in Berlin. The last prospect of democratic government had ended in May, 1932, when Heinrich Brüning, by then ruling through emergency decrees requiring Presidential approval, was dismissed by the Reich President, Hindenburg. Minority governments were formed, first under Franz von Papen and then under General Kurt von Schleicher. In the meantime, there were elections in July, 1932, when the Nazis captured 230 out of 608 seats in the Reichstag, and again in November, 1932, when the Nazi vote surprisingly decreased, leaving them with 196 seats. But this was only an illusion of ebbing fortunes; the von Schleicher Government had the pledged support only of the Nationalist and People's Parties, with 62 Reichstag seats between them. Hitler and the Nazis could count on Nationalist support if von Schleicher made way for them, and early in January they secured the promise of the support of von Papen and leading industrialists at a meeting held at the Cologne home of the banker, Freiherr von Schroeder. On January 30, 1933, Hindenburg called on Hitler to form a new Government. The Nazi Era had begun; it was to last for just over twelve years.

Hitler dissolved the Reichstag and fixed the date of March 5 for new elections. In the meantime he conducted a barn-storming election campaign, in which the full might of the Nazi Party was blatantly displayed, with brown-shirted storm-troopers parading the streets and brass bands playing. On February 17, he arrived in Cologne. His private aircraft touched down at around 11 p.m. Adenauer did not meet him; he had

21, 22, 23......Cologne City Archives.
24.........'Justice is the foundation of public affairs.'

decided that Hitler was in Cologne electioneering and not in his capacity of Reich Chancellor. He sent instead the City Councillor in charge of police – Dr. Heinrich Billstein. Hitler ignored Billstein at the airfield and drove away to the Hotel Dreesen in Bad Godesberg in a rage.

On February 19 Hitler was due to speak in Cologne. During the previous night two Nazi swastikas were hoisted on pylons of the bridge from Cologne to Deutz. This was municipal property, and Adenauer had already given instructions that no 'party' flags were to be flown from any municipal building. He ordered municipal workers, under police protection, to take the flags down. This was done on the morning of February 19. As a compromise, Adenauer allowed Nazi flags to be flown from flagpoles in front of the Fair Ground buildings, where Hitler made his speech, but not on them.[25]

This was in fact Adenauer's second act of open defiance, and it was astonishing that Hitler did not at once remove him forcibly from his office of Mayor. His first act of defiance took place a fortnight earlier, in Berlin. It was provoked by the decision of the Nazi Government to dissolve the Prussian Land Parliament.

It could be argued that there was something anomalous about the Prussian Land Parliament. To some extent, it was a 'State within the State': Prussia was far larger than any other component of the German Reich, it was centred on the Reich capital of Berlin, and it might even act as a counterweight to the government of the country. These, of course, were not the reasons why the Nazis wished to dissolve it; they were afraid that it could become a focus of democratic survival in the authoritarian, corporate State which Hitler intended to create. In October, 1932, von Papen had himself, as Reich Chancellor, confirmed as Reich Commissar for Prussia with special powers. This gave the Nazis their cue; when Hitler came to power on January 30 he was already committed to destroying the Prussian Government. He still regarded von Papen, mistakenly, as potentially dangerous.

From the first, Adenauer opposed this Nazi plan. On February 6, however, he was overruled at a two-hour session in Berlin of the three-man Commission appointed to decide on the fate of the Prussian Government and Parliament. The two other members of the Commission were Hitler's Vice-Chancellor, von Papen, and the President or Speaker of the Prussian Land Parliament, Dr. Kerrl, who had been won over to the Nazi cause. Von Papen argued that a hopeless situation had arisen in which servants of the State tried to work for two masters, the Reich and Prussia. He pointed out that Prussia had been without a Minister–President for nine months,

25..........*Konrad Adenauer*, Paul Weymar, p. 98–9.

and he called the situation 'intolerable'. He demanded the dissolution of the Prussian Land Parliament with effect from March 4.

Adenauer argued boldly against this course and asked that the Prussian Parliament should be allowed to choose a new Minister–President. He added that his Centre Party was even prepared to support the candidature of Hermann Goering, Hitler's henchman. With the utmost firmness, he demanded that the statehood of Prussia should not be violated.[26] And when von Papen put the matter to the vote, Adenauer pointedly abstained – an action which drew down on his head the wrath of the whole Nazi Press.

The fate of the Prussian Parliament had been settled, but Adenauer did not give up. On February 9 the *Vossische Zeitung* warned him that his efforts were doomed; the paper compared them with 'formalities at a funeral'. On February 18 the French Socialist leader, Edouard Herriot, tried to help in a speech in which he expressed deep concern over Prussia's fate. (He must have been just about the first Frenchman in history to say such a thing!) Adenauer regarded this intervention as ill-timed; he wrote a sharply worded memorandum in which he stated that interference in the affairs of another country was usually counter-productive.[27] On February 25 Adenauer made another journey to Berlin to try and talk round von Papen and Goering, who was Prussian Minister of the Interior. He got nowhere. Nor did a letter of March 1 to von Papen help, in which Adenauer voiced his misgivings about the coming elections, believing as he did that there would be considerable interference with the rights and freedoms of citizens by the armed thugs of the SA and the Communist Red Front.[28] Von Papen could be relied upon only to betray any confidence. It is highly probable that from then on Adenauer was on the Nazis' black list.

Immediate action was taken against him after the March 5, 1933, elections, in which the Nazis captured 44 per cent of the vote and, together with their Nationalist allies, commanded a majority of the seats in the Reichstag. A detachment of storm-troopers was quartered on him, living in his house, ostensibly to protect him. There was another guard on his office in the Town Hall. He received a number of anonymous letters, probably inspired by the Nazis. One choice item was the following poem:

'Dieb, Verräter, Separatist,
Und was du sonst noch alles bist.
An Rom verkaufst du deutsches Recht,

26..........Cologne City Archives. There is something ironical about Adenauer, who had in the past fought for the freeing of the Rhineland from Prussian domination, fighting now for Prussia's preservation.

27, 28.....Cologne City Archives.

Gewissenslump und Pfaffenknecht!
Jetzt wird's dem deutschen Volk zu bunt;
An den Laternenpfahl mit Dir,
Du Schweinehund!'
(*Thief, traitor, separatist,*
And whatever else besides you may be.
You sell Germany's interests to Rome,
You conscienceless clod, and priest's toady!
Now it's become too much for the German people;
To the lamp-post with you, you pigdog!)

Adenauer was warned by friends that his home might be attacked on February 12, the day when local elections were being held, unless he resigned his post and left Cologne. He did not resign but he took his children to the Roman Catholic Caritas hospital and left them there in the charge of its director. He went on March 12 to a memorial service for the dead of the First World War, showing no slightest sign of fear – 'Although he had been warned that it might not be safe for him to attend, Adenauer duly appeared. I accompanied him and with my own eyes saw the complete isolation in which he found himself. People avoided him like a leper.'[29]

At the memorial service he was warned again, this time by a man who had joined the Nazi Party, that the Nazi SA had been instructed to 'liquidate' him. He was to be thrown out of the window of his office in the Town Hall when he arrived there on the following Monday morning.

It seems, on the whole, unlikely that the Nazis were preparing this spectacular defenestration. It would have damaged their public image, and this was something about which they still worried, with less than half the German electorate behind them. Certainly, they wanted him out of the way, especially as they were making preparations for the passing of the 'Enabling Act' which, on March 23, gave Hitler the powers of a dictator. The Act laid down that for a period of four years the Government would have the right to decree any law or sign any treaty without reference to the Reichstag. Since this meant the virtual abrogation of Parliamentary rights, by a radical amendment of the constitution, the Act required a two-thirds majority in the Reichstag. Adenauer's resolute defence of Prussian parliamentarianism suggested that he could have become the focus of Centre Party resistance. As it happened, the Centre Party members of the Reichstag voted for the Act; the only party which did not was the Social Democrats. There was a comfortable majority for the Act, as the Communist Party had already been outlawed.

29..........*Konrad Adenauer*, Paul Weymar, p. 102. Evidence of Dr. Billstein.

By then Adenauer was, in fact, out of the way. On the afternoon of March 12, he asked for police protection. It was refused. Now, when it was too late, Adenauer must have bitterly regretted his own opposition, two years earlier, to the proposal that the Prussian Government should set limits on Nazi demonstrations and meetings. To resist them any further would have been useless, and it could imperil his family. He decided to go to Berlin. There he might be able to put his case to Hermann Goering, now Reich Minister of the Interior. What he hoped to gain by this vain quest can only be surmised. At the best, he might be reinstated in office, at least for the time being; at the worst, he would lose nothing and could lie low until the Nazis had forgotten about him.

He told Gussi only that he was going to Berlin for a few days. He told his office nothing and ordered his official car to pick him up, as usual, at 9 a.m. on March 13. But by 7 o'clock he had gone, creeping out of the house in the dark and being driven fifty miles in the car of his close friend Robert Pferdemenges to Dortmund station, where he caught the train for Berlin. The Nazis immediately announced his dismissal, and appointed a Dr. Günther Riesen as Acting Mayor. Riesen at once instituted an inquiry into the running of the municipal finances, and proceeded to sack one official after another. The city's administration had been firmly in the hands of the dominant Centre Party; the purge carried out by Dr. Riesen was designed to fill all key posts with Nazis and their sympathizers.

In Berlin Adenauer achieved nothing. Goering was that most unpleasant and dangerous type of being, a *faux bonhomme*; someone who pretends to be a nice guy but isn't. For all his girth and superficial geniality, he was one of the most vicious of the Nazi leaders – utterly unprincipled, vain and cruel. He kept Adenauer waiting for three days before he saw him. What he had to tell Adenauer was in no way encouraging: the incident of the removal of the swastika flags from the Cologne–Deutz bridge had not been forgotten; Adenauer's administration of Cologne was now being investigated; and he was suspected of having embezzled city funds. Goering had himself ordered the investigation in February. It was based on an accusation made in the Prussian Parliament in September, 1932, that Adenauer had never repaid a 15 million Mark credit granted in 1930 by the 'Prussian Cooperative Bank' (*Preussische Zentralgenossenschaftskasse*). Adenauer's accuser, a Dr. von Winterfeld, claimed that much of the money had gone into the pockets of prominent members of the Centre Party.[30] He asked that a legal inquiry should be made into the matter.

This was now, in fact, being done. Around March 18 Adenauer wrote to his successor, Dr. Riesen, and asked why loyal members of the city

30..........Cologne City Archives.

administration in Cologne were being dismissed. Riesen's answer confirmed that preliminary inquiries had shown that Adenauer and his officials were guilty, at the very least, of 'reckless extravagance' and 'monstrous corruption'.[31] Riesen concluded his letter by telling Adenauer that he was 'in the dock', that he, Riesen, was Counsel for the Prosecution and the German people would be his Judge.

Riesen's charges were taken up, in May 1933, by a regular commission of inquiry, headed by a Nazi official, a Dr. Adolf Miller. This commission made exhaustive inquiries, even investigating the wages paid to Adenauer's gardener in the Max Bruch Strasse. Every important item of city expenditure during the previous ten years was scrutinized. So was every lunatic accusation against Adenauer, including those made by members of the Communist Party. The commission of inquiry wasted an immense amount of time. It discovered nothing, and it terminated its activities sometime in 1934.

After his flight from Cologne, Adenauer stayed only a short time in Berlin. According to one biographer,[32] he was very much alone, but was able to fall back on his religious faith, and paid frequent visits to the Church of St. Hedwig. If so, he may have had meetings – which have never been recorded – with ex-Chancellor Brüning, who was living as a kind of unofficial pensioner at St. Hedwig's Hospital, which was attached to the church. It was while he was there that Brüning told Fabian von Schlabrendorff (a future member of the German 'resistance' to Hitler), that 'a man has to choose now whether he wants to stand under the swastika or under the cross of Christ. He can decide for only one of them.'[33] Both Brüning and Adenauer were courageous men; both realized that they were in deadly danger. Brüning was to leave Germany in June, 1934. Adenauer had ample opportunity to leave too. But, unlike Brüning, he had a family, a large one. This may have been the operative reason why he decided to remain in Germany, and somehow to survive the Nazi Era.

The official inquiry being conducted by Dr. Adolf Miller may have helped to convince Adenauer that he had to lie very low indeed. Gussi came up to Berlin to talk things over. Adenauer's position was parlous. He no longer had a single friend in political high places. The Centre Party was in process of dissolving itself; it had signed its own death-warrant by voting for the Enabling Act, for Hitler had no intention of allowing a primarily locally-based, Roman Catholic party to go on subsisting on the Roman Catholic vote in the Rhineland. The Nazis had begun to round up their enemies. Their secret police arm, the Gestapo, was now active.

31..........Letter of Dr. Gunther Riesen, dated March 21,1933.
32..........*Konrad Adenauer*, Paul Weymar, p. 108.
33..........*The Secret War against Hitler*, Fabian von Schlabrendorff, p. 52.

Lord Mayor of Cologne, 1931

Opening the Cologn
Fair, 1924

Accompanying President Hindenburg at a ceremony marking the British evacuation of Cologne, 1926 (*above and opposite*)

Attending the Cologne Fair with President Ebert, 1924

The Adenauer family at the dining table. A photograph taken in the mid-thirties, during the Nazi era.

Adenauer, for that matter, had no hope of finding a job and a means of subsistence in Berlin. He turned for help at this bleak moment to a former school friend, the Abbot of the monastery of Maria Laach, Ildefons Herwegen. He asked for sanctuary at the abbey, tucked away in the hills of the Eifel.

Herwegen told him that he would be welcome. At almost the same time, another old friend of Adenauer's paid a surprise visit to Berlin. This was Danny Heinemann, who had in the past put him in touch with French diplomats and businessmen. He had heard of Adenauer's plight. He brought him 10,000 Marks in cash, refused to accept an IOU, left again almost before Adenauer had finished thanking him. Under Nazi instructions, Adenauer's bank had refused him credit and had apparently 'blocked' his account. Heinemann's ten thousand Marks tided him over the first financial crisis of his life.

Robert Pferdemenges had risked something by putting a car and chauffeur at his disposal and getting him out of Cologne. Danny Heinemann risked nothing by his gift, but showed great goodwill and confidence in him. Ildefons Herwegen took a major and calculated risk by accepting Adenauer into the monastic life of Maria Laach. It has been written, very often, that Adenauer was a man who did not make friends. Well, he found three – and very good friends at that – when he needed them most. They did more for him, when it mattered, than most people's friends do for them in a lifetime.

Maria Laach is a Benedictine abbey, in the foothills of the Eifel and about fifteen miles west of the Rhine. The abbey sits on the western side of a deep lake, believed to be the crater of an extinct volcano. The country round it is thickly wooded, and scenically beautiful. Seeking refuge there meant that Adenauer would lead a remote, monastic life. In order not to attract attention, his family would remain in Cologne, and would communicate with him through third persons – their mail was likely to be censored. The maximum precautions were observed, too, in getting Adenauer to Maria Laach; he came by train from Berlin to Neuss, twenty miles north of Cologne, and he was met there by the faithful Pferdemenges and his car. They did not drive through Cologne on their way to the abbey; Adenauer had been officially 'expelled' from his native city.

Maria Laach was total exile and virtually total seclusion for a man who had led an intensely active life, mainly in the public eye. Yet there were compensations. There was a good library in the abbey, and Adenauer's reading had been somewhat neglected for years past. Now he read a great deal, particularly books on German and Roman history. There was lovely countryside around, and he walked often and far. He talked much with the monks, and in Herwegen found a man not only bound to him by the tie of personal friendship but with an alert, liberal and far-ranging mind.[34] In many countries of the world, Catholic laity 'go into retreat' under religious supervision, usually for a week or two. Adenauer's enforced 'retreat' was an extended one; it lasted for the best part of a year.

During the school summer holiday he was joined by Paul, his 10-year-old first-born from his marriage with Gussi. Paul was already showing an interest in the Church, and it was felt that the absence of one child from the Adenauer home in Cologne would not be noticed. Then for Christmas, 1933, the whole family joined him, cramming into a couple of rooms at a small hotel by the lakeside. For Paul, the summer holiday had been a treat – with the long rambles in the hills with Adenauer, the manner in which he was treated as a companion by his father, the feeling of sharing a worthwhile experience and mutual trust.[35] The Christmas reunion went very well, too, with the usual tree, small gifts and a feeling of an exciting and protracted picnic in the snow-covered hills. Christmas can still be a time of good cheer, even in humble or unusual circumstances. For the four younger children, certainly, this particular Christmas was fun. If it were less so for the three children from his first marriage – they were, after all, all in their twenties and well aware of the dangers which threatened Adenauer – they were still put at their ease by their father. 'He showed,' according to one of them, 'an almost incredible tact; to us he simply did not suggest that he had any fears at all for himself. He was absolutely determined not to involve us in them, but they existed all right.'[36]

Adenauer's stay at Maria Laach may indeed, as one of his children believes, have been 'character-forming'.[37] He was thrown back entirely on himself. His natural stoicism was deepened and enhanced. He had time to think, and think hard (really for the first time in his adult existence) about the basic problems of his country. He certainly drew considerable comfort from his religion and from the atmosphere of peace and purpose which pervaded Maria Laach.[38] The whole Nazi Era was to be a tremendous test of character for him; the test began now.

The family reunion at Christmas, unfortunately, did not pass unnoticed. A little later Herwegen received a formal 'complaint' from the Governor of the Rhineland, Freiherr von Lüninck, and a demand that Adenauer should be told to leave Maria Laach at once.[39] Herwegen wrote a dignified letter of refusal, but Adenauer decided himself not to cause his friend any possible embarrassment. He had just heard of a house which he would be

34, 35.....Dr. Paul Adenauer, in private conversation with the author.
36...........Dr. Max Adenauer, in private conversation with the author.
37...........Dr. Paul Adenauer, in private conversation with the author.
38...........Frau Ria Reiners, in private conversation with the author.
39...........*Konrad Adenauer*, Paul Weymar, p. 112.

able to use while its owners went into temporary emigration. They wanted to keep their property and leave someone in charge of it whom they could trust.[40] The house was at Neubabelsberg, a small place on the south-western outskirts of Berlin. The place's sole claim to fame was that it housed the studios of the biggest German film corporation, Ufa. After the Second World War it featured much in the news as the nearest place to the Soviet 'check-point' on the autobahn from Berlin to West Germany.

A suburb of Berlin might seem a curious place for Adenauer to choose for a temporary home for himself and his family. It was only a dozen miles from the centre of Berlin and the seat of the Nazi regime. Adenauer was a West German Rhinelander. Berlin was inimical to him, although he knew the city tolerably well as a result of his frequent visits there as President of the Prussian State Council. He was virtually in a 'foreign' country at Neubabelsberg, in a land of gloomy forests and fens, the heartland of Protestant Prussia. One picture taken of him during this interlude of near-exile shows him sitting in a wood, his hands clasped round his knees and his back against the trunk of what looks like a birch-tree. There is snow on the ground, and on Adenauer's face an expression of brooding melancholy and deep resignation. For once, he failed to hide his feelings from the camera.[41]

He hid them pretty successfully from the family. The two oldest sons were now off his hands, and Ria was studying at Heidelberg University and was home only for the holidays. She remembers plenty of happy days at Neubabelsberg; so does his youngest daughter, Libet, although she was only 6 years old at the time.[42] To Paul, Neubabelsberg was menacing and strange. He seems to have been the member of the family most keenly aware of his father's feeling of helplessness; the others were charmed by the fact that he was spending so much more time with them, showing so much interest in their personal problems and organizing a 'family collective' with gusto (Paul cleaned the shoes, Lotte was chief washer-up and little Libeth did the dusting).[43] Adenauer helped them with their homework, took them for walks and picnics in the forests, taught them all to swim and encouraged the 4-year-old Schorsch (George) in his engaging gift as a mimic. There was, indeed, plenty of gaiety in the family, whose different members got on well with one another. A sense of family solidarity was something which Adenauer valued very highly indeed, and

40...........Adenauer does not seem ever to have divulged the name of the owner, or to have left any written reference to it.

41...........*Konrad Adenauer*, Georg Schröder, p. 69.

42...........Frau Ria Reiners and Frau Libeth Werhahn, in private conversation with the author.

43...........*Konrad Adenauer*, Paul Weymar, p. 112.

it was something which he liked to bring out on any 'special occasion', with a little speech to each one of them, a small joke or a compliment on some personal achievement.[44]

Living under the permanent fear of reprisal against him and his family, Adenauer had a minor shock in March, 1934. Some weeks earlier, a former manager of the 'Deutsche Bank' in Cologne (Adenauer had been on the bank's Board of Directors) Anton Brüning, was arrested on a charge of embezzlement. Adenauer received a court summons, to make himself available for a call to appear as a witness. Adenauer's lawyer brother, August, learnt that his 'evidence' was to be presented 'in camera'. Acting on his brother's behalf, August Adenauer managed at least to arrange that this interrogation – for it amounted to this – should take place at the house of the third brother, Hans Adenauer, Canon of Cologne Cathedral.

Three officials of the Court, including a judge and the Public Prosecutor, arrived at Hans Adenauer's house. They carried out a preliminary interrogation of Anton Brüning, in which he accused Adenauer of having accepted bribes to a value of 35,000 Marks from the Bank. The money was, allegedly, used to pay off a mortgage; Adenauer repaid the Bank by giving it preferential treatment over the municipality's business. It was at once obvious that Adenauer had not been brought to Cologne as a 'witness' at all; he was himself on trial, and he was in deadly danger.

According to his biographer[45] Adenauer was allowed to cross-examine Brüning. He did so with great ability, but Brüning would not withdraw his accusation. The supposition must be that Brüning was hoping to secure a remission of sentence for himself, or perhaps a pardon. Finally, Adenauer appealed to Brüning 'in the name of all that is sacred to you', pointing at the same time to the crucifix hanging on one wall of the room. Brüning, in spite of the imprecations of the Public Prosecutor, withdrew his accusation against Adenauer. He was marched out of the house, on his way to prison.

This was a lucky escape for Adenauer. He had a luckier one three months later. On June 30, 1934, Hitler perpetrated what has been known ever since as the 'Röhm Blood-Bath'. Ernst Röhm, a veteran member of the Nazi Party, an ex-member of the post-1919 'Free Corps' and a soldier of fortune who had served in South America, had become head of the brown-shirted SA on January 1, 1931. By 1933, when Hitler came to power, the SA had nearly three million members and Röhm was the most powerful man, next to Hitler, in the whole Nazi movement. He was, in addition, perhaps the only leading Nazi who had no fear of Hitler and

44..........Frau Ria Reiners, Frau Libeth Werhahn and Dr. Paul Adenauer, in private conversation with the author.

45..........*Konrad Adenauer*, Paul Weymar, p. 114–18.

regarded him, indeed, with a leavening of contempt. An openly active homosexual, Röhm was a man of brutal appearance, blazing courage and able to exert considerable charm when he wanted to.

He had organized the SA on para-military lines, and packed its higher échelons with his own nominees (quite a few of whom shared his homosexual tastes). A student of history, he believed, according to one authority,[46] in instilling a truly revolutionary spirit into the SA and turning it into the spiritual equivalent of those ragged but indestructible French revolutionary armies which won their most sensational victories even before Napoleon appeared on the scenes. Röhm made it clear, at the end of 1933, that he wanted the Nazi revolution to move into a 'second stage' in which privilege would be swept away and a truly socialist ideology imposed in order to create a wholly unified community. When this kind of talk began to be shaped into concrete plans, and Hitler got wind of them, he acted with sudden and savage violence. Röhm and his associates were seized and murdered on the spot. Hundreds of his followers were killed, and Hitler took the chance of striking down all sorts of political opponents who had nothing to do directly with Röhm. General von Schleicher and his wife were murdered; so was Edgar Jung, a personal assistant of von Papen. Prominent Social Democrats were flung into the newly created concentration-camps, and two of Adenauer's former Centre Party colleagues narrowly escaped with their lives. Ex-Chancellor Heinrich Brüning was warned that his life was in danger, and left a few days before the 'Blood-Bath', bound for the United States. Gottfried Treviranus, dressed for a tennis-party in white flannels, escaped over the wall of his garden as a detachment of black-shirted SS men drove up to his front door. He, too, fled the country.

Adenauer was arrested by a single member of the Gestapo at his house in Neubabelsberg. It was a warm summer evening, and the whole family were in the garden. Adenauer was watering his flowers. The Gestapo agent tried the garden-gate, thought that it was locked, and climbed over it. He told Adenauer he was under arrest, let him put a few things into a bag and took him away in his car. Only a short time later, the rest of the family heard some shots fired; they were those that killed General von Schleicher and his wife, living only a few hundred yards away.[47]

Typically, Adenauer was utterly matter-of-fact and calm when he was driven off. He had nothing on his conscience, and said so to his wife as he left. He was held for two days, along with twenty-nine other 'suspects', in a villa outside Potsdam. All the prisons in the town were full. Twice he

46..........*The Nemesis of Power*, Sir John Wheeler-Bennett, p. 307–8.
47..........Dr. Paul Adenauer, in private conversation with the author.

was briefly interrogated and the second time, in Potsdam police headquarters, he was threatened with a 'further' interrogation in the cellar. By this he was meant to understand that he would be tortured, but he refused steadfastly to admit any guilt which he did not feel. The fact that he manifestly had nothing to do with any 'plot' against the Nazi regime may not have been the factor which saved him. The details of the 'Blood-Bath' had shocked the outside world; Hitler probably decided that there had been enough 'executions' for the moment. He was still interested in preserving some illusion of Nazi pseudo-respectability in the eyes of the rest of the world.

Soon after his release, Adenauer received a message from Abbot Ildefons Herwegen, warning him that he was in danger. His recommendation was that Adenauer should keep on the move.[48] One of the most unpleasant features of this was the complete uncertainty of the situation – Adenauer had no idea what charge might be made against him, nor could he tell whether the signal given by Herwegen was justified, or whether a Nazi *agent provocateur* was merely carrying on a private war of nerves against him. At all events, he left Neubabelsberg and spent some weeks travelling from one small place to another. This was the least documented period of his life, and even members of his family have little idea of exactly where he went.

It could hardly have been a long period, for some time in August he made a written application for payment of his pension, or at least a part of it, to the Minister of the Interior in Berlin, Wilhelm Frick. According to one biographer,[49] this was on August 9, eight days after the death of President Hindenburg and the abolition of the post of President by Hitler, who became *Führer*, or 'Leader', as well as Reich Chancellor. In his letter to Frick, Adenauer allegedly protested that he did not deserve the epithet applied to him of 'nationally unreliable', and argued that he had declared in the Prussian State Council that the Nazi Party would take over the leadership of the Reich. Adenauer – or so the story goes – added that his dealings with the Nazi Party had been 'correct' and that he had allowed their swastika flag to be flown on appropriate occasions.

Subsequently, Adenauer admitted that he wrote to Frick for restoration of his pension rights, but he never alluded to the terms of his letter. It is possible that he found a form of words which helped his case, without in any way compromising his conscience. A pension was subsequently paid

48..........Just who informed Herwegen has never been made clear. Dr. Paul Adenauer believes it may have been a member of the Provincial administration in Coblenz, where Herwegen had good friends.

49..........*Konrad Adenauer*, Rudolf Augstein, p. II. In *Adenauer, Democratic Dictator*, Charles Wighton gives the date as August 10, 1934.

to him – the sum of 12,000 Marks a year has been mentioned[50] and he received an unspecified sum in compensation for the two houses in Cologne which the Nazis had 'requisitioned'. It was with this money that he now, in 1935, bought a plot of ground in the village of Rhöndorf on the east bank of the Rhine opposite Bonn, and built the house, No. 8a Zennigsweg, which became his home for the rest of his life. It remains a matter of doubt whether Frick or the municipal authorities in Cologne made the operative decision about his pension. It was, in any event, a matter about which he hardly needed to reproach himself afterwards; he was fully entitled to his pension, and fully justified in asking for his rights.

There were some uncomfortable vicissitudes before No. 8a Zennigsweg, was built. In 1935 Adenauer rented an old and uncomfortable house in Rhöndorf. He had to leave it at a moment's notice when an order was issued expelling him from the *Regierungsbezirk*, or administrative district of Cologne. This area just included Rhöndorf, and Adenauer, leaving his family there, moved four miles upstream to Unkel (in the administrative district of Coblenz) and lodged at the Roman Catholic 'Pax' holiday home. The weather that winter was bad, the roads were difficult for members of his family who had to cycle to see him and he was much alone. One former Cologne municipal official, Josef Giesen, recounted how on the 'Day of Prayer and Repentance' (*Buss und Bettag*) in November, 1935, Adenauer seemed totally forlorn and at last beginning to lose heart. He told Giesen that he felt like a tree which had been torn up by the roots and tossed into the river of life to drift aimlessly downstream.[51]

The two 'funny men' of Rhineland folk-lore are called Tünnes and Schäl. The jokes about them are legion. One which was current at this time was –

> TÜNNES: 'What do you hold of the Third Reich?'
> SCHÄL: 'My tongue!'

A great many Germans, apart from Adenauer, were holding their tongues. Dachau concentration-camp had opened in April, 1933. Five years later there were a dozen such places, into which opponents of Nazism simply 'vanished'. Millions of Germans knew of one or more of these places, but relatively few Germans knew much about what went on inside them. The 'Brown Book of the Hitler Terror', published by Messrs Gollancz of London, was banned in Nazi Germany and would have gone on to the

50..........*Konrad Adenauer*, Rudolf Augstein. The 12,000 Marks figure is confirmed by Weymar (p. 125). But Weymar says that the restoration of his pension rights resulted from talks between the Cologne administration and Dr. August Adenauer, the lawyer who was Konrad Adenauer's brother.

51..........*Konrad Adenauer*, Paul Weymar, p. 124.

bonfires of 'subversive' literature organized by Hitler's Minister of Propaganda, Josef Goebbels. The Rhineland was not a keenly Nazi area, but there was no overt spirit of resistance to Nazism. Only handfuls of the inquisitive gathered in front of the Jewish shops which were pillaged and the synagogues which were burnt down in the Roonstrasse, the Glockengasse and at Mülheim, Deutz and Ehrenfeld during the 'Crystal Night' of November 9, 1938. The people of Cologne were shaken out of their scared apathy only when the Nazis decided to turn their beloved 'Carnival'[52] into a 'party occasion' and formed a monolithic 'Cologne Carnival Association'. There was an immediate counter-attack by the Carnival societies, which secured permission to continue in being. It would have been more apposite had the citizens of Cologne shown a similar energy in defending their civil liberties.

When the building of his home in Rhöndorf was completed, Adenauer had something to occupy him at last. He planned the garden, carted stones for its steep terraces, planted it, grew vegetables as well as flowers in profusion. He worked hard in the house as well, turning it into a comfortable and charming home at the minimum cost, with a truly magnificent view across the Rhine to the faint blue line of the Eifel hills in the distance. Bonn lay almost beneath him. Cologne was away to the right, never out of mind but out of sight behind the crags of the Drachenfels, the mountain from which the mythical dragon had once dominated the river valley until he was slain by the Knight Roland. Creating his home gave Adenauer a real sense of satisfaction; he was doing something for the family; giving it a base and re-establishing some sense of security and continuity when it was most needed.

For Adenauer had little doubt that the Second World War was coming, and it was no surprise to him when it broke out in 1939. He predicted it a few months earlier, and took his wife with him to Switzerland on holiday in the summer.[53] In the back of his mind was the thought that the outbreak of war would be followed by another mass round-up of 'suspects' by the Nazis. It would be as well to lie low for a time. He warned friends of what might happen, but he seems to have had no idea of emigrating in order to avoid persecution. Members of his family agree that he never spoke of it,

52..........Carnival traditionally takes place during the week leading up to Ash Wednesday. 'Rose Monday' is the true climax of the Carnival, and Shrove Tuesday completes the celebrations. In some parts of the Rhineland Carnival has become something of a fetish, spreading over many weeks and involving wildly inflated municipal and personal expenditure.

53..........His son, Max, remembers him predicting war, 'in 3 or 4 years time', in 1935. He told Max that the Nazis, by their excesses, were certain to blunder into war by then. Dr. Max Adenauer, in private conversation with the author.

never planned for it and almost certainly never thought of it. They agree, too, that the principal reason why he intended to stay in Germany was not because he thought himself too old to make a new start – he was, admittedly, 63 when war broke out – but because he could not bring himself to leave his family. By 1939 all three children from his first marriage were entirely independent of him – his daughter, Ria, was married to a successful engineer. But his two youngest, Libeth and 'Schorsch' were only 11 and 8. And Gussi, a devoted and affectionate mother, was a little defenceless, and more than a little dependent on his experience and judgement.

The theory is tenable that Adenauer went on holiday to Switzerland just before the Second World War in order to make himself 'unavailable' when the wave of arrests which he expected should take place. If he calculated so precisely, he was remarkably prescient, and very well-informed about Nazi psychology. When the Nazis believed that someone was really dangerous to them, they hunted him down remorselessly; but when they had to round-up sexagenarians merely because their names were on a 'black list', they were not much interested. Adenauer was allowed to go on living quietly in Rhöndorf, while first two of his sons, and then the third, went to the front to fight for a German Government in which none of them believed any more. His youngest daughter, Libeth, intelligent and impressionable, probably has the clearest recollection of just how Adenauer himself felt about 'Hitler's War'. Her evidence was: 'He told us that the Nazis could not win it. He believed that they should not, and he made this very clear to all of us. We prayed for the war to be lost by Germany, not our Germany but Hitler's. That was our only source of hope for the future.'[54] Adenauer – and this did him credit – was one of a relatively small percentage of Germans who did not complain bitterly after the war of the Allies' insistence on unconditional surrender. In this, he was entirely consistent.

Prayer, as Adenauer saw it, was all that was left to him. He knew that his name was on the Nazi 'black list'.[55] If he had ever thought of taking part in the resistance to Hitler, this fact alone precluded it; he would have been a liability to those infinitely gallant Germans who plotted Hitler's downfall and death. But there were three other reasons why he never joined them, although – as one of his sons maintained – he knew plenty of people who would have put him in touch with them.[56] He did not believe that Hitler could be brought down by his German opponents, and he distrusted in

54...........Libeth Werhahn, in private conversation with the author.

55...........*The Order of the Death's Head*, Heinz Hoehne, p. 142. An SS report of August, 1937, is cited, showing that a watch was being kept on Adenauer and the Freiherr von Schroeder by the Nazis.

56...........Dr. Max Adenauer, in private conversation with the author.

particular Dr. Karl Gördeler, one of the leaders of the 'resistance', whom he had known in the German *Städtetag* and who almost certainly sent an emissary to Adenauer sometime in 1943. He was not a conspirator by nature. And he feared that the Nazis would take reprisals on his family, were he to participate in an unsuccessful plot. This, as it happened, was exactly what the Nazis did do to the families of the 1944 conspirators.

Paul Adenauer remembers his father telling him after the war that an approach had come from Karl Gördeler, through a third person.[57] His recollection is that his father regarded Gördeler as 'indiscreet'; it seems certain too that Gördeler's emissary showed him one of those 'lists' of members of a future non-Nazi government which Gördeler so enjoyed compiling.[58] Other associates of Adenauer's have pointed out that he was 'too careful' to involve himself in a project over which he would have no personal control, that he believed instinctively that it would not bring about Hitler's death or downfall, and that the vague hopes of the conspirators of securing a fair peace from Germany's enemies were bound to be disappointed.[59]

Adenauer himself maintained a total silence about whatever relations may have existed between him and the German Resistance. Obviously he would not have wanted it known that he had been approached by the resisters – because, equally obviously, he made no move to join them. It is significant that he seems never to have tried to communicate with foreign countries during the war. His friends put this down to discretion, his enemies, to calculated cunning allied to an instinct for survival. He could have died an anti-Nazi martyr; he chose to survive as a non-active 'non-Nazi' instead.

On July 20, 1944, the conspirators struck, but their almost perfectly planned attempt to kill Hitler miscarried. While hundreds of suspects were rounded up and Gestapo torturers were extracting more and more names of anti-Nazis from their victims, the Adenauer family waited in trepidation. On July 24 six Gestapo officials searched the house in Rhöndorf and found nothing (Adenauer was far too careful to have left the list of Gördeler's 'shadow Cabinet' lying around!). On August 23 two police officers arrived and arrested him. He was escorted first to Gestapo headquarters in Bonn, briefly interrogated, and from there was taken to a temporary detention-centre in the Trade Fair grounds at Cologne-Deutz.

57...........Dr. Paul Adenauer, in private conversation with the author.

58...........Dr. Hermann Pünder, in private conversation with the author. Pünder recalls discussing one of Gördeler's lists with Adenauer, but non-committally.

59...........Dr. Heinrich Krone, Dr. Hermann Pünder and members of Adenauer's family, in private conversation with the author.

He was put into a room with a Communist, Eugen Zander, an alert fellow who made it his business to know everything that was going on in the camp. He was responsible for saving Adenauer's life, for he learnt that a party of prominent prisoners was going to be transported to Buchenwald concentration-camp, and that Adenauer's name was on the list. With the connivance of a Dr. Richartz, a fellow prisoner who had access to the dispensary and was allowed to give medical treatment under supervision, Adenauer shammed illness and was moved to the Hohenlind Hospital. He arrived there depressed, emaciated and terribly anxious about his family – he had had one glimpse of Gussi and Libeth through the barbed-wire fence surrounding the detention-centre. But at the hospital he had another stroke of luck; the head doctor was a personal friend, Professor Paul Uhlenbruck. He was given his own room and as much food as could be spared, and was excellently looked after.

What was more, he was able to organize his escape. He was fetched from the hospital by a highly official-looking car of the *Luftwaffe* (German Air-force), driven by a Major Hans Schliebusch, a friend of the family. Schliebusch had a forged document which showed that Adenauer was needed in Berlin for interrogation. Instead, he took him to an old mill, the Nister Mühle, forty miles south-east of Cologne. The miller and his wife knew who he was, but discreetly accepted him as guest under the name of 'Herr Weber'. The plan was for him to lie low there until the war was over.

On September 25 two members of the Gestapo called at his home in Rhöndorf, demanded to know where Adenauer was and, when told that nobody knew, removed Gussi to Brauweiler prison, on the outskirts of Cologne. There she was thrust into a cell filled with prostitutes, taken out and threatened with reprisals, including the imprisonment of the 16-year-old Libeth, and forced to confess where her husband was. The Gestapo fetched him from the Nister Mühle early the next morning. Possibly for the only time in his life, Adenauer lost his nerve when the Gestapo car arrived in the dark hours of early morning. He dodged up to the loft and tried to hide behind a chimney stack. There the three Gestapo officials found him, after searching the whole house. They took him to Brauweiler prison, releasing their 'hostage', Gussi, on his arrival there.[60]

Adenauer spent just two months in Brauweiler. Later in life, he claimed that he had been put into a concentration-camp by the Nazis. Brauweiler was not exactly that, but rather a staging-post on the way to the concentration-camps. Adenauer could have been moved at any moment, and no more would have been heard of him. He was put into a dirty, damp cell, wretchedly fed and frequently interrogated. His braces, tie and

60..........*Konrad Adenauer*, Paul Weymar, p. 156–9.

personal belongings were taken away from him, which was standard practice in German wartime prisons, and the prison-commissar told him that it would cause him personal inconvenience if he committed suicide. In Adenauer's own words: 'I asked him what made him think that I might take my life. He replied that as I was now nearly 70 years old and had nothing more to expect from life, it seemed reasonable to suppose that I would put an end to it.'[61]

In fact, Adenauer showed amazing composure and fortitude at Brauweiler. When Libeth visited him – she often had to wait two to three hours outside the prison before being allowed a two- to three-minute talk with him – he had no complaints about his living conditions and no thought of recrimination against Gussi for having disclosed his hide-out at the Nister Mühle. At his interrogations he continued to insist, courteously but firmly, that he had committed no crime, and to demand his release. He instructed Libeth to get in touch with her brother Max, now a Lieutenant in the Army. Max visited him on October 26, then called at Gestapo headquarters in Berlin and suggested there that army morale must suffer if fathers of serving soldiers were arrested for no reason at all and flung into prison. This may have contributed towards Adenauer's release, but in the meantime he had another shock. Major Hans Schliebusch and his young son were brought into Brauweiler prison. The Major's part in Adenauer's escape from Hohenlind Hospital had been discovered. He and his son contracted typhus in prison and died shortly after the Americans took Cologne.[62]

On November 26, 1944, there was a heavy air-raid on Cologne and the prisoners at Brauweiler trooped down to a shelter in the basement. After the raid was over, Adenauer was told that the order for his release had come from Berlin. The camp stores were closed as it was a Sunday, and Adenauer left on foot, without his tie or his braces. He was given a lift home by a Cologne friend who was lucky enough to have some petrol left. He arrived back to a house full of women – the wives of Max and Koko had joined the rest of the family. He was weak, undernourished but philosophical. With luck, the Gestapo would take no further interest in him, and the war was undoubtedly almost over. The Americans were only sixty miles from Cologne.

His womenfolk nursed him back to something like reasonable health. He listened avidly to the broadcasts of the BBC working out the likely course of the Allied advance into Germany, and deciding that the Ameri-

61..........*Memoirs*, Konrad Adenauer, VOL 1, p. 17.

62..........*Konrad Adenauer*, Paul Weymar, p. 165. But in his *Memoirs*, VOL 1, p. 19, Schliebusch was still serving in the German High Command *after* his own release from Brauweiler.

cans would cross the Rhine at Mainz and the British at Wesel. This meant, he supposed, that Rhöndorf would simply be by-passed, but there was one dramatic incident still in store for him. According to his own version [63] he had gone up the hill above his house to his personal observation post, looking west across the Rhine. The Americans were on the far bank and there had been some intermittent firing across the river.

Now, three shells arrived in quick succession, hitting the ground twelve, seven and five yards away from him respectively. He later claimed that he had seen the first shell 'hurtling towards me' and had flung himself to the ground. When the third shell exploded, he jumped up and ran down to the house, where there was a make-shift shelter in the garden. He was temporarily deaf, but unhurt. According to his daughter, Ria, it was the only time during the last weeks of the war that she saw him at all excited. It was, in fact, impossible for Adenauer to have seen a shell coming straight at him, although it is just possible that he saw a tracer shell fired as a marker. Later in life, he was to assert that the shells had been deliberately fired at his house, possibly because it was an obvious place for an observation-post.[64]

The Americans arrived eight days later. There was no fighting in Rhöndorf and the defending German troops withdrew to the east. The Adenauer family emerged from the air-raid shelter, where they had spent most of their time during the previous three weeks. They found that the house had been struck one glancing blow by a shell, and that several trees in the garden had been hit. About a week later [65] two American officers drove up to the house in a jeep. They came with the request that Adenauer should accompany them to Cologne and take over the administration of the city again.

63..........*Memoirs*, Konrad Adenauer, VOL 1, p. 19.
64..........*Memoirs*, Konrad Adenauer, VOL 1, p. 19, in private conversation with the author, Weymar.
65..........*Memoirs*, Konrad Adenauer, VOL 1, p. 20. Weymar (p. 171) writes that the two Americans arrived on the day after the German withdrawal. Either version may be correct, since Weymar's information came from Adenauer in 1955, whereas Adenauer only began writing his memoirs in 1964.

6 A new Germany, a new Party

In his prison cell in 1944 Dietrich Bonhöffer, one of Hitler's most courageous opponents, wrote that 'Terror is one of the "pudenda", one of the things that ought to be concealed.'[1]

In another letter, he had this to say: 'It was God who made clothes for men, which means ... there are many things in human life which ought to be kept covered over. To uncover is a mark of cynicism ... since the Fall, reticence and secrecy are essential.'[2]

Adenauer would have agreed with both of these sentiments. He had, for sure, known terror during the Nazi era – when the Gestapo came for him in Neubabelsberg, when he was taken from his home in Rhöndorf, when he skulked in the loft of the Nister Mühle. But he believed in extreme self-control and in hiding any feeling of weakness. The war may have treated others worse than him, but he had paid several visits to the Valley of the Shadow of Death. When Hitler's armies overran Poland, Scandinavia, the Low Countries and France, then Yugoslavia and Greece, he remained mute. He was equally, commendably silent during the years of defeat and of brutally destructive Allied bombing of his homeland, most of all of his home-town of Cologne. Adenauer had learnt how to keep quiet, and never subsequently made a virtue of his discovery. At the end of it all, in 1945, he was a haggard ghost of the immensely self-confident, stiff-necked Mayor of Cologne who had been described, before the Nazis came to power, as the 'strongest character in Germany'. He was in his 70th year. It would have been reasonable to suppose that his active career was over.

The Cologne to which Adenauer returned had suffered even more than its former Mayor. Adenauer had paid a visit to it about six months before the war ended, and had been sickened by the destruction caused by repeated Allied bombings – Cologne was the target for the first British one thousand bomber raid.[3] The French writer, André Gide, drove through it shortly after the war ended, and was so horrified by what he saw that he stayed only a quarter of an hour and asked to be driven out of the city as quickly as possible. If a Frenchman could feel like that about Cologne, how much more appalling must the sight of his native city have

1............*Letters and Papers from Prison*, Dietrich Bonhöffer, p. 47.
2............*Letters and Papers from Prison*, Dietrich Bonhöffer, p. 51.
3............*Konrad Adenauer*, Paul Weymar, p. 127.

been to Adenauer, who had lived in it for nearly sixty years and ruled it for sixteen?

Almost every Romanesque church had been pulverized and the massive Cathedral had suffered several direct hits. Over 60 per cent of all houses had been totally destroyed; another 30 per cent were rendered uninhabitable. This scale of destruction is the more fantastic when one considers that Cologne was spread over the biggest area of any city in Germany save Berlin – only a third of it was built-up. In other cities in the Rhineland the damage done by Allied bombing was grim; in Cologne it was catastrophic. Even its streets had disappeared; mountains of rubble had piled up in them and turned them into lunar landscapes, over which ran the meandering paths made by the feet of the thousands who returned to search for their homes in the ruins. All the bridges over the Rhine had been destroyed and all public services – transport, gas, electricity and to some extent, water supply – had ceased to function. The pre-war population of Cologne was three quarters of a million; when the United States Army moved in it was about 32,000.

Adenauer seems to have had a notion that the American occupation authorities had been furnished with some special 'white' list of anti-Nazi Germans whose co-operation they could secure. The reason why the Americans sought out Adenauer and asked him to become Mayor again was much simpler – he was the last pre-Nazi Mayor. In dozens of other towns American, British and French Military Government re-installed the man who had been in office until the Nazis removed him. Adenauer, predictably, went to work with a will; he has given his own account of these early weeks in his *Memoirs*.[4] His first task was to secure enough food to keep alive a population which grew at a formidable rate as people streamed back to the city from the surrounding countryside. The Americans helped with supplies from their military depots. They helped with transport too, but there was little they could do about the city's other principal need, housing. Makeshift huts sprang up everywhere, and people even scrabbled holes in the ground and fought their way down to relatively undamaged, barely habitable basements. It was to take Cologne nearly ten years to restore its outward appearance to normal.

Round him Adenauer assembled a small but dedicated staff. He moved temporarily into two rooms in Cologne-Lindenthal, and worked an eighteen-hour day. According to one Cologne official, Johannes Albers, 'Adenauer was always available, and always had time'.[5] He organized the gangs of rubble-clearance workers, he sent fleets of buses to half a dozen

4.............*Memoirs*, Konrad Adenauer, VOL I, p. 20–5.
5.............*Konrad Adenauer*, Paul Weymar, p. 177.

concentration-camps to collect citizens of Cologne and bring them home, he obtained supplies of steel in order to begin work on one of the Rhine bridges, he hired architects to produce the first blueprints of the virtually new city which had to be built. He established excellent relations with the American authorities, but on June 21, 1945, they left and were replaced by British Military Government. There was, Adenauer subsequently maintained, an immediate change of climate – 'Conflicts soon arose between me and the British administrative officers. In my opinion the British were treating the population badly. Their attitude towards me was also very negative.' [6]

The change of climate was, of course, going on everywhere in occupied Germany. Human beings have a natural urge to help their own kind when they are in dire distress, even if they are ex-enemies. Relief measures were desperately needed in the early months. After that, military occupation tended to drop into a more bureaucratic routine. Adenauer had not been the British nominee for the Mayor's post, and the British authorities knew less about him than they should have done. On their side, it must be remembered that Adenauer had the reputation of an autocrat, an absolute ruler in his own domain, brooking no argument. By the time the British moved in, he was undoubtedly a great deal readier to assert himself than fifteen weeks earlier.

The British made a bad start by tapping the telephone line to Adenauer's home in Rhöndorf, and doing it so ham-handedly that he was informed about it by the German postal authorities. In Adenauer's view, the British showed a marked preference for local Social Democrats and allowed themselves to be influenced by a memorandum of July, 1945, composed by his old opponent in the City Council, Robert Görlinger. In this memorandum[7] Görlinger maintained that Adenauer and his former associates of the Centre Party were insisting on denominational schools, were carrying on 'underground' political organization (political parties were still banned by Allied order) and were trying to bring back Nazi Party members into positions of authority. Adenauer learnt of the Görlinger memorandum some time after the Labour Government came to power in Britain at the end of July. He was acutely suspicious of the British Labour Party's instinctive sympathy for German Social Democracy.

It was in any case inevitable that differences should arise between Adenauer and British Military Government. The task of an occupying power is always invidious. In the case of post-1945 Germany it was impossibly difficult. The British authorities had to urge reconstruction of the

6............*Memoirs*, Konrad Adenauer, VOL I, p. 25.
7............*Memoirs*, Konrad Adenauer, VOL I, p. 26.

With friends and family

siting the prison at Brauweiler

'he Berlin exile

At war's end: in front of Cologne Cathedral, 1945 →

Above At the Schoneberger Rathaus with the three Allied Commanders, Generals Taylor, Ganeval and Bourne. *Below* A relaxed moment with son George and daughter Lotte, 1950.

life of the community at a time when all materials were in short supply; when dismantling of German industry was under way; and when Allied regulations made it impossible for the Germans to produce the steel, building materials and consumer goods which were so badly needed. Allied aims were in large part defeated by Allied regulations, and at the same time a vast social upheaval was being instigated by Allied measures to obliterate the Nazi Party. It was this paradoxical situation which prompted the many wry German jokes about Allied 'occupation'. One standard jest related to a British offer to help build a temporary bridge across the Rhine. How long, the British officer asked, would it take the German municipality? The answer: three weeks. But how long, then, if the British authorities gave all the help that they could afford? Answer: three years.

Adenauer's suspicions of the British were reciprocated. There were rumours – unfounded, as far as one can judge – of his having established personal contact with the French Government. A more tendentious and trivial story was that he accepted food parcels from the French. There was talk, once again, of his alleged connexions with the Rhineland separatists in the 1920s. The British authorities did not like the peremptory tone of his 'requests' for more coal and building materials for Cologne. Nor could they have been favourably impressed by the final passage of the speech which he made when the first meeting of the Cologne City Council took place on October 1, 1945, under British auspices, and which Adenauer himself quoted with satisfaction in his memoirs – 'Let us, then, go to work together, bowed low, but unbroken.'[8]

Then, at the end of September, Adenauer refused to order the felling of trees in his beloved 'Green Belt', running round the city's western perimeter, for the people to burn in their grates. There were already severe shortages of fuel, and now came the first frosts of what turned out to be a very cold winter. The austere Adenauer insisted that the trees of the 'Green Belt' would not keep Cologne warm, and that they were a long-term investment of real value. On October 5 Adenauer gave an interview to two foreign newspaper correspondents, one British and the other American. He told them that there was a case for the formation of a 'Rhine–Ruhr State', linked economically with France and Belgium, but only if this were done within the framework of a federation which should include all parts of Germany other than the Soviet-occupied Eastern Zone. He suggested 'a system of international control' in place of military occupation,[9] and expressed the wish that some 'British statesman' would talk and, presumably think, of Germans as 'Western Europeans'.

8............*Memoirs*, Konrad Adenauer, VOL I, p. 31.
9............*Memoirs*, Konrad Adenauer, VOL I, p. 32.

On the day following, October 6, the British Military Government's chief administrative officer for North Rhine, Brigadier John Barraclough, summoned Adenauer to his office, told him that he had failed to fulfil his responsibilities or to do his 'duty to the people of Cologne', dismissed him summarily and ordered him to leave Cologne 'as soon as possible, and in any case not later than 14th October'.[10] Adenauer was at the same time instructed not to engage, 'directly or indirectly, in any political activity whatever.' This ban, and his dismissal, were at once confirmed by the British Corps Commander, General Thomas.

This was, possibly, the most momentous step taken by any of the Western Occupying Powers in the field of German domestic politics. For Adenauer was, literally, driven out of Cologne, the birthplace which he intended to serve with his remaining strength and capacity. Cologne's problems were so hideous that he would have found it hard, probably impossible, to have forsaken his native city during the next five years. But the history of Western Germany as a whole advanced a giant stride in that period. Adenauer could always, of course, have moved into the wider political arena after 1950. But by then – had he meanwhile been totally occupied in Cologne – he might have found a political constellation where he was unwanted.

The 'Barraclough affair', then, was so significant that it deserves as full an examination as possible. One concrete piece of evidence has been supplied by Brigadier Barraclough. Having previously said that he would make no statement on this subject while Adenauer was still alive, he spoke on British television after Adenauer ceased to be Federal German Chancellor in October, 1963, and also gave an interview to the *Daily Express* newspaper in London. This interview was republished in a short biography of Adenauer.[11] Barraclough's account reads as follows:

'I was Regional Commander of the Rhineland. The British authorities were working to bring order out of chaos. The German authorities in most of the cities and towns were co-operating. But for some reason the city of Cologne was lagging far behind.

'General Templer (then Director of Military Government and later Field-Marshal Sir Gerald Templer, Chief of the Imperial General Staff) came to my HQ in Düsseldorf and told me that he was disturbed by the lack of progress in Cologne.

'The devastation in Cologne was almost indescribable. Public transport was non-existent. Electricity and gas supplies had broken down. The navigation channel of the Rhine, one of the main arteries of communication, was completely blocked.

10..........*Memoirs*, Konrad Adenauer, VOL 1, p. 33.
11..........*Konrad Adenauer*, Rudolf Augstein, p. 14–15.

'The sewers were open. Thousands of Germans were starving. Hundreds of thousands of refugees were moving on the roads.

'I arranged a meeting with Adenauer.

'We met in the office of the local commander in Cologne. I think that this is the first time Adenauer and I had seen each other. Although I was impressed by his personality, I freely admit that I did not realize that I was face to face with a man who was to become one of Europe's dominating politicians.

'He came into the room carrying a book under his arm. We shook hands and sat down.

'I did my best to impress on Dr. Adenauer the desperate urgency of the problems facing us, and appealed to him to co-operate.

'His immediate reaction was to show me an album of drawings entitled "The Cologne of the Future", or something to that effect. Apparently he thought it impracticable to rebuild the city on the existing site. His plan was to build a new Cologne outside the boundaries of the old city.

'I remember pushing the book back across the table and saying: "Show me that in ten years time. In the meantime you must tackle the immediate problems."

'We talked for the best part of two hours, but made no progress.

'Surrounded by the chaos which I have described, here we had the senior paid official with his head well in the clouds.

'With great reluctance, I decided that for the good of his own people he would have to go.

'This was my own unaided decision. It has since been said that I was influenced by political reasoning and by Dr. Adenauer's advanced age. Both charges are false.

'I dismissed Dr. Adenauer for one reason only: because he was not doing his job as the leading paid administrative official of the city.'

So much for the testimony of Brigadier Barraclough, to which one must return in due course. Adenauer's own account has already been given, paraphrased. Adenauer stated, in addition, that Brigadier Barraclough did not ask him to sit down, that there were a number of other British officers present who remained seated as if they were a kind of tribunal, and that the interview was very short indeed – involving only the reading and translating of the Brigadier's 500-word statement, after which Adenauer at once left the room. The two versions of the incident, then, are at almost total variance with one another.

Two points in Barraclough's statement are easily dealt with. It was perfectly true that Adenauer had produced a memorandum on the rebuilding of Cologne. But this was produced well before the day of his dismissal, and if he happened to be carrying a copy of the memorandum on

October 6, this was purely fortuitous – or he brought it along believing that it might be the subject-matter for the interview. The memorandum did not, of course, suggest in any way that Cologne was to be left in ruins and some 'substitute city' built outside its previous confines. On this point Barraclough's statement was totally misleading.

It was misleading, too, on the subject of General Templer's visit to Cologne. Templer did, indeed, comment on the devastation of Cologne and ask why more was not being done to put the city in order again. His conducting officer was appointed by British Military Government and was in a position to explain that Cologne had suffered far more than any other city in the Rhineland from Allied air-raids. This did not need to be explained to Barraclough at all; he was the chief administrative officer for the area, living at Düsseldorf, only twenty-five miles away. The inference must be that Barraclough used Templer's expression of concern as a pretext for getting rid of Adenauer.

The question as to whether Adenauer really was asked to sit down and have a cosy chat with Barraclough might seem to be of minor importance. But veracity has its own standards; if Barraclough misreported his interview with Adenauer on this salient point, then his testimony becomes suspect. It is absolutely impossible to square the two accounts; one of which has Adenauer chatting comfortably for two hours, and the other places him standing upright before his 'judges' for under ten minutes. What is the truth on this point?

One has to reach it by a roundabout route. With an astonishing lack of tact, Barraclough invited Dr. Willi Suth to be Adenauer's successor. It is scarcely conceivable that he did not know that Suth was Adenauer's brother-in-law. If he did, it makes his choice weirder still. Suth, at all events, was not prepared to take the job. It was offered to Dr. Hermann Pünder. What happened to Pünder is indicative. He was summoned by Barraclough and informed that he was to become Mayor of Cologne. An interpreter translated the short, clipped passages of Barraclough's 'invitation'. Pünder replied in very passable English, and only when he did so, did Barraclough, agreeably surprised, offer him a chair. Up till then, Pünder was kept standing.[12]

It is, to say the least, most unlikely that Barraclough would have offered a chair to the man whom he was sacking, when he was so loath to offer one to the man whom he was asking to become Mayor in his place. Unlike Pünder, Adenauer did not speak English! Pünder's only other comments on Barraclough were that he conformed to the 'military martinet' type referred to by Germans as a *Komisskopf*; and, more revealingly, that he

12..........Dr. Hermann Pünder, in private conversation with the author.

instructed Pünder to have potato patches planted round Cologne Cathedral! Pünder flatly refused.[13] As far as Adenauer's performance went, Pünder's view was that he had almost certainly been 'fractious' (the German word used by Pünder was *boeckig*). This may well have been true, too.

The local British Military Government authorities took sole responsibility for sacking Adenauer. Neither General Sir Brian Robertson, the chief policy-maker in the British administration, nor his political adviser, Sir Christopher Steel, were informed. Sir Christopher first heard of the sacking two days later. Then, for prestige reasons, it was too late to reverse Barraclough's decision. Sir Christopher compared Templer's part in the affair with the stray remark of King Henry II of England, which resulted in the murder of Thomas a'Becket.[14] Sir Brian's succinct comment was, 'I was lucky to miss that party.'[15]

There was a thoroughly unpleasant sting in the tail of this sorry affair. Gussi Adenauer was in hospital in Cologne. Adenauer's banning from his native city meant that he had to get special permission to visit his wife, and according to his own story, it was granted grudgingly and he was restricted to two visits a week.[16] According to his own story, again, one of the secretaries in the Town Hall, a Fraülein Goldkuhle, was dismissed because she wrote a letter to Barraclough in which she boldly stated her belief that Adenauer had done everything he could for the people of Cologne.

Did the Barraclough incident seriously affect Adenauer's feelings towards Britain? Members of his own family, on the whole, think not. Frau Ria Reiners remembered him making a joke of the affair only a couple of days afterwards. Both she and her brother Max believed that he was 'too big' a man to be influenced in his real political views. Paul Adenauer felt that it 'did rankle a bit', but that his father's sense of humour helped him to make light of it.[17] Frau Libeth Werhahn was told by her father that he

13..........Dr. Hermann Pünder, in private conversation with the author. Lord Pakenham (later Earl of Longford), British Minister for German Affairs, produced a curious sidelight on Barraclough. When Pakenham first visited the British Zone he remarked to Barraclough that the only possible policy towards the Germans was 'one of friendliness'. Barraclough answered, 'I couldn't agree more' (*Born to Believe*, Lord Pakenham, p. 175). The author of this book knew Barraclough's Düsseldorf headquarters well. It contained some good administrators, but it did *not* radiate 'friendliness' to the Germans.

14..........Sir Christopher Steel, in private conversation with the author.

15..........Sir Brian Robertson (later Lord Robertson), in private conversation with the author.

16..........*Memoirs*, Konrad Adenauer, VOL I, p. 34.

17..........Members of Adenauer's family, in private conversation with the author.

had been sacked as a result of Social Democratic machinations. This was the attitude which he decided to adopt in his published *Memoirs*, in which he claimed that the British Labour Government regarded him, an anti-socialist, as 'inconvenient for their policy' and suspected him of being too friendly with the Americans.[18]

Adenauer retailed the story of his sacking a great many times afterwards. Sometimes he tried to make a joke of it, as when he told Brigadier Barraclough years later that he had two files in his office, one headed 'Dismissal by the Nazis' and the other 'Dismissal by the Liberators'. But there was a note of bitterness, too, on many occasions. If there were two human qualities which Adenauer really loathed they were rudeness and stupidity. He believed that Barraclough had been guilty of both. Lord Robertson and Lord Longford, both of whom got to know Adenauer well, and liked him, believed that he regarded his dismissal as an affront and that it left a mental scar which never entirely healed.[19] He knew that the accusation of having failed his beloved Cologne and its people was monstrously unjust.

What is quite sure is that his dismissal had the vastly important indirect result of launching Adenauer into the party-political arena. For the moment, indeed, he was expressly banned from all political activity. But Sir Christopher Steel and the head of the 'German Political Branch' of Military Government, Lt.-Colonel Noel Annan (later Lord Annan) had talked his case over. Also consulted was Mr. Ronald Grierson, the local British political officer in the Rhineland. In December, 1945, Lt.-Colonel Annan went to Adenauer's home. Adenauer explained to him that he could not 'talk politics' in the British Zone, but that he would accompany the erudite Lt.-Colonel to Bad Honnef, only three miles away and just inside the French Zone. There, they had a long talk. Its upshot was that, after Annan had explained matters to Barraclough, the ban on Adenauer's political activity was lifted.[20]

For Adenauer, this was not a moment too soon. He had been totally inactive for two months, at a time when – as he saw it – his country needed men of his calibre most. He was acutely suspicious of British Military Government, believing it to be the instrument of the British Labour Party in sponsoring the German Social Democrats and making them hot favourites for future political power. And the organization of the party to

18..........*Memoirs*, Konrad Adeneur, VOL I, p. 34.

19..........Lord Robertson and Lord Longford, in private conversation with the author.

20..........*Memoirs*, Konrad Adenauer, VOL I, p. 35, contains the statement that an 'Oxford Don' came to see him from Buende. Annan was in fact a Cambridge don. His headquarters was in Berlin, with a branch office in Buende.

which he would naturally belong, the 'Christian Democratic Union', was already under way with men much younger than himself bidding for its leadership.

One must, for a moment, go back in time to explain what had happened in this connexion. When the victorious Allies arrived in Germany they laid down that there should be no political parties – indeed, no political activity at all while the remnants of Nazism were being swept away. On May 16, 1945, Sir Winston Churchill confirmed this position for the British Zone by stating that there could be no 'regional' or central German Government during the whole period of Allied occupation (at that time it was expected to last twenty years). Gatherings of six or more people were forbidden. The Social Democrats were scandalized, for they considered that their party, which alone voted against the 1933 Enabling Act giving Hitler a dictator's powers, had never ceased legally to exist. In May leading Social Democrats in Hamburg asked the British Military Government if they could re-form their party on a formal basis. Permission was refused.[21]

But even before then German conservatives began a clandestine political activity. In April, 1945, three former members of the former Catholic Centre Party formed what was probably the first 'cell' of a new, more broadly-based, interdenominational party. These three – Leo Schwering, Dr. Wilhelm Warsch and Joseph Frings – met in secret in Königswinter, only a mile from Adenauer's home, even before the American forces arrived. On April 1 they decided to lay the groundwork for a 'Christian People's Party' (*Christliche Volkspartei*), which would take the place of the Centre in its old strongholds and could spread to Protestant Germany. Later, Schwering approached Adenauer, who told him that there were considerable obstacles other than Allied Military Government edicts.[22]

It may well be that Adenauer did not want even the nucleus of a Christian party formed while he was otherwise engaged. As Mayor of Cologne, he was much in the public eye and could take no part. But Schwering's ideas were not new to him. In the early 1920's he and Adam Stegerwald had discussed plans for just such an interdenominational party, to be called the 'Christian-National People's Party'. In 1922 at the 'Catholic Conference' in Munich, Adenauer appealed openly for its creation. From April, 1945 Adenauer carefully scrutinized the plans of Schwering and his friends, and of men with similar ideas in other parts of Germany.

In May and June other Christian 'cells' were organized in several places

21..........*Die Entstehung der* CDU *und die Wiedergründung des Zentrums im Jahre* 1945, H. G. Wieck, p. 35.

22..........*Frühgeschichte der Christlich-Demokratischen Union*, Leo Schwering, p. 14.

in the Rhineland, including Essen, Dortmund, Münster and Paderborn. On June 17, 1945, a number of leading men in the new movement were allowed to hold a meeting in the Kolpinghaus in Cologne. They decided that the old Centre Party should be jettisoned (in fact, it lingered on in some parts of the Rhineland for several years to come). This was not an easy decision to take, especially not in the Rhineland where the Centre Party had for so long been the guardian of Catholic principles and interests. As Schwering put it – 'We had to do battle with precisely those people who had been our best friends.' They also laid down certain guiding principles (*Leitsätze*), delineating the new party as Christian, democratic and 'social', rather than Socialist. It formally constituted itself as the 'Christian Democratic Union' on September 2, 1945, in Cologne.

So much for the Rhineland CDU, which was in effect the successor-party to the pre-war Catholic Centre. Meanwhile, much had been happening in other parts of Germany, notably in Berlin. There, the Berlin branch of the CDU was officially founded on July 22 and quickly opened offices in the Jaegerstrasse. It called itself 'all-German' and this was encouraged by the Soviet Military Government, which hoped to control the central organizations of all the principal political parties (it had automatically secured control of the re-founded Communist Party). The leading lights of the Berlin CDU were three former Centre Party members, Jakob Kaiser, Andreas Hermes and Otto Nuschke, and a former Liberal, Ernst Lemmer. The Berlin CDU had two big advantages over its Rhineland rivals; it was supplied with premises, paper and petrol by the Soviet authorities, and it had established itself in the old Reich capital.[23]

Until early October Adenauer was Mayor of Cologne. From then on he was active in the affairs of the CDU, first behind the scenes only, but then openly and with increasing vigour and authority. Late in September he intervened to frustrate what he considered a dangerous diversionary initiative. This was when the pre-1933 Reich Minister of the Interior, Karl Severing, organized discussions between leading Social and Christian Democrats, with the evident idea of forming a 'democratic front' which would work out guide-lines for a future 'national' government. Adenauer attended a conference, held at Bad Godesberg to sum up the results of these discussions. He did not speak at it, but made it clear that he disapproved of any 'pre-emption' of clear-cut party-political programmes. Severing's well-meant initiative petered out.[24]

In Bavaria the effort to form an inter-denominational party nearly came to nothing. A bitter rearguard action was fought by the ultra-conservatives

23..........*Der Spiegel*, weekly, October 18, 1961.
24..........H. G. Wieck, p. 145.

of the former 'Bavarian People's Party (BVP) led by Alois Hundhammer. They were out-manoeuvred by Josef Müller, who was determined to build a powerful branch of the CDU with the support of Protestant North Bavaria. The Bavarian section of the new party, however, insisted on its own name – Christian Social Union (CSU). Bavarians have to 'be different'; the CSU remained a semi-autonomous branch of the CDU from then on. In Hesse, progressive conservatives nearly joined up with the Social Democrats and were only deterred by the thought that the SPD remained, ideologically, a Marxist party. In Hamburg, Herr von Schlange-Schöningen emerged as the leader of a right-of-centre branch of the CDU. In 1946 the Berlin CDU made a determined effort to win over the Hamburg branch; this was repelled by Adenauer.

There were further jockeyings for power, for it was clear that the Berlin branch wanted to gain overall control and believed this to be in the national interest, whereas the West German branches were instinctively federalist and became increasingly unwilling to involve themselves in any part of Germany in which the Soviet Union had even partial control. In December, 1945, Andreas Hermes organized an 'all-German conference' – *Reichstagung* – of the CDU in Bad Godesberg. The Soviet authorities had become suspicious of this upright and clear-sighted man, and refused to grant him a permit of exit from the Soviet Zone. Adenauer attended the Bad Godesberg meeting, and most adroitly blocked moves towards union of the CDU under Berlin management. Hermes was accordingly 'deposed' by the Soviet authorities.[25] Unwittingly, they removed the most dangerous rival of the man who subsequently became the greatest thorn in their flesh, Adenauer.

On January 8, 1946, it was decided to convene a CDU executive meeting for the British Zone for January 19 and 20 in Herford. Adenauer was nominated as one of the five delegates from the Rhineland. According to one authority,[26] 'for the friends of the former Cologne Lord Mayor it was clear that he was preparing himself for duties to come', and in Bad Godesberg, a professor coined the phrase – *Conradus ante portas* – 'Konrad is at the gates'! As a political prophet, the professor was no slouch. On January 6 Adenauer had sent a confidential letter to seven key members of the CDU, in which he explained that he was reserving himself for the 'major' tasks which lay ahead: the union of the CDU with the remnants of the Centre; a 'family compact' with the Christian Democrats of Bavaria and the French Zone; and then – restoration of a free press in Germany, the settlement of Germany's economic problems, the restoration of the

25 ....*Der Spiegel*, weekly, October 18, 1961.
26...........H. G. Wieck, p. 171.

rule of law and the development of a 'national' foreign policy.[27] This was quite a list, and it made plain that Adenauer regarded himself as a force to be reckoned with. He was not apt to underrate himself; nor did he overrate his powers.

What was really intriguing was that Adenauer considered that control of the CDU in the Britizh Zone was vitally important. He was absolutely right. The British Zone contained the whole of the industrial Ruhr and all West German ports, with the exception of Bremen, which remained an American 'enclave'. Even more relevant was Adenauer's thought that, to build up one's political potential, one needed a *Hausmacht* – a political base. In face of the centralizing aims of the Berlin CDU and the deviationist trends in Southern Germany, the British Zone seemed to Adenauer an appropriate base. He set out to gain control of it.

Adenauer obtained this necessary control at the January 19–20, 1946, Herford meeting. The organization of this meeting was a trifle haphazard; it was not at once clear that the issue was the choice of a chairman of the British Zonal executive. Nobody present, save Adenauer, seems to have realized that what was being chosen was really the future leader of the whole CDU. Hamburg had its candidate, Hans von Schlange-Schöningen. Westphalia had Friedrich Holzapfel, and Berlin had Andreas Hermes. Adenauer was not an official candidate at all.

But when the delegates assembled at Herford, Adenauer took the chair as *Alterspräsident*, or 'senior' at the meeting. He did it with an easy grace. Many of the delegates did not know each other; the 'chair' was left vacant and Adenauer seated himself in it, remarking that, as the oldest delegate present, it was natural for him to give a lead. The chairmanship of this zonal executive led to chairmanship of the whole CDU. This was to be Adenauer's political base for the next two decades. Schlange-Schöningen left the meeting on the second day, to become chairman of the British Zonal Food Office. Hermes, who had no official status at the meeting because he was no longer a CDU executive member in Berlin, left of his own accord and disappeared for good from the political stage. Holzapfel vanished into obscurity too – Adenauer was later to send him to Berne, as the first West German Ambassador to Switzerland. Nothing happens in Berne, nothing happened to Holzapfel, ever again. That was how his Chairman wanted it, after he had been given the consolation prize of deputy to Adenauer, whose post was confirmed at the CDU Zonal Council meeting of February 26.

From then on, Adenauer moved with inexorable momentum towards complete control of the CDU. In March, the Hamburg and Schleswig-

27..........H. G. Wieck, p. 172.

Holstein groups integrated themselves fully in the Zonal organization. In the same month, Adenauer chaired a meeting of CDU leaders in Stuttgart at which it was decided that the CDU in Berlin should be merged with other Zonal branches of the party. More important, Adenauer laid down that the seat of leadership should not be Berlin or any city in the Soviet Zone. Nor should Berlin become the headquarters of the CDU, even if Berlin ceased to be occupied by the Russians.[28] In June, 1946, Adenauer coolly ignored a CDU meeting in Berlin, at which Kaiser forced through aims which were acclaimed as 'Christian Socialist'. Only a handful of West German 'observers' attended. Kaiser was made to realize that the CDU of West Germany would make no concession to Socialist aims in order to placate the Soviet occupying power. Adenauer was playing it safe; he did not believe that any fair compromise could be reached with the Russians, and he preferred to risk the splitting of the CDU, into a West German party which would play a decisive role in Germany's future, and an East German branch doomed in any event to satellite status and political impotence.

Single-mindedness usually pays off. Adenauer knew what he wanted. His rivals in Berlin tried to calculate in all-German terms–while all their calculations were vulnerable to Soviet whim and design. Adenauer scotched a Berlin attempt to secure a regular exchange of information with Hamburg,[29] he won over the CDU in Hesse by promising that Frankfurt would be the future capital of Germany and he helped to put an end to the North Bavarian Protestant drive for a left-of-centre social programme. Under Adenauer, the Rhineland CDU was beginning to emerge as the dominant power inside the party.

'He appeared to us as a statesman who knew what he wanted.' This was the phrase used by Leo Schwering, after Adenauer spoke to a mass rally in Cologne earlier in 1946.[30] In that speech Adenauer talked for two hours at Cologne University to an audience of 4,000 about Germany's future. He spoke in a quiet, reflective manner, without bombast and without a trace of resentment over the past. His message was clear: the State was no longer to dominate the individual, who should be allowed to show his initiative in every facet of his existence; and the Christian ethic should once again become the bastion of the German community. Adenauer called for the restoration of reasonable living standards, for no annexations of German territory, for a Federal State with sufficient central authority and for progress towards a United States of Europe. He used one evocative phrase – 'Occupation is neither a pleasure for those who endure it, nor

28...........*Adenauer and the* CDU, Arnold J. Heidenheimer, p. 73.
29...........*Adenauer and the* CDU, Arnold J. Heidenheimer, p. 82.
30...........Leo Schwering, p. 190–3. The speech was made in March.

for those who exercise it.' His speech was the first evidence of real statesmanship, still surviving in a German nation which under the Nazis had been enslaved, disgraced and spiritually gelded.

The speech marked Adenauer out as perhaps the only man who could successfully forge the widely differing groups within the CDU into a cohesive political party. At this stage of history Adenauer must have had two fears about the CDU. The first was that it would develop into a large but leaky umbrella, under which would cluster people of all sorts of differing political persuasions, who would in due course drift away to form a multitude of new parties. This would lead to the same impotence and sectionalism of the parties of the centre which took place in the Weimar Era. This danger could only be banned if the CDU were led with real authority and sense of purpose.

The second danger, as Adenauer saw it, was that of the party being centrally directed from Berlin, coming under Soviet influence there and so proving unable to evolve a philosophy and policy which made sense. This danger was very real; in May, 1946, the Soviet Military Government forced a split between the West German and East German Social Democrats. The East German branch of the party was compulsorily merged with the Communist Party to form the Socialist Unity Party (SED). Kurt Schumacher defiantly set up the headquarters of the West German Social Democratic Party in Hanover and successfully prevented the Berlin branch from being swallowed up by the SED. The Russians, therefore, were intent on intervening in internal German politics. But they would probably not make the same mistake twice. With the CDU they were likely to proceed with more caution, if they could have a united party centred on Berlin.

Adenauer had never deviated in his belief that a counterweight to Berlin and its Prussian hinterland should be created in the Rhineland. In July, 1946, the British authorities took a significant step in this direction by creating the *Land* of North-Rhine–Westphalia. This linked the industrial Ruhr and the agricultural areas of Westphalia with the Rhineland. The new *Land* was to become the fulcrum of economic power in West Germany; its borders were very similar to those drawn on the map in 1919 by Adenauer, when proposing the creation of a Rhine–Rühr state within the Reich. The British authorities consulted Adenauer and Schumacher as the leaders of the two principal emergent political parties. They were flown in a British military aircraft to Berlin, where Adenauer readily accepted the British proposals, while Schumacher sharply and typically rejected them.[31] Prussia, as it happened, had already been officially

31...........Allegedly, Schumacher declared that Germany would now be governed by 'three Cardinals' – Cardinal Faulhaber in Munich, Cardinal Frings in Cologne and the Communist 'red Cardinal' Pieck in the Soviet Zone.

'abolished' by Allied Control Council Law No. 46 of February 25, 1946. More than 150 years earlier the philosopher, Johann Gottfried von Herder, prophesied that the work of Frederick the Great, who lifted Prussia into the top league of European powers, would in course of time disintegrate. Herder called for the 'dismemberment' of Prussia, the 'un-German' warrior-state, and its integration into the Holy Roman Empire. Prussia was regarded as an 'enemy' by all four Occupying Powers after the Second World War. Approximately half of its territory – in the shape of the old provinces of Silesia, Pomerania and East and West Prussia – was lost when Poland's western frontier was advanced to the line of the Oder and Neisse rivers. The Russians carved up their zone into five *Länder* and the post-1815 Prussian domains in West Germany were, in the course of 1946, to be split up between the three *Länder* of North-Rhine–Westphalia, Lower Saxony and the Rhine–Palatinate.

Well before the creation of *Land* North-Rhine–Westphalia, Adenauer had decided to co-operate with the Allied Occupying Powers as far as he possibly could. One useful medium of co-operation was the British Zonal Advisory Council, set up in March, 1946, in Hamburg. Adenauer attended its meetings regularly, where he argued strongly for increased food supplies for the desperately hungry German population, for the re-activation of industry and commerce and for the lifting of Allied restrictions and controls. Schumacher took no interest in the Zonal Advisory Council, discouraged what he regarded as 'collaboration' with the Occupying Power, and lost a golden opportunity of informing himself of British policies. The Zonal Advisory Council was a purposeful body and not, as Schumacher supposed, a mere talking-shop.

In the autumn of 1946 there were municipal elections in Berlin, the Soviet Zone and the British Zone. The CDU obtained nearly 20 per cent of the votes in Berlin and the Soviet Zone, but around 40 per cent in the British Zone. There were angry exchanges between the Berlin and Rhineland branches of the party, with Kaiser arguing that the CDU should boost its chances in Berlin and the Soviet Zone by establishing its headquarters in Berlin and by declaring itself unequivocally in favour of the 'socialization' of heavy industry in the Ruhr.

Adenauer answered the first demand in an interview which he gave to the Hamburg newspaper, *Die Welt*, in November.[32] He said that his most important difference with Kaiser concerned Germany's 'centre of gravity'. He rejected Berlin as the physical and spiritual centre for the CDU because of its 'Prussian spirit'. He went on:

'It is my belief that Germany's capital should be situated in the south-

32..........*Die Welt*, daily paper, November 30, 1946.

west rather than in Berlin, far to the east. The new capital should lie somewhere in the region of the river Main, where Germany's windows are wide open to the west. If, on the other hand, Berlin becomes the capital once again, distrust of Germany abroad will become ineradicable. Whoever makes Berlin the new capital will be creating a new spiritual Prussia.'

The issue of socialization of heavy industry was more complex. As early as August, 1945, Adenauer had written to a political supporter in Munich, Dr. Wilhelm Scharnagl, that the common objective must be 'progressive social reform, but not Socialism'.[33] Yet he was prepared, at least temporarily, to pay lip-service to the somewhat vague ideas about 'public ownership' of industry that were being propagated. These ideas owed much to the even vaguer general desire for a 'new start' for German society and to the confused arguments that a defeated and impoverished Germany could no longer afford the 'luxury' of a capitalist form of society. (The idea that state-run industries were more 'economical' was to be quickly disproved by the experiments of the post-war Labour Governments in Britain.)

Within the CDU were a number of influential people who believed that heavy industry, meaning primarily coal, steel and chemicals, should be 'socialized'. They included the Christian Trade Unionists, Jakob Kaiser in Berlin, Karl Arnold in Düsseldorf and, with less conviction, Josef Müller in Munich. Early in 1946 a CDU supporter, Otto Heinrich von der Gablentz, produced a pamphlet entitled *Über Marx hinaus* ('On from Marx') which proposed communal ownership of key industries, co-determination rights for industrial workers and large-scale economic planning. Adenauer's reaction to the pamphlet was to declare that 'Socialism' was unacceptable – 'If we use it we may win five people, but twenty will run away.'[34] Later he stated that 'the transfer to public ownership of the means of production is not in our eyes necessarily equated with social progress'. And he pointed out that nationalization had not benefited Britain's coal industry, and that any British interference in the structure of Germany's basic industries might constitute a breach of international law.

In February, 1947, however, the CDU's British Zonal Council took what appeared to be a momentous step. On the advice of an 'economic committee' which it had set up, it approved in principle the so-called 'Ahlen Programme' which seemed to ordain the revolutionary restructuring of German heavy industry. The three most important points in this programme were the transfer of the coal industry to a system of public ownership; the reorganization of steel, chemical and other key industries

33..........H. G. Wieck, p. 73.
34..........*Adenauer and the* CDU, Arnold J. Heidenheimer, p. 120.

on the principle of a 'mixed economy'; and acceptance of the rule that public bodies should hold a majority of shares in all such undertakings.

Adenauer's subsequent handling of the 'Ahlen Programme' was a masterpiece of diplomacy, and can best be dealt with at this point of the narrative. When a *Land* Government for North-Rhine–Westphalia was formed in 1947, Adenauer introduced, as leader of the largest political party, three bills implementing the Programme. He thereupon proposed that planning and control of key industries should be kept down to a minimum. Grasping what appeared to be a golden opportunity, the Social Democrats tabled their own far more comprehensive socialization bill. Adenauer secured the backing of his party in opposing this, and in offering amendments which held up legislation. Only in August, 1948, did the Social Democratic bill pass its third and final reading. By then it was too late; the London Foreign Ministers' Conference two months earlier had pointed the way to the creation of a West German State, and the British *Land* Commissioner in North-Rhine–Westphalia, General Alec Bishop, regretfully informed the *Land* Government that he could not approve the socialization of heavy industry in one particular *Land* – when all heavy industry had to be regarded as a 'national asset'. That was the end of the 'Ahlen Programme'; Adenauer's discreet 'filibuster' had worked.

In the meantime Adenauer had also won his battle against Kaiser and the 'centralists' in the CDU. But they did not give up without a struggle. Kaiser shifted the weight of his effort from making Berlin the CDU's headquarters, to reaching the longer-term objective of German reunification. On February 5 and 6, 1947, a meeting of CDU representatives from all four zones of occupied Germany and from Berlin took place – mainly at Kaiser's initiative – in Bad Königstein, near Frankfurt. They proclaimed the indissoluble unity of Germany, and Kaiser thereupon demanded discussion of where the CDU should have its headquarters. Once again, Adenauer insisted that it should be not Berlin, but Frankfurt. Kaiser's strongest supporter, Ernst Lemmer, noted that at this meeting 'Adenauer sat in the farthest corner of the room, from where he sent his most trusted aides into the firing-line'.[35] Nor was Adenauer above using diversionary tactics of a questionable kind – he suggested that Kaiser had been indulging in indiscreet consultations with leading ex-members of the Wehrmacht and officials of Soviet Military Government, and that he had learnt this from a 'Lord Mayor in the northern Rhineland' whose name could not be given. Lemmer, who was in a position to know, claimed that this tale was untrue and might even have been invented by Adenauer.[36]

35..........*Manches war doch anders*, Ernst Lemmer, p. 290.
36..........*Manches war doch anders*, Ernst Lemmer, p. 291.

The Bad Königstein meeting decided, by a narrow majority, against Berlin as CDU party headquarters. The majority accepted Adenauer's thesis, that the consolidation of the three western zones was the right way to work for German unity, and that the CDU must not expose itself to the forceful intervention of a totalitarian power, the Soviet Union. Still Kaiser did not give up hope. In March, at the Leipzig Trade Fair, he proposed the creation of a 'National Assembly' by the four main parties, the CDU and SPD of West Germany, and the SED and LDP (Liberal Democratic Party) of East Germany. Adenauer took evasive action; he merely waited until Schumacher, on behalf of the Social Democrats, rejected this plan. All that came of it was a stultifying conference of Prime Ministers of East and West German *Länder* in Munich on June 6, 1947. The East Germans left the conference when their proposed agenda was not accepted.

A last, fugitive effort was made from within the CDU to work for German reunification. Kaiser's chief supporter in Bavaria, Josef Müller, formed the so-called 'Ellwanger Circle' with this purpose in view. Adenauer's answer was to attend one of this group's meetings, at Bad Brückenau, and point out with destructive irony that plans for reunifying all four zones were hopelessly premature.[37] Kaiser had already come to the end of this particular road; in December, 1947, he and Lemmer were ejected from their offices of CDU Chairman and Deputy Chairman in the Soviet Zone and banned from any further political activity there. The pretext was Kaiser's demand that an officious Soviet Military Government 'observer', Captain Kratyn, should leave a meeting at which West German CDU representatives were present.[38] Long before this, in June, the 'Marshall Plan' of the US Secretary of State General George Marshall, for large-scale economic aid to Europe, had been tabled. The Soviet Union had rejected the plan on its own behalf and on that of countries under Soviet Occupation. They included the Soviet Zone of Germany, which was to be economically amputated from the three western zones. Unwillingly, Kaiser abandoned his plans for working, through a unified CDU, for a unified Germany.

Kaiser's challenge to Adenauer's leadership of the CDU disappeared from that moment. There was no one else to take it up. Hermes and Schlange-Schöningen had dropped already out of the party political arena. Karl Arnold, in Düsseldorf, had the moral fibre but not the necessary political acumen and ruthlessness. Josef Müller, in Munich, schemed but did not plan. Heinrich Brüning had not returned from exile in America, and Ludwig Erhard had not yet emerged as a recognizable political figure

37..........H. G. Wieck, p. 193.
38..........*Manches war doch anders*, Ernst Lemmer, p. 312.

from the Frankfurt fastnesses of the Bizonal Economic Council, set up in June, 1947, when the economies of the British and American zones were merged.

Within the CDU Adenauer was pre-eminent and he intended that the CDU should become the political arbiter of West Germany. Adenauer's pre-eminence had a personal as well as a political side. Here is one description of him at that time:

'At seventy he appeared to be physically frail. Like his fellows he had too little to eat in those first three post-war years ... The Adenauer of those days made a singular impression on me. He moved and spoke with a relaxed grace and restraint, while the mass of his fellow politicians were indulging in hysterics over dismantling, denazification and the lack of bread. In the midst of men who spent their time looking for extra rations or getting prematurely drunk at the first 'mixed' Allied cocktail parties, Adenauer seemed an obvious choice for the Chancellorship. He preserved in the face of the occupiers of his country a dignity that was virtually unique, thus marking himself out as the best man to deal with them on behalf of his fellow Germans. In them he inspired confidence alike by his refusal to complain about material discomforts and by his steely insistence on getting on with the tasks of political organization. Work and responsibility were making him into a younger, healthier man.'[39]

And this was how Brian Connell, the German Correspondent of the London *Daily Mail*, saw him at about the same time:

'I remember being struck at this first meeting by the high, serene brow, the curious Mongoloid cheek-bones and the bright, intelligent eyes of this spare, reserved man, already in his seventies. At a time when the propagation of political panaceas reached buzz-saw pitch in any private gathering, he was quiet, dignified, clipped in speech and to the point; the curious inverted diphthongs of his Rhineland accent – forcing one's attention as much as the clarity of his mind and his unexpected gifts as a witty *causeur*.'[40] Connell noted that Adenauer 'does not get his way by pounding the table; he uses men by flattering them, charming them with silky good humour or freezing them with quiet contempt.'

And a mere vignette – Julius Hollos, of *Die Welt* and later of the London *Financial Times*, was struck by Adenauer's amazing nonchalance. Late in 1946 he had an interview with Adenauer, who had come from one meeting and was on his way to another. With a deprecatory gesture, he took two *Butterbrots* (jumbo-sized sandwiches) out of a small bag, and ate them gracefully and without embarrassment while he answered Hollos'

39..........*The Atlantic Monthly*, magazine. Article by Terence Prittie. September, 1957

40.........*Watcher on the Rhine*, Brian Connell, p. 242.

questions.[41] Adenauer's critics and enemies misunderstood this gift of being unembarrassed; they imagined that he merely had a very thick skin.

Two British administrators who saw much of Adenauer during these early post-war years had a high regard for him. One, General Sir Brian Robertson had much to do with him; first as Deputy to the British Military Governor, Air-Marshal Sir Sholto Douglas, who loathed Germans and kept his dealings with them down to the minimum, and later when Robertson himself became Military Governor. Adenauer, Robertson considered, was 'eminently reasonable, highly intelligent and flexible in negotiation. He was not a man who liked everyone, and he sometimes took offence. But – I got to grow fond of him.'[42] Robertson added wryly – 'Schumacher helped me to appreciate Adenauer. He – Schumacher – just wouldn't let me get to know him; he remained constantly, unremittingly hostile. I went a long step out of my way to try to understand him. I went to his little house – no good.'

The other, Lord Pakenham, as the British Minister responsible for Germany, was struck at first by Adenauer's steely reserve – 'I first met him at an official British luncheon; he watched me very carefully, very appraisingly. Then, in due course, I got to know him. I suppose one tribute I can pay to him is that my Foreign Secretary, Ernie Bevin, began to worry about my having been turned into a "pro-German" by a man whom he regarded as a "Catholic Nationalist".'[43] Pakenham realized the depth as well as the determination of Adenauer – 'In many talks I had seldom, I felt, done more than scratch the surface of his mind.'[44]

Pakenham, again, was impressed by his dignity. When Adenauer met Sir Winston Churchill at The Hague in 1948, he said nothing to him personally about how Hitler's German opponents had looked to the British Prime Minister as the man who could topple the Nazi regime. Adenauer explained why: Churchill had said that Germans were either at one's throat or one's feet. Therefore, he politely requested Pakenham to convey discreetly to Churchill his feelings of admiration and gratitude.[45]

Finally, Pakenham hit on one strange facet to Adenauer's character – 'He showed me something unique in my experience, a power to stand outside the Germans, like a beloved father or even grandfather. He knew, none better, the weaknesses that had betrayed them.'[46] This facet may not have been altogether fatherly or grandfatherly; more than once during the

41..........Julius Hollos, of *Die Welt*, in private conversation with the author.
42..........Lord Robertson, in private conversation with the author.
43..........Lord Longford, in private conversation with the author.
44..........*Born to Believe*, Lord Pakenham, p. 194.
45..........*Born to Believe*, Lord Pakenham, p. 198.
46..........*Born to Believe*, Lord Pakenham, p. 199.

Nazi Era Adenauer complained bitterly of the moral cretinism of so many of his countrymen. He did not suffer fools or cowards gladly.

Yet patience and persistence were the two qualities which he was called upon to put to the most use of all during those first post-war years. At the end of them, a man of 72 found himself at the head of one of the two potentially strongest political parties in the 'rump-Germany' west of the Elbe. He had already laid down guide-lines for his party, the CDU, which it never forsook during his lifetime. He had secured the understanding of the British occupiers of the part of Germany in which he lived – even after they had dismissed and disgraced him. He had put up an impeccable performance as a German citizen, in the hour of his country's defeat. He was ready to move on to the next stage in his long political Indian summer. In 1948 he was confronted with the tasks of framing a democratic constitution for West Germany, fighting the first elections held under its terms, and forming a government which was to be the model for the foreseeable future. No man of 72, in the whole of history, has faced such a daunting challenge. No man, whether septuagenarian or not, faced it with such blithe awareness.

7 Midwife of the Federal Republic

Early in 1948 Adenauer suffered, for the second time in his life, a bitter personal loss. From 1945 onwards his wife, Gussi, had been seriously ill. She suffered from what her family called 'a disease of the blood'. The probability is that it was leukaemia, and she may have worsened her condition – the understandable outcome of Nazi persecution and the desperate worries which it caused – by overdoses of sleeping tablets.[1] In the autumn of 1946 she was ill with double pneumonia, but in the spring of 1947 she seemed to be in better health than for years past.

In June, Adenauer, who had been promising her a holiday in Switzerland for nearly ten years, was able to take her for three weeks to Chandolin, in the valley of the Rhône, where they had spent their last holiday abroad together. But in September she was much worse and had to go into the Johanniter Hospital in Bonn. She died on March 3, 1948, after a week in a state of coma. Adenauer behaved with the devotion and courage which one would have expected of him. According to his youngest son, George; 'In those days, after my mother's death, we felt how deeply attached he was to us. Without wasting words he quietly rearranged his whole working day so that he could at least spend the lunch hour with his family, and we should not feel too lost and lonely.'[2] This is a remarkable tribute; for it was Adenauer, aged 72 and a widower for the second time in his life, who had most reason to feel 'lost and lonely'. The eldest of his children was only 40; all seven of them had lives still to lead, families to raise and no necessity to feel lonely at all.

There is a tendency to underrate the wives of 'great' men. Gussi was recognizably affectionate and loyal. But she was also a person of strong convictions. Mr. John McCloy, whose wife was a distant cousin of Gussi's Zinsser family, and who himself became US High Commissioner in Germany, regarded her as a 'very remarkable woman. She was more aggressively anti-Hitler and anti-Nazi than Adenauer himself, although both were put in prison.'[3] Human feelings and sheer decency of character as marked as Gussi's were a real prop to Adenauer in the dark days of the Nazi Era.

1............Letter from Dr. Max Adenauer, December 11, 1969.
2............*Konrad Adenauer*, Paul Weymar, p. 231.
3............Letter from Mr. John McCloy, December 23, 1969.

By mid-1948, when Adenauer was firmly in control of the Christian Democratic Party, the international situation – in so far as it affected Germany – was radically different from that of 1945. The war-time 'Grand Alliance' had broken down completely. Adenauer had, indeed, predicted that it would, while a prisoner in the Cologne Trade Fair detention centre in 1944.[4] In the countries which it occupied, the Soviet Union suppressed democratic liberties, violated the United Nations Charter, installed Communist administrations by brute force and established police states. The Soviet Union deliberately fomented revolution in Iran and maintained troops there contrary to treaty arrangements, and applied violent pressure on Turkey to surrender bases in Thrace and on the Dardanelles. The Soviet Union, again, used its veto to sabotage the work of the United Nations Security Council, denied Marshall Plan economic aid to Eastern Europe and carried out the coup of February, 1948, which destroyed the democratic Czechoslovak state.

In Germany, the Soviet Union blocked all effective action by the Four Power Allied Control Council. Admittedly, the Russians were given their cue by the French. During the last three months of 1945 the French vetoed all constructive proposals to create centralized administration of Germany. They turned down the Anglo-American proposal to allow free passage of individuals between different zones of occupation; they refused to authorize political parties to be organized on a national basis, or a nation-wide trade union authority, or a national railways directorate. They demanded the control of the Rhineland, the annexation of the Saar and the expropriation of the Ruhr's heavy industries.

France, without a doubt, had suffered bitterly from the war – psychologically as well as materially. The Soviet Union had suffered far more, and was determined to secure the maximum compensation. Its government maintained that Germany should pay $10 billions in reparations as a 'first charge' on its economy. A Four Power 'Level of Industry' plan was agreed, under which the Soviet Union was allocated reparations from western zones in the shape of a dismantled industrial plant, as well as the reparations accruing from the Soviet Zone. At the same time, the Soviet Union took reparations out of current production, which was in any case insufficient to meet the straitened needs of the German population. At Allied Control Council meetings the Soviet Union refused to subscribe to the principle of economic unity laid down by the 1945 Potsdam Agreement, or to agree to a joint policy for imports and exports.

On May 3, 1946, the American Military Governor, General Lucius Clay, suspended all reparations deliveries from the US Zone to the Soviet

4............*Konrad Adenauer*, Paul Weymar, p. 138.

Union. In July, the Soviet Union rejected the American offer to merge zones of occupation economically. The Allied Control Council became the scene of endless, futile quarrels which need not be described here. At the Moscow Conference of March 10–April 24, 1947, the Soviet Union reiterated its demand for $10 billions of reparations (approximately £86 million). The only concrete progress achieved at this conference was the agreement that all German prisoners-of-war should be repatriated by December 1, 1948. The Soviet Union had no scruples about breaking this agreement.

The all-out drive by the Soviet Union to turn its German zone into a Communist satellite, combined with Soviet pressure in Eastern and Central Europe and total Soviet non-co-operation in settling Germany's future, was bound to produce a reaction on the part of the Western Powers. In September, 1946, Churchill appealed in his famous speech at Zurich for some kind of 'United States of Europe' – the tragedy was that he was no longer Prime Minister and could not follow it up himself. In January, 1947, came Marshall Aid. On March 12, President Harry Truman of the United States enunciated his policy of 'containing' Soviet pressure. In October, 1947, the three 'Benelux' countries of Holland, Belgium and Luxemburg, formed a union. On March 17, 1948, the Western European Union agreement on mutual defence was signed in Brussels by Britain, France and the Benelux states (Italy and West Germany were later included in it). In April, 1948, the Organization for European Economic Co-operation was founded.

Just one year later, twelve nations concluded a mutual defence pact as members of the North Atlantic Treaty Organization (NATO). To the original five of the Brussels Agreement were added the United States, Canada, Denmark, Iceland, Italy, Norway and Portugal. Finally, in May, 1949, the Council of Europe was founded, as a consultative body which would work for the establishment of a European Parliament.

These last two events run ahead of the story. On March 20, 1948, the Soviet Military Governor, Marshal Vassily Sokolovsky, stormed out of the Allied Control Council. It was the signal for ruthless Russian pressure on West Berlin to begin. On April 1, the first road and rail restrictions on Allied traffic between Berlin and West Germany were imposed. On June 16, the Russians left the Allied *Kommandantura*, or joint administration in Berlin. On June 23, East German Communists staged a riot round the Berlin City Hall, situated in East Berlin. On the same day the Western Allies introduced the new 'deutschmark' currency into their sectors of Berlin – they had introduced it in the three western zones of Germany, but not in Berlin, on June 18. The Soviet riposte was to introduce their own new 'East Mark' into both their zone and sector on June 23.

On June 24 the Russians severed all land and water routes to West Berlin. The answer of the Western Allies was to launch the 'Berlin air-lift' which, in the course of the next year, brought nearly two and a half million tons of food, fuel and other goods into the city in 277,000 flights. Apart from breaking the 'Berlin Blockade', the air-lift created a bond between the Western Allies and the Germans which had not existed before. On the German side there was genuine gratitude for the successful and immensely costly Western effort to preserve the liberties and the independence of free West Berlin; on the Allied side there was full recognition of the pluck and sturdy common-sense of the Berliners.

Adenauer had no part in the Berlin Blockade. His energies were entirely absorbed in what was happening in West Germany. On April 7, 1948, the British Military Governor, General Robertson, made a speech before the *Land* Parliament of North-Rhine–Westphalia, in Düsseldorf, in which he called for the fullest German support of the ideals of Western European civilization, in face of the 'common enemy'. He did not need to name the Soviet Union, when he declared: 'Make up your minds to stand together against these gentlemen who, with democracy on their lips and truncheons behind their backs, would filch your German freedom from you ... The prospects are good. Go forward and seize them.' The prospects, as General Robertson indicated in his speech, were economic recovery and political self-determination, which should be sought in co-operation with the Western Powers. He added: 'We must accept it as a fact that an Iron Curtain splits Germany.'[5]

General Robertson's speech made it clear that the Western Allies had begun to think in more positive terms than just carrying on a military occupation of Germany for an indefinite period of time. The French Zone was to be brought into a 'trizonal' area of economic administration. More important, plans were in preparation for giving the three western zones a unified political administration – a German one. In May and early June a six power Conference took place in London. Its communiqué, on June 7, announced the intention of giving the Germans 'the political organization and institutions which will enable them to assume those governmental responsibilities compatible with the minimum requirements of occupation and control.' On July 1, 1948, the three Western Military Governors summoned the Prime Ministers of the eleven West German *Länder* to Frankfurt and handed them the three 'London Documents' drafted by the six power Conference. Two of these dealt with recommendations for boundary revisions among the *Länder*, and for 'reserved powers' for the occupation authorities under an 'Occupation Statute'. The third, and by far the

5............The *Manchester Guardian*, April 8, 1948.

most important, provided for the *Länder* Prime Ministers to convene a constituent assembly by September 1 to draft a democratic constitution and set up a Federal State.

The *Länder* Prime Ministers met at Herrenchiemsee, forty miles east of Munich, from August 10 to 25 and drew up a preliminary report on the work of drafting a constitution. The 65 members of the constituent assembly, or 'Parliamentary Council', were elected by the *Länder* Parliaments. They consisted of 27 members of the CDU, 27 Social Democrats (SPD), five Free Democrats (right-wing liberals), two Communists and two members each of the right-wing conservative 'German Party' and of the last remnant of the Catholic Centre Party. The stage was set for the struggle for power between the CDU and SPD, a struggle which was to be the central feature of West German politics from this time onwards. In its initial stage, this struggle was to revolve round two men, Adenauer and the leader of the SPD, Kurt Schumacher. Something must, at this point, be said about the latter, for he was Adenauer's only contemporary rival of real stature.

The first thing to note about him was that he was a Prussian, inimical for that reason to Adenauer, if for no other. He was born at Kulm, on the Vistula. In addition, he was a Protestant, a bachelor and a chain-smoker (Adenauer loathed the habit of smoking). Unlike Adenauer, too, he had fought in the First World War and had lost an arm. His physical handicap and his sexual fastidiousness probably contributed to his aggressive temperament, in which his emotional excitability was matched by a penchant for savage and wounding sarcasm. He was a dedicated socialist, with an ingrained dislike of privilege and capitalist power of any kind. Too many warring qualities seemed to have been poured into him, and not sufficiently stirred to settle. He was sincere, honest, fundamentally decent, and at the same time, erratic, intransigent and extremely impatient.

The impression which he made on relative strangers was almost invariably a bad one. General Robertson's views about him have already been cited. The American Secretary of State, Dean Acheson, met him in 1949 and was appalled by his virulence.[6] Without losing a moment, Schumacher launched into 'an unrestrained and bitter attack against Adenauer, on the strange ground that Adenauer was working smoothly with the occupation authorities'. Schumacher's American biographer, Lewis Edinger, writes of his 'tortured body', his 'fanatical eyes' and 'jerky gestures'.[7] Robertson's successor, Sir Ivone Kirkpatrick, thought Schu-

6............*Sketches from Life of Men I have known*, Dean Acheson, p. 172.
7............Kurt Schumacher, Lewis J. Edinger, p. 135–6.

macher was almost pathologically touchy and truculent.[8] He found rational discussion with him next to impossible.[9]

There was probably one overriding reason for Schumacher's shortness of temper; he was obsessed by the feeling that he had little time left to do what he believed was necessary for the German people. He regarded Adenauer as double-dealing and Jesuitical, as a reactionary and a man who had allegedly been ready to detach the Rhineland from Germany after each World War. A note of comedy was supplied by one of Adenauer's well-meaning efforts to find common ground with Schumacher by praising his Alsatian – Schumacher was inordinately fond of his dog. On at least two occasions, conversations between Adenauer and Schumacher were prefaced by a long disquisition on dogs by the former. Schumacher, instead of expanding on this theme, was at first astonished and then acutely suspicious. But it is doubtful whether Schumacher on his side wanted to understand Adenauer at all. Worn down by the years which he had spent in Nazi concentration-camps, racked by pain which led later to the amputation of one leg and unhappily conscious of the fact that he might not have long to live, Schumacher was appalled by what seemed to him to be Adenauer's leadership of a bourgeois 'restoration', his readiness to see ex-Nazis restored to positions of trust and his irritating ability to win the ear of the Western Allies. It must have been maddening for Schumacher, having much of Martin Luther's fervour, to see the chances of a 'Socialist Reformation' ebbing away just as his own vitality was doing.[10]

Schumacher, again, genuinely believed that his Social Democratic Party could be the only torch-bearer of a new German democracy. As he saw it, the 'bourgeois' political parties had betrayed German democracy in 1933, by voting for the Enabling Act which gave Hitler the powers of a dictator. He regarded them as collaborators, and he was convinced that they would

8............Sir Ivone Kirkpatrick, in private conversation with the author.

9............The author's personal experience of Schumacher was very different. If he was aware of interest and sympathy, Schumacher responded in a most friendly and forthcoming manner. Basically he was warm-hearted as well as being dedicated to the cause of social justice. In spite of his erudition there was often an engaging simplicity about him. In a number of talks with him, the author did not find him always strictly practical, but he believed passionately in human dignity and freedom. He could on occasion let his hair down too. One long-serving member of the British Military Government, Mr. Lance Pope, remembers him at a beer and sausage party, standing on the table and leading the chorus of 'Here's a health unto his Majesty'.

10..........*Würdigungen*, Theodor Heuss, p. 220. The author, Federal President from 1949 to 1959, recalled that when Schumacher 'grasped one's hand, with his left hand turned over to the right, one had a sense of feverish clutch on life itself'.

now automatically be infiltrated by ex-Nazis. He therefore demanded recognition of the SPD's 'precedence' before other political parties, and it was this demand – made with a certain arrogance – which infuriated and antagonized Adenauer at one of their early meetings.

There was another circumstance which irked Schumacher. This was what he regarded as the 'non-recognition' of the special mission of the SPD by the British Labour Government. Adenauer, as has already been made plain, had a very different view. He believed that the Labour Government had collaborated with Cologne Social Democrats in organizing his dismissal as Lord Mayor in 1945. Adenauer's subsequent distrust of Britain and British politics is so much a feature of his diplomatic philosophy, that this question of British Labour 'preference' for the SPD must be given some consideration.

In the first place, the British Labour Government certainly ensured that a good proportion of Military Government planners in Germany were Labour men themselves. The British Political Branch was literally packed with them. So was Military Government's important Education Branch. A number of Labour Party nominees were given high administrative office; some of them, perhaps, not of the highest calibre.

These Labour Party nominees showed an understandable tendency to establish contact with German Social Democrats. There was a certain, again understandable, aversion to anyone who had had anything to do with the Nazi Party; and the SPD was, alone among the new parties, 'Nazi-free'. It helps, too, to talk a common language, the language of socialist idealism and ideology. Another link between the British Labourites and the German Social Democrats was the fact that a number of the latter had sought refuge in Britain during the Nazi Era. Schumacher gave several of them key posts in the party headquarters in Hanover. These men may have helped very particularly in 'placing' their nominees in the British-supervised press and radio. SPD men went into key positions in the first British-sponsored daily newspaper, *Die Welt*, the British-sponsored news-agency, DPD, and the leading German radio corporation, NWDR. All this, incidentally, was noted by Adenauer, and much resented.

But liaison between the British Labour Party and the SPD failed at one level, the top. The British Foreign Secretary during these early post-war years was Ernest Bevin. Sir Ivone Kirkpatrick has supplied a clue to Bevin's attitude to the SPD – 'One thing which left its mark upon him was the bellicose attitude of the German Social Democrats in 1914, for which he never forgave them. He felt betrayed, and it made him more anti-German than anything else the Germans ever did.'[11] Lord Robertson

11..........*The Inner Circle*, Sir Ivone Kirkpatrick, p. 205.

supplied a more human touch; he remembers Bevin saying to him, with ponderous seriousness – 'I try to be fair to them (the Germans); but I 'ates them, really.'[12] There was no settled British policy in favour of building up the SPD, because Bevin had no wish to build up any section of the German community. Possibly Schumacher's most bitter grievance was that the British Government did not treat the SPD simply as friends.

Schumacher was a very sick man when the Parliamentary Council met for the first time on September 1, 1948. In addition, he had in July directed the SPD *Land* Prime Ministers to reject the idea of a separate West German State, on the grounds that this would deepen the East–West rift and make German reunification even more difficult to attain. He therefore delegated the plump, personable Professor Carlo Schmid to lead the SPD members in the Parliamentary Council. By doing so, he abdicated in favour of Adenauer. It is a curious commentary on SPD tactics that Schumacher opted out of the Assembly which gave the new Germany its constitution, and instructed his supporters to vote for Adenauer to becomes its President – believing that he, Adenauer, was too old to have anything of a political career afterwards.

Misreading the portents, the *Manchester Guardian* reported that Adenauer had been elected 'after prior consultations between the two parties, and this may be an indication of future co-operation and the sinking of party differences in the interest of the German people'.[13] It was nothing of the kind; the direct confrontation of SPD and CDU, of Adenauer and Schumacher, began at this moment.

The Parliamentary Council was to sit for just under nine months. By the end of that time it had hammered out the 'Basic Law of the Federal Constitution', and had prepared the way for the holding of Federal elections and the convening of a Federal Parliament for the whole of West Germany. On the whole, the Council did a remarkably good job; it produced a constitution which has stood the test of time and has produced an effective system of government. It took much longer than had been expected; the Western Allies hoped that it could be finished in three months and Federal elections could be held in December, 1948.[14] But there were a great many problems to solve, and competing views among the Western Allies as well as among the German parties had to be brought into line with each other.

Adenauer's comment on the position at the outset of the Council's deliberations was as follows: 'We followed the general principle that we must learn the lessons of the mistakes of the Weimar Republic. The position of the future Federal President was not to be endowed with the

12 ....Lord Robertson, in private conversation with the author.
13..........The *Manchester Guardian*, September 2, 1949.
14 ....*German Parliaments*, Sir Stephen King-Hall, p. 122.

powers possessed by the President of the Weimar Republic. Another principle was the strengthening of the position of the Federal Chancellor compared with that of the Reich Chancellor of the Weimar Republic. The future Basic Law was to make it impossible to remove individual ministers by a vote of no confidence ... it would have to table a vote of no confidence against the Federal Chancellor himself. However, the Weimar Republic also served as a warning of what happens when it is too easy to bring down a government; to guard against these dangers we included a provision to the effect that parliament could only table a vote of no confidence, if at the same time it could propose a new Chancellor commanding the necessary majority to form a government.'[15] There was, in fact, to be no repetition of the disastrous experience of the Weimar Era, with governments falling on the average at six-monthly intervals and legislative authority finally reverting to a nominee of the President, ruling by decree.

There were other problems to consider beside the powers of Parliament, President and Chancellor. The CDU favoured decentralization and as federalist a system of government as possible; the SPD wanted the maximum centralization. The Parliamentary Council wanted to give West Berlin full membership in the Federation; the Western Allies were prepared to let West Berlin send only 'observers' to a Federal West German Parliament, knowing that Allied control in West Berlin, isolated in the middle of Soviet-occupied territory, must not be weakened. The CDU wanted a direct system of voting, the SPD favoured proportional representation. And when the Council ironed out differences over taxation, the Western Allies intervened in order to give the *Länder* a wide measure of financial independence.

This last subject was one of two which produced sharp differences of opinion between the three Western Allies. On taxation the United States favoured decentralization. Britain, whose own Civil War was fought in the seventeenth century over the 'power of the purse', believed that control of taxation must be vested in the Federal Government. France, after initial wavering, came down on the American side – not for altruistic motives, but because a West German State would be weakened by decentralized control over taxation.

France stood on her own in a much more important, but much less publicized controversy. Both the British and Americans, according to the British Military Governor and his Political Adviser, were prepared to have had a provisional government in the first place, and let it appoint the necessary 'special committee' to draft a constitution.[16] Proposals to this

15...........*Memoirs*, Konrad Adenauer, VOL 1, p. 122–3.

16...........Lord Robertson and Sir Christopher Steel, in private conversation with the author.

effect were actually made at the end of 1947, and a provisional government could have been formed early in 1948. France insisted on a written constitution being first prepared, and a constituent assembly being formally elected afterwards – hoping in this way to string out deliberations, possibly over a period of years. During the protracted work of the Parliamentary Council, the French continued to counsel the maximum reflection and the minimum haste. France's motto for dealing with the German question was, according to one American observer:[17] 'Let us drag our feet, now and then.' In Paris the French slowing-down policy was called *La guerre tiède*, the 'tepid war'. A struggle went on behind the scenes among the Western Allies, about which the outside world knew nothing. At the same time, the Western Allies were drafting the 'Occupation Statute', which would reserve certain powers to them after a Federal Government began functioning.

Adenauer took control of the Parliamentary Council as soon as he was elected its President. With charming irony, he complimented the Council's 'senior', Adolf Schönfelder of the SPD, on his 'youthful freshness and energy', when the latter was elected Vice-President.[18] Schönfelder was only two years older than himself. He was, too, sadly lacking in energy of a physical nature, and was out-shouted at the inaugural session by the Communist leader, Max Reimann, who successfully drowned the noise of his feebly ringing bell. Adenauer, according to one authority, displayed precisely those qualities needed to manage the Council – personal authority, quick reflexes, firm handling of both people and situations, apt touches of his own 'Cologne humour' and remarkable staying-power during sessions which sometimes dragged on far into the night.[19]

In addition, Adenauer showed remarkable skill in dealing with the Communists – as he was later to show when the first Federal Parliament came into being. In the Council, there were only two Communists, but they were committed to disrupting its work by every means in their power. Fortunately, one of them, Heinz Renner, was a Rhinelander; he found it very hard to resist Adenauer's gentle appeals to him 'as a Rhinelander and gentleman' and his interjections, to the annoyance of his fanatical boss, Max Reimann, tended to degenerate into slapstick comedy. One example: when Adenauer quietly chided him with not really meaning anything that he said, Renner replied – 'When one has a totally private talk with you [he used the German phrase *unter vier Augen*, meaning no one else present], then one is well-advised to have a couple of witnesses.'

There were two particularly critical controversies in the Parliamentary

17..........*This is Germany*, Ed. Arthur Settel. Chapter by James O'Donnell, p. 350.
18 ....*Zeitgeschichte*, quarterly, Rudolf Morsey, January, 1970, p. 68.
19..........*Zeitgeschichte*, quarterly, Rudolf Morsey, January, 1970, p. 69–70.

Council. The first took place in December, 1948, and was known as the 'Frankfurt Affair'. The SPD accused Adenauer of having made use of the access which he had to the three Military Governors to argue the CDU's case for financial decentralization, and to invoke their help against his opponents in the Council. Adenauer maintained that he had done no more than tell the Military Governors that certain differences of opinion existed in the Council and that its work would therefore take longer to finish than had been hoped. Adenauer added that he had been 'completely taken aback' when accused of asking the Military Governors to arbitrate.[20] He successfully fended off an SPD vote of no-confidence and a Communist demand that he should cease to be President.

The second controversy was more serious. From afar, in Hanover, Schumacher had been fulminating against Adenauer's evident control of the Parliamentary Council. He was especially incensed over the above-mentioned vote of no confidence – the Bonn SPD group rejected his proposal to back this vote by threatening to leave the Council. Schumacher was further annoyed by the obviously excellent relations which Adenauer had established with the Military Governors. In March, 1949, the Military Governors stood out for greater financial decentralization than had been agreed, after endless wrangling, by the Council. Shortly afterwards, they transmitted the now completed 'Occupation Statute' to the Council, listing their reserved powers but promising to end Military Government and transfer Allied authority to High Commissioners. The SPD insisted on withholding their decision on accepting or rejecting Allied terms until their Party Congress, which was to be held in Hanover on April 19 and 20. Adenauer argued in favour of accepting the Allied terms, in order not to endanger the successful work on the constitution and the prospect of Federal elections in the summer.

On April 20 Schumacher uttered in Hanover what Adenauer called 'a kind of ultimatum'.[21] He demanded the minimum interference in the future work of a Federal Government by the Allies, 'adequate' sources of revenue for the Federal Government and a guarantee of the legal and economic unity of the West German State. Adenauer spoke the next day on the North-West German Radio (NWDR), deploring the SPD attack on the Allies, and appealing to the SPD not to cause a rift in the German nation by accusing the CDU of pursuing an 'anti-national' policy of fulfilment (*Erfüllungspolitik*). But on April 22 the Military Governors announced that they were empowered by their Governments, in directives sent to them before the SPD Party Congress, to make certain concessions –

20..........*Memoirs*, Konrad Adenauer, VOL 1, p. 128.
21..........*Memoirs*, Konrad Adenauer, VOL 1, p. 135.

at their own discretion. The concessions, in effect, met Schumacher's demands. In making them, the Allies managed to avoid a 'loss of face' on their own part, but they inflicted a grievous loss of face on Adenauer. For the SPD acclaimed the Allied concessions as the direct consequence of what Schumacher called 'our historic No'.

What had happened to make Allied concessions so suddenly possible and give the SPD this heaven-sent chance of posing as the only true guardians of Germany's national interests? Adenauer produced his explanation in a speech which he made during the election campaign, on July 21, in Heidelberg. He subsequently confirmed what he said then in his *Memoirs*.[22] The Allies had, indeed, considered in advance the possibility of making concessions. They had therefore prepared two Notes, the second of which was withheld until after the SPD Congress in the hope that it need not be used. But, Adenauer insisted, the SPD was informed of the contents of the second Note; he, Adenauer, was not. Their informant had been a 'British officer'. He had enabled Schumacher to proclaim his so-called 'historic No' in Hanover.

This explanation was too trite. Both Lord Robertson and Sir Christopher Steel have subsequently denied that information was channelled to the SPD.[23] Sir Christopher pointed out that the days were long since past when British Military Government had given special help and encouragement to the SPD; such help and encouragement had, moreover, been intended essentially to help make the SPD a bulwark against Communism. One authority has suggested that it was not the British, but the Americans who 'tipped off' the SPD; but that this was not done deliberately, and it was more a case of the SPD forming an impression that Allied concessions were under debate and could therefore be obtained by making a firm stand.[24] The author's own view is that this firm stand was the logical climax of growing SPD disillusionment. On April 3 the leader of the SPD group in the Council, Professor Carlo Schmid, told him the SPD had already made too many concessions – 'We cannot always be the party to give way. We still have a responsibility to the German working man and further concessions would be a betrayal of his interest.'[25] Professor Schmid thought that Allied intervention 'destroys the judicial and economic unity of Western Germany', and he declaimed against the 'absurdity' of over-decentralization of tax-control. The author was able to forecast,

22..........*Memoirs*, Konrad Adenauer, VOL I, p. 136.

23..........Lord Robertson and Sir Christopher Steel, in private conversation with the author.

24..........*Der Spiegel*, weekly of April 2, 1949, and April 30, 1949, quoting the CDU member of the Parliamentary Council, Heinrich von Brentano.

25..........The *Manchester Guardian*, April 9, 1949.

on April 12, the SPD 'time-bomb designed to explode on April 20'.[26] And that was what happened.

Adenauer's anger over what he regarded as an 'unfair' SPD triumph had a comic sequel. On April 23 he summoned a number of British newspaper correspondents to his office in Bonn. With him was his political adviser, Herr Herbert Blankenhorn, who gave the British newspapermen a view of the situation which he had already explained to the author eleven days before.[27] Adenauer then proceeded to deliver a devastating attack on the London *Times*, which had 'celebrated an SPD victory'. The SPD, Adenauer pointed out, had been ready to jettison the draft constitution and produce a substitute 'administrative statute'. But, whatever the rights or wrongs of CDU/SPD differences, it should be understood that the Allies were dealing with a body, the Parliamentary Council, which was trying to represent German interests and reach a fair and sensible agreement.[28]

The excitement caused by this incident died down, and the Council was able to reach agreement with the Military Governors on the system of Parliamentary voting – 60 per cent of the seats in the Federal Parliament, or *Bundestag*, would be filled by direct vote, and the remaining 40 per cent would be 'made up' from party lists on the basis of proportional strength. On May 8, 1949, the Basic Law was approved in the Parliamentary Council by 53 votes to 12, and the Military Governors gave their approval on May 12. The *Länder*, whose influence had been carefully excluded from the work of the Council by Adenauer, voted between May 18 and 21 on the Basic Law. Ten out of eleven approved it; the eleventh, Bavaria, joined the Federation, since Article 144 of the Basic Law laid down that it should be valid if two-thirds of the *Länder* gave their approval. The stage was set

26..........The *Manchester Guardian*, April 13, 1949.

27..........The *Manchester Guardian*, April 13, 1949. Blankenhorn explained on April 12 to the author that the SPD was sabotaging the possibility of a fair compromise between the Parliamentary Council and the Allies. He said: 'After 1919 the German people were divided into two camps – those who refused to recognize the Versailles Treaty and those who tried honestly to fulfil its conditions. This situation may repeat itself today. Above all, we are afraid of a rupture between the principal German parties, which will last for years to come and embitter social relations.' As *Guardian* correspondent, I added in my report: 'These words might well give more than a passing twinge of conscience to all those who have given surreptitious backing to some German party in the interests of their own security or for the propagation of their own forms of Constitution.'

28..........From the author's own notes. *The Times* correspondent, it has to be recalled, sat silent and embarrassed throughout this strange meeting. The author suggested that the next time that Dr. Adenauer had a quarrel with *The Times*, he should not summon other British correspondents to his presence.

for Federal elections; the date chosen for them was August 14, and electioneering started in July with the Basic Law out of the way and a short respite allowed for the Parliamentarians who had been responsible for framing it.

Before the Parliamentary Council dissolved, it had one more decision to make. This was to choose a 'capital' and seat of government for the Federal Republic. The issue appeared, at first sight, to be pre-ordained. Frankfurt had played the key role in Germany's very first, fleeting essay in democratic government – during the Revolution of 1848. The city had remained a centre of liberal thought and political enlightenment. In the early post-war years, Adenauer had himself advocated a new German capital on the banks of the river Main, and had specifically mentioned Frankfurt as being preferable to 'Prussian' Berlin. The SPD were wholeheartedly in favour of Frankfurt, which was centrally placed and a great city in its own right. For the SPD, it had the additional advantage of being the capital of *Land* Hesse, which had a Social Democratic Government.

But Adenauer had decided on Bonn. He was able to produce all sorts of arguments in favour of it. It was not an Allied garrison-town, whereas Frankfurt was a centre of both American civil and military administration. It was so manifestly unsuited to being a permanent capital that it would be much more an obviously provisional seat of government – pending the reunification of Germany and the creation of an all-German government in Berlin. Bonn was relatively unscathed by the war; whereas Frankfurt had been more than 50 per cent destroyed and was expected to take ten years to rebuild. Finally, Adenauer appointed a special representative of the Government of North-Rhine–Westphalia, a Dr. Wandersleb, to argue the case for Bonn on financial grounds. Dr. Wandersleb, a small, Figaro-like person, engaging, highly optimistic and readily available to the press, produced figures which purported to show that installing a capital in Bonn would cost under a half of what it would cost in Frankfurt. The figures which he produced amounted to about one-tenth of the actual cost in the next ten years – at the end of which Bonn was still very much a 'provisional' capital, with Ministries and government and party offices scattered in wild profusion round an overblown university town.[29]

The truth was that Adenauer was utterly determined to have the new capital in his beloved Rhineland. Bonn was only twenty miles from his

29..........Wandersleb's first 'budget', which admittedly provided only for makeshift arrangements sufficient to enable a government to start functioning in September, 1949, was of only 3 million Marks. Twenty years later it was estimated that over 300 million Marks had been spent on government installations.

native Cologne, which would benefit tremendously from having the new capital so close. And it was just across the river from his house in Rhöndorf. He had some useful allies. The SPD leaders in the industrial Ruhr preferred a capital within easy distance – petrol and cars were still in short supply. So did the chairman of the newly formed Trade Union Congress, Hans Böckler. When the issue became acute, Schumacher tactlessly declared that the selection of Frankfurt would be a 'defeat' for the CDU. This resulted in CDU solidarity in the Parliamentary Council vote, which decided in favour of Bonn by 33 to 29. At the same time, Adenauer secured the old Weimar colours, black, red and gold, for the new Federal German flag. His only reverse was over the character of the Second Parliamentary chamber, or *Bundesrat*. Its members were to be chosen by the *Länder* Governments; Adenauer would have preferred the second chamber to have been an independent 'Senate'.

Adenauer went into the 1949 election campaign on the crest of the wave. He had a united CDU behind him. He had gained tremendously in prestige as a result of the successful work of the Parliamentary Council. He was able to show that even the Occupation Statute represented a real advance on previous conditions; the apparatus of military government would be cut down, there would be an Allied civil administration in place of the military one and the French Zone would be fully integrated with the British and American in a united West German State. Finally, Adenauer had emerged as the principal spokesman of the German people, by virtue of his speech in Berne, on March 23, 1949.

The speech gave a sober and painstaking account of the German situation. It also contained plenty of criticism of Allied policies in Germany. Adenauer said that the Allies should not have transferred all governmental authority into their own hands, or planned the economy 'down to trouser buttons', or carried out dismantlings of industry which seemed intended to eliminate German competition in world markets, or purloined German trade patents. The rest of the speech was positive in tone: Adenauer appealed for *rapprochement* with France, for the union of Western Europe including Britain, for the 1948 Ruhr Statute (which set up a 15-man 'Authority' to regulate heavy industry) to be treated as a start in European co-operation and for the German people to be helped to develop a healthy sense of nationhood.

The speech caused a stir. Those few Germans who had been able to travel abroad had kept tactfully silent, and had not dimly considered using international occasions – Adenauer was speaking at a meeting of the Inter-Parliamentary Union – as platforms for criticism of Allied administration in Germany. Part of the London press deplored the Berne speech as 'anti-Allied', and some Swiss newspapers – one referred to him as 'the pale lean

German with the hard Tartar face' – evidently thought that he had abused Swiss hospitality. But the speech commended him to a great many Germans; secretly, they had been feeling that it was high time that a German should say something on behalf of his countrymen. They needed a champion. Lord Pakenham was right when he wrote that Adenauer was 'morally unimpressed with the Occupation, with the credentials of the British or any other foreigners for setting everything in Germany right'; and, again, that 'If he (Adenauer) had been "persona grata" with the Allies in the days of the great hunger and dismantling he would never have kept his people together.'[30] The worst of the 'great hunger', admittedly, was over since the middle of 1948, but dismantling was still going on. And the German people still bore a great load of blame, shame and guilt on their shoulders.

The election campaign of July-August, 1949, was fought mainly on economic issues. This was inevitable. Foreign policy remained an Allied preserve while the political parties of the Weimar Era retained their ideologies and sectional interests. Of the West German parties in 1949 only the Communists (KPD) and the SPD had reasonably clear-cut ideologies. Both were Marxist, and the SPD's retention of outworn notions about the 'class struggle' and the dangers of clericalism, as well as their belief in public ownership of industry, limited their appeal to the working class and a minority of intellectuals. Yet the SPD confidently expected to emerge as the strongest party in the Federal Parliament. It had a party machine manned by the 'old hands' of Weimar days. It had a vastly greater membership than any other party – even though it had fallen in two years from 875,000 to around 750,000. It had the support of the Trade Unions. In 1932 the Social Democrat, Rudolf Breitscheid, had prophesied – 'After the Nazis, us.' The party was especially well-entrenched in northern Germany, where SPD Mayors controlled three great cities, Wilhelm Kaisen in Bremen, Max Brauer in Hamburg and Ernst Reuter in Berlin, while Hinrich Kopf was the 'uncrowned king' of *Land* Lower Saxony.

Until only a short time before the election, the CDU's only big card looked to be Adenauer himself. Then he was joined by Professor Ludwig Erhard, head of the Bi-zonal Economic Council and the main force behind West Germany's gathering economic recovery. Erhard was a huge acquisition for the CDU. Even before the Allied-instituted 'Currency Reform' of June, 1948, he had come out boldly in favour of the abolition of economic controls and had enunciated his theory of a 'Free Market Economy'. He was violently opposed to the nationalization of industry and determined to encourage individual initiative. His Free Market

30..........*Born to Believe*, Lord Pakenham, p. 197.

Economy was based on cheap imports, boosting exports, reducing tariffs and liberalizing trade. By mid-1949 his theories had borne fruit. There was more food and consumer goods in the shops, more jobs and the first beginnings of a building boom. With his rosy cheeks, his ample girth and his confident predictions of better times on the way, Erhard was the man to appeal to the floating vote as well as to confirmed anti-socialists.

Sectionalism, however, died hard. The old Hanoverian, or *Guelf* Party regrouped itself as the 'German Party' in Lower Saxony. The Bavarian Party insisted on maintaining itself as a separate entity in its south-eastern corner of the Federal Republic. The much diminished Catholic Centre Party continued to survive in the Rhineland, in spite of the efforts of its leader, Dr. Karl Spiecker, to fuse it with the CDU. And the Free Democratic Party (FDP), which was to become the only real political force in West Germany apart from the CDU and SPD, was in reality an amalgam of sectional, middle-class interests; in Southern Germany these interests were coloured by a traditionally deep-rooted liberalism, whereas in North-Rhine–Westphalia and Hesse the FDP branches were conservative and stood to the right of the CDU.

There was one paramount reason why the CDU entered the election campaign with much greater confidence than seemed justified to many outside observers. (The British authorities, for instance, were tipping the SPD to win by a considerable margin.) The SPD had lost most of its traditional supporters, who lived in areas under Soviet control, or in Berlin – which could only send 'observers' to the Federal Parliament. As long ago as 1912 the SPD, with well over four million votes and 35 per cent of the seats in the *Reichstag*, was the strongest single party in Germany. But its main areas of strength, apart from places like Hamburg, Bremen and the big cities of the Ruhr, were Saxony, Anhalt, Thuringia and Greater Berlin. Admittedly, there had been a big influx of refugees into West Germany since 1945, most of them Protestant North Germans. But they had mostly come from the provinces to the east of the new, temporary Oder–Neisse frontier with Poland. These provinces had traditionally been conservative and not Socialist strongholds.

Adenauer believed that the CDU could beat the SPD in the elections. He thoroughly enjoyed himself in the campaign, speaking up to four times a day, paying particular heed to local problems and prejudices, concentrating on the simple economic questions which interested his listeners most – housing, employment and the strength of the currency. While Schumacher was accusing him of political dishonesty, Adenauer refused to indulge in personal recrimination. One of his biographers maintained that the factors which won the election for the CDU were Adenauer's guile, good luck and ruthless suppression of opposition.[31] The truth was less colourful; the CDU won because Adenauer had had just enough time to weld it into a reasonably united party, and because he led it with such unwavering confidence. Long before the election campaign was over, all notion of Adenauer as a prestigious but powerless Federal President had disappeared. He was the only logical choice to lead a government formed under CDU leadership.

The election results were a grievous shock to Schumacher and the SPD. The CDU vote, at 7,360,000, was more than 400,000 higher than the SPD's; 139 members of the CDU, against 131 of the SPD, gained seats in the *Bundestag*. The FDP, fortified by the votes of many of the East German refugees, won 52 seats. The other 80 seats were divided among a motley collection of parties; with the exception of 15 Communists (KDP) they were mainly right-wing in character. This was something for which Adenauer had already made due allowance; he saw that the CDU would be in a position to form a right-of-centre coalition. The SPD did not have any chance of taking part in government, save with the CDU as senior partner. This was a crippling blow to Schumacher's hopes and pride. His reaction was typically embittered. He was to dub the creation of the new Federal Republic 'Western counter-action to Russian action in setting up a totalitarian regime in the Eastern Zone'.

On August 21 Adenauer assembled a number of leading members of the CDU at his Rhöndorf home. In his memoirs he has given his own account of the meeting.[32] The views of those who attended were fairly evenly split between a group which believed that something like a 'national' government should be formed with the SPD, and other parties too, if desired; and a group which believed that a right-of-centre coalition should be formed without the SPD. Adenauer backed the second group, without reservation. He advanced arguments which were unanswerable. The SPD had, since the election, made it clear that they would require the Ministry of Economics if they joined a 'big' coalition. Adenauer pointed out that 13 million Germans had voted against the policy of socialization of industry preached by the SPD, and only 8 million had voted in its favour. Adenauer argued against the CDU being dragged into some kind of compromise on public ownership, which in his opinion would not work. He regarded the SPD as impossibly awkward partners.

Reading between the lines, it is obvious from Adenauer's account of this meeting that he had decided in advance exactly what was to happen. After letting everyone have his say he produced, like a facile conjuror, the

31..........*Adenauer, Democratic Dictator*, Charles Wighton. There are several references.

32..........*Memoirs*, Konrad Adenauer, VOL 1, p. 177–82.

names of the parties which would join in a coalition. They were the CDU, the FDP and the Lower Saxony 'German Party'. Between them, they would have 208 out of 402 seats in the *Bundestag*, and such a coalition could count on the general support in economic matters of another 30–40 members. Equally casually, Adenauer produced as his candidate for President, Theodor Heuss of the FDP, and fended off a question on his unfriendly attitude towards organized religion with a joke – 'His wife is a good Christian, and that's enough.'

Although he claimed to have been surprised[33] when someone present suggested him as Federal Chancellor, Adenauer at once declared that he had consulted his personal physician, Dr. Martini, and that gentleman had stated that his health was good enough for him to fulfil the duties of Chancellor. He would be able to 'carry on for two years'. In reality, Adenauer was to be Chancellor for more than fourteen. There was only one untoward incident at this Rhöndorf meeting of CDU leaders which, again, Adenauer turned into a joke. The report was circulated that a 'Papal envoy' had been present at the meeting. Adenauer's subsequent explanation was that the 'intruder' was a member of a Dutch monastic order who turned up to have a personal word with Dr. Hermann Pünder, one of the CDU leaders present. 'I never saw, nor do I know, this gentleman,' Adenauer wrote in his memoirs. 'My family told me he was not wearing any socks. I could hardly imagine that a representative of the Vatican would turn up without socks.'[34] The rumour of 'Papal intervention' died stillborn.

A 'President' or Speaker of the *Bundestag* was elected at the inaugural session of the *Bundestag* on September 7, 1949. He was the CDU's nominee, Dr. Erich Köhler. The election of the Chancellor was fixed for September 15. But so sure was Adenauer of his own election that on September 8 he gave an interview to the correspondent of the *Manchester Guardian* in which he outlined some of the features of his future government's policies,[35] with particular reference to its relations with the Western Powers. The CDU-led Government would, he said, press for the scaling-down of Allied dismantling, for an early settlement of the question of ownership of heavy industries based on 'a balance between private capital and public control' and for the removal of Allied restrictions on the German economy and the German citizen. He would ask for German diplomatic representation abroad, for increased freedom of Germans to travel, for the freeing of Germany's export-trade from the control of the Allied 'Joint Export–Import Agency', for the ending of the Allied ban on ship-building and for

33..........*Memoirs*, Konrad Adenauer, VOL 1, p. 180.
34..........*Memoirs*, Konrad Adenauer, VOL 1, p. 182.
35..........The *Manchester Guardian*, Terence Prittie, September 9, 1949.

a peace agreement between the Federal Republic and the Western Allies – 'If we must wait for a peace treaty with the Soviet Union, our wait is liable to be a very long one.'

Adenauer rejected the Oder–Neisse line as Germany's eastern frontier, claiming that it restricted Germany 'both economically and as a people'. He called for freedom of economic competition as a necessary adjunct to bringing Germany 'into the wider world economy', and he accepted Allied organs of control like the Military Security Board and International Authority for the Ruhr with the proviso that the one should restrict its activities to genuine security measures, and the other should be the base for 'international control in a wider area of Europe'. Finally, Adenauer sharply denied reports that he had tried to drive a diplomatic wedge between Britain and France. He added: 'I should consider such a policy utterly mistaken. Only a united Western European front can secure the rebuilding of the new Europe. I would be glad if the British Government and British public opinion would accept the facts that England is a European power, that her history is bound up with that of Western Europe, and that she is bound in duty to play her part in European development.

'I must add here that the British Government has openly supported the German Social Democrats in their Zone of Occupation. Its representatives have influenced the North-West German Radio, the news agencies and the military paper *Die Welt*, which has been given special advantages and which pursues a definitely Socialist policy. As a member of the CDU I must oppose this policy energetically.'

Adenauer, it was clear, was not going to be an altogether 'comfortable' negotiating partner for the Western Powers. As the *Manchester Guardian* correspondent noted: 'The most significant interest in his answers is that he is prepared to assert the German point of view in all questions in which the Western Allies still feel themselves vitally concerned. Only by the friendly solution of these questions can Germany re-win her place among the European nations.'

On September 15, 1949, Adenauer was elected Federal Chancellor by the *Bundestag*. He had already prepared his Cabinet list and had secured the promise of FDP and 'German Party' participation in his coalition Government. But there were some last-minute jockeyings over the vote for the Chancellor. The South German Liberals of the FDP regarded Adenauer as altogether too conservative for their taste. There may even have been backsliders among his own CDU following, whose left-wingers were finding it hard to swallow their disappointment that a CDU/SPD coalition was not to be formed. In the event, only 202 out of the 402 members of the *Bundestag* voted for Adenauer's candidature; 142 voted against, 44 abstained, there was one invalid vote and 13 members were absent. Later a Frau Margarethe Hütter, an FDP member from Stuttgart, was to claim that her vote was decisive. She was appointed, from the party's reserve list, to take the place of Professor Heuss, designated to be Federal President. She arrived at the Parliament building, or *Bundeshaus*, in breathless haste and cast her vote for Adenauer. Another contender for the distinction of having given Adenauer that last, vital vote was Herr Johann Wartner, of the Bavarian Party.[36] His party's orders were for its 17 members of the *Bundestag* to abstain – Adenauer was, believe it or not, insufficiently 'federalist' for their taste. Wartner – there is only his own word for it, since the ballot was secret – voted for Adenauer.

More operative, perhaps, was Adenauer's own comment – 'When I was later asked whether I had voted for myself I replied: "Naturally; anything else would have been hypocrisy."'[37] The narrow margin of his victory – it amounted to one vote, since 201 would not have been an absolute majority – suggested a precarious balance of power during the impending four year term of the first Federal Government. This was underlined by three resolutions put forward by the SPD, immediately after Adenauer's election. They were for the revision of the dismantling programme, the inclusion of West Berlin as an integral part of the Federal Republic and the removal of the seat of government from Bonn to Frankfurt. As Chancellor, Adenauer was going to be put under instant, heavy and continuing pressure. He was nearly 74 years old. The average man of that age would have long since retired to the shelter of home and family and such harmless hobbies as the writing of memoirs and the growing of roses.

36...........*Konrad Adenauer*, Georg Schröder, p. 30.
37...........*Memoirs*, Konrad Adenauer, VOL I, p. 182.

8 Ending the Allied Occupation

Adenauer made his first speech as Federal Chancellor on September 20, 1949, to the *Bundestag*. His statement of government policy was as concise, as straightforward and as unemotional as the hundreds of speeches which he would subsequently make in the same drably formal Parliament Chamber. His Government's principal aims, as he outlined them, were: to win further concessions from the Western Allies in the form of greater political and economic equality, to be loyal to them as partners in Western Europe, to develop good relations with all neighbours, to encourage economic progress, to modify de-Nazification measures in the course of welding a more unified community and to end anti-Semitism in any shape or form. In his speech Adenauer said: 'There is no other path to freedom and equality for the German people, after the total collapse endowed us by National Socialism, than by ensuring that we win our way back alongside the Allies. The only path to freedom is by way of seeking to expand our freedom and our authority step by step, in agreement with the High Commissioners.'

There was only one mildly jarring note – at least to Western ears – in the speech. This was the reference to the unacceptability of the provisional frontier in the east, the 'Oder–Neisse line'. Around nine million Germans who had been expelled from their homes in the eastern provinces, (placed by the 1945 Potsdam Agreement specifically under provisional Polish administration), and from the Sudetenland in Czechoslovakia, sought refuge in the Federal Republic. Like any other West German politician, Adenauer was acutely conscious of the importance of the refugee vote. The London *Times*, pointed out that, 'Whatever may be thought of the justice or injustice of the (Oder–Neisse) line, it must clearly be understood from the start that if Germany is to be welcomed into the European union it does not follow that Europe accepts and supports all Germany's claims for frontier revision.'[1] Otherwise, Adenauer's statement of government policy was given a cautious welcome in the Press of the free world.

Elected Chancellor by the smallest possible majority of the *Bundestag*, Adenauer had to compete with a difficult and delicate balance of power. Quite apart from his Free Democratic and 'German Party' coalition part-

1............The London *Times*, September 21, 1949.

ners, there were all sorts of factions within his own CDU whose wishes had to be taken into account. Paradoxically, the CDU had still not formally unified itself as a party, and Adenauer may well have deliberately postponed its unification until he felt that he possessed the necessary personal authority. Adenauer had to strike a fair balance between the Roman Catholics and the Protestants in his party, between North Germans and South Germans, and between the Conservatives and the Trade Unionist left-wing. He had to give special consideration to the Bavarian branch, which remained semi-independent under its title of the Christian Social Union (CSU). And he had to 'squeeze out' of the *Bundestag* those leading members of the CDU whom he foresaw being unable to remain in step with his policies – Karl Arnold, Hans von Schlange-Schöningen and Werner Hilpert, the leader of the recalcitrant *Land* Hesse branch. Arnold, whom the left wing would have liked to have had as Chancellor, was conveniently 'kicked upstairs' to become President of the Second Chamber, the *Bundesrat*.[2] Hilpert and Schlange-Schöningen surrendered their *Bundestag* seats when passed over for Cabinet posts.

The Cabinet consisted of fourteen members, including Adenauer. Nine belonged to the CDU, three to the FDP and two to the 'German Party'. In his appointments Adenauer showed a sureness of touch in taking party and sectional feelings into consideration, which was never quite so necessary in his later Cabinets. There were six Bavarians – a tribute to the CSU's sense of special identity and to the fact that Bavaria was the only *Land* which had hesitated to join the Federal *Bund*. The left wing of the CDU was mollified by the appointment of Jakob Kaiser, Minister for All-German Affairs, Gustav Heinemann, Minister of the Interior, and Anton Storch, Minister of Labour. The FDP might have been thought to have come out badly, with only three Ministers. But as a sop Franz Blücher became Vice-Chancellor, and he and Heinrich Hellwege of the German Party slipped naturally into the position of liaison men between Adenauer and the CDU's two coalition partners. A refugee from Silesia, Hans Lukashek, was appropriately given the Ministry for Refugees.

About half of this first Cabinet were political nonentities, but at the same time sound and hard-working administrators. This suited Adenauer's

2............The author regarded Arnold as a man of probity, courage, commonsense and compassion. He made an admirable Prime Minister of *Land* North-Rhine–Westphalia, where the major industrial concentration of the Ruhr and the heavy burden of dismantling made a spirit of enlightened compromise especially necessary. According to Sir Ivone Kirkpatrick (*The Inner Circle*, p. 234), Arnold 'lacked the killer instinct' as a politician. The British publisher, Victor Gollancz, described Arnold to Lord Pakenham (*Born to Believe*, p. 193) as a 'saint'.

book, for he was to impose a personal authority which was certainly needed at the time if the Government were to hold together. In fact, only one Minister in his well-drilled team was ever prepared to question his views during Cabinet meetings. This was the peppery Bavarian Minister of Finance, Hans Schäffer. One other Minister, Gustav Heinemann, was subsequently to resign, and Jakob Kaiser more than once threatened to do so; but both men remained disciplined and docile at Cabinet meetings. A feature of these was Adenauer's absolute readiness to decentralize to a limited extent. He gave Ludwig Erhard virtual *carte blanche* in the economic field where he had already proved so resoundingly successful, and about which Adenauer professed and preferred to remain ignorant. Schäffer had almost equally total authority in the realm of finance, and the Ministers of Posts, Transport, Housing, Food, Bundersrat Affairs, Refugees and Marshall Plan aid were encouraged to get on with their jobs, with a minimum of direction. The picture of Adenauer as an interfering autocrat is an entirely false one. He was frankly uninterested in various functions of government, and had no time for them. He placed great reliance on his key Ministers, Erhard, Schäffer and Heinemann, and was justified in doing so. Meanwhile he took exclusive control of the business of negotiating with the three Allied High Commissioners, entailing the winning of one concession after another along the road leading to the restoration of West German sovereignty and independence.

There is another popular but misleading picture of Adenauer as head of Government. This is the picture of him monopolizing the actual sessions of his Cabinets. Germans who observed his conduct of Cabinet meetings very closely have a very different story to tell.[3] He let ministers have their say, and only cut them short when they were obviously long-winded. His own comments on their statements were invariably carefully and courteously phrased. Admittedly, he always made it plain that he expected results by the end of the four-hour weekly Cabinet meeting. He drew a distinction between discussion and actual argument, and discouraged the latter – in fact, Schäffer was probably his only Minister who argued and who embarked on argument over subjects which were not his direct concern.

Adenauer had his foibles. He loathed smoking, for he suffered from youth onwards from a weak chest and a tendency towards bronchitis. But there was no formal ban on smoking at Cabinet meetings; Ministers simply respected his feelings. According to one of his advisers, 'We used to go out and smoke in the corridor.'[4] There were occasions when he

3............Hans Globke and Felix von Eckardt, in private conversation with the author.

4............Felix von Eckardt, in private conversation with the author.

realized that one or two Ministers felt badly in need of a cigarette, and he would then tell them to smoke, as long as enough windows were open. Fresh air, for that matter, was another subject on which he felt strongly, and a window usually stayed open, even in winter. Adenauer was a stickler for punctuality and for the maintenance of formal good manners at all times.

His first Cabinet worked well for him. It might even be regarded as too pliable. Adenauer had dealings with two other bodies who were anything but that. These were the *Bundestag*, and the three power Allied High Commission. First, then, a word on the *Bundestag*:

An excellent description of it has been given by one particular British writer.[5] It was housed in what he called 'the most garish parliament building in the world,' an enlarged cubist block of white concrete. Its Parliament Chamber contained the coats of arms of *Bund* and *Länder*, and it's podium was 'painted black and studded with gold-headed nails, rather like a Max Reinhardt set for a production of *Julius Caesar*'. The Members sat in black and green leather chairs, which were screwed to the ground. Likewise built in were ink-wells and desk-tops – the Bonn planners had evidently noted the experience of French and Italian Parliaments and the free fights for which they used justly to be famed. The roof of the Chamber 'was divided into a chequer-board design with a square of blinding neon-tubing in each alternate recess, which acts as a grill for the unfortunate journalists and spectators who occupy the raised gallery on the opposite side of the hall from the Speaker'.

The same writer claimed that 'the wranglings of the Bonn assembly have been marked by an acerbity and lack of sense of compromise which often appal spectators. The members bring to their task of stabilizing a nation in the solar plexus of Europe more complexes than they do ideals, more ambition than they do zeal, and more turbulence than enthusiasm.' His description of a *Bundestag* debate was 'a desk-slamming, feet-thumping, brawling 'brouhaha'.

The description was not altogether unjust. One qualified British observer thought the quality of his first *Bundestag* 'abysmal'. It was largely composed of 'freaks and dullards'. Its standard of debate was pathetic, for the cardinal rule was for nobody to listen to what anyone else had to say. In this observer's view, the pitiful uncertainties of mind of these 'Parliamentarians' were clear illustration of the debacle of the Weimar Republic repeating itself.[6] The new British High Commissioner, Sir Ivone Kirkpatrick, who succeeded General Robertson soon after the *Bundestag*

5............*Watcher on the Rhine*, Brian Connell, p. 229–30.
6............Sir Christopher Steel, in private conversation with the author.

came into being, put it more prosaically – 'the *Bundestag* was in a "state of euphoria", redolent with wild "policies" and wilder declamations.' In his dry phrase, 'The antics of the German parliamentarians brought home to me the demoralizing effects of a long occupation.'[7]

Certainly, the *Bundestag* was a strange place in 1949. Its very first debate, on September 22, offered an illustration of this. It was opened by Schumacher, who was by way of explaining the Opposition's views on Adenauer's government statement of two days earlier. Schumacher managed to work in a few concrete points, but his speech as a whole was a masterpiece of misplaced rhetoric. Chuckles began on the government benches, and developed into idiot mirth. Maddened, Schumacher assailed his opponents, calling them 'the real Nazis'. (The pity of it was that he lost his temper, for in private he had a much more telling phrase for them – the 'Neanderthal benches'.) The place fairly erupted, and it was minutes before the Speaker could restore order.

Apart from their leader, the Social Democrats were a fairly peaceable lot. Not so the fifteen Communists led by Max Reimann. They were bitterly disappointed by their poor showing in the elections; they had expected to win around forty seats, including at least two in the Ruhr, Solingen and Remscheid, by direct election. But their chances were ruined by the brutal and revolting performance of the Red Army during the early days of the Occupation, by the Soviet blockade of Berlin and by Soviet wrecking of Four Power administration of Germany. Much more than the pre-1933 party, the KPD was steered from Moscow. Its natural policy, therefore, was to disrupt the workings of the *Bundestag*. A start was made in its very first session, with the demand to dissolve the *Bundestag* as an 'unconstitutional' body. Adenauer became a particular target, and his speeches were subject to almost continuous interruption, often of the most primitive kind.

There was plenty of noise from the right-wing benches too. There were half a dozen extreme right-wingers who were camouflaged ex-Nazis, and a dozen members of a so called 'Economic Reconstruction' party led by a weird demagogue, Alfred Loritz – weird, because he seemed to have no recognizable policies at all. There was, in general, a tendency to indulge in cat-calling at the least provocation, and to spend much of the time in between outbreaks of mirth and anger ostentatiously reading newspapers and writing letters. Speeches were generally read, and bore no relation to what went before or after. There was little conception of real debate. A fortnight after its first session, the *Bundestag* was 'invaded' by two ex-prisoners-of-war just returned from the Soviet Union. These 'ragged men',

7............*The Inner Circle,* Sir Ivone Kirkpatrick, p. 228–9.

as British and American newspapers called them, attempted physical assault on Max Reimann. The KPD exploited the incident by claiming that they had been 'hired' by the Chancellor for 50 Marks apiece.

In all this sort of hurly-burly Adenauer remained calm, self-possessed and restrained. His patience in the face of Communist provocation was remarkable. As in the Parliamentary Council, he showed frequent flashes of sardonic wit. 'Irony', Hillaire Belloc has written, 'is a sword, and must be used as a sword ... it is a form of jest in which we ridicule a second person in the presence of a third'. In Adenauer's irony there was a mischievous element. One knew when he was enjoying himself, and one knew when a pungent wisecrack was coming. His voice took on 'false note, a yellow note', to quote George Orwell; his Cologne accent became exaggerated and a nasal quality crept into it. On such occasions he then proceeded to annihilate the enemy verbally.

But this gift of irony was not over-used. A valuable asset should always be hoarded. Adenauer had other assets, too. Sitting at the end of the 'Cabinet rank', his face maintained an invariable inscrutability. He sat upright, but relaxed. When he was listening attentively to a speaker, he turned his head a little to the left, and let his eye dwell on him, unblinkingly, dispassionately. He never sought to catch the eye of the *Bundestag* President; he never had to, for eyes veered automatically towards him when he rose to answer a question, or intervene with the minimum fuss and the maximum dispatch in a debate. Very occasionally, he came down from his Cabinet seat and took his place below, in the front row of the CDU members. This had an instant effect on party morale; his followers became, like their leader, attentive and alert, subtly more responsible. He had the same effect on the front benches of his party as a good manager has on his football team.

A fortnight after the *Bundestag* came into existence, I wrote that Adenauer had 'in a few weeks, grown in stature'. I stressed his 'poise, moderation and purely objective approach to problems of Germany's external relations', and placed his speeches – along with those of Professor Carlo Schmid of the SPD – 'on the credit side of the German Parliamentary balance-sheet'.[8] There was precious little else to place on that side of the ledger.

Adenauer established a personal supremacy in the *Bundestag*, which he exercised with discretion and which only began to desert him in his last years in office. But he had, at the outset of his Chancellorship, the more immediately important task of dealing with the three power Allied High Commission. The High Commissioners, it should be recalled, were the

8............The *Manchester Guardian*, October 7, 1949.

successors of the Military Governors. In a personal sense, two of them were that too. Generals Clay and Pierre König were recalled to the United States and France respectively, and were replaced by Mr John McCloy and M. André François-Poncet. General Robertson, now wearing civilian clothes, continued to serve as Britain's chief representative, and was replaced in 1950 by Sir Ivone Kirkpatrick.

A word should be said about these four men and Adenauer's relations with them. For these relations were all-important. Only through the High Commissioners could Adenauer secure the step by step progress towards a restoration of German sovereignty which he believed to be so necessary. Only through them could he obtain badly needed economic concessions, in particular the revision of the oppressive dismantling programme. And only through them could he bring the Federal Republic into the European community as a fully entitled partner.

By the end of 1949 Adenauer had grown to know Robertson well and to like him. This had not been the case at first, when Adenauer's impression was that Robertson was a 'typical' British senior officer, ultra-reserved in speech and thought, and probably instinctively anti-German. Robertson, he discovered, was nothing of the kind; and Adenauer grew to value his keen brain, as well as his integrity, good manners and dignity.

His successor, Kirkpatrick, was a very different character – a Catholic, and highly professional diplomat, with a razor-sharp awareness of people's feelings and motives and the same sardonic humour as Adenauer himself. Kirkpatrick was a skilled and persistent negotiator, and plenty of negotiations between Adenauer and the High Commissioners lay ahead. When he introduced Field-Marshal Lord Montgomery to Adenauer, Montgomery, holding Kirkpatrick's coat lapel, remarked jovially – 'Does this chap give you much trouble?' To which Adenauer replied – 'Not half as much as I intend giving him.' They were, in fact, a good match for each other in many a battle of wits. Kirkpatrick paid him this tribute:

'In negotiation I always found him a redoubtable but charming adversary. He certainly enjoyed the clash of wits at the conference table. He relished his brushes with the High Commission and he told me more than once that he had enjoyed our long and often dreary sessions over the Bonn treaties.

'He was always quick to detect any weakness in the opponent's armour and to drive his weapon through the chink. On the other hand, he was equally quick, generous to recognize the strength in the opponent's case.

'He is always the rational man. The argument is conducted on the plane of reason with courtesy, humour and understanding. The tall figure sits stiff as a ramrod at the table. In carefully articulated German the sentences fall from his lips – impassive, authoritative sentences with a flavour of Chinese detachment. But from time to time events seemed to provoke him to anger. I once told him that he must never allow himself to get angry because the excitement was bad for his health. "On the contrary", he replied with an impish grin, "that is what keeps me young".' In Adenauer, Kirkpatrick saw a man of principle, a brilliant diplomatic tactician and a man who enjoyed using his own cunning as a means to a worthwhile end.[9]

The French High Commissioner, M. François-Poncet, took a full part in the periodically renewed duel of wits. Often, with him, a certain acidity crept in, and he did not hesitate to be deliberately rude, if it served his purpose. French diplomacy is an exact science, and a cold, calculated rudeness is one of its weapons, used with discretion and a spiteful elegance. Small, porcine but as immaculate as an Edwardian roué, François-Poncet had a sharp mind as well as a sharp tongue, and a pretty turn of wit. In one passage of arms with Adenauer, he suggested that the latter would be delighted to get rid of the High Commissioners. 'That's putting it too strongly,' Adenauer retorted. 'But I wouldn't mind if they turned into gay butterflies, or something of the kind.' François-Poncet came back with – 'That wouldn't do: you'd catch us in a butterfly-net.' Adenauer capped the exchange: 'In that case you'd declare butterfly-nets to be banned weapons.'[10]

François-Poncet's feline spitefulness was well illustrated in the remark which he made one day on arrival in Adenauer's office, that he was 'bringing greetings from a dead man'. As Adenauer waited, he went on: 'He is not exactly dead, but he has left the political stage. M. Schuman has resigned.'[11] Schuman was the one Frenchman whom Adenauer was able to trust as a friend, until de Gaulle became France's leader nearly a decade later. François-Poncet was aware of their friendship; his malice was deliberate.

It was Adenauer's strength that he was able to swallow affronts – as long as they came from Frenchmen. He had set his heart on Franco-German understanding thirty years before he met François-Poncet. He must have had a certain admiration for the latter's barbed jests, and it may have been some consolation to him that François-Poncet involved himself in a real vendetta with Adenauer's own arch-enemy in the field of domestic politics, Schumacher. The French High Commissioner called Schumacher a 'Faustian schizophrenic'. In return, Schumacher accused him of having

9............*The Inner Circle*, Sir Ivone Kirkpatrick, p. 230.
10...........*Gar nicht so pingelig*, Walter Henkels, p. 100–1.
11...........*Gar nicht so pingelig*, Walter Henkels, p. 98.

'appeased' the Nazis from 1933 to 1939, posing as an apostle of Franco-German understanding and giving a most unconvincing repeat performance after 1945.[12] There was more than a morsel of truth in this.

With the American High Commissioner, John McCloy, Adenauer had a very different kind of relationship, in which a warm personal friendship became the operative, if underlying factor. McCloy's wife was a distant relation of Adenauer's second wife, Gussi, but McCloy does not seem to have been aware of this link before his arrival in Germany.[13] McCloy, a banker and a somewhat unpolitical choice for his post, found Adenauer at first reserved and austere, and 'not above striking a pose or two for political effect'.[14] But Adenauer mellowed to a man who clearly wanted to understand his and Germany's problems, and was ready to help in a practical way. McCloy was impressed by his wisdom, courage and native shrewdness. Only very rarely did Adenauer vent his irony on him, as when McCloy, in all good faith, told Adenauer that he 'felt at home' when entering the Petersberg offices of the High Commission, and Adenauer riposted – 'In *that* case, Mr McCloy, after *you*!'[15]

McCloy was of very special help to Adenauer in one particular field. American Governments wanted to give the Germans a fair chance of making economic progress; it seemed futile to them to contribute Marshall Plan economic aid while at the same time imposing penal restrictions on German industry and commerce. In his memoirs Adenauer quotes a memorandum of his personal adviser, Herbert Blankenhorn, of November 30, 1949, which began: 'At every meeting between Federal Chancellor Adenauer and the High Commissioners, the Chancellor invariably raised the question of dismantling, but met always with an absolutely negative response.'[16] This was not correct. Already, early in October, McCloy had indicated that dismantling of the Ruhr's industries was 'purposeless' and that the control of the Military Security Board was all that was needed.[17] McCloy had lost no time in making his Government's view on this matter plain. From then on, Adenauer knew that he could count on American sympathy over dismantling.

At his very first meeting with the High Commissioners, on September 21, 1949, Adenauer asked for 'economic opportunity to earn a livelihood', for international help in solving the refugee problem, for European economic co-operation based on the hub of the Ruhr, and for movement

12..........*Kurt Schumacher*, Lewis J. Edinger, p. 163.
13, 14.....Letter from Mr. John McCloy to the author, December 23, 1969.
15..........*Gar nicht so pingelig*, Walter Henkels, p. 98.
16..........*Memoirs*, Konrad Adenauer, VOL 1, p. 197.
17..........The *Manchester Guardian*, October 10, 1949.

towards European federation.[18] Almost at once, he was engaged in complex negotiations with the High Commissioners on these and other subjects. These negotiations resulted in the so called 'Petersberg Agreement' of November 24, under which Allied dismantling of German industries was considerably reduced in return for concessions made by the Federal Republic which were mainly for show. The agreement was the result of hard bargaining, and was largely drafted by Herbert Blankenhorn on the German side, and Sir Christopher Steel on behalf of the High Commission. Its terms require some analysis, for this was the first agreement reached by Adenauer on his step by step progress towards the sovereignty of the Federal Republic.

First, the concessions made by the Federal Republic. Adenauer undertook to co-operate fully with the Allied Military Security Board in steps to ensure and maintain Germany's demilitarization. He had no option in the matter; the Board would have operated in some form or other in any event. Adenauer recognized the 'Ruhr Statute' which provided for the use of the area's economic 'potential' on a fair basis, under the supervision of an international authority in which the United States, Britain, France, West Germany and the three Benelux countries participated. Again, he did so because there was no alternative. It was clearly better for the industrial area of the Ruhr to be administered by a body which included Germans, than by one which did not. Admittedly, acceptance of the Ruhr Statute brought bombastic wrath in the *Bundestag* down on Adenauer's head. Carlo Schmid of the SPD called the Statute 'the hand at the throat of Germany' and claimed that 'its fruits will be the nationalism of a dog on a chain'.[19] For once more prosaic, Schumacher argued that the real problem was not the internationalization of the Ruhr, but the internationalization of Europe.

Then, the Federal Republic was to be integrated in Western Europe in all possible ways. On the Allied side there was talk about this part of the

18...........A curious and significant scene took place when Adenauer and his 'team' of five Ministers and five officials were greeted by François-Poncet, the High Commission 'Chairman of the month'. In the Petersberg Hotel, which had been requisitioned by the occupying powers, a carpet had been laid down in the middle of the drawing-room. The three High Commissioners were lined up upon it when the German delegation arrived. Adenauer evidently believed they were 'reserving' the carpet for themselves (*Memoirs*, VOL I, p. 184), but he managed to step nimbly on to it when greeting François-Poncet, and remained there while introducing his Ministers. The carpet, for the record, was made by a German firm in Bielefeld and, like the furniture, crockery and fittings in the Petersberg, placed at the disposal of the occupying powers.

19...........*This is Germany*, ed. by Arthur Settel. Chapter by Terence Prittie, p. 279.

agreement entailing some surrender of German independence. In reality, it suited Adenauer's book perfectly: the Federal Republic was now free to join the Council of Europe in Strasbourg and a number of international organizations like the World Bank and Monetary Fund. It was also allowed to establish consular representation abroad. The High Commissioners may have wanted to integrate the Federal Republic in Western Europe, to prevent a future fully-fledged German State from re-emerging as a potential danger in Central Europe. But Adenauer wanted integration as much as they did.

The most immediate German gain from the Petersberg Agreement lay in the economic field. Seventeen major industrial plants were struck off the dismantling list, three others were to be almost totally spared, and all dismantling was to end in West Berlin. For the first time since the war, too, West Germany would be allowed to build ocean-going ships both for her own use and for export, although some restrictions on size and speed were still kept in force. The level of steel production, admittedly, was to be held down to 11 million tons a year; but this level had been previously agreed after first being very considerably raised. As Adenauer himself correctly noted, what mattered most 'was the psychological effect of these concessions on our "entrepreneurs" and other leaders of economic life and on the will to work of our labour force'.[20]

Even more significant, as Adenauer pointed out in the *Bundestag* debate on the same day, the Federal Republic had been treated as an equal partner for the first time. Nevertheless, it was a stormy debate. The SPD and the Communists claimed that Adenauer had surrendered too much and had left the 18 million East Germans out of his reckoning. The SPD was incensed that the Agreement had been signed before the *Bundestag* had been consulted. A storm in a tea-cup was caused by Adenauer's production of the text of a United Press report; it quoted the Trade Union Congress in Düsseldorf as saying that the Agreement represented a 'serious effort' on the part of the High Commissioners to meet German needs and that the Government was justified in accepting the Ruhr Statute. Adenauer called the agency report a 'telegram', and Schumacher at once denounced it as a forgery, and an 'objective and subjective untruth'. The *Bundestag* Secretariat telephoned Trade Union headquarters. They confirmed that the United Press had reported their statement correctly.

Adenauer announced this at 3 a.m. on November 25, with the debate still continuing. This led to a wild slanging match on the floor of the house. It culminated in Schumacher calling Adenauer 'Chancellor of the Allies', being called to order and refusing to withdraw this epithet, and later

20..........*Memoirs*, Konrad Adenauer, VOL 1, p. 221–2.

being suspended for the next twenty days in session of the *Bundestag*. The bile which had been boiling up inside Schumacher spilled over in this frantic outcry – he was maddened beyond endurance by the obvious success of Adenauer's negotiations with the Allies and by the total exclusion from them of himself and his party. It must be remembered, in extenuation, that – already without a right arm – he had been obliged to have his left leg amputated in the previous year. This had completely undermined his already poor state of health; he could be said to be already a dying man. It must be remembered, too, that Schumacher sent Adenauer a written apology a few days after the debate.[21]

Nor was Schumacher alone in making wild statements. In Adenauer's memoirs this passage occurs: 'After the Petersberg Agreement it was indeed possible to repeat General Robertson's words, that we had broken out of the ring. I am convinced that the German people would have fallen to Communism from sheer misery and despair, if unemployment and distress had continued to mount, if the glimmering of hope in a better future to which they still held had been extinguished by failure over the Petersberg Agreement.'[22] Distress was not mounting at the time. Nor was there a real danger of the German people falling to Communism; they had been taught to regard it as the ultimate evil during the Nazi Era, and it remained an easily recognizable enemy. Still, the Petersberg Agreement remains a really valuable achievement, not least for the speed and efficiency with which it was negotiated.

With the Agreement signed, Adenauer was able to turn his attention to two problems of major importance. The first was relations with France, and this will be dealt with in a later chapter. The second was the Federal Republic's share in the defence of her own territory, and of Western Europe. Both subjects were to cause endless heart-searching, and, latterly, to become interwoven with one another.

One must return for a moment to the tribulations of the Western Allies in 1948, and to what one authority called the 'state of near-panic' existing then, with a French Minister telling him that the Russians would be in Paris by August.[23] The Berlin Blockade was menacing enough to suggest an acute danger of world war. In addition, the Russians were applying pressure, brutally if not always successfully, on Czechoslovakia, Turkey, Norway and Iran. The North Atlantic Treaty, signed on April 4, 1949, set up a defensive alliance; and NATO plans to produce sufficient conventional forces to defend Western Europe were apologetically modest when compared with actual Soviet armed strength at least 200 divisions still on

21..........*Memoirs*, Konrad Adenauer, VOL I, p. 230.
22..........*Memoirs*, Konrad Adenauer, VOL I, p. 231.
23..........*The Inner Circle*, Sir Ivone Kirkpatrick, p. 205.

a war-footing and more than 25 in the 'advance bastion' of East Germany alone. With Communist parties highly active in France, Italy and other West European countries, the Communist threat to Western democracy was a real one.

Adenauer could not fail to have given careful thought to this threat. Rather ingenuously, he writes in his memoirs that 'in November 1949 the foreign press suddenly began to discuss the question of the rearmament of Germany'.[24] He had himself already begun to discuss it. The first occasion would seem to have been on November 13, when the American Secretary of State, Mr. Dean Acheson, was in Bonn. Acheson's message for Adenauer was that Europe must help itself more effectively, if the United States were to go on helping Europe. It seems sure that Acheson sounded Adenauer on a future German defence contribution. This served as the 'lead-in' for the interview which Adenauer gave on December 3, 1949, to the correspondent of the *Cleveland Plain Dealer*, John P. Leacacos. In it he stated that, although he could not agree to the creation of an independent West German Army or to 'German mercenaries' serving in foreign armies, he was ready to consider the possibility of a German contingent in the army of a European Federation. Adenauer repeated this, in more guarded terms, at a press conference on December 5 and again, to the *Frankfurter Allgemeine Zeitung*, on December 7.

His technique with the press was an intriguing one. It had already become his habit to 'fly a kite', by giving a piece of 'exclusive' information to a single correspondent, usually one who was not especially well-known or serving a leading newspaper. By doing this, Adenauer gave himself the chance of sounding opinion, as he saw it, discreetly, always allowing himself the chance of claiming to have been misunderstood or misreported. He did this so often during his political career that one has to assume that it was a calculated technique. On this occasion, he countered the inevitable hubbub by explaining that he had been misreported. But he had broken the ice over the question of West German rearmament, and that was probably all that he had intended doing.

It was perfectly true that there had been some talk of rearming West Germany, for that mental state of near-panic about which Kirkpatrick wrote persisted long after the Berlin Blockade was lifted. Sir Winston Churchill had discussed the subject in general terms. The former American Military Governor, General Lucius Clay, was more explicit in a speech at Harvard University on November 20. Even Field-Marshal Sir William Slim, Chief of the British Imperial General Staff, said early in December that German rearmament could be effectively organized. Slim, it may

24...........*Memoirs*, Konrad Adenauer, VOL 1, p. 267.

be remembered, coined the phrase for the Germans of 'bloodthirsty sheep'.

Having once taken up the subject, Adenauer was not going to let go. On December 8 he told a CDU meeting in Düsseldorf that a West German contribution to Europe's defence in no way diminished the absolute opposition of the German people to war. On December 9 he urged the need to preserve the Federal Republic's security, especially in view of the creation of a para-military 'People's Police' in East Germany which was 'nothing less than a regular army'.[25] On December 10 he posed the question to the *Neue Zürcher Zeitung*, 'Which is the greater danger – the Russian threat to the Western world, or the existence of German military contingents brigaded with the armed forces of other nations?'[26]

On December 16 he told the *Bundestag*: 'Even in the event of the Allies demanding in a categorical form a German contribution to European security, there can be no question whatever of the establishment of a German army. The utmost we would be prepared to consider would be a German contingent within the framework of a European army.'

The truth was that Adenauer had pondered long and carefully over the question of German rearmament, and had come to the conclusion that it was an absolute necessity. He had three good reasons: it would give the Federal Republic, in time, political equality and independence; it would bind West Germany more closely into Western Europe; and it would help to provide an effective defensive shield for both the Federal Republic and Western Europe. His country was, after all, in the front line of the Cold War. But, where priorities were concerned, Adenauer's view was clear-cut – 'Rearmament might be the way to gaining full sovereignty for the Federal Republic. This made it the essential question of our political future.'[27]

After his burst of hectic activity in December, 1949, however, Adenauer seemed to lose interest. This was not really the case, but there were plenty of reasons for him to tread warily. Certain sections of the Western press, particularly some British newspapers, assumed that the Germans were longing to get back into uniform. This was not so at all, although there was a small minority of ex-officers and NCO's who still thought of the armed forces as the only worthwhile career. After the First World War people of this kind formed the 'Free Corps', the 'Green Police' and the 'Black Reichswehr', looking for a substitute for regular military service. But there was a much greater readiness to take up arms again after 1918 than after 1945. Defeat in the Second World War had been total and

25..........*Konrad Adenauer*, Paul Weymar, p. 333.
26..........*Neue Zürcher Zeitung*, daily paper, December 11, 1949.
27..........*Memoirs*, Konrad Adenauer, VOL I, p. 270.

devastating; even twenty years later the ravages of war had not entirely disappeared.

German women – and after the war-losses, nearly 55 per cent of the population were women – remembered only the horrors and deprivations of war, and none of its comradeship and sense of achievement. The younger generation were instinctively anti-war and anti-military; they were quickly showing an aversion to those old, sonorous cracker-mottoes about 'Fatherland' and 'Germany's destiny', and they had no desire to become prospective cannon-fodder. The Evangelical Churches were taking an increasing interest in the subject of German reunification, and saw in rearmament a barrier to its attainment. A strong body of intellectuals took the same view, and among the ex-soldiers there was a reaction against military red tape and routine – the Germans talk of *Kommisz* and *Barras* and one of the most successful novels published in Germany after 1945, *Null-Acht-Fünfzehn*, was a parody of the military life. All too many ex-soldiers remembered being pushed around by their own leaders, forced to fight in suicidal last-ditch actions, and demeaned by the uncomfortable experiences of Allied prisoners-of-war camps.

Among the political parties, the SPD feared that rearmament would bring the rebirth of a military caste, with that sense of superiority and exclusiveness which was far more negative than insistence on toughness and perfection in drill. The SPD, too, was remembering something of the pacifist principles which it so blithely discarded in August, 1914. The Free Democrats and German Party were angling for the ex-soldiers' vote and shied away from the idea of rearmament while German ex-soldiers were still being sentenced for war-crimes by Allied tribunals. The Communists, of course, opposed rearmament violently; they realized that the one military combination which their Russian masters could fear was that of disciplined German conventional forces and American nuclear weapons. Even in the CDU there was an actively pacifist group, as Adenauer was shortly to discover. And there were the beginnings of neutralist stirrings, some of them Soviet-inspired.

In the spring of 1950 Adenauer decided to aim at a more modest target than a West German contribution to a European army. In June he proposed the creation of a Federal police force, which would be armed and would be additional to the local police maintained under *Länder* control. General Robertson was on the point of leaving Germany and it was to him that Adenauer first turned. He pointed out that the Russians had started arming 'Peoples' Police' under the ex-Nazi General, Hermann Rentsch, in July, 1948, and had raised this force to a strength of 48,000 in the summer of 1949. This force was organized in 'alert squads' of up to 1,200 men, stationed in barracks and given infantry weapons and light tanks. By early 1950 it had its own reconnaissance aircraft, its first fully mechanized regiment and a new commander in the shape of the formidable Wilhelm Zaisser, who had fought under the pseudonym of 'General Gomez' in the Spanish Civil War. In the course of the next two years, the 'Peoples' Police' was to be doubled to a strength of over 100,000 men and was given medium tanks, artillery and its first YAK fighter aircraft.

Robertson and his political adviser, Sir Christopher Steel, were ready to forward Adenauer's request for a roughly equivalent West German force to the British Government.[28] But British foreign policy was the reverse of forceful, and while France wanted nothing done for the time being, the United States Government favoured a package deal. This was for a German armed contribution in Europe, United States reinforcements for their existing army in Europe of four divisions, and the appointment of General Dwight Eisenhower as Supreme Commander in Europe.[29] This package deal was blocked by the British Foreign Secretary, Ernest Bevin. All that happened was that the High Commission approved the reinforcement of *Länder* police forces by a mere 10,000 men. It was at this moment, in June, 1950, that the Korean War broke out. It produced a mood of deep concern among the Western Allies, and of real fear in West Germany. For Germany, like Korea, was a bone of contention between East and West, a much more important one too. The zonal frontier through the middle of Germany was long, rambling and indefensible. And there were around 25 Red Army divisions in East Germany, against a bare seven Allied divisions in the Federal Republic. Something, it seemed, needed to be done.

In July, 1950, Adenauer instructed ex-General Hans Speidel, once Rommel's second-in-command of the *Afrika Korps*, to produce a memorandum on the Federal Republic's external security. It was ready by August 14, three days after Adenauer returned from a holiday in Switzerland (he went to the Bürgenstock, near Lucerne, after a bout of pneumonia). Speidel's findings were that Soviet preponderance in conventional arms was overwhelming, that American nuclear supremacy was only assured up to 1952, and that NATO's forces in Europe should be 'firmed-up' by a German contribution of 15 divisions, with a tactical air-force and a small naval command, to be produced in the next two years.

Adenauer implicitly believed Speidel's assessment of the situation (indeed, it was remarkably accurate and to the point). On August 17, 1950, an interview was published in the *New York Times*, in which he spoke of the need for a West German military contribution, to offset the East

28..........Sir Christopher Steel, in private conversation with the author.
29..........*The Inner Circle*, Sir Ivone Kirkpatrick, p. 240.

German Peoples' Police. On the same day, he confronted the High Commissioners with a proposal for 'a German defence force made up of volunteer units to a total strength of 150,000 men.'[30] Such was his haste – something altogether unusual for Adenauer – that he did not make it clear what form this volunteer force would take. François-Poncet assumed that it was some kind of para-military police-force, and Adenauer confirmed on August 23 in a press conference that this was so. That he had acted without his otherwise invariable forethought was indicated by a remark that he made to the High Commissioners on August 17. McCloy asked him whether he could raise 150,000 volunteers if the SPD were against it; and Adenauer answered that he had already discussed the matter with Schumacher, and that he 'had acquired great respect for Dr. Schumacher's judgement!'[31] If such a thing had really happened, it was more sudden and more startling than the transformation of Saul to Paul on the road to Damascus. Until then Adenauer never ceased to claim that Schumacher possessed no judgement at all!

On August 29, Adenauer acted, once more, without caution. He had sensed a connexion between a German armed contribution and the watering-down of the already modified Allied 'Occupation'. In double-quick time he compiled a memorandum urging a German military contribution to a European army and linked this with the proposal that the High Commissioners should be turned into Ambassadors and the Federal Republic should enter into normal diplomatic relations with its Western partners. In the memorandum, Adenauer implied that it was 'grotesque' that the Federal Republic had to address itself to a 'Trinity' instead of to the representatives of friendly powers.

There was nothing the matter with the memorandum itself. The three High Commissioners had for long been nicknamed the 'Unholy Trinity', and the Petersberg headquarters 'Monte Veto'. But there was a Western Foreign Ministers' Conference in New York on September 12, and McCloy, as 'Chairman of the month', was about to leave for the preparatory talks. Adenauer sent a special courier to Frankfurt to catch McCloy before he left. It was August 30, and on September 1 François-Poncet became 'Chairman of the month'. He would, Adenauer knew, hold up his memorandum, since France was still instinctively opposed to any form of West German rearmament.

The courier arrived in time. Adenauer's memorandum was studied in Washington. Moreover, it bore fruit quickly. On September 19, the communiqué of the Western Foreign Ministers referred to a 'new step' on

30..........*Memoirs*, Konrad Adenauer, VOL I, p. 274.
31..........*Memoirs*, Konrad Adenauer, VOL I, p. 277.

the road to West Germany's return to the comity of nations, forecast the revision of the Occupation Statute, and suggested that the Federal Republic would soon have its own Foreign Minister. The Foreign Ministers asked only that the Federal Republic should acknowledge pre- and post-war debts and be ready to pool defence equipment and materials in the common cause of Western European security. All this was to the good; but Adenauer had, in his haste, failed to tell his Cabinet what he was doing. His Minister of the Interior, Gustav Heinemann, was strongly opposed to rearmament, in any form. On September 4 he offered his resignation to Adenauer, which the Chancellor refused to accept. But on September 11 he insisted on resigning. He repeated his opposition to rearmament, but it may well have been that he was even more angered by Adenauer's disregard for the feelings of himself and others, who needed convincing.

Heinemann, basically, was a pacifist. He was also deeply concerned with finding ways of bringing German reunification closer. Quite rightly, he saw that West German rearmament was an irrevocable step. It was something which the Western Allies, unwilling to muster adequate conventional armed forces to defend themselves, could not put into reverse. It placed West Germany squarely in the Western camp, in an East–West confrontation which was liable to last a lifetime at least. Heinemann left politics altogether, then formed a neutralist party of his own,[32] eventually joined the SPD and won his way back to Cabinet office and, finally, became Federal President.

Maybe Adenauer could argue that he was well rid of Heinemann, who was already becoming a thorn in his flesh. Heinemann had irritated him by talking about God having 'twice dashed the weapons from the hands of the Germans' and proposing that the Federal Republic should not oppose 'the will of God'. Adenauer, according to his own version, had retorted that God had 'given us our heads to think with and our arms and hands to act with'.[33] But Adenauer was certainly wrong in claiming that Heinemann resigned 'in a moment of agitation'. Heinemann was a sober and serious man, and he resigned on what he believed were cardinal issues of policy and of treatment of the Cabinet.

The 'Heinemann crisis' passed quickly. Adenauer does not seem to have given it another thought, as he was engrossed in the subject of rearmament.

32..........Heinemann explained his views to the author in two interviews, after he had formed his neutralist 'All German People's Party'. He argued that Adenauer's big mistake had been his failure to explore possible paths to German reunification. Heinemann was not dogmatic on this question during these interviews, although he sounded so in one or two other statements made at this time.

33..........*Memoirs*, Konrad Adenauer, VOL 1, p. 292.

With Britain now prepared in principle to accept a German defence contribution, much hinged on the attitude of France. Pestered with her colonial problems and able to contribute no more than a 'shadow' division to NATO's forces in Germany, France knew that if she stalled all proposals for German rearmament she might provoke the Americans to pull out militarily from a Europe unwilling to defend itself. Fifteen years later, de Gaulle would have relished such a prospect of killing two birds with one stone; but the governments of the Fourth Republic were weak and unsure of themselves. France therefore put forward its own proposals, embodied in the 'Pleven Plan' of October 24, 1950 (René Pleven was Prime Minister at the time). This was for European 'mixed divisions' to be created, in which German units would be at company strength. Europe's defence would, in effect, be conducted by a kind of European 'Foreign Legion'.

Few words need be wasted on the 'Pleven Plan'. It was utterly unpractical, and it was a sad reflection on the French National Assembly which approved it. From the language point of view alone, mixed divisions would have been unworkable; on top of that there would have been problems of manning, command and equipment. This was pointed out to France's Defence Minister, Jules Moch, at the NATO Ministerial conference in Washington on October 28. But Britain was again wavering over the German defence contribution, and at a further NATO meeting in Brussels on December 18 and 19 it was decided to re-examine the possibility of mixed divisions, based on a new proposal by the American Ambassador to NATO, Charles Spofford, of 'combat teams' of 5,000–6,000 men. Christmas, and the usual recess afterwards, passed without any decision being reached.

During this period of shilly-shallying Adenauer kept his head and his patience. His ability for reading the mind of the 'man-in-the-street' was never more apparent than at this time. In spite of the campaign launched against rearmament by the SPD and members of the Evangelical Churches like Pastor Niemöller, Adenauer felt that a great many Germans were slowly coming round to the belief that it was logical for them to take a part in their own defence, especially if this gained the Federal Republic political advantages. The SPD were propagating the *Ohne mich* ('Leave me out of it') movement, but there were signs that their attitude on rearmament was not as rigid as before. In Stuttgart in September, Schumacher declared that 'We are ready to bear arms once again if, with us, the Western allies take over the same risk and the same chance of warding off a Soviet attack, establishing themselves in the greatest possible strength on the Elbe.'[34] Rearmament, in fact, was a practical matter and not one which should be decided on principle alone.

34..........*The German Phoenix*, William Henry Chamberlin, p. 204.

To the High Commissioners Adenauer explained that the 'negative' attitude of the German people would be overcome, if the Federal Republic were given back its independence. It suited him to underline the strength of purpose of the SPD and the effects of that party's arguments. In a series of speeches and interviews, he urged the immediate replacement of the Occupation Statute by a system of treaties, and the recognition of absolute equality for Germans in the common defence of Europe. In October, 1950, he instructed ex-Generals Hans Speidel and Adolf Heusinger to review the possibility of organizing a 500,000 strong German army within the framework of European defence. On December 22 he nominated these two men, along with ex-Colonel Johann Count von Kielmansegg and the Trade Unionist member of the CDU, Theodor Blank,[35] as a 'select committee' on defence. And he sharply rejected Soviet notes of November 3 and December 15 which accused him of breaking the Potsdam Agreement, sabotaging all hope of Four Power agreement over Germany, and planning military aggression.

In the early months of 1951 Adenauer kept up his steady pressure on the High Commissioners to institute talks on the revision or replacement of the Occupation Statute. He had a new argument which he pressed persistently. In *Land* elections in Schleswig-Holstein, Wurtemberg-Baden and Bavaria, the CDU had lost seats and votes. This, Adenauer claimed, showed that his 'policy of fulfilment' was becoming increasingly unpopular, because it was not paying sufficient dividends. In Bavaria, a 'Refugee Party' had appeared (the BHE) which had picked up 10 per cent of the votes. Adenauer argued that political extremism was becoming a danger. On March 6, 1951, the High Commissioners revised the Occupation Statute. The most important provision was that the Federal Republic should now have charge of its own external relations. Adenauer accordingly became Foreign Minister, in addition to being Chancellor, on March 15. He would now conduct foreign relations on two different levels, through his contact with the High Commissioners and through normal diplomatic channels with countries other than Britain, France and the United States.

This was a big step on the road to West German sovereignty. Another was the acceptance on May 2, 1951, of the Federal Republic as a full member of the Council of Europe. In this, Adenauer later wrote, 'I saw confirmation of my policy of tenacious patience.' And he went on to take a side-swipe at Schumacher – 'It was not the policy of banging a non-

35..........Count von Kielmansegg was an anti-Nazi. One of his ancestors had fought gallantly on the battlefield of Waterloo. He subsequently served as Chief of Staff on NATO HQ in Europe. Blank was to head first the 'Defence Office' set up in Bonn, and later the Ministry of Defence.

existent negotiating table, but the indefatigable manifestation of our will to co-operate in the safeguarding of peace and social progress in Europe which had brought back to us that measure of sovereignty.'[36]

More important, a new, long and vital round of talks between Adenauer and the High Commissioners began on the Petersberg on May 10, 1951. The aim of these talks was nothing less than the ending of the Allied occupation and the replacement of the Occupation Statute by contractual and freely negotiated agreements between the Federal Republic and the three Western Powers. Weeks were, indeed, wasted over tiresome preliminaries, in particular an agreed agenda. The summer holidays intervened. In August, holidaying again on the Bürgenstock in Switzerland, Adenauer summoned his advisers and discussed with them the details of contractual agreements and a possible mutual security pact between the Federal Republic and the Western Powers. But concrete progress was forecast at last when the three Foreign Ministers met in Washington from September 10–14 and agreed that talks should go ahead, from September 24, on the Petersberg, and that these talks should be designed to bring the Federal Republic into a European Defence Community and to replace the Occupation Statute.

Adenauer, in his own words, 'was determined to adhere to the large perspectives, that must be the criteria of our decisions. I entered these negotiations with optimism and confidence.'[37] The talks were the third, and most crucial step on the road to West German sovereignty; the first was the establishment of a West German State, and the second the 'Petersberg Agreement' of November 24, 1949. The talks, which began on September 24, 1951, were the most difficult which Adenauer had yet undertaken. They were to drag on far into 1952.

There were valid reasons for this. The first and by far the most important, was that the Western Powers were trying to secure German approval for an agreement, necessarily involving some unwelcome sanctions on a nation accounted guilty of provoking the war in which it was defeated. But at the same time, the Western Powers were inviting that same nation to take up arms again, in defence of its conquerors as well as itself. This gave Adenauer considerable bargaining power.

The Western Powers did not at once appreciate this, and the draft agreements which they at first offered were unacceptable. It took them time to realize that the Federal Government was negotiating as an equal, and they were jolted out of their stride by Adenauer's skilful citation of demands by his Free Democratic partners which were hard to meet and

36...........*Memoirs*, Konrad Adenauer, VOL I, p. 362–3.
37...........*Memoirs*, Konrad Adenauer, VOL I, p. 365.

others by the Social Democratic Opposition which were even more radical.

The third reason for the long duration of the negotiations was the complex nature of the Western proposals. Military Government had intervened in almost every side of German life, and there was an inevitable tendency to try to cling on to some 'Occupation' powers while surrendering others. In the end, five main 'Conventions' were agreed. The 'General Convention' defined the aims of the Western Powers, their trusteeship of Berlin, and their pre-emptive right to settle questions concerning Germany's relationship with the Soviet Union. A second Convention regulated the 'rights and obligations' of Western armies, a third dealt with questions arising out of the war. Then there was a Convention to settle the Federal Republic's economic and financial contributions to Western defence, and another to arbitrate on foreign interests in Germany.

One British newspaper noted at the time that the agreements were reached, (May 1952), that it was the third Convention which contained 'the stings and sanctions which any Treaty must impose on account of the hardships and injustices arising out of Nazi brutalities and the last war. Into these Conventions have had to be written quantities of Allied legislation – on the break-up of the industrial trusts, restitution to victims of Nazism, the position of the war criminals, the safeguarding of non-German industrial interests. The statesmen at Versailles had an easy task compared to this – and they did not have to condition every action they took with the reflection that they were dealing with a divided country and that nothing they did must prejudice the chances of that country being reunited.'[38]

The writer of this article offered a ludicrous example of German insistence that the Conventions should be absolutely 'fair'. More than one German newspaper had printed an alleged statement by an official that an American soldier should not get one cigarette more than the future German soldier 'because they might find themselves one day in the same fox-hole, and the German might have nothing to smoke!' Fortunately, Adenauer did not negotiate agreements with Western partners on this principle of potential deprivation in fields which did not matter. Then, the negotiations would have been even more long drawn-out. But Adenauer fought every difference on matters of crucial importance with tremendous pertinacity.

It would be tedious to deal in detail with the negotiations which culminated in what became known as the Bonn and Paris Agreements of May 26 and 27, 1952. In the course of these negotiations Adenauer paid visits to

38..........The *Manchester Guardian*, Terence Prittie, May 29, 1952.

Rome, Paris and London. The Paris visit belongs to another chapter. That to London, in December 1951, might have been a memorable milestone. Churchill had again become Prime Minister in October. Adenauer must have been delighted that the Labour Government, insular, awkward and hostile to Germany, had gone. Adenauer's visit was the first by a German head of government since that of Brüning in 1931.

In his bluff but intuitive way, Churchill had decided that Britain must make friends with 'good' Germans: when Adenauer arrived, he expressed himself in terms which a Catholic Rhinelander was bound to appreciate. He asked Adenauer if he were a Prussian. Adenauer denied it. Churchill said that Prussians were 'villains'. Nothing could have been more pleasing to Adenauer's ears; he remarked, slyly, that his one great political opponent, Schumacher, was a Prussian.[39] This exchange took no account of the paradox in Anglo-German relations, that the British have for the last century and a half forgotten that the Germans who understand them best, and are ready to understand them better still, are precisely those Prussians whom Churchill classified as 'villains'.

There were some half-hearted anti-German demonstrations in London and Oxford during Adenauer's visit. They counted little against the fact that King George VI, clearly in ill-health, made a special effort to meet Adenauer and be amiable towards him, and that Churchill was spontaneously forthcoming and friendly.[40] But Adenauer, in his memoirs, added a revealing postscript. He described how, later, he had another talk with Churchill and the latter made a drawing on a menu-card of what western civilization comprised.[41] Churchill drew three concentric circles – representing the United States, a united Europe, and Britain with her Commonwealth. Nothing, Adenauer noted cryptically, had changed in the British attitude. What he really meant was that Britain still did not feel or think in European terms. This had long been his rooted belief.

Under Churchill and Eden (Sir Anthony Eden, later Lord Avon, was Foreign Secretary and the recognized 'Crown Prince' of the Conservative Government), Britain approached the Bonn and Paris agreements in a reasonably confident spirit. It meant certain sacrifices – Allied military costs of occupation would not in future be levied but would have to be negotiated; Allied organs of control like the Military Security Board would be abolished; restrictions on the German economy would be

39..........*Memoirs*, Konrad Adenauer, VOL I, p. 397.

40..........The fact that King George died only a few weeks later made a deep impression on Adenauer. It showed that the King had gone out of his way to have a talk with him. Adenauer said later that he 'liked him very much'.

41..........*Memoirs*, Konrad Adenauer, VOL I, p. 399.

removed and German competition in world markets would undoubtedly become fiercer. The High Commissioners would become Ambassadors. But Britain would not be directly involved in a military sense with the Federal Republic, for Britain would not belong to the European Defence Community which was to be formed. France would; and the French Government had hesitations, up to the last minute, about signing the agreements. Typical of these hesitations was a statement made on May 25, 1952, only a day before the Bonn Agreement was to be signed (the Paris Agreement was signed a day later, on May 27), by the veteran French Socialist, Edouard Herriot. He said:

'The rearmament of Germany fills me with great anxiety. If we were as convinced that Germany will honour the obligations to which she has subscribed as we are of her will to restore her former greatness we would feel no disquiet. But the obligations agreed on paper are insufficient ... I implore our American friends not to drag us into a series of the kind of experiments whose pained and powerless witness I was between the two wars. It is said that the Americans are businessmen. This is not so. They are idealists, with a slightly naïve idealism.'[42]

The United States Government had, indeed, made up its mind. Eden helped Acheson to dispel France's fears, at least for the moment. The Agreements were signed, as planned, on May 26 in Bonn and May 27 in Paris. When the latter was signed, Britain added an undertaking to come to the help of the European Defence Community, should it or any part of it be the object of armed attack. What seemed a modest contribution was nevertheless a unique event in British history. In Bonn there were neither flags nor fireworks. A mood of reasoned satisfaction was tempered by the reflection that Germany remained as much divided as before – perhaps even more, as a result of formal West German rearmament. The SPD argued the case against the Agreements with lack of imagination, and the party's attitude was compared by one observer with that 'of a hungry man who refuses a reasonable meal because he has not ordered it himself'.[43]

The same observer had already analysed reasons for Adenauer's success – he had set himself attainable objectives: the establishment of effective government, the regaining of sovereignty and the integration of the Federal Republic in the 'Europe of Charlemagne'; and he had gone about his task with a sense of historical perspective, an invariable political moderation and a renunciation of high-sounding phrases and self-important gestures.

42..........*Memoirs*, Konrad Adenauer, VOL 1, p. 413.
43..........The *Manchester Guardian*, Terence Prittie, June 6, 1952.

Another reason for Adenauer's success was the fact that the situation of the Federal Republic, although delicate, was simple in essence – nothing could be won without the help and understanding of the Western Powers. Adenauer had an aptitude for seeking and finding the simple way out of his problems. He had thrown in his lot unreservedly with the West in the Cold War, accepting United States leadership and seeking reconciliation with France as a basis for a united Europe. More of this in the next chapter. One should, perhaps, pay a passing tribute to the High Commissioners, who showed on the whole a remarkable understanding of the realities of the situation and a fair degree of tact in dealing with Adenauer and his advisers. The French Foreign Minister, M. Robert Schuman, remarked that never in history had men worked with such zeal to abolish themselves.[44]

Almost in the hour of Adenauer's triumph his great rival, Schumacher, died. This was on August 22 while Adenauer was taking a well-earned rest on holiday in Switzerland. He paid suitable tribute to his patriotism – 'Despite many differences which divided us in our political concepts, we were yet united in our common goal, to do everything possible for the benefit and well-being of our people.'[45] In reality, Schumacher had been an irritant almost up to the last. In January 1952 he had instituted an appeal to the Federal Constitutional Court in Karlsruhe, to rule that rearmament was unconstitutional and would require the revision of the Constitution by a vote of two-thirds of the members of the *Bundestag*. This constitutional controversy was to drag on until March 1953. Even when the Agreements had been signed, Schumacher had refused to abandon his total opposition, in which he had intemperately declared that 'Whoever approves the *Generalvertrag* (the Bonn Agreement) ceases to be a German.'

But verbal excesses should not blind one to Schumacher's services to post-1945 Germany. His moral integrity and blazing courage helped to prevent any drift from the ranks of the SPD to Communism. In a sadly demoralized country he set a fine example of personal probity, civic courage and faith in the future. He identified his Party with the root-beliefs of the Western democracies, and he spoke out fearlessly against the wrongs perpetrated by the Soviet Union – the maintenance of concentration camps in East Germany, the failure to return hundreds of thousands of German prisoners-of-war, the abuse of human dignity and the trampling in the dust of human rights. He opposed the merger of the SPD and Communist parties under Soviet sponsorship and so played a key role in saving West Berlin.

44..........*The Inner Circle*, Sir Ivone Kirkpatrick, p. 246.
45..........*Konrad Adenauer*, Paul Weymar, p. 479.

Schumacher was a political animal, and it seemed that he lived for politics alone. If he made tactical blunders, it should not be thought that they could ever outweigh his sturdy championship of human freedom. Physically broken by Nazi persecution, bruised by what he regarded as Allied cold-shouldering of him and his Party, distressed by his inability to secure popular participation in a new golden era of social justice, he died a bitterly disappointed man.

9 Rough Road to Rapprochement

One must, for the moment, go back in time. While Adenauer was negotiating the sovereignty and independence of the Federal Republic, a new picture was unfolding itself of a matter very close to the Chancellor's heart, namely Franco-German relations. The tradition of friendship between the German Rhineland and France is an old one. In the Thirty Years War the Catholic Rhineland looked to Catholic France as their protector against the 'heathen' Protestants of North Germany and Sweden. The French blotted their copy-book badly in their wars of conquest in the late seventeenth and early eighteenth centuries, yet a hundred years later one finds Heinrich Heine thinking of himself as a potential intellectual intermediary between France and Germany (Heine talked, by way of contrast, of 'infernal' England and called the English 'the most loathsome people which God created in his wrath'.[1]) One finds the same trend of thought in Goethe's utterances, tinctured with an ingrained distrust of his own German people; while the Krupps of Essen did not hesitate to sell cannon to Napoleon.

The Germany of Bismarck and Wagner, Karl Marx and even the early Thomas Mann, preaching 'cultural nationalism', and a Russo-German Union during the First World War, recoiled from France, from French liberalism, cosmopolitanism and supposed French 'decadence'. Adenauer represented a reaction against this primarily Protestant, North German animosity towards France. He was essentially a West European, and one of his early speeches in 1919, after becoming Lord Mayor of Cologne is as good an illustration as any of this fact:

'Whatever the ultimate shape of the peace treaty, here on the Rhine, at the ancient international crossroads, German civilization and the civilization of the Western democracies will meet during the decades to come. Unless a genuine reconciliation is possible between them, unless the European nations learn to recognize and cultivate that which is common to all European civilization ... unless it becomes possible once more to unite the nations through cultural understanding, unless in this way we shall be able to prevent a new war among the nations of Europe, European leadership will be lost for ever.'[2]

1............*The Mind of Germany*, Hans Kohn, p. 123.

2............Speech at Cologne University, June, 1919, Cologne City Archives.

In speaking of the Western democracies, Adenauer was thinking primarily of France; to a lesser extent – because they were smaller – of Holland, Belgium and Luxemburg; and lesser still – because they were remote – of Britain and the United States. What he believed in 1919 he believed, even more strongly, in 1945. For whereas the First World War devastated France, the Second struck at the very existence of his own country. Like Goethe, Adenauer had a profound distrust of human nature in general and of the German national character in particular.[3] It was all to his credit that he always believed that there was something positive to be done. The quest for Franco-German reconciliation became one of the most positive and productive aspects of his thinking.

He spoke his mind on this subject often. Thus in November 1949 he gave an interview to the Hamburg weekly paper, *Die Zeit*, which included the following passages: 'I must work for Franco-German understanding. Such a policy should not be misinterpreted as being pro-French, let alone anti-British. It is certainly not a question for us of playing off one foreign power against another ... But friendship with France requires greater efforts because it has so far laboured under inhibitions.'[4] A little ingenuously, Adenauer went on: 'I think I can say that reconciliation with France is more popular today in Germany than at any moment before 1945.' Perhaps it was even more popular immediately after the collapse! But his message was plain, and he made it plain that he believed that German youth, above all, desperately wanted reconciliation and a new start.

Only a few days later Adenauer told the *Baltimore Sun* that France should be allowed to invest in up to 40 per cent of German industry, especially the steel industry. The United States might help France to find the necessary capital. He realized that France regarded the German steel industry as potential for a reorganized armaments industry and as a factor which disturbed the balance of power in Western Europe.[5] On March 7, 1950, Adenauer went much further; he proposed, in an interview with the *Inter-*

3............Professor Ludwig Erhard saw the dark side of this distrust of Adenauer's. He told the author that his outstanding characteristic was 'contempt for beings' (*Menschenverachtung*). Others of Adenauer's advisers (for instance, Hans Globke, Felix von Eckardt and Professor Walter Hallstein) put it very differently. The sum of their views, as expressed to the author, was that Adenauer was able to look at his fellow-countrymen dispassionately, evaluate their good and bad qualities, and guard against their weaknesses.

4............*Die Zeit*, weekly paper, Hamburg, November 3, 1949.

5............*The Baltimore Sun*, daily paper, November 7, 1949. These interviews had a significantly favourable reception from the French Gaullists. In the French National Assembly on November 24, 1949, Louis Terrenoire proposed a 'direct' Franco-German entente, without reference to other Western governments.

national News Service, a union between France and Germany which 'would give new life and vigour to a Europe that is seriously ill'. Britain and the Low Countries should be free to join this union as well, so that there should be no question of merely creating a Franco-German 'power bloc' in Western Europe. He urged Britain, in particular, not to 'ignore her responsibilities in Europe'.

Having once embarked on his policy of Franco-German reconciliation, Adenauer never relaxed his efforts to get something done. Thus one finds him, four years later, preaching this gospel with undiminished fervour – 'There is no European policy without France or against France, just as there can be no European policy without or against Germany. Franco-German understanding, in the fullest meaning of the word, is for me a matter of rational conviction, as much as it is a matter of the heart.' [6]

Adenauer's interest in Franco-German reconciliation was essentially a political one. He was not especially attracted by the 'French way of life', although he may have liked, to some extent, the idea of it. He simply knew very little about it. His mainly parochial existence for the greater part of his life meant that he had only been once to France before reaching the age of 70, and had then spent only two days in Paris, in conference.

His was, in the early post-war years, very much a lone voice. His Ministers said little on the subject of reconciliation, although at least one of them developed an unfortunate predilection for the bright lights of Paris.[7] One member of his Cabinet, Thomas Dehler, Minister of Justice, made a typically tactless speech at the Free Democratic Party Congress on January 22, 1950. He said that France was as much responsible as Germany for the First World War, and that French petty-mindedness at the Paris Peace Conference had helped to launch Hitler. The French High Commissioner, François-Poncet, wrote Adenauer a shocked letter, saying that one would 'expect more equity from a Minister of Justice'.

François-Poncet himself was not much of a help to Adenauer in his quest. Astute, politically amoral, alternately icily rude and wickedly gay, the French High Commissioner was the ideal tool for the human

6.............Interview with Ernst Friedlaender, broadcast nationwide. July 2, 1954

7.............This particular Minister, who obviously cannot be named, had an unhappy 'home life'. He formed the habit, when visiting Paris in Adenauer's entourage, of visiting what is euphemistically called a 'house of ill fame', allegedly just off the Boulevard des Italiens. On one occasion French Surêté officers followed him, interested only in his 'protection'. They were trailed, in turn, by one of Adenauer's staff, who duly reported the affair to the Chancellor. Adenauer's attitude was typical; he did not censure his Minister for profligacy but for stupidity. He ceased to be a candidate for a key post in the Cabinet for, as the Chancellor remarked, 'one can't have a Foreign Minister who is quite as indiscreet and silly as *that*'.

computers of diplomacy in the 'Quai d'Orsay', France's Foreign Ministry. He had posed as a 'friend' of Germany, notably during the Nazi era. But he was, in reality, the utterly loyal and ruthless servant of his country's interests. His part in the principal dispute, over the Saar (which was to hold up realization of Adenauer's statesmanlike aims), was negative and could have been catastrophic. He had a penchant for lecturing the Germans, as this extract from a speech made in Paris in April, 1950, shows: 'The German people has not learned the taste for liberty. It has more appreciation for command and obedience ... Liberty is a strong wine which it does not quite know how to handle and which goes to its head. It has no political experience.' If François-Poncet wanted reconciliation with Germany, it was with a dutiful Germany which had learnt its lesson and given way to every material French demand.

France joined the Soviet Union in blocking all early attempts to secure effective Four Power control of Germany, through centralized 'agencies'. France carried out industrial dismantlings in her zone of occupation with cold efficiency, and according to one (as it happened pro-French) politician, removed 22,000 machines in 1946 and 1947 which were not even on the dismantling list.[8] French dismantlings were so rigorous that two *Land* Governments resigned, of South Baden and South Wurtemberg. At the town of Kehl, on the Rhine, opposite Strasbourg, a German population of 13,000 was displaced by a French one of 9,000, and unilateral annexation was clearly envisaged. Much more important, France detached the industrial region of the Saar, with a population of one million, from her Zone of Occupation and made it plain that it was her intention to link the Saar economically with France, and later, perhaps, politically.

The dispute over the Saar was to become a burning and bitter issue, which could easily have wrecked Adenauer's hopes of Franco-German reconciliation and held up the much wider plans for Western European integration. Something should, therefore, be said about the origins of this dispute.

In the first place, the one million inhabitants of the Saar were Germans. In 1919 the French Prime Minister, M. Georges Clemenceau, had propagated a myth of the '150,000 Frenchmen in the Saar'. They did not exist. They were German in speech, political loyalty and way of life. But for France the area was economically interesting. In very rough terms, the Saar's output in coal and steel, if added to that of France, equalled the coal and steel output of West Germany. But if the Saar remained in West Germany, West German coal and steel capacity would be nearly double

8............Professor Carlo Schmid (SPD), who was half French, told this to the author on September 5, 1948.

that of France. The French, particularly after their severe loss of prestige in the Second World War and their very real sufferings, genuinely believed that there should be a 'fair balance' of industrial power between their country and the new Federal German Republic.

The Saar had already been detached once from Germany, in 1919. Its economic assets were then mainly sequestrated by France and had to be bought back by their previous owners in 1935, when the area was returned to Germany after sixteen years under League of Nations administration and after a plebescite in which over 90 per cent opted for Germany. The plebescite was conducted under international supervision, but was to some extent prejudiced by the weight of Nazi propaganda. Only 9 per cent voted for a continuation of League administration, and just half of 1 per cent for transfer to France.

In 1945 France imported into the Saar a number of former 'Saar separatists'. They included Johannes Hoffmann, who was brought from Brazil, and Edgar Hector, who had become a French citizen. Their return produced a standard music-hall joke in the Saar – 'What is the difference between 1935 and 1947? Answer: Last time we had the people who marched in, and this time the ones who ran out.'[9] These men were installed in control of pro-French, puppet 'Christian People's' and 'Socialist' parties. They were promised that no East German refugees would be allowed into the Saar, that there would be no dismantling of industry and that France would import foodstuffs (the Ruhr was close to starvation at this time), invest capital and promote trade. These were formidable bribes, and the people of the Saar were bound to be impressed by them.

In 1946, in January, the Saar was brought into a 'customs-union' with France. The ostensible reason was that this would stop imported French food from being 'smuggled' into the rest of Germany. At the same time, the Saar's coal-mines were, for the second time, sequestrated by France. In July, 1946, the actual area of the Saar was increased by 48 per cent, bringing its 'borders' up to the Luxemburg frontier and to the very gates of Trier. This unilateral action was modified in June, 1947, after the United States' and British Governments had raised objections; the eventual increase in the Saar's area was cut down to 32 per cent.

In October, 1947, Saar elections were held. They were a triumph for what German critics called *Magen-Politik* (stomach-politics).[10] A parliament of 50 members was elected, of whom 48 favoured France's policies. The other two were Communists, which did not make their connexion with a defeated, disgraced and bankrupt Germany any more respectable. Pro-German democratic parties were not allowed to exist. The French

9, 10.......*The Listener*, weekly, London. Article by Terence Prittie, March 13, 1952.

franc was at once introduced as the legal currency; the coal-mines were reorganized under a French directorate; and in January the French Military Governor was replaced by a High Commissioner, M. Gilbert Grandval. In April, 1948, the economic union of the Saar with France was officially completed. It had already been proclaimed in December under the new Saar constitution. Its 59th article read: 'The Saar is an autonomous state, organized on a democratic and Socialist basis. It is economically united with France.'

In June, 1948, the Saar's railways were put under French management, and in July Saar 'nationality' was created (a Saar flag, with a white cross superimposed on the French *tricouleur*, was to be added a year later). In December the teaching of French was made compulsory in all schools. Plenty of French aid was given during this period to an organization which called itself the *Mouvement pour la rattachement de la Sarre*, favouring annexation of the area to France. But France used this only as a make-weight to counter the first feeble stirrings of a pro-German spirit. The real French purpose was explained in the Chamber of Deputies in Paris by Jacques Bardoux: 'The Saar is not yet a free state; she must become one without delay. In fact, she must become a second Luxemburg.'[11] He should have added – 'but under total French control'.

To Germans concerned about the Saar, even more to the Saarlanders themselves, there was a nightmarish quality about this inexorable French drive towards the final severing of the Saar from Germany. Each new step was backed by a display of impeccable French logic, and explained away as being purely 'provisional'. Even though the United States had expressly declared in October, 1948, that the Saar remained legally part of Germany,[12] Germans felt helpless and forsaken. But in Germany, particularly in the right-wing parties and among the Free Democrats, voices began to be raised, first in consternation and then in increasing anger.[13]

Adenauer remained as discreetly silent as he could afford to be. Until he

11..........*The Listener*, weekly, London. Article by Terence Prittie, March 13, 1952.

12..........*Memoirs*, Konrad Adenauer, VOL 1, p. 232.

13..........Loudest among such voices was that of Prince Hubertus zu Löwenstein, whom the author once described as a 'German leprechaun'. A man of great charm and culture, the Prince was to embark on a series of personal demonstrations against French policy in the Saar. These led to his own arrest and temporary imprisonment, and to massive rallies on the borders of the Saar as expressions of solidarity with the Saarlanders. The Prince was mistakenly thought to be a knight-errant of lost causes. His views on the Saar proved to be right, and he assisted, more dramatically, in 'liberating' the island of Heligoland, which had been used as a bombing practice target by the British Royal Air Force.

Above Discussions with Bishop Dibelius at Königswinter, November, 1951.

With Sir Winston Churchill at Number Ten Downing Street, 1952.

Below Seated between Lord Avon and Dean Acheson at the Foreign Ministers' Conference of 1952.

Left, top to bottom: A private talk with US Secretary of State John Foster Dulles in Paris, December, 1953 – The State Visit to Paris, October, 1954: *Left to right* Professor Hallstein, French Premier Mendès-France, Dr. Adenauer and Professor Erhard – With Khruschev, Bulganin and Malenkov in Moscow, September, 1955 – Adenauer meets Indian Premier Nehru – Putting his favourite flower – a rose – in Harold Macmillan's buttonhole.

became Chancellor, this was easy. Afterwards he was much influenced by a meeting which he had in October, 1948 with the French Foreign Minister, Robert Schuman. In his own words, 'Schuman intimated that France regarded the return of the Saar to Germany as possible. France's main concern was the securing of her economic interests. Robert Schuman's views on this nerve-point of Franco-German relations had put my mind at rest. After our conversation I observed the greatest reticence on the Saar in my speeches and was under constant attack for it from Dr. Schumacher.'[14]

This was a rational explanation, up to a point. Writing nearly twenty years after the event, Adenauer was trying to prove that his Saar policy – in reality, an Achilles Heel – was justified. That the return of the Saar was 'possible' should scarcely have sounded reassuring, and one cannot accept Adenauer's statement that his mind had been 'put at rest' without reservations. Adenauer maintained, when later under fire, that he always realized that there could be 'no final settlement of the Saar question that prejudged the peace treaty'.[15] This was a laudable aim; but what the French were intent upon doing was to cut the Saar out of Germany with a surgeon's expertise. Probably, Adenauer should not be too much blamed; he only became Chancellor late in 1949, and on January 13, 1950, Robert Schuman paid his first visit to Bonn. Adenauer, according to his own account, expected the visit to 'yield the beginnings of a solution of the Saar problem'.[16] To say that he was wide of the mark would be an ultra-British understatement.

The Gaullist newspaper *Rassemblement* called it a 'jaunt' of Schuman, and depicted the *comme il faut* Minister, accompanied by a possé of cocktail-craving journalists and being ushered into Adenauer's presence by the 'familiar silhouette' of High Commissioner François-Poncet, 'now suddenly eleven years younger' – a blatantly obvious reference to his punctilious presence at the court of Adolf Hitler in 1939.[17] The Gaullists were in opposition to the Fourth Republic. Their denigration of François-Poncet was still understandable; they saw in him the small-time careerist and bureaucrat, who may have believed in 'Vichy France' and 'Collaboration' in his heart. Their disapproval of Schuman needs more explanation. For who was Robert Schuman, and why did a man preaching Franco-German reconciliation, as he did, merit their dislike?

Schuman was from Lorraine, born a German citizen as a result of the annexation of Alsace-Lorraine by Germany after the 1870 war. He grew up as a German, and German was the 'language of the home' of most northern

14, 15, 16 *Memoirs*, Konrad Adenauer, VOL 1, p. 233.
17..........*Rassemblement*, newspaper, Paris, January 21, 1950.

Lorrainers anyway. He served, as an officer, on the German side in the First World War. (His father, conversely, served as a French officer in the war of 1870.) In 1919 he became a Frenchman, for the first time, in early middle-age. To French Gaullists he was an object of suspicion, a 'frontiersman' with, almost certainly, the mixed loyalties which such people sometimes have. To most Germans he was something which they would, under normal conditions, have rejected with scorn – a German-speaking German, who threw in his lot with France when there was no easy alternative. Adenauer, of course, saw him very differently, as one of the latter-day inheritors of the 'Middle Kingdom' of Lothar, Charlemagne's grandson. In that historically remote 'Middle Kingdom' was the germ of Franco-German understanding. Schuman's Lorraine and Adenauer's Cologne had both belonged to it.

On January 14, 1950, Adenauer gave a luncheon for Schuman, at which the latter made a speech of some length, containing nothing beyond a vague commitment to Franco-German understanding. In this speech he called the Rhine 'our Rhine, the German and French Rhine', a geographical definition which takes no account of the fact that the Rhine does not, and did not ever flow through one single yard of French territory. After the speech came talks. In them, lasting two hours, Schuman expressed amazement over German doubts about the Saar. He defended every step so far made by France in the Saar and outlined some completely new ones. The French Government had drafted certain 'Conventions' with the Government of the Saar. They were the work of Maurice Couve de Murville, one of the most 'expert' brains of the Quai d'Orsay and a man who would have taught Machiavelli's Prince much about the art of diplomatic guile. Schuman was apparently able to accept these bogus 'Conventions' in good faith, which can be read as a tribute either to his credulity or his cunning. And he added a rider, that there should be no plebescite on the future of the Saar, since the 'people of the Saar did not want one'.[18] A convenient concession, this, to the principles of orthodox democracy, which was not being practised on the Saar.

Adenauer undertook some anxious soundings of Allied views about the Saar during the next few weeks. He got nowhere. Then on March 2 the French High Commissioner informed him, peremptorily, that the 'negotiations' between the French and puppet Saar Governments had been concluded in Paris and the 'Conventions' would be signed the very next day. So much for Schuman's sweet nothings about Franco-German understanding. François-Poncet, never a man to resist the temptation of landing a kick at a punch-drunk adversary, urged Adenauer not to become over-

18...........*Konrad Adenauer*, Paul Weymar, p. 339.

excited; in his words, 'The first impulse is not always the best, especially in a country as nervous and excitable as yours.'[19]

On March 4 Adenauer gave a Press Conference calling the Conventions a 'decision against Europe'. In his memoirs he skates over it, and does little more than mention a quite erroneous impression which he had gained, that the Saar conventions took away from Germany 'coalmines which we needed for an economic balance inside the Federal Republic'.[20] This was not a relevant consideration. Schuman made this clear in a Press Conference in Paris on March 6. He outlined four 'Saar Conventions', proclaiming an independent status for the Saar, its economic union with France and agreements on French control of the Saar's coal-mines and railways.

To inquiries from Adenauer, the British and United States High Commissioners gave it as their opinion that the 'Conventions' had only a temporary character and needed confirmation by a Peace Treaty. Addressing the *Bundestag* on March 10 Adenauer claimed that France was a 'trustee' in the Saar and that nothing which had been, or could be done would prejudice the terms of a final Peace Treaty. He asked for the restoration of democratic freedoms in the Saar, an overdue request. His speech was interrupted by Social Democratic deputies driving a right-wing member, Wolfgang Hedler, out of the Chamber for alleged anti-Semitic utterances and throwing him into the road outside, on his head. Democracy was thus vindicated in Bonn, more violently than even the sorely-tried Saarlanders might have desired.

Meanwhile, on March 7, Adenauer had given his first interview to the *International News Service*, urging Franco-German union, and repeated this in a second interview on March 21. In between, on March 16, General Charles de Gaulle gave his support to Adenauer's proposal. While welcoming the Saar conventions, he said that the Saar was of minor importance compared with the wider European interests which were at stake. He endorsed the idea of a Franco-German Union in historical terms which Adenauer well understood – union could revive and perpetuate the bygone empire of Charlemagne and could bring together again those 'Franks, Gauls and Romans' who had defeated Attila the Hun, and who were now confronted by a new menace to European civilization.

This was heady stuff, but it did not alter the awkward facts of Adenauer's position. The question of the Federal Republic's admission into the Council of Europe as an associate member had now to be settled. Adenauer had concealed the fact that his Government would not be formally invited

19..........*Konrad Adenauer*, Paul Weymar, p. 340.
20..........*Memoirs*, Konrad Adenauer, VOL I, p. 240.

to join, but would have to submit a request for admission.[21] At the same time, France was demanding that the Saar be admitted to the Council of Europe too. In his talks with the High Commissioners, and especially with François-Poncet, Adenauer now insisted on his Government being invited to join the Council of Europe; otherwise, he declared, the *Bundestag* would reject German membership. He asked, too, for an undertaking that the Saar's membership would be provisional, pending a final settlement of the Saar question at a Peace Treaty. But the French Government would not agree to this. For the moment there was impasse.

It was broken by Schuman. On May 9, 1950, he proposed a Franco-German Coal and Steel Authority which would be the framework for a wider Western European organization. It would pool the entire coal and steel output of France and West Germany and, incidentally, of the Saar as well. Two years earlier both Adenauer and the CDU Prime Minister of *Land* North-Rhine–Westphalia, Karl Arnold, had broached the idea of an international control body for heavy industry in which a number of West European countries could participate. Instead, there had been an international Authority for the Ruhr alone – a discrimination against Germany which was a not un-natural consequence of 'Hitler's War'. Schuman's proposal was sensational for, in the words of one authority, he 'broke completely with the foreign policy that since Richelieu's time had been based on the axiom that the weakness of Germany is the strength of France'.[22] It was a bold step, too, on economic grounds. The German coal-mines and steel works were more efficient than the French; for instance, the West German miner's output per shift was over one ton while the French was under three-quarters of a ton, and the pithead price of coal was $7 (£2 16s.) a ton in Germany against $10 (£3 6s.) in France. A pooling of coal and steel resources could lead to uneconomic French pits and plants going out of business, and French workers drifting to the same German industries to which they had been forcibly deported by the Nazis between 1940 and 1945.

Adenauer's reaction to Schuman's proposals was predictable. This was, as he saw it, a chance for a real breakthrough for the 'European idea'. It could help to create the European 'Third Force', which Adenauer did not envisage as the equal of the United States and the Soviet Union but as a powerful factor in the preservation of peace.[23] In addition, it would help Adenauer to bring the Federal Republic into the Council of Europe and would at least mitigate the adverse effects of the Saar Conventions which Adenauer, by implication, realized would have to be accepted. Adenauer

21..........*Memoirs*, Konrad Adenauer, VOL 1, p. 249.
22..........*France, Germany and the New Europe*, F. Ray Willis, p. 81.
23..........*Memoirs*, Konrad Adenauer, VOL 1, p. 258.

was given fresh encouragement by the real architect of the Schuman Plan, M. Jean Monnet, who paid a visit to Bonn on May 23. With his gift for cutting through red tape, Monnet decided that the countries who would be represented at the first 'Schuman Plan Conference', in Paris on June 20, should send no technical experts. This was to eliminate needless and wordy argument over details when the purpose of the Conference was to lay down general principles.

The publication of the Schuman proposals did, as Adenauer hoped, help the Federal Republic into the Council of Europe. The *Bundestag* vote in favour of entry was 220–152. Work on the Schuman Plan itself, was bound to take time and the West German delegation, led by Professor Walter Hallstein, was only able to report in March 1951, that the draft treaty for the 'European Coal and Steel Community' had been approved and initialled. Nor was this the end of the matter. On April 9 Schumacher made a fighting speech, pledging total SPD opposition to the Schuman Plan. He called it 'a second capitulation, six years after the end of the war' which would bring 'the perpetuation of the Occupation Statute for fifty years'.[24]

'I warn you,' Schumacher went on, 'not to misuse the word "European" in connection with a plan which embraces only this south-west corner of Europe.' This 'corner' was the home of 'capitalism, clericalism and cartels'. Clericalism (and there was an eerie echo of the Middle Ages in his voice), was 'rampant' in the Schuman Plan countries. Therefore he demanded the inclusion of Britain and Scandinavia (although Britain and the Scandinavian countries were showing no interest), and he took a final smack at France by describing the shipment of some dismantled machinery from the French zone to Czechoslovakia as 'immoral, senseless, primitive and a negation of all policy'.

Verbal barrages from Schumacher were nothing new. Two days later Adenauer was in Paris. It was his first official visit, and only the second time in his life that he had been there. The two main subjects to discuss were the Schuman Plan and the Saar. Adenauer set out to secure what concessions he could, knowing that it was impossible to induce the French Government to put its Saar policy into reverse. On the whole, he was reasonably successful.

From Schuman he secured a letter which contained this passage: 'The French Government declares that it acts in the name of the Saar, on the basis of its present status, but that it does not regard the signing of the (Schuman Plan) Agreement by the Federal Government as a recognition of the present status of the Saar... It does not consider that the Agreement

24..........The *Manchester Guardian*, Terence Prittie, April 10, 1951.

anticipates the final status of the Saar, which is to be settled by a Peace Treaty or by an agreement concluded in place of a Peace Treaty.' Adenauer's comment was that, like Schuman, who had already said something to this effect, 'in the treatment of the Saar question what mattered most was to keep one's nerves steady'.[25] He was writing long after the event and, reading between the lines, one may detect the hint of an uneasy conscience. For the troubles of the Saar were far from ended, and France's determination to separate the area from Germany in perpetuity was unshaken. There was nothing 'final' about Schuman's letter; it was essentially of tactical value in enabling Adenauer to continue along the path leading to total Franco-German reconciliation.

And it helped to secure the *Bundestag*'s approval of the Schuman Plan, on January 11, 1952, by 232 votes to 143. The Schuman Plan, which set up a six nation common market for coal and steel, consisting of France, Italy, the Federal Republic and the three Benelux countries had been signed in Paris on April 18, 1951. Without the implicit understanding that the status of the Saar was 'provisional' and would need to be confirmed by a Peace Treaty (which the Federal Republic, presumably, would only sign if the terms were fair), the right-wingers in the *Bundestag* must have rejected the Schuman Plan. In the *Bundestag* debate Adenauer intervened repeatedly; his two strongest arguments were that the Schuman Plan gave the Federal Republic 'industrial equality', and at the same time confirmed the demise of the mildly repressive International Authority for the Ruhr.

Adenauer's Paris visit had an added significance, in that it made a most pleasant personal impression on the Chancellor. The French Press was kind to him; so were his official hosts. His relationship with Schuman was by now good; the two men spoke the same political language, each accepting the element of foxiness in the other. Adenauer was charmed by Monnet, friendly, honest and at the same time prodigiously efficient, as a planner. He was given a stately luncheon at the Elysée Palace by President Vincent Auriol, and was shepherded round the 'sights' of the city by a calculatingly affable François-Poncet. The French can be truly unique in marrying intellectual interest with taste and elegance. It was no small thing that Adenauer was given the right food and wine; he was a connoisseur of wine, with a special taste for the lighter fine Moselles, but in London he had been given *Liebfraumilch*, a 'branded' name for any blend of only passably drinkable Rhine wines. Acting as his host at dinner in a small, exclusive restaurant, François-Poncet commented on his own menu – *Simple, mais correcte*. Adenauer, delighted, turned to one of his advisers:

25..........*Memoirs*, Konrad Adenauer, VOL I, p. 336.

'We'll have that on a plaque, above the door of the Foreign Ministry in Bonn!'[26]

Adenauer established fruitful contact with the other signatories of the Coal and Steel Community Agreement, Joseph Bech of Luxemburg, Paul van Zeeland of Belgium, Dirk Stikker of Holland and Count Carlo Sforza of Italy. The Chancellor was, to some extent, being 'initiated' into the European diplomatic world – whereas he had so far dealt with 'Occupying Powers' of whom only one, France, was European. Finally, Adenauer was deeply touched by a seven-page letter from a student, Simone Patouilles. She sent him her dead father's *Croix de Guerre* as a 'token of remembrance' of a visit which this girl believed was 'the first real step on the road to peace and salvation, not only for Germany, your fatherland, but for France and all nations that are conscious of the joint heritage which we have a solemn duty to defend'.[27] Taste and elegance are not the only virtues of the French; they are past-masters in the art of making a graceful gesture.

For the Saar, Adenauer – as he saw it – had done all that he could for the time being. The Saarlanders may have thought otherwise. The only pro-German political party, the Democratic Party of the Saar, had been banned in 1950, and the ban was formally confirmed early in 1952. In the meantime, no pro-German newspaper was allowed to be printed, and the import of German newspapers of the Federal Republic was limited to 80,000 a month, or one a day to every 300 Saarlanders. In the first five years after the war, more than 2,000 people were expelled from the Saar by the French and French-sponsored authorities, and even in 1951 around 200 heads of families were still debarred from returning home. Leading members of the press were dismissed because they were German nationals, and students of Saarbrücken University were refused permission to study at German universities, without any reason being given.

The Saar police, under the instructions of the Minister of the Interior, Herr Hector, a French citizen, invaded the privacy of the homes of people adjudged to be too pro-German. Telephone lines were systematically tapped and mail censored. The separatist Saar authorities had two reverses: pro-German 'Christian' Trade Unions split from the 'United' Trade Unions under government control, and the Vatican blocked all efforts to detach the Saar from the Roman Catholic see of Trier, in Germany. But, as one British newspaper put it, the 'Saar's economy was tied to that of France with all sorts of sailor's knots'.[28] Industries, railways, posts were

26..........Erwin Wickert, West German playright, author and diplomat, in private conversation with the author.

27..........*Konrad Adenauer*, Paul Weymar, p. 420.

28..........The *Manchester Guardian*, April 21, 1952.

all put under French management. The Saar's coal output was leased to France for 50 years, and plans were made for placing the important Warndt coalfields under complete French ownership, and for actually taking the coal out, under the frontier, on to the French side.

The Saarlanders remained, on the surface, phlegmatic. In Saarbrücken's few dingy night-spots, people bumped their beer-mugs to the rhythm of German march-tunes (paradoxically, they were increasingly unpopular in Germany itself), and sang about the 'long, hard road back to the homeland'. Just below the surface was a fatalistic belief that the Saar would go back to Germany some day. As frontiersmen, the Saarlanders admitted that they had the best of both worlds immediately after the war, consumer goods from France but the certainty that their origins and sentimental attachments would remain German. They managed to stay remarkably unresentful, but there was often more than a hint of unease in their outward manner.[29] Even frontiersmen cannot always conceal their feelings.

On November 30, 1952, carefully rigged elections were held in the Saar. All genuinely pro-German parties were banned. The Communist party was allowed to take part, and was denigrated by the Saar separatists as being both pro-German and anti-European. The official parties campaigned on a ticket of 'Europeanization' of the Saar, with Saarbrücken the prospective coal-dust 'capital' of Europe. The thought that this grubby, provincial town could be the capital of anything more than the tiny puppet-state of the Saar was patently absurd. Roughly 60 per cent of the electorate voted for the pro-French parties. Far more significant, over 25 per cent deliberately spoiled their ballot-papers on the advice of the loosely organized, pro-German political groups. One foreign journalist condemned the elections as 'undemocratic, unnecessary and unfortunate. They are undemocratic because three pro-German parties have not been allowed to take part. They are unnecessary because they could have been postponed until Franco-German talks had been given a better chance of succeeding. They are unfortunate because, whatever their result, they have embittered

29..........During numerous visits to the Saar the author had a number of personal experiences which indicated how people really felt. Typical was the demeanour of the staff of the French bank, the Crédit Lyonnais, established in Saarbrücken in 1945. Its members cultivated deliberately vacant expressions, avoided all but formal conversation with clients, and cast hunted glances when they did not know they were being observed. When the Saar declared itself in favour of reunion with Germany in 1955, the author was greeted in the bank with smiles, lively conversation and expressions of real joy. The bank employees, it turned out, were well-informed; they knew that the author was the only British correspondent from Bonn who had maintained that the Saar would return to Germany.

Franco-German relations and set back the process of European integration.'[30]

The same observer concluded that, failing the restoration of satisfactory conditions in the Saar, 'all talk of Europeanizing the Saar is claptrap, and these elections are no more than an ingenious way of wasting people's time and trying their temper'. In retrospect, that seems a fair summing-up.

The issue of the Saar was, for the time being, put on ice. In January, 1953, a new French Prime Minister, René Mayer, declared that acceptance of the 'European status' of the Saar was a prerequisite for acceptance by France of the Bonn and Paris Agreements. In May, the Saar Conventions were revised by France, but only in order to give the Saar the right to conduct its own foreign policy and maintain diplomatic representation abroad. The emphasis was still on making the Saar into a 'Second Luxemburg'.

For the next nine months to a year, the Saar, as a diplomatic issue, slumbered. It seemed to be a minor matter, compared with the question of European defence and budding European economic integration. Early in 1954 one finds Adenauer having earnest discussions with the American Secretary of State, Mr. John Foster Dulles, about what should be done over the Saar. But Dulles, with that childlike simplicity which occasionally interrupted moods dedicated and obsessive, frankly admitted that he did not understand the problem at all![31] He urged Adenauer to do whatever was necessary. One wonders if any Foreign Minister of any great power could ever have talked with more disarming candour.

By early 1954 it looked as if the French Government would settle for a 'Europeanized' Saar, economically linked with France. A French Foreign Minister, M. Georges Bidault, had proposed a 'statute' for the Saar, underwritten by France, Britain and the United States, and accepted by the Federal Republic as an integral part of a future German Peace Treaty. A Belgian, Van Naters, asked by the Council of Europe to produce some new thought, recommended the progressive reduction of customs duties between the Saar and Germany and the Saar's conversion into a kind of 'joint entrepôt' between France and Germany. In an interview given on March 17, 1954, the Saar premier, Johannes Hoffmann, put his own gloss on these plans. He said that Saarbrücken should be turned forthwith into the 'European capital'; he would build a 'European garden city' on the hills to the south of the place. The area should have a 'European statute' approved by France and Germany, and voted on by the Saarlanders in a

30..........The *Manchester Guardian*, Terence Prittie, December 1, 1952. In the December 2 edition of his paper the author noted that a great many 'ballot paper spoilers' wrote Saarbrücken Football Club 'as their contribution to an election which they regarded as despicable'.

31..........*Memoirs*, Konrad Adenauer, VOL 2, p. 263.

referendum. Economic union with France should be preserved until France and Germany 'grew together'.

The Special Correspondent of the *Manchester Guardian*, to whom Herr Hoffmann gave these thoughts, remarked on his astonishing optimism. He did not seem in the least worried that the Saarlanders had voted 90 per cent in 1935 for return to Germany; he was convinced that they would now be overwhelmingly in favour of the sort of 'Statute' which he envisaged.[32] Here was an important clue to subsequent French policy. The French trusted Hoffmann implicitly; he had, after all, been their nominee in the Saar for nearly ten years and he should surely have known how *his* people felt. In October, 1954 Adenauer had protracted talks with the new French Prime Minister, Pierre Mendès-France, who proposed a 'package' agreement, over German rearmament, membership of NATO and the Saar. The talks were among the toughest that Adenauer ever had to conduct. They lasted for four days, from October 19 to October 23.

Adenauer wanted to secure implementation of the Bonn agreement of May 26, 1952, and of the London agreement of October 3, 1954, on Western European Union. The latter had superseded the Paris agreement of May 27, 1952, which had been rejected by France. The Federal Republic was now to be brought into NATO, and the original idea of a European Defence Community had been abandoned. But more of this later.

Where the Saar was concerned, as his own memoirs show, Adenauer was now intent only on gaining political freedom for the sorely-tried Saarlanders and obtaining France's acceptance of his new doctrine – that the future of the Saar could not be decided without reference to its inhabitants. He was ready to play these two cards openly in his negotiations with Mendès-France; he held another turned face downwards, his original demand that the future of the Saar could only be 'finally' decided at a Peace Treaty.

Mendès-France held, as he saw it, one trump card too, which he now boldly played. This was his intention to refuse signature of the Bonn agreement and the London agreement on the now extended Western European Union, unless Adenauer met his minimum demands on the Saar question. These were that the Saarlanders should vote in a referendum on the Statute, which would effectively 'Europeanize' the area, and that a positive vote would be followed by the detachment of the Saar from Germany.

France was due to sign the two agreements, giving West Germany sovereignty and bringing her as a partner into Western Europe's military alliance, on October 23. On October 22 Adenauer and Mendès-France were closeted until after midnight, and the only small concession that Adenauer was able to wring from his agile and implacable adversary was

32..........The *Manchester Guardian*, Terence Prittie, March 18, 1954.

that free elections should be held in the Saar within three months of the referendum on the Statute. In his memoirs Adenauer maintained, much later, that he knew he could rely in the referendum on the Saarlanders, as 'good Germans', knowing how to vote.[33] In his view, 'The Saar was in no way sold. The population of the Saar was given the opportunity of freely developing politically and economically, freely forming a political opinion and implementing their chosen decision at a peace treaty.'[34]

This was simply not true. The Saarlanders were put under great pressure, with their economy linked with that of France, their half-fledged political institutions under the control of French-sponsored separatists and their morale undermined by nearly ten years of calculated if genteel intimidation. In addition, Adenauer distrusted Mendès-France, with his Napoleonic manner, his aggressive blue jowl and his total disregard for human factors.[35] He must have realized that if Mendès-France could 'Europeanize' the Saar, there was no slightest chance of it ever returning to Germany. At the same time, Adenauer got what he wanted most: France's signature of the enlarged Brussels Pact treaty on Western European Union on October 23, 1954, and French ratification of this and the Bonn agreement which followed in December. In May, 1955, the Saar referendum was fixed for October 22, 1955, and the *Bundestag* in the meantime approved the Adenauer–Mendès-France agreement on the Saar by a majority of 61 votes, while the Federal Constitutional Court in Karlsruhe decided that it did not infringe the West German constitution.

In May, too, Adenauer made one further concession, when he agreed on German participation in the building of a Moselle Canal, which would operate almost exclusively to France's benefit. For France the value of a Moselle Canal was obvious. Good Ruhr coking coal could be cheaply transported to the industrial area of central Lorraine. A small gesture was made in return by the puppet government in the Saar, which announced that it would abolish the censoring of mail and the tapping of telephone-lines. It had hitherto stubbornly denied that such things were being done![36]

The 'Saar question' was entering its final phase. On October 2, 1955, the three pro-German parties, which were now allowed to function without direct hindrance, formed themselves into a *Heimatbund*, a 'front' whose

33..........*Memoirs*, Konrad Adenauer, VOL 2, p. 377.
34..........*Memoirs*, Konrad Adenauer, VOL 2, p. 381.
35..........The ascetic Adenauer distrusted him for another, surprising reason. Mendès-France was a teetotaler. But in the early hours of the morning of October 23 he was so exhausted when arriving back at his hotel that he took a stiff whisky in place of his usual glass of milk.
36..........The *Manchester Guardian*, Terence Prittie, May 2, 1955.

main demand was that the Statute should be rejected and the Saar brought back into Germany. Even in the late spring the leader of the most active pro-German group, Heinrich Schneider of the Democratic Party, told the correspondent of the *Manchester Guardian* that he had not yet made up his mind whether to reject the Statute – this could mean the Saar reverting to more rigid French control. The new *Heimatbund* campaigned with the fervour which had been pent-up for years past, with a justified sense of grievance and with a solid and perfectly understandable German patriotism.

Yet up to the last moment the issue remained in doubt. At the beginning of October Adenauer was sharply criticizing the Hoffmann regime in Saarbrücken. But a few days before the referendum he told an amazed audience in Bochum that the Saarlanders would be wise to accept the Statute. He was getting wildly conflicting advice from his Foreign Ministry 'experts' and from the Ministry for All-German Affairs. The former believed that the Statute would be approved by the Saarlanders; the latter was convinced that it would not. Adenauer, obviously, decided that the Foreign Ministry was the better informed. He had some justification. According to one authority 'No one seemed to doubt that the Saar population would ratify Europeanization ... most observers assumed that it would be endorsed by 70–80 per cent of the electorate.'[37] In the event, 63 per cent of the Saarlanders rejected the Statute. On December 18, 65 per cent voted for the pro-German parties in *Land* elections. On January 31, 1956, the new Saar Government declared the area to be part of Germany, and formal reunion took place on January 1, 1957, as a result of an agreement between Adenauer and the French Socialist Prime Minister, M. Guy Mollet. This agreement was ratified by the French and West German Parliaments in December, 1956.

How badly did Adenauer miscalculate over the Saar? Some Germans who knew him well maintain that he did not miscalculate at all. Thus, Dr. Gerhard Schröder, Minister of the Interior at the time and later Foreign Minister, felt that Adenauer did his best, by securing a free vote in the Saar and by seeking a solution in the interest of Europe as a whole.[38] Adenauer's closest personal adviser, Dr. Hans Globke, agrees with this view. He could not tell the Saarlanders to vote against the Statute, without breaking the spirit of his agreement with Mendès-France, and his Bochum speech was

37..........*France, Germany and the New Europe*, F. Ray Willis, p. 204. The author's own experience in Saarbrücken gave him a diametrically opposite view, which he reported in the *Manchester Guardian*. The Saarlanders were at last beginning to talk freely, and the author predicted a 2–1 majority against the Statute.

38..........Dr. Gerhard Schröder. In a letter to the author, April 20, 1970.

made as a proof of his honest intentions towards France. He was, in addition, afraid of France's possible reaction to rejection of the Statute.[39]

Professor Walter Hallstein, another close confidant, believed that Adenauer regarded 'Europeanization' of the Saar as a 'fair contribution to Europe'. He was 'completely composed' when the result of the referendum was announced.[40] Dr. Erich Mende, later the leader of the Free Democratic Party, was convinced that Adenauer was ready to sacrifice the Saar – with the reservation that he was an expert political poker-player and may have hoped for a change of feeling in the Saar at the last moment.[41] The Ministry for all-German Affairs was horrified by Adenauer's Saar policy, and the Minister, Herr Jakob Kaiser, risked his neck politically by helping clandestinely to finance the pro-German parties in the Saar. As for the Saarlanders themselves, Hubert Ney, the leader of the pro-German CDU, subsequently praised Adenauer's policy of Franco-German understanding, which created the atmosphere of confidence needed for a fair solution of the Saar question. Heinrich Schneider, the leader of the pro-German party, the DPS, on the other hand, refused thereafter to attend any function where Adenauer was present.

Adenauer himself remained discreetly silent. Even in his memoirs he has little to say in his own defence, a fact which may be regarded as significant. On his 1965 election-tour, he visited the Saar, and looking down from the hillside at the great bend of the river at Mettlach, was heard to say, 'Thank God that it has been possible to reunite this land with Germany.'[42] That utterance, too, may have been significant; his conscience may have pricked him often in the years between.

The truth was that, in seeking a solution for the Saar, Adenauer was playing for much higher stakes – the return of German sovereignty, acceptance of the Federal Republic as a military partner of the Western Powers and progress towards a unified Europe. Nor should one forget that Adenauer had suffered a shattering reverse, when French shilly-shallying and intransigence led to the collapse of plans for the European Defence Community. One must, for a moment, return to that sombre and dramatic episode.

The Bonn and Paris agreements, it will be recalled, had been signed on May 26 and 27, 1952 by the U.S., Britain, France and the Federal German Republic. The Federal Parliament ratified them on March 19, 1953. By the summer of 1954 the three Benelux countries had ratified the Paris, or EDC

39..........Dr. Hans Globke, in private conversation with the author.
40..........Professor Walter Hallstein, in private conversation with the author.
41..........Dr. Erich Mende, in private conversation with the author.
42..........*Adenauer. Ein Porträt*, Will McBride and Hans Werner Graf Finck von Finckenstein, p. 101.

agreement; Italy's ratification was regarded as a matter of time. These countries were, of course, not party to the Bonn agreement. Only France had obstinately refused to take the plunge. In June the Foreign Affairs Committee of the French National Assembly rejected the EDC agreement by 24 votes to 18, and three days later, on June 12, the Laniel government fell. Joseph Laniel's place was taken by Pierre Mendès-France, of whom mention has already been made.

As Adenauer himself said: 'The European idea faded, because it was put on the shelf.'[43] For him the situation was maddening, and a certain testiness was creeping into his *Bundestag* speeches and Cabinet meetings. With immense difficulty he had repelled the SPD's anti-rearmament popular campaign, that party's efforts to block rearmament on constitutional grounds and the wayward jockeyings of some Free Democrats who sought to exploit the issue for party ends. Now Mendès-France submitted, in August, 1954, a fresh list of French conditions for ratifying the agreements. The EDC agreement was to be valid for 20 instead of 50 years, and could be terminated at one year's notice; the only 'integrated' armed forces were to be those on German soil; the EDC Headquarters was to be in Paris; all EDC decisions would have to be unanimous, implying a right of veto by any member; finally, any EDC member would be free to leave the organization if Germany were reunified.

Adenauer's view was that Mendès-France was trying to sabotage the EDC Paris agreement, but was afraid to do so openly.[44] History will probably judge Adenauer to have been right. With all his swagger and superficial panache, the French Prime Minister does not seem to have known his own mind. From August 19–22 Adenauer was in conference with Mendès-France and other EDC country leaders in Brussels. Adenauer urged action on the part of the French government but the talks ended in deadlock. When the meeting was over, Mendès-France had a personal talk with Adenauer, in order to play a confidence-trick on him which, for once, seems to have partly bamboozled the wary and suspicious Chancellor. Mendès told him that he was all in favour of the 'European idea', that his mother was Alsatian and German had been the language of his family-home (this was untrue), and that he would never let his 18- and 20-year-old sons be cannon-fodder in another war. He offered to put the EDC treaty fairly and squarely before the French National Assembly. Adenauer gave this proposal a cautious welcome; there was nothing else that he could very well do.

On August 29 and 30 the French National Assembly debated the EDC

43...........*Memoirs*, Konrad Adenauer, VOL 2, p. 271.
44...........*Memoirs*, Konrad Adenauer, VOL 2, p. 274.

treaty. The French Prime Minister put up a performance worthy of Pontius Pilate, washing his hands of the EDC agreement and leaving the bewildered and apprehensive members of the Assembly to make up their own minds. He said that he had failed to secure adequate military guarantees in the Brussels talks, and had not obtained the requisite assurances over either the Saar or the proposed Moselle Canal. By giving every reason for withholding support for the EDC agreement, while not calling for its rejection, Mendès-France helped to secure a vote of 319 against 264 against any resumption of talks on the EDC. The French National Assembly was unable even to give a straight vote on an honest motion, and reject the agreement. It merely swept it under the table.

According to one biographer,[45] Adenauer was so incensed that he did not speak for two days. Another authority suggests that the Chancellor seriously considered resigning.[46] Certainly, he was bitterly disappointed and very angry. He summoned the whole Cabinet to his Black Forest hotel on the Bühlerhöhe where he was holidaying and secured unanimous support for an immediate demand for the full restoration of German sovereignty. This demand was repeated in an interview which he gave to a special correspondent of the London *Times*. In it Adenauer claimed that France had wrecked the European idea, that the German people were being forced to turn to outdated nationalistic attitudes and to seeking an accommodation with the Soviet Union and that France's 'destiny' had been sabotaged by the French Communist Party.[47] A day or two later Adenauer told the US Secretary of State, Mr. John Foster Dulles, that the 'best Europeans' were in America.[48]

45...........*Adenauer. Democratic Dictator*, Charles Wighton, p. 206.

46...........*Aussenpolitik in Adenauer's Kanzler-Demokratie*, Arnulf Baring, p. 334.

47...........*The Times* of London, September 4, 1954. It is interesting that Adenauer turned at this moment to a British newspaper. He asked specially for Mr. John Freeman, the only British journalist with whom he had really friendly relations and to whom he gave his signed photograph. Adenauer's biographer, Weymar, called the interview the most controversial ever given by the Chancellor. After due reflection, Adenauer made no mention of it in his own memoirs.

48...........The author's personal relationship with Adenauer requires, perhaps, a footnote at this point. After a fair beginning in 1947 it ran, temporarily, into difficulty. The reason for this was an 'incident' at a dinner-party given by the Chancellor early in 1950. These dinner parties were given in order to influence the world press, and it was the second of this kind presided over by Adenauer. Each time, six foreign journalists were present, along with six Germans. Each time, Adenauer answered questions as soon as the coffee was served. The first such dinner was a complete success; Adenauer answered questions with great frankness and the journalists went home highly satisfied.

At the second dinner-party, a Swiss journalist set the ball rolling, asking

As it happened, the British Government saved the situation by springing into action in a way in which it had not done for years. Sir Winston Churchill, now in his third year of restoration as Prime Minister, sent Adenauer a message of encouragement in September (he had already told the House of Commons in July that the Western Powers must keep faith with the Federal Republic). On September 11 his Foreign Secretary, Eden, started on a lightning round of European capitals. His aim was to call a nine-power conference and extend the Brussels Pact to include the Federal Republic and Italy. Britain offered to keep four divisions and a tactical air force in Germany for fifty years – an unprecedented step for any British Government to take and one to which the British Treasury agreed with

---

whether it was a fact that British foreign policy was sadly weak. Adenauer agreed that it was, and gave his thoughts on the subject. The Swiss asked whether British foreign policy had not been lamentable since before 1914. Once again Adenauer agreed; he blamed Britain for short-sightedness in 1914, for complacency at the time of the Locarno Pact, and for cowardly appeasement of the Nazis by Chamberlain. His strictures were accompanied by a repetitive *Ja-Ja, Herr Bundeskanzler* from the correspondent of the London *Times*. I began to get both embarrassed and angry.

Still the Swiss persisted – had British foreign policy not been largely responsible for the Second World War, because the British failed to 'stop Hitler'? Once again Adenauer agreed, maintaining that Allied cowardice discouraged the German people from rising against Hitler and overthrowing his régime. Unwisely, I rose to my feet at this point and suggested that Allied threats against Hitler would merely have further united the Germans under him, and that primary responsibility for the war rested with the German government. I sat down again very quickly.

Adenauer was pink with annoyance. 'You were only a young man at the time, and I was then an experienced statesman,' was his riposte.

'Just who would have risen against Hitler, then?' I asked.

'Consider my own Catholic Centre Party,' was his answer. '*We* never gave up our struggle against Hitler, even when Britain and France did at Munich!'

'But isn't it a fact,' the *Christian Science Monitor* correspondent asked, 'that your own Catholic Centre Party voted to a man for the Enabling Act which gave Hitler the powers of a dictator?'

There was a hideously long, strained silence and then a buzz of meaningless chatter. The dinner-party dispersed prematurely (there was never another one of its kind). As I was leaving, Adenauer's Press Chief advanced on me and informed me that I would never again be 'received' by the Chancellor. I had shown a total lack of consideration for an older man – and a statesman at that – and gross discourtesy by getting up at his dinner-table (he was right about that). I protested that I could not sit silent while my country was accused of responsibility for the Second World War; my protest was shrugged aside.

The 'incident' had a comic sequel. For two years I was, where Adenauer was concerned, 'in disgrace'. Then, suddenly, I was invited to tea, along

Left top to bottom: Willy Brandt, Lord Mayor of Berlin, reporting on his world tour at the Schaumburg Palace, March 11, 1959 – The Chancellor confers with Sekou Touré, President of Guinea, November 1959 – Received by the Emperor and Empress of Japan at the Imperial Palace, Tokyo, March 1960 – De Gaulle and Adenauer: a portrait displayed during the French President's State Visit to Germany, September, 1962 – The two elder statesmen – *Below, right*: Welcoming US President Kennedy at Cologne Airport, June 23, 1963.

Appointed a Knight of the German Order in the Andreaskirche, Cologne,
March 10, 1958

the greatest reluctance. Eden caught a guilty French Government and parliament on the rebound; the Brussels Pact was signed on October 3, 1954. West Germany was to be re-armed within the framework of NATO, and German armed forces were, provisionally, fixed at twelve divisions, with 1,350 aircraft and small naval units. On October 22, at the Paris Conference, the Federal Republic was invited to join NATO, on undertaking not to produce atomic, biological or chemical weapons. The Occupation Statute was abolished and the High Commission formally ended its work. West German sovereignty was fully restored.

All this happened at breath-taking speed. It showed what could be done when one Power – in this case, Britain – knew exactly what it was doing and possessed a first-class diplomat, in this case Sir Anthony Eden. French delaying actions, including an effort by Mendès-France to introduce an arms-control scheme of impossible complexity, were swept out of the way. French feelings of guilt were illustrated yet again at the end of December, when the National Assembly ratified the Bonn agreement by 380 votes to 180, the Saar agreement by 368 to 145 and the acceptance of the Federal Republic into NATO by 287 to 256. Having once caught France on the rebound, Eden rushed negotiations ahead so fast that the French had no time to collect themselves for a new delaying action. For once, the Quai d'Orsay was found wanting.

Adenauer never ceased to regret France's rejection of the EDC agreement. He firmly believed that it would have been an immensely significant step on the road to full European integration. Some acute observers held a different view; they thought that the proposed European Army would not have functioned properly and that France would have used the maximum diplomatic ingenuity to delay its organization – even if she had agreed to it in principle. More operative, perhaps, is the thought that by settling the thorny questions of West German sovereignty and rearmament, and the future of the Saar, the European Powers removed all serious obstacles to Franco-German understanding and reconciliation. How to complete his own contribution to it became one of Adenauer's main preoccupations during the next decade and up to the time of his death.

---

with the correspondents of the London *Times* and *Daily Telegraph*. Adenauer received us with his usual courtesy, and we stayed about an hour and a half. Shaking hands with *The Times* correspondent at the door, he complimented him on his paper's editorial policy. He then praised the *Telegraph* correspondent's reports on the German domestic scene. Finally he turned to me and dismissed me, with sardonic abruptness. He had not forgotten. Years later, after a number of useful meetings, he relented a little. Shaking hands with me, he looked me very straight in the eye. With a twinkle in his own he said: 'I think we understand each other rather better now.' (*Ich glaube, wir verstehen uns jetzt ein bischen besser.*)

10 Consolidation

During his lifetime it was said, often enough, that Adenauer took too little interest in home affairs. If one compares him with contemporary European statesmen – say Harold Macmillan in Britain, or Charles de Gaulle in France – one is bound to notice Adenauer's lack of public pronouncements on domestic matters. The Federal Republic has been described as an economy without political being. Its Governments were confronted with greater economic and social problems than any in Europe – one need think only of the rebuilding of its shattered cities, the resettling of around twelve million refugees, the 'equalization' of war-losses, the adjustment to democracy by eliminating the remnants of Nazism or the settlement of the war-crimes question. Had Schumacher and the SPD come to power, they might well have concentrated almost exclusively on problems like these, building or trying to build a new society in Germany and cold-shouldering the Western Powers until they got what was necessary out of them.

The truth is that Adenauer did take a keen interest in domestic as well as foreign policy problems, with the exception of what he regarded as strictly and academically economic and financial matters. But his interest was mainly concentrated into Cabinet sessions, when he himself laid down the guide-lines of foreign policy but allowed Ministers to explain and then get on with their own concerns. Ludwig Erhard was given a totally free hand in the economic field (according to Erhard, Adenauer did not merely take next to no interest in economics – 'he did not want to know about such matters').[1] Adenauer had a succession of highly efficient Ministers of the Interior – Gustav Heinemann, Robert Lehr and Gerhard Schröder. They needed it is true, periodic support, but little direction. The same was true of Ministers for Refugees and Housing. Material problems were going to be solved in any case, however daunting they looked at the outset. For the immense energies of the German were being concentrated on regaining a material well-being which had not been theirs since 1914. They intended to make good the privations of two World Wars, of the Weimar period of financial and economic instability and near-chaos and the Nazi Era of 'Guns before butter'.

Whole books have been written about the 'German Economic Miracle'.

1............Professor Ludwig Erhard, in private conversation with the author.

Relatively little need be said here. But one or two domestic problems, political as well as economic, require brief mention. The first is the resettlement of the refugees.

Nearly ten million arrived in West Germany after 1945 from the lost provinces east of the Oder–Neisse line, from the Sudetenland in Czechoslovakia and from German 'colonies' in other East European countries. To these were added, progressively, several million inhabitants of Communist East Germany. This second category of refugees voted, as it was said, 'with their feet'; they came to West Germany of their own accord, leaving homes and belongings, often their families too, in what was still part of Germany. Such was the effect of Soviet-enforced Communist tyranny.

This great flood of refugees produced a number of problems. First, they had to be resettled, given new homes and jobs and integrated in the West German community. They produced a considerable, if only temporary unemployment problem – the figure reached two million early in 1950. The Federal Government could not finance resettlement out of normal tax revenue. So special legislation was framed and the so-called 'Equalization of War Burdens' bill became law in August 1952, providing for a 50 per cent levy on all surviving pre-war capital assets, 'spread' over a period of thirty years. This money financed Government spending on the refugees, to the tune of around 3,000 million Marks a year. Total government borrowing for refugee resettlement was eventually more than 50,000 million Marks.

The refugees, mostly tough Easterners or thrifty Sudetenlanders, helped to deal with their purely material difficulties in a decade. But they saddled the Federal Government with two awkward political obligations. The first was the need to consider the 'refugee vote' at any and every election. The second was to maintain, as an article of faith, the right of the German refugee to return – at a date unspecified – to his old 'homeland'. Adenauer had played a purely constructive role in guaranteeing the right of every German refugee to seek asylum in the Federal Republic (the Allied High Commissioners at one stage began to question this principle[2]), and he helped to push through the 1952 'Equalization of War Burdens' bill. But the political implication of the refugee question was a manifest liability. The importance of the refugee vote forced him to do a deal with the BHE Refugee Party. His refusal to consider recognition of Germany's existing eastern frontier eliminated all possibility of a forward-looking policy in Central Europe. For this refusal meant that the Polish–East German frontier, the so called 'Oder–Neisse line', remained purely

2............*Konrad Adenauer*, Paul Weymar, p. 406–7.

provisional. Poland had to rely on Soviet 'protection' as a counter to possible German claims for the return of the lost eastern provinces, and the Soviet Union exploited Poland's fears. The East German refugees kept these claims alive and Adenauer, always a realist when allowed to be, was obliged to pay lip-service to refugee slogans which were often provocative and very quickly became meaningless.

That the refugee problem did not become a social running sore may have been primarily due to the single-minded concentration of the average refugee, like the average West German citizen, on finding a good job, working very hard at it, earning well and putting money aside, buying some of the things that he had wanted for so long – a home, equipment for it, a car, even a holiday abroad. This concentration on material well-being, culminating with the breakthrough into the 'affluent society', acted as an inoculation against social unrest. It might, for instance, have been thought that the Trade Unions would have become a focus of opposition to Adenauer and his CDU-led government. For by 1951 the West German Trade Union Congress (DGB) had a membership of over six million, and had united within itself the pre-Nazi socialist, liberal, Christian and 'free' unions. It was, potentially, one of the most powerful labour organizations in the world, precisely because it was so unified.[3] The DGB wanted socialization of heavy industry, the institution of a 'welfare-state' along the lines followed in Britain and the strict curtailment of the political power of industrial and commercial pressure-groups. Adenauer was rigidly opposed to socialization and the welfare-state, and regarded the existence of pressure-groups as a natural symptom of capitalism.

The DGB may have been impressed by Adenauer's insistence on the creation of property for the lower income-groups, on the building of cheap 'social' housing in spite of its inflationary effect[4] and by his keen interest in obtaining financial credits for the refugees and other 'have-nots'.[5] But a more important factor may have been Adenauer's personal friendship with Hans Böckler, who became chairman of the DGB in 1949. Adenauer always possessed the ability to cultivate a good working relationship with people of very different character from his own; John Foster Dulles was probably the outstanding example of this. Hans Böckler was the son of a miner and began his working life in the metal industry. He 'belonged' to the Ruhr. Heavily-built, slow of speech, phlegmatic, wedded heart and soul to the cause of social justice and the interests of the working class, Böckler was a kind of German Ernest Bevin, but mercifully lacking Bevin's argumentative disposition and built-in prejudices. He

3............*Konrad Adenauer*, Paul Weymar, p. 393.
4............*Adenauer und die Folgen*, Hans Joachim Netzer, p. 154.
5............*Adenauer und die Folgen*, Hans Joachim Netzer, p. 155.

knew Adenauer of old, and served for years on his pre-war Cologne City Council. This may have been the link between them which really mattered; in addition he was an exact contemporary, born – like Adenauer – in 1876.

In the German Trade Union movement Böckler possessed the same unquestioned authority as Adenauer did in the political field. Under his firm and logical direction the Unions developed a practical philosophy on the all-important question of wage-claims. The wild inflation of the Reichsmark in the 1920s and again after the Second World War had taught a worthwhile lesson. This was that any wage–price spiral was damaging to the economy and promoted inflation. Broadly speaking, wage increases had to be linked with increased productivity – something which British Governments only began to understand in the 1960's and were still not implementing as a policy by 1970. With certain exceptions, German Unions adopted the view that it was better to accept a little at a time rather than force through major wage increases by the threat of strike action. This view was based on the belief of Böckler and his lieutenants that the Unions and the working class which they represented must take their full share of responsibility in rebuilding the German economy.

Böckler and the Unions believed, understandably, in the socialization of the heavy industries. But they were not prepared to make this a crucial issue while, from 1948 onwards, the German economy was being restored to normal. Socialization disappeared from the CDU programme well before the party became the hub of Adenauer's first Government. Without saying so, Böckler tacitly dropped the socialization issue, and concentrated instead on securing *Mitbestimmung*, or co-partnership, for workers in heavy industry.[6] Over this issue, indeed, the strike weapon was threatened, but in January, 1951 Böckler and Adenauer reached agreement on the bones of a 'Co-partnership Law'. The law was drafted by a small committee of Trade Unionists and Cabinet Ministers, Adenauer himself, Erhard and the Minister of Labour, Anton Storch. It was put before the *Bundestag* on February 14, 1951. The law applied only to the coal and steel industries. It provided for three-man boards of management (*Vorstand*), of whom one would be a Trade Union nominee and would be in charge of labour relations, and for five workers' representatives to sit on the eleven man supervisory boards (*Aufsichtsrat*). The eleventh man on the supervisory board would be chosen jointly by management and workers.

On April 10, 1951, the Co-partnership Law was passed by the *Bundestag*. Adenauer's part in this was crucial. His Free Democratic and German Party allies decided to vote against the Bill; it was passed by the combined votes of the CDU and the Opposition SPD. Clearly, the coalition was put

6............*Gar nicht so Pingelig*, Walter Henkels, p. 161.

under a severe strain.[7] One should not forget that it had a majority of only 14 in the *Bundestag*. The defection of even the small German Party might have left Adenauer II short of a bare majority. The Chancellor took a calculated risk. Only the help of the SPD made Adenauer's risk pay off; the Co-partnership Law became a key factor in maintaining a degree of industrial peace enjoyed by no other West European country during the next twenty years. This achievement probably outweighs Adenauer's relative lack of interest and action in the overall social field; in 1952 he ordered a select committee to draw up recommendations on the radical reorganization of social security, jettisoned its report and thereafter allowed social legislation to be framed on a patchwork basis.[8]

One other facet of Adenauer's relations with Böckler requires mention. From him Adenauer obtained a ready understanding of the Federal Republic's need to align itself with the Western Powers, make real friends of them and, in order to do that, fulfil the demands of the High Commission while always seeking to modify them through negotiation. The SPD opposed the Petersberg Agreement in both its original and revised versions, the International Authority of the Ruhr and the Schuman Plan for a Coal and Steel Community, the Federal Republic's entry into the Council of Europe and West German re-armament and its corollary, the Bonn and Paris agreements. Only over re-armament did the SPD have a fair measure of Trade Union support. Böckler was as much convinced as Adenauer that the Federal Republic should opt unequivocally for a place in the West European community. He showed, in general, a more mature political judgment than did Schumacher.

Industrial peace and a fair degree of understanding with the Trade Unions are achievements for which the first Adenauer Government can claim a great deal of credit. It had another, more unusual social problem to deal with – what Germans called the *Uberwältigung der Vergangenheit*, the coming to terms with the country's Nazi past. This problem took two forms; a vast number of ex-Nazis had to be 're-integrated' in the life of the community, and a small and fractious minority of ex-Nazis had to be combated on the political front. Both these problems were unique to Germany.

The Western Powers had carried out a far-flung programme of so called 'de-nazification' in their Zones of Occupation. Every Nazi Party member was examined by panels set up by the Western Powers and subsequently kept in function under German direction, placed in some particular category (major offender, minor offender, passive member), and in special cases denied a citizen's normal privileges or even imprisoned for criminal

7............*Konrad Adenauer*, Paul Weymar, p. 401.
8............*Adenauer und die Folgen*, Hans Joachim Netzer, p. 159.

activity as a Nazi. To 'root out' Nazism was, of course, an impossible task; the best that could be done was to label all dangerous ex-Nazis and debar them from positions of authority and influence. Even this objective was over-ambitious. In the view of one observer: 'De-nazification was drawn out far too long and became so tortuous and inequitable that it finally defeated its own purpose. The sufferers were almost invariably the "small Nazis" with harmless records but too little wherewithal to bribe their way through the de-nazification panels. Such absurdities were perpetrated as forcing widows to "de-nazify" their dead husbands. Quite understandably, reasonable Germans were revolted by the futile attempts to purge the entire population.'[9]

The confusions of de-nazification resulted in a psychological reaction and a swing of feeling in favour of people who were being called upon to answer for the 'crime' of blind obedience to the government of the day, or of mere complaisance. Adenauer took a practical view of the question of de-nazification. Never much impressed by its efficacy, he used its findings as pointers to the selection of suitable people for his governmental apparatus. His object seems to have been to keep obviously unrepentant ex-Nazis out of all important posts, but not to disqualify a candidate for a particular post simply because he had once been a member of the Nazi Party. A future Minister of the Interior, Gerhard Schröder, suggests that Adenauer had a constructive approach to this vexed question – he regarded someone as 'cleansed' from his Nazi taint if he was wholeheartedly prepared to serve a democratic government and democratic cause.[10]

Ex-Nazis found their way back into government service from the outset of the Federal Republic's existence. As early as December, 1949, Adenauer had to order the suspension of a Dr. Ehrich from the Ministry of *Länder* Affairs; he turned out to have been one of the former high-ranking Nazi officials nicknamed the 'Golden Pheasants'.[11] In May 1950 he ordered the formation of a cadre for the future German Foreign Service, and learnt that its organizer, a Dr. Haas, had chosen 14 ex-Nazis among his 31 executive staff.[12] Two years later, it transpired that 39 out of 49 senior members of the re-formed Foreign Ministry had belonged to the Nazi Party.

Adenauer was subsequently to install ex-Nazis in the Cabinet, and among his personal staff. His original view on this matter remained, indeed, absolutely unshaken. Only ex-Nazis who had committed criminal acts or who remained unrepentant could not be entrusted with positions of responsibility and influence. Adenauer was often bitterly criticized for

9............The *Manchester Guardian*, Terence Prittie, June, 195(.
10...........Gerhard Schröder, in a letter to the author, April 20, 1970.
11...........*Germany Divided*, Terence Prittie, p. 228.
12...........*Germany Divided*, Terence Prittie, p. 227.

this attitude. His critics claimed that he should have reserved good jobs for 'good democrats' and that he was himself guilty of a complaisance which discouraged Germans from 'overcoming' the past. Perhaps these critics tended to forget that vast numbers of Nazi Party members were 'non-political', that the infant Federal Republic needed all the help that it could get from the best available administrators, and that Nazism would be 'bred out' of the German people by good government, intelligible aims and a democratic ideal. Adenauer believed in creating positive factors, as the best means to counteract the negative elements of a situation which he had inherited.[13]

Just how the problem of the ex-Nazis should have been tackled is a question which probably cannot be answered for a long time to come. The answer will depend on the way in which the German community develops. In 1971, one can only say that the signs are that Adenauer's optimism will be proved justified. Of course, the sheer passage of time has helped and the gradual disappearance of ex-Nazis, as they have died off.

Of more immediate relevance was the question whether ex-Nazis could win their way back to political power and threaten the still semi-fledged democracy of the Federal Republic. A few ex-Nazis crept into the first Federal Parliament, when four million votes went to parties of the Right with a fairly obvious nationalist flavour. Ex-Nazis began to win positions of influence in the Free Democratic and BHE Refugee parties too. But there were only two serious threats to West German democracy up to 1953. The first was in 1951–2, when a blatantly neo-Nazi 'Socialist Reich Party' was organized by the ex-Nazi General Otto Remer. The second was in 1953, when Werner Naumann, the former right-hand man of Hitler's Propaganda Minister, Josef Goebbels, sought to infiltrate right-of-centre parties, with the hope of engineering a future political coup. He wanted thus to infiltrate, then overset the democratic government of the Federal Republic.

First, the SRP and General Otto Remer. The latter was in command of the "Wachregiment" or "Guard Regiment" in Berlin at the time of July 20, 1944, plot against Hitler. He marched his men to the Defence Ministry and arrested the conspirators. With his wolfish jaw and glaring eye, Remer was the epitome of Nazi dynamism and virility. He began organizing the SRP in 1950. He dressed up his followers in jack-boots and

13..........An angle on Adenauer's attitude towards ex-Nazis was given by the US High Commissioner, Mr. John McCloy (letter to the author, December 23, 1969). He compared Adenauer's attitude to that of Abraham Lincoln after the American Civil War towards American southerners. Adenauer had no sympathy for real criminals, but some for 'passive' Nazis. He did not want the German people to be divided irrevocably into 'sheep' and 'goats'.

riding-breeches and formed them into strong-arm squads. A tub-thumping orator in the Goebbels tradition, he demanded the rehabilitation of ex-Nazis, the restoration of the 'honour' of the ex-soldier, the release of war-criminals and the condemnation of 'those blackguards', as he called the few surviving members of the German Resistance to Hitler. He and his followers ridiculed the German democratic parties and vented scorn and hatred on the Western Powers.[14]

On May 7, 1951, the SRP won 16 seats in the *Land* Lower Saxony elections and polled 400,000 votes. This was 11 per cent of the poll, a frighteningly large proportion for a party campaigning openly on a Nazi ticket. Other extremist parties collected another 27 per cent of the votes, suggesting that almost two of every five voters in this backwoods land were opposed to democratic rule. A few months later, the SRP was almost equally successful in *Land* elections in Bremen. The Federal Government took appropriate action. Remer was indicted for slandering the men of the Resistance and sent to prison for three months. The SRP was banned as an anti-democratic organization. Its lineal successor, the 'German Reich Party' (DRP) did not attract anything like the same support. Never again in Adenauer's life-time was a serious challenge mounted by an extremist political party.

The second serious threat to West German democracy came two years later. Towards the end of 1952 the Free Democratic Party set out to capture a larger proportion of the extremist vote by drawing up a so-called 'German Programme', calling for more centralized government, a cut-down of the *Länder* from 11 to 5, the end of 'discrimination' against ex-Nazis, an amnesty of political prisoners and a more independent foreign policy. The 'German Programme' looked certain to become official party policy, but the liberal wing of the FDP attacked it vigorously and much of it was discarded. The FDP Conservatives thereupon entered into negotiations with a small group of unrepentant ex-Nazis led by Dr. Werner Naumann. These people were, in Naumann's own words, 'dedicated' to the ideal of single-minded service to a new 'Leader'. They had links abroad with Nazi 'cells', and a following in intellectual circles and the press.

Naumann's plan was to infiltrate at least three political parties, of which the FDP was the most important, prior to the 1953 Federal elections. In this way Naumann hoped to organize a body of around 40–50 *Bundestag* members who would hold the balance in the *Bundestag* once the elections were over, and might even be able to dictate the course of German history. The subsequent rallying of extremist elements in the *Bundestag* would, Naumann hoped, enable him to form a single nationalist Party which

14..........*The Listener* London, Terence Prittie, June 28, 1951.

would emerge as the victor in the 1957 elections. Trained by Goebbels, utterly ruthless, with a sinister charm and suave, mock-modest manner, Naumann was potentially far more formidable than Remer and the rough-neck hobbledehoys of the SRP.

The British Intelligence services, well-fed with news by their representatives in Düsseldorf, informed the High Commissioner, Sir Ivone Kirkpatrick, about all operative details of the 'Naumann conspiracy'. On January 14, 1953, Kirkpatrick ordered the arrest of Naumann and seven of his leading followers. With wry humour, he called them 'a pirate gang, which intends to seize the ship by gaining control of the bridge, then board other ships and collect a nice little navy'.[15]

Kirkpatrick knew exactly what he was doing. His action would cause him some unpopularity, but this was preferable to letting matters slide, or even to placing the onus of action on Adenauer and his Government. In a personal interview, he had this to say: 'I see no reason why we should wait for these gentlemen to put into action all the plans which they have religiously committed to paper. Those plans speak for themselves and their purpose is, in their own words, to achieve those ideals for which they once stood and for which their comrades fell.'[16] British Intelligence officers collected thirty crates of documents from the houses and offices of the Naumann group. They included detailed studies of Nazi methods of administration and plans for the future – a great deal more evidence than was needed to show that this was the last plot during the Adenauer era aiming at a Nazi restoration.

Adenauer talked to members of the British press about the affair on January 19. The Chancellor was in a difficult position. His authority had been by-passed, even if with the best of motives. Two dangers were apparent to him; he might be blamed for failure to act on his own when German democracy was in danger, or for allowing the British authorities to rope in some relatively harmless German citizens (thus the highly respected *Frankfurter Allgemeine Zeitung* wrote that the men of the Naumann group were 'only merchants' and the British had feared their commercial competition). Adenauer said on January 19 that the Naumann group had been under careful observation for at least six months. He had discussed its activities three times with Kirkpatrick, but had only been notified of the impending arrests on the evening before they took place.[17] He agreed that there was one obvious advantage in action being undertaken by the British, rather than the German authorities; the former could hold them without legal charge and examine them at their leisure.

15..........*Germany Divided*, Terence Prittie, p. 324.
16..........Sir Ivone Kirkpatrick, in private conversation with the author.
17..........The *Manchester Guardian*, Terence Prittie, January 20, 1953.

There was a certain ambivalence in Adenauer's further remarks. He said that the British action had been carefully timed, and that there was no 'ulterior motive' behind it. His view was that Naumann and his cronies should not be allowed to return to political life, but at the same time he believed that they would have had small chance of successfully infiltrating right-wing parties. As a footnote to this press conference Adenauer complained about a public opinion survey carried out by the American High Commission and published almost simultaneously with the uncovering of the Naumann conspiracy. This survey showed that 44 per cent of Germans who had been questioned thought there was 'more good than bad' in Nazism, whereas only 34 per cent thought Nazism bad, without qualification. Adenauer said that he had not been informed in advance of publication – the survey was a confidential document and would not normally have been published at all – and that a survey in which only a 'sample' of 1,200 people had been questioned was misleading.[18]

Adenauer broadcast to the nation on January 30, 1953, repeating his view that the Naumann conspiracy had not been a serious danger for West German democracy. He told the interviewer that it 'would be a miracle, if no convinced National Socialists existed any more in the Federal Republic. Neither fools nor criminals die out as quickly as that. But a real threat to the security of the Federal Republic does not exist in any way. There can be no question of a new seizure of power. A few Nazis still don't add up to National Socialism ... We have a viable, a watchful democracy.'[19] A year later Adenauer was to say that not only did a re-created National Socialism not exist in Germany, but he would guarantee that this would not happen.[20] On the whole, his optimism was justified, at least during his tenure of power. Neo-Nazism in its open political form ebbed after the ban on the SRP was imposed; it ceased to be a danger lurking in the shadows after the Naumann conspiracy.

The neo-Nazis represented one aspect of the problem of 'overcoming' the past. Another was the need to redress, in whatever way possible and to whatever extent possible, the atrocious sufferings inflicted by Hitler's Germany on the Jews. It should, of course, have always been clear that there was no question of 'compensation' being paid so that a balance-sheet could be drawn and the German account with the Jewish race 'squared'.

18 A grotesque circumstance was that the US High Commission had published the results of this survey by mistake. It annoyed Adenauer even more than the arrests, as it seemed to be designed solely to embarrass him, only a few months before Federal elections were due to take place.

19 Interview with Ernst Friedlaender, broadcast nation-wide, January 30, 1953.

20 Broadcast on Suedwestfunk, August 6, 1954.

Six million European Jews, all of them innocent of any crime or offence, had been murdered. Countless others had been subjected to hideous sufferings. The thriving Jewish community in Germany, once 600,000 strong, had been reduced to a pathetic remnant of around 30,000. The Jewish community in Poland had been even more cruelly decimated, from 4 million to under 25,000. The Jewish community in Austria was virtually wiped out.

Compensation, in the ordinary sense of the word, was impossible. What was possible was to make the maximum material restitution, within Germany's available means. Adenauer seems always to have understood this, and to have regarded this task as his duty. Dr. Nahum Goldmann, the President of the World Jewish Congress, appears to question this with the statement that 'Soon after the end of the war, a group of German Jews persuaded Dr. Adenauer to state that the German Government was prepared to make an appropriation of ten million dollars. This offer was, of course, declined as completely inadequate.'[21] Although he was later to play a leading part in negotiating a financial settlement with Adenauer, Goldmann appears to have been mistaken. The true story was published by the Jewish *Allgemeine Wochenzeitung* in Düsseldorf shortly after Adenauer became Chancellor. The editor, Karl Marx, quoted Adenauer as saying:

'The State of Israel has come to represent Jewry as a whole. The Federal Government, as an earnest of its intention to make amends for the wrongs which Germany have inflicted on Jews from all over the world, will put development aid to the value of ten million Marks at Israel's disposal.'[22] This was a purely preliminary gesture; Adenauer was prepared for the negotiations which were to come.

During October and November, 1949, Adenauer had several discussions about restitution to the Jews with his personal adviser, Herbert Blankenhorn. The latter, an astute observer of foreign opinion, believed that generous treatment of this matter would do more to restore Germany's good name than anything else. Early in 1950 Blankenhorn had a meeting with Noah Barou, who was acting for the newly formed 'Conference on Jewish Material Claims against Germany'. This confirmed his view, although there was a setback a few weeks later when German and Israeli Parliamentarians met at a Congress in Istanbul, and Itzhak Ben-Zvi, later Israel's President, complained that it was an insult to every honest and decent human being to have to meet Germans and pretend to ignore the terrible crimes committed in their name. Later during the Congress, a

21..........*Memories*, Dr. Nahum Goldmann, p. 254.

22..........*Allgemeine Wochenzeitung*, Düsseldorf, November 11, 1949.

meeting was arranged between Ben-Zvi and two German delegates, Heinrich von Brentano and Carlo Schmid. Although he spoke German perfectly, Ben Zvi insisted on the discussion being in French.[23]

On July 1, 1950, Dr. Hendrik van Dam, the General Secretary of the 'Central Council of Jews in Germany', prepared a memorandum for negotiations between Israel and the Federal Republic. Among other things he proposed that an Israeli Reparations Mission should be sent to Germany.[24] There the matter rested for the moment. One reason for this was the Israeli Government's feeling that most Israeli citizens would regard the idea of accepting any help from Germans as utterly repellent. But on March 12, 1951, the Israeli Government found a formula; it asked for a contribution from both German states for resettling refugees in Israel (the East German State was never to pay a penny).[25] Its note was sent via the four Occupying Powers. It pointed out that from 1938 to 1950, 380,000 European Jews had sought refuge in Israel, and it proposed a round sum for resettlement of $1,500 million (£600 million).

There could have been a further setback to hopes of agreement, as a result of a meeting which Adenauer had in Paris in April 1951 with the Israeli Ambassador, Dr. Maurice Fischer, and the representative of the Israeli Ministry of Finance, Dr. David Horowitz. According to one authority, they reproached Adenauer with a long catalogue of German crimes and implied that the Federal Republic was under a legal obligation to make restitution.[26] Adenauer might have taken offence. He did not; and on September 27, 1951, he addressed the *Bundestag* on the subject of restitution and announced the intention of his Government of working out details in conjunction with the Government of Israel.

On November 30, 1951, the Israeli Government sent a second Note to the four Occupying Powers. It gave Jewish material losses as a result of Nazi action at $6,000 million (£2,400 million), and repeated its proposal of compensation of $1,500 million. Adenauer's answer was to invite Goldmann to meet him on December 6, at Claridge's Hotel in London.

There, Goldmann stated Israel's case. When he had finished, Adenauer told him: 'While you were speaking, I felt the wings of history beating in this room.'[27] The Chancellor, who reminded Goldmann of 'a medieval Gothic figure', promised to give him a letter explaining his intentions. This was done, and Goldmann was later to pay tribute to his 'undeviating straightforwardness and logical consistency'. Goldmann, admittedly,

23, 24, 25. Dr. Rolf Vogel, in the Wiener Library Bulletin, 1968–69, VOL XXIII, No. 1.
26..........*Konrad Adenauer*, Paul Weymar, p. 433.
27..........*Memories*, Dr. Nahum Goldmann, p. 260.

seems to have failed to state a figure for compensation; he had gone to London intending to propose $1,000 (£400 million).[28]

The next move took place in March, 1952, when German and Israeli delegates met at The Hague. Their discussions were fitful and, on the Israeli side, sometimes heated. The German delegates received their instructions from the banker, Dr. Hermann Abs, who evidently regarded the negotiations as an occasion for detailed financial haggling, without any suggestion of moral responsibility on Germany's side. According to Goldmann, Abs at one stage made a derisory offer of 100 million Marks, and at another, claimed that the Federal Republic could produce no foreign currency until there was an overall settlement of German pre-war and post-war debts.[29] Adenauer intervened by summoning Goldmann and Abs to Bonn on June 10, 1952, and the sum to be paid by the Federal Republic was finally fixed at 3,000 million Marks ($762 million), payable mainly in kind over a period of twelve years. Another 500 million Marks were to be paid to the Jewish Conference on Claims for distribution to Jews living outside Israel.

The Agreement was signed in Luxembourg on September 10, 1952, and ratified by the *Bundestag* on March 4, 1953, after a debate in which three small parties (including the Communists) opposed the Bill, while the bulk of the FDP abstained from voting. Adenauer's personal interventions in the debate, and his readiness to make common cause with the SPD Opposition, resulted in the Bill being approved by 288 votes to 34, with 86 abstentions. In the next twelve years the Agreement was loyally fulfilled by the Federal Republic. Among the capital equipment which Israel received, and was allowed to select through its Reparations Mission established in Cologne, were 60 passenger ships, 41 merchantmen, four tankers, a floating docks, a steelworks and a copper smelting plant. Adenauer's final comment on the Agreement was contained in a broadcast made on November 12. In it he said that threats which had been made by the Arab League to break off trading relations with West Germany would have not the slightest effect – 'There are higher things to think about than good business deals. And we want a different sort of Germany from the Germany of Hitler.'[30]

The story of the Luxembourg Agreement deserves two footnotes. The first relates to the attempt on Adenauer's life in March, 1952. Two schoolboys, Werner Breitschopp, aged 12, and Bruno Beyersdorf, aged 13, were

28...........*Memories*, Dr. Nahum Goldmann, p. 260. Goldmann told Weymar (*Konrad Adenauer*, p. 439) that he did ask for $1000 million. The letter which Adenauer sent to Goldmann mentioned no figure.

29...........*Memories*, Dr. Nahum Goldmann, p. 265–6.

30...........The *Manchester Guardian*, November 13, 1952.

handed a parcel on the Bayerstrasse in Munich by a stranger. It was addressed to 'Dr. Konrad Adenauer, Federal Chancellery, Bonn', and they were given a tip and asked to post it. A bogus 'sender's' name was given as 'Dr. Berghof, Frankfurt-am-Main'.

The two boys asked a tram official what they ought to do with the parcel; they sensed there was something strange about being handed it on the street to post. The official told a traffic policeman, a police car was called and the boys and their parcel were taken to police headquarters in the Ettstrasse. There the explosives expert of the Munich fire-brigade, Karl Reichert, tried to dismantle the parcel. It exploded, and he died four hours later from his injuries.

The grateful Chancellor entertained the two boys to tea on April 1, thanked them and presented them both with gold wrist-watches. Bruno said later: 'This Herr Dr. Adenauer was very nice to us, like a father. He wasn't at all haughty or stuck-up. You can talk to him just like you can to anyone.' The police offered a reward, but the only clue was a letter posted in Geneva on March 29 to several French newspapers, claiming that 'a book filled with explosives was sent to Dr. Konrad Adenauer, the Chancellor of the Nation of Assassins'. According to his official biographer,[31] Nahum Goldmann confirmed that the man who handed the parcel to the two boys was a Jewish fanatic. Adenauer knew that the Federal police had established his identity, but refused to blame the Jews in any way. He refused, too, to let the incident deter him from supporting and signing the Luxembourg Agreement.

The second footnote has to do with German–Israeli relations after the Luxembourg Agreement. According to one of his closest advisers,[32] Adenauer tentatively offered Israel diplomatic relations with the Federal Republic at the time of the Agreement. The offer was turned down. Adenauer bided his time; he believed that Arab intransigence – the states of the Arab League made it plain that they would regard opening diplomatic relations with Israel as a highly unfriendly act – would diminish if the Federal Republic were a sound and useful commercial partner. But Adenauer feared that damage done to Arab–German relations would damage Western interests in general in the Middle East. At least once, according to this same adviser, he asked the American Ambassador in Bonn, Mr. David Bruce, to sound his Government on the subject of the Federal Republic seeking diplomatic relations with Israel. American advice was allegedly against this proposal. Once again Adenauer waited, although he had by then learned that Israel was ready to open diplomatic relations – through Felix Shinnar, the head of the Reparations Mission in Cologne.

31..........*Konrad Adenauer*, Paul Weymar, p. 448.
32..........Dr. Hans Globke, in private conversation with the author.

Meanwhile reparations continued to be paid, not only direct to the State of Israel but to individual claimants to compensation under the terms of Federal legislation. In 1962 one expert, Hendrik van Dam, was to assess total West German payments at 24,000 million Marks.[33] Eight years later Nahum Goldmann estimated that the final 'bill' would be from 50,000 to 60,000 million Marks.[34] This, as far as it went, was satisfactory. In addition, contact had been established in 1957 between the West German Minister of Defence, Herr Franz-Josef Strauss, and the Director-General of the Israeli Defence Ministry, Shimon Peres. Between them they worked out details of a secret Arms Agreement, under which the Federal Republic bought the Israeli 'Uzi' sub-machine gun, Israeli mortars and small arms.[35] The Federal Republic, again, granted Israel loans for the development of the Negev desert, after Adenauer's meeting in March 1960 with the Israeli Prime Minister, David Ben Gurion, at the Waldorf-Astoria Hotel in New York. The Federal Republic became a firm friend to Israel, even though the establishment of full diplomatic relations had to wait until 1965, when Adenauer's political career had ended.

Adenauer's work in helping to restore something approaching normal German–Israeli relations may have owed a little to sentiment – Louis Hagen, a Jew, had been his close friend in the early days after he became Lord Mayor of Cologne, and Daniel Heinemann, a Jew, had come to his aid financially when he was being persecuted by the Nazis. By contrast, Adenauer's work in restoring normal German–American relations probably had no sentiment behind it, for he believed implicitly that the United States was the natural leader of the Western world, and that Europe needed American help and friendship for an indefinite period to come. His personal relations with the United States took a significant step forward in April, 1953, when he paid his first visit there.

He set off by sea from Le Havre on April 2 in the liner, the *United States*. His entourage included his daughter Lotte, his State Secretary, Professor Walter Hallstein and his Press Chief, Felix von Eckardt. The crossing was extremely rough, which did not affect Adenauer in the slightest. He was in mischievous mood too. One morning he passed the open door of Hallstein's cabin, and saw 'the Professor's' thick brief-case lying there invitingly. He opened it, found that it contained highly confidential documents and thereupon annexed and kept it for two days – while the distraught Hallstein suffered badly from both the weather and the knowledge that he had lost his brief-case.[36]

33..........*The Realities of Post-war Germany*, Walter Stahle, p. 288 *et seq.*
34..........*Memories*, Dr. Nahum Goldmann, p. 280.
35..........Rolf Vogel, The Wiener Library Bulletin, 1968–69, VOL XXIII, No. 1.
36..........*Ein unordentliches Leben*, Felix von Eckardt, p. 207.

The ship docked at New York on April 6. Adenauer was 78 years old but he had a stripling's enthusiasm for action. He was not expected in Washington until the next day. In a few hours he took in the Metropolitan Museum (he was already forming his own private collection of paintings) and a visit to his old friend Daniel Heinemann at his home in Greenwich, Connecticut. In the evening a dinner party at the Union Club, and then on to Washington.

In Washington he met President Eisenhower and the members of his Administration. It was an emotional occasion; one must remember that Eisenhower had decided, two years before, to 'forgive' the 'new' Germany and was now riding the tide of his own graciousness. There was plenty of goodwill too, and Adenauer demonstrated his 'total lack of any sort of inferiority complex'.[37] From the President he went on to the State Department for talks with John Foster Dulles, whom he regarded by now as an old friend. This was a strange friendship, and one which can only be explained by the fortuitous attraction of opposites – Dulles impulsive, temperamental but at heart a down-to-earth, low-church New Englander; Adenauer calm, reserved, symbolic of a much older civilization than that of the United States, suspect – absurdly – of being the agent of the Vatican. Perhaps the strongest bonds which united them were their dutiful belief in God and their hatred of Communism. Yet that would seem a peculiar base on which to build the warm friendship and trust which united them.

His self-control and crystal clarity of thought did most to make Adenauer's American visit a complete success. At the National Press Club in Washington he made a deep impression on his hard-bitten audience, answering question after question with gravity and good humour for more than an hour. At Arlington National Cemetery he made an imposing figure, laying a wreath of red roses on the tomb of the 'Unknown Soldier' and standing straight-backed while the massed military bands played the *Deutschland-Lied* (Adenauer had caused some controversy by reintroducing the old national anthem while visiting West Berlin in April, 1950). In San Francisco he addressed a gathering of 700 at the Commonwealth Club. He was delighted with the city, and told Hallstein that the Foreign Ministry could reserve the post of Consul-General there for him, when he was no longer Chancellor.[38]

His sang-froid was well illustrated on the flight from Washington to San Francisco. His plane had to land at Denver to refuel. But there was a snowstorm raging, and the pilot made two unsuccessful efforts to land,

37...........*Ein unordentliches Leben*, Felix von Eckardt, p. 212.
38...........*Ein unordentliches Leben*, Felix von Eckardt, p. 230.

taking off again each time when he found himself overshooting the runway. There was too little fuel to go on over the Rockies to San Francisco and, while everyone else remained deathly still, one of the journalists travelling with the Chancellor's party began to jabber with fright. Adenauer sat placidly in his corner, reading a book on botany.[39]

His tour took in Boston, Chicago and Ottawa. From his talks with America's leaders Adenauer brought back two clear, correct impressions – his Federal Republic was adjudged to have come of age at a tender four years, and the United States Government would henceforth treat it as an equal partner. The threat of the two super-powers, the United States and the Soviet Union, doing a deal at Germany's expense, was banished, virtually for good. (It must be admitted that this particular fear did recur in Adenauer's mind once or twice.) Adenauer was charmed by everything that he saw in America – although a little surprised at being slapped on the back and called 'Good old Connie!' in Washington. His comment – 'Sometimes they're just children.'[40]

His return to Germany was triumphal. He flew straight to Hamburg, where the CDU Party Conference had just begun. There, he retailed his experiences in America with obvious satisfaction and was given a tumultuous reception. The Federal elections were only five months away and campaigning would start in July. Before that happened, there were to be sensational events in East Germany (see Chapter 12), but the East German rising would have no direct effect on the West German elections. For Adenauer had already decided on his Election programme: prosperity, security and 'no experiments'. Prosperity could be spelled out in detail; industrial and agricultural output doubled in three years, nearly half a million new homes being built each year, new jobs provided for two and a half million refugees, a strong currency and rising living standards. Security was represented by the growing friendship with the Western democracies, and the Federal Republic's prospective place in the European Defence Community (the demise of the EDC was still a year away). 'No experiments' was a useful slogan, and Adenauer judged the psychology of the electorate correctly. Things were going well for the man in the street, and he knew it.

During the election campaign it became clear that Adenauer was the central figure; people were going to vote for or against him, rather than for Parties or principles. His only great rival, Schumacher, was dead; his mantle had fallen upon the worthy but inadequate Erich Ollenhauer, only to smother him. Adenauer campaigned tirelessly, never getting to bed

39..........*Ein unordentliches Leben*, Felix von Eckardt, p. 228.
40..........Sir Christopher Steel, in private conversation with the author.

before 2 a.m. and preserving his good humour. Towards the end of the campaign he told von Eckardt: 'Do me a favour, and don't sit in the front row at my meetings. When I see your bored face, I can't think of a thing to say.'[41] He drew huge and enthusiastic audiences, and he played up to them, with touches of *Koelsch* or Cologne dialect drollery interspersing heart-warming production figures and sombre warnings of disaster if power were placed in the hands of the lesser mortals of the SPD.

Several factors helped Adenauer and the CDU. The first was the disarray of the SPD. Deprived of their leader, they were reduced to putting the face of a dead man on their election posters.[42] Their policy of 'Opposition at all costs' to every Western plan or proposal did not commend them to an electorate which, especially after the failure of the East German rising, felt isolated in the front line of the Cold War. The SPD's jaundiced view of the movement to secure European unity was especially unpopular among the youth, to whom 'Europe' was a more appealing idea than nationalism in a divided country. And the SPD were still tarred with the ideological Marxist brush.

No other party but the SPD could have taken votes away from the CDU in 1953. The FDP had been shaken by the Naumann conspiracy, and the battle between its right and left wings was grinding along. There was no party to the right of the FDP with anything to offer the electorate, save outdated cracker slogans and woolly-minded appeals to futile and fading resentments. The small Parties were bound, too, to suffer from the change in the Electoral Law. In 1949 it was possible to pick up seats in a single *Land*, with a vote of over 5 per cent in it. In 1953 the 5 per cent clause applied to the Federal Republic as a whole – unless a party managed to win a seat by direct election. To give an example – a small party gaining over 5 per cent of the votes in Bavaria would, up to 1953, have been given a Bavarian seat in the Federal Parliament. This seat would not have been won by direct election, but would have been awarded from the reserve list. After 1953 the reserve list seats were awarded on a 'national' basis and a small party with a local following in only one, or a very few of the *Länder* would get no reserve list seats at all. Right-wing nationalists, congenitally incapable of uniting, were placed at a disadvantage which has kept them out of the political arena in Bonn ever since.

The elections took place on September 6, 1953. Adenauer cast his vote on a beautiful morning in Rhöndorf. He retired to bed that evening, having asked to be woken at his usual hour of 6.30 the next morning. An over-enthusiastic State Secretary telephoned him at 5, and his Press Chief

41..........*Ein unordentliches Leben*, Felix von Eckardt, p. 272.
42..........The *Manchester Guardian*, Terence Prittie, September 4, 1953.

did the same thing half an hour later. They were both chagrined when Adenauer answered, with a note of asperity in his voice, just 'Thank you very much', and then went back to sleep.[43]

For the results were sensational. Four out of every five adult West Germans had voted. The CDU share of the poll had jumped from 31 to 45 per cent. As a result, moreover, of the 'wasted' votes for parties which secured no seats, the CDU now had an absolute majority in the *Bundestag*, 244 out of 487 seats. The party had made big gains in parts of the country where it was already strong in 1949, and inroads into the SPD strongholds of Hamburg, Hanover and Hesse. Of the other parties with *Bundestag* seats, the SPD with 150, the FDP with 48 and the German Party with 15, had only just about held their own. The remnant of the Catholic Centre Party was left with three seats in the Rhineland, and the new BHE Refugee Party polled 6 per cent of the votes and secured 27 seats.

It was an impressive victory, and very much a personal one for the man who had once called himself 'seventy per cent of the Cabinet'.[44] In a flowery and flatulent tribute Hans Zehrer, the editor of *Die Welt*, wrote that, 'We are witnessing in Germany today a mysterious process by which an entire people is fusing with the person of its Chancellor.' More appositely, *Time* Magazine selected Adenauer as its 'Statesman of the Year'. In Washington the State Department issued an official statement to the effect that – 'The results of the elections in West Germany constitute an overwhelming endorsement by the German people of the policies of the Adenauer Government: that is to say, of German membership in the European Community, of democratic reconstruction, and of uncompromising opposition to Soviet designs.'[45] The Federal Republic was no longer a temporary makeshift; it had consolidated itself as the first durable German democratic state. In that sense, this may have been Adenauer's greatest hour.

43...........*Konrad Adenauer*, Paul Weymar, p. 505.
44...........*Watcher on the Rhine*, Brian Connell, p. 245.
45...........US State Department, September 7, 1953.

11 Chancellor-democracy

It would be a reasonable generalization to say that the five years, 1948 to 1953, were the most productive of Adenauer's life. During those five years he took part, always in the key role, in organizing the Christian Democratic Party, framing a West German constitution, regaining sovereignty for the Federal Republic, earning for it a place in the Western Alliance, laying the foundations for lasting friendship with the traditional foe, France, and winning two Federal elections. It would be an equally fair comment that the next five years, from the end of 1953 to early in 1959, were those of his greatest authority and prestige. His critics would claim that his mastery was too complete; it encouraged him to mould West German democracy in his own image and to govern by means which were only nominally democratic. It was a five year period during which Adenauer, with much more justification than Louis XIV of France, could have said *L'état c'est moi.*

Much has been written about his personal routine. In fact, there was nothing especially interesting about it. He rose early – most great statesmen have done likewise (an obvious exception was Churchill). He had more reason than most to leave his bed at 6 to 6.30 a.m. – he remained a bad sleeper all of his life and depended, rather too much, on sleeping tablets. From 8 to 9 a.m. he dictated letters to his personal secretary in his Rhöndorf home. Then, half an hour for breakfast, with a couple of newspapers to read, and off at 9.30 to his Bonn office in the Palais Schaumburg, happiest when his chauffeur was getting there in record time. Unless the *Bundestag* were in session, he was at his desk until 1.30 p.m., save on Wednesday morning when there was a three-hour Cabinet meeting.

Lunch was served to him, alone, in a small room next to his office. He ate, as always, frugally, and he cared nothing for large, official luncheons (One of his favourite phrases was *Man muss masshalten* – the equivalent of the English proverb, 'Moderation in all things.') After lunch, an hour's rest, changing into pyjamas (Churchill had the same habit). Then came a cup of tea and a fifty minute walk, nearly always with State Secretary Hans Globke. Adenauer's devotion to his daily walk was equalled by his need of fresh air – an open window was to him a necessity. And he had a certain contempt for non-walkers – hence his remark when his Foreign Minister, Heinrich von Brentano, came panting up the 53 steps to the front door of his Rhöndorf home, 'And this is the new German youth I'm always hearing about!'[1] Typically, Adenauer always 'invited' Globke for their stroll in the gardens of the Palais Schaumburg, with a *Wollen wir, Herr Globke?* ('Shall we?'). This grave courtesy was as natural to him as fresh air and brisk exercise.

On a normal working day their walk ended at around 3.30 p.m. and from then until 8 p.m., Adenauer was at his desk again, sitting always very upright yet surprisingly relaxed. On a normal day, he drove straight home, ate a good but not heavy supper, read books and listened to music until bedtime at 11.30. But sometimes there was company; sometimes, too, there were late night debates in the *Bundestag*, when the Chancellor remained wary and alert until all was over, putting to shame men not much more than half his age who slept in their seats or sought periodic refreshment in the *Bundestag* restaurant.[2] Adenauer was very much a creature of habit, but dining with him, one gained the impression that he did not mind a break in his routine at all – as long as there was some purpose to the occasion.

He had his idiosyncrasies and his foibles. One of the more pleasant was to take Ministers, or others who disagreed with him, aside, have a bottle of good wine opened, and chat over it. Then, when everyone was in good humour after downing his glassful, he would suggest that 'we start all over again on the business'. His Minister who described this little manoeuvre, called him 'a master of diversionary tactics'.[3]

He believed in a calculated display of good manners, but done 'naturally'. He always rose to greet a guest, rose to see him out and saw him to the door. He shook hands as if he meant it, looking one straight in the face. He won many admirers by doing this with an easy grace. It was not only his advisers, like his Press Chief, Felix von Eckardt, but even political opponents, who used the phrase – *Er war ein richtiger Herr*: (He was one of nature's gentlemen.)[4]

Like the Spanish he paid particular attention to his footwear, and was liable to cast a pitying and disapproving glance at unpolished shoes on the feet of his Ministers. Though he had a penchant for dark colours where his personal attire was concerned, in the world around him he

1.............*The Unquiet Germans*, Charles Thayer, p. 128.
2.............Members of the British House of Commons complain frequently about the catering service. The food in the *Bundestag* restaurant has always been eatable, but the service there is as bad as anything outside the frontiers of the Soviet Union and the confines of its grisly Intourist hotels.
3.............Dr. Erich Mende, in private conversation with the author.
4.............Felix von Eckardt and Prince Hubertus zu Loewenstein, in private conversation with the author.

loved pastel shades, and his particular delight was a Rhineland sunset, with the sky shading into tones of palest gold, primrose, pink, blue and grey. He watched many sunsets, looking westwards across the Rhine from his house. To trap a moment of beauty, he knew, is to catch part of the purpose of life.

Adenauer's love of flowers, and particularly roses, is so well-known that nothing new can be said about it. This love began when he was a small boy, and it remained with him for the best part of a century. There are many photographs of him smelling a rose, savouring its fragrance and loving it, maybe paying a tribute to it later in that inimitable, slurred and yet slightly nasal Cologne accent. Once again, one must guess that it was his love of beauty which gave him his very special appreciation of flowers. For him, clearly, an essential part of life; he was lucky.

Adenauer's instinctive attachment to the family unit was, obviously, much more significant. For it led to him forming what was, in effect, a second political 'family' in the Federal Chancellery. Patriarchal in his rule as well as his private life, Adenauer has often been criticized for ruling through advisers, rather than through his Cabinet, let alone through Parliament or party. The truth was that Adenauer believed, where overall policy was concerned, that he knew what had to be done. Where details had to be filled in, he turned naturally to certain advisers whom he trusted implicitly. The men of this inner Cabinet, or political family, played an immensely greater part in the running of the country than the general public realized.

The least important of them was Otto Lenz, a man with a brilliant legal brain and a deep, almost obsessive interest in news-media. Lenz was not, at first sight, the sort of man whom one might expect Adenauer to choose as a State Secretary in the Chancellery. He had been a member of the Catholic resistance to Hitler and was closely connected with Adenauer's early rival for leadership of the CDU, Jakob Kaiser. He was, initially, a 'Berliner' and wanted the CDU headquarters in the old Reich capital. He was immensely gregarious and often indiscreet.[5] His unpunctuality and unpredictability made the sedate, sober Hans Globke's hair stand on end. He built up a number of information media, dabbled in secret service work, interfered incessantly with the Federal Press Office and eventually shook and then lost the Chancellor's confidence when he angled to create a 'Super-Ministry' for news and information at the end of 1953 and caused a Government crisis.

Lenz was the cuckoo in the Chancellery nest. He became, quite simply, too active for the Chancellor to keep track of his plans. This, rather than the sharp reaction of the High Commissioners and the foreign Press to

5............*Aussenpolitik in Adenauer's Kanzler-Demokratie*, Arnuld Baring, p. 8.

his 'Super-Ministry' plan, was the reason why Adenauer got rid of him. He was the only man in whom Adenauer placed real personal reliance who was occasionally undependable.

This could not be said of Herbert Blankenhorn, on whom Adenauer leaned heavily in the early post-war years. Blankenhorn stood perhaps closest to Adenauer during the formation of the CDU, and became its General Secretary in the British Zone. From there he moved to the post of Adenauer's personal adviser. Emotional, vivacious, well-versed in foreign affairs and with a nimble mind, Blankenhorn was more interested in policy-making than influencing public opinion. He was an apostle of *Erfüllungspolitik* – in colloquial terms, playing ball with the High Commissioners – and he was of particular use to Adenauer in keeping contact with the foreign press. (He had less to do with the West German press, whose members distrusted him because he had once been a member of the Nazi Party.) Adenauer valued perhaps most of all his urge to get things done – 'Tell that to Herr Blankenhorn,' was one of his favourite phrases.

Blankenhorn had a wonderful memory, and this was a characteristic shared by most of Adenauer's intimate circle of advisers. Another man to whom he could turn with invariable success was Professor Walter Hallstein, rector of Frankfurt University from 1946 to 1948 and recommended to Adenauer by the Swiss economist and academician, Wilhelm Röpke.[6] Hallstein was precise, pernickety, sometimes garrulous – although not in the Chancellor's presence. He was probably the most convinced 'European' in Adenauer's entourage, with tremendous faith in the ideal of political as well as economic union. His immense knowledge of international law was valuable, as was his easy mastery of foreign languages.

With his sly wit and periodic spells of mischievousness, Adenauer needed a 'butt' among his close advisers. He selected Hallstein unerringly, for 'the Professor' had a kindly disposition and became what one of Adenauer's daughters called a *dankbares Opfer* (literally, a willing victim).[7] He never resented Adenauer's jests; indeed, they were not ill-intended, and the two men remained the best of friends up to the Chancellor's death.

Felix von Eckardt, Adenauer's only long-standing and really successful Press Chief, had his own niche in this band of assistants. Press relations were poorly handled during the first years of the Federal Republic, and Press Chiefs came and went with monotonous regularity. They were, invariably, men who inspired no confidence in members of the press and were totally incapable of projecting government policy. Von Eckardt was a man of exceptional social ease and grace; he loved company, had a

6............*Aussenpolitik in Adenauer's Kanzler-Demokratie*, Arnuld Baring, p. 18.
7............Frau Libeth Werhahn, in private conversation with the author.

sparkling wit, and was a deft and articulate government spokesman. What Adenauer admired most in him was that he was never at a loss.[8] Von Eckardt became a close confidant on party politics and even on the internal affairs of the Cabinet. He was closely consulted before major Cabinet changes were made in 1956,[9] and Adenauer often talked over problems within the CDU with him.[10]

There can be little doubt that neither Blankenhorn, Hallstein nor von Eckardt was Adenauer's 'key' adviser. This place belonged to Dr. Hans Globke, the head of the Chancellery from 1953 onwards. Because of his power, his past and his permanency, Globke became perhaps the most controversial character in the short history of the Federal Republic.

For a man without ambition, his power was tremendous. He was a former Aachen city councillor, a zealous Roman Catholic and member of the Centre Party, and he was recommended to Adenauer by the Minister of Finance in *Land* North-Rhine–Westphalia, Dr. Heinrich Weitz. Adenauer offered him the post of State Secretary in the Chancellery in 1949, but Globke (for reasons connected with his past) turned it down. When he reconsidered his decision he was given as many tasks as Adenauer could unload on him, tasks which he accepted cheerfully and discharged with robot-like efficiency. He informed Adenauer on the work of the different Ministries, briefed Ministers on Adenauer's own decisions, looked after personnel policy (hence the massive dossiers which were kept locked away in the Chancellory *Panzerschrank*, or safe), and supervised the tactical and administrative co-ordination of government business. He was the master-mechanic who kept the machinery of government well-oiled and running smoothly. He was, equally, a Chief of Staff, with an exact knowledge of all the forces and weapons at Adenauer's disposal.

8............In his book *Ein unordentliches Leben* (p. 188) Felix von Eckardt has a story which aptly illustrates this characteristic and Adenauer's reaction to it. He was due to accompany Adenauer from Bonn to Paris on May 26, 1952, the moment after the Bonn Agreement was signed. Von Eckardt's car broke down on the way to the airfield. He was given a lift, but left his suitcase in the car which had broken down. It held his dinner-jacket and morning-dress, and von Eckardt was a man who dressed elegantly. An official car was sent back to fetch his things and von Eckardt, playing frantically for time, induced Adenauer to pose three times on the tarmac for the benefit of an applauding crowd. When the perspiring chauffeur came running with von Eckardt's suitcase, Adenauer sized up the situation in one glance. 'Well, well,' he said to the relieved but apprehensive von Eckardt, 'now that you have your luggage, world history can go on again.'

9............*Ein unordentliches Leben*, Felix von Eckardt, pp. 439–42.

10...........*Ein unordentliches Leben*, Felix von Eckardt, p. 331. In one aside to von Eckardt, Adenauer remarked: 'Do all that you can for our evangelical wing. You don't need to bother about the Catholics; they'll look after themselves.'

He was the soul of discretion. Dedicated to his work, he never forgot a detail, never mislaid a document.[11] His dossiers on political personalities in Bonn included details of their private lives which were unknown even to their nearest and dearest. Thus, Adenauer was able to take a prominent member of the CDU aside and tell him, in a fatherly way, not to go on paying such frequent visits 'to a certain address in Cologne'. This side of Globke's work was resented in some quarters, understandably. It may be that even Ministers had an unhappy suspicion that they were being watched. What is sure is that Globke was totally objective and, in giving Adenauer information, totally honest. The comment may not have been justified of the US High Commissioner, Mr. John McCloy, that 'Adenauer always had a tendency to give credence to a report if it came from devious sources. I once accused him of going to the caves of Adullam for his information.'[12] In reality, Adenauer normally relied on sources which he knew were reliable. He knew, too, that Globke was not a seeker after office; he asked several times to be allowed to resign, on grounds of failing health.[13]

When Adenauer was seriously ill in the early winter of 1955, Globke was the only man whom he consulted in his sick-room.[14] Perhaps there was, indeed, something molelike about his capacity for creative work in the twilit, private world of his own secluded office in the Chancellery. But the ostensible objection to Globke was that he had helped to produce, as a Prussian civil servant, the commentary to the infamous Nuremberg 'Racial Decrees' of the Nazis in 1936. In the 'Ministerial Gazette of the Reich and the Prussian Ministry of the Interior' of March 11, 1936, Globke and his civil service senior, Dr. Wilhelm Stuckart, were commended for their drafting of the Decrees.[15] These decrees relegated the Jews of Germany to the status of second-class citizens, and prepared the way for their bitter and brutal persecution. They constituted a document of hideous racial intolerance.

The 'Globke case' cannot be satisfactorily summed-up.[16] One vital

11...........During a personal talk with the author, Globke went to his very extensive archives to trace a newspaper report and could not find it. *Einfach unglaublich* (frankly unbelievable) was his comment. But this was long after his retirement.

12...........Mr. John McCloy, in a letter to the author, December 23, 1969.

13...........*Ein unordentliches Leben*, Felix von Eckardt, p. 169.

14...........*Germany Divided*, Terence Prittie, p. 205.

15...........*Konrad Adenauer*, Rudolf Augstein, p. 40.

16...........Dr. Globke is most unwilling to take an active part in defending himself. This has been the author's experience in interviews with him. Many people who have examined the facts, including Dr. Rolf Vogel, believe that he did his best to help victims of Nazism.

witness in this 'case' is Cardinal von Preysing, who made the following statement:[17] 'Dr. Hans Globke has been known to me for many years. He has always correctly appraised the dangers and errors of National Socialism. Over and above his fundamental opposition, he has always sought to obstruct or render impossible unlawful actions and acts of injustice and violence on the part of the Nazis, to the fullest extent possible to him within the scope of his activities. He disclosed to me and my fellow workers plans and decisions made by the Ministry, and certain proposed Bills of a highly confidential nature ... He rendered valuable assistance in our relief work for the persecuted Jews and half-Jews by giving timely warnings.'

Cardinal Preysing was one of many of Dr. Globke's contemporaries who believed in his innocence. Thus Dr. Heinrich Weitz, who became Minister of Finance in *Land* North-Rhine–Westphalia, made a deposition six months after the end of the war in which he asserted that he had turned to Dr. Globke for help and advice on various occasions during the Nazi era. Weitz, and others, knew of Globke's close association with a number of members of the German resistance against Hitler. Two of them gave evidence on his behalf – Jakob Kaiser, who became Minister for All-German Affairs in the Federal Republic, and Otto Lenz, one of Adenauer's closest advisers. Kaiser's deposition, made on December 31, 1945, is of particular significance. In it he said that he had himself put Globke in touch with three other leaders of the German resistance, Dr. Gördeler, General Beck and General von Hammerstein, that Globke would have become Secretary of State for Education in the post-Nazi Government planned by Gördeler, and that Globke had given valuable information to Hitler's opponents and had worked indefatigably to help Trade Unionists against the encroachments of the Nazi 'Labour Front'. Otto Lenz was among those who maintained that Globke only remained in the employment of the Nazi State at the wish of himself and others who wished to destroy it, because he needed all the information which he could procure in his post in the Ministry of the Interior. On several occasions Globke helped to secure the release of people imprisoned by the Nazis and earmarked for a traitor's trial. All this evidence was available to Adenauer, and it seems certain that it strengthened his determination to keep Globke in his employment.

A personal view may not be out of place here. I interviewed Hans Globke on June 15, 1960. He told me that he had realized, in retrospect, that he could have refused to produce the commentary to the Nuremberg Racial Decrees. But he imagined that the Nazi regime would become more

17..........*The Vanishing Swastika*, Christopher Emmet and Norbert Mühlen, p. 33.

liberal as time went on, and he knew that he could 'water down the ideas in the head of Herr Stuckart,' his superior. Globke maintained that he was responsible for excluding from the application of the decrees people who were one-quarter Jewish, and the 'marriage ban' – Jews were not to marry Gentiles – was lifted from these people too. He collaborated with the Ministry of Defence to gain concessions for half-Jews, on the ostensible grounds that they were needed for the armed forces in the event of war. Globke showed me a letter from a Jewish professor to whom he had given desperately needed help. He told me much besides, and it had to do with that terrible dilemma of the 'un-Nazi' official confronted with the ruthless pressure of Nazi 'administrative indoctrination'. I believed what he told me.[18]

Globke's case is relevant to this story, because he played so large a part in the running of Adenauer's Chancellery. Adenauer came under heavy fire for retaining his services, but never for one moment considered jettisoning him. Loyalty to a subordinate is at least as important as loyalty to one's 'boss'.

In his book *Aussenpolitik in Adenauer's Kanzler-Demokratic*, Arnulf Baring has painted a lurid picture of the Chancellery offices in the Palais Schaumburg. He suggests that the Chancellor – like a bad schoolmaster – enjoyed exploiting human weakness and playing-off one 'favourite' against another, (p. 20), that he swopped favourites and encouraged them to conspire against each other, and that the Chancellery became a hotbed of envy, intrigue and confusion.

There seems to be something very wrong with this picture. In the first place, the Chancellery functioned very smoothly. Indeed, the chief complaint against it is that it functioned too smoothly, and so deprived Ministries of their responsibilities. A Chancellery presided over by a demented pedagogue could not have done what Adenauer's office did.

In the second place, the principals who have already been named (Otto Lenz died some years ago and so was not consulted by the author) were frankly amazed by the thought that Adenauer exploited them and played them off against one another. Hallstein's view, for instance, was: 'Adenauer loathed wasting time. He made his decisions quickly – in my case for instance, he talked to me about the Schuman Plan and three days later asked me to lead the German Delegation. When he gave you work to do, he expected you to get on with it. He would not have had time to play us off against each other. He was much too interested in the job to be done, much too busy. Of course, he liked teasing people sometimes. Who cared? He didn't mind being teased himself.'[19]

18..........Terence Prittie, *Manchester Guardian*, June 17, 1960.
19..........Professor Walter Hallstein, in private conversation with the author.

Globke, too, scouted the idea of any internal struggle in the Chancellory for the favour of the Chancellor – 'This is wrong, and absurd. The real truth is that Adenauer was tremendously open and frank with his advisers. When he wanted something put right, he said so very directly. He intended to get work that mattered done with the least possible delay.' As for any jockeying over competences, there was a fairly clear-cut division within the Chancellery between administrative and domestic affairs on the one hand, and foreign policy matters on the other. Globke and Lenz looked after the first, Blankenhorn and Hallstein the second.[20]

The Chancellery staff advised Adenauer on the 'background' of any political personality whose appointment to some post was under consideration; in Globke's view, there was no attempt to prejudice Adenauer's decisions in this field. Globke did, of course, keep his detailed dossiers on personnel, and Adenauer did sometimes say – 'And who knows what Herr Globke may have in his safe?' This, in Globke's view, was typical of Adenauer's gentle persiflage. For his part, the accusations and denunciations which reached the Chancellery were dealt with on an intelligible basis; he filed away purely personal complaints, but took steps to investigate anything with a 'political content'. A file was closed just as soon as it was clear that there was no purpose in keeping it.[21]

Adenauer liked to give his advisers a 'tag' as a part of the 'family relationship in the Chancellery. Hallstein was the learned professor, with an academician's semi-ethereal aura. Blankenhorn was the ever-busy factotum, Globke the 'grey eminence' with secrets locked away in his brain. Felix von Eckardt, looking in a little from the outside at the Chancellery, agrees that it was a kind of second family to Adenauer. These were 'his' people, whom he could trust implicitly, whom he regarded with a paternal benevolence and chided occasionally, but whom he always treated as human beings and to whom he was always prepared to listen.[22]

His paternalism sometimes reached out beyond the confines of the Palais Schaumburg. Gerhard Schröder, who became his Minister of the Interior in 1953, holding that post for eight years before he moved to the Foreign Ministry, speaks of a 'father–son relationship',[23] in which there was much sympathy and understanding. So, more surprisingly, does Erich

20...........Dr. Hans Globke, in private conversation with the author.

21...........There is no clear evidence of Globke's own meticulous system breaking down. The outstanding instance of a Chancellery *Panne* – the German word for a gaffe – occurred before the 1953 elections. Otto Lenz procured information that two SPD *Bundestag* candidates were in treasonable contact with the East German Communists. Adenauer used this information in an election speech in Frankfurt. It was subsequently discovered to be false.

22...........Felix von Eckardt, in private conversation with the author.

23...........Dr. Gerhard Schröder, in private conversation with the author.

Mende, the leader of the FDP – although Adenauer evidently decided to like him only after an initial period of suspicion. Mende's favourite story about Adenauer relates to an argument in a Government Coalition Conference in 1952, when Mende – greatly daring – asked him why he was contradicting something which he had said himself an hour earlier. The other leading members of the FDP were horrified when Mende, the youngest among them, produced his diary and read out what Adenauer had said.

Adenauer retorted at first that the best thing to do with a diary was to throw it away. He never kept one himself. Then he found a formula – 'If I really did say it as you maintain, then you must be right. But I didn't mean it the way that you do!' For some time afterwards Adenauer took an impish pleasure, when meeting Mende in company, in saying to bystanders – 'You must be careful with Herr Mende; he keeps a diary.'[24]

Part of Adenauer's secret in dealing with people was his ability to 'keep his distance from them.[25] He never allowed a human relationship to become, in a purely superficial sense, too warm. When he set out to charm someone, he still maintained a certain reserve. This habit, paradoxically, gave greater, and not less scope for the really worthwhile gesture of friendliness. When he made it, it really meant something. He had other attributes in dealing with people. His interpreter, Herr Weber, noted in particular the directness of his glance, the deep concentration with which he listened, the flattering interest which he took in the small, personal affairs of those around him, his powers as a conversationalist, and his courteous and elegant manner with women.[26] According to one adviser, he was 'never rude in a personal sense'.[27] And, although he sometimes had to waste time with professional politicians who were bores, he was adept at not wasting time when it could be avoided. Thus his principle in granting interviews to journalists – 'If he's important, he can stay an hour. If he's not, then he needn't come.'[28]

His gift for repartee was famous. Some of the best stories about him were collected in a book, *Gar nicht so pingelig*, by Walter Henkels, a German journalist who knew the personal side of the Bonn scene better than any. One or two may serve as illustrations of his humour:

Of journalists, he said in 1960, 'One should be careful with small children and journalists. They will always take a shy at you with a stone afterwards.'[29] Of a government spokesman, his phrase was that he suffered

24..........Dr. Erich Mende, in private conversation with the author.
25, 26.....Herr Weber, in private conversation with the author.
27..........*Ein unordentliches Leben*, Felix von Eckardt, p. 162.
28..........*Ein unordentliches Leben*, Felix von Eckardt, p. 165.
29..........*Gar nicht so Pingelig*, Walter Henkels, p. 121.

'from having his tongue too near his brain.'[30] As a piece of political philosophy – 'In politics it's not a matter of being in the right, but of having the right.'[31] Again, when an importunate journalist went on applying to see him: 'Tell the chap I was buried yesterday, and nobody knows yet. Then he's got his scoop.'[32] On the Soviet foreign Minister, Molotov – 'He always makes a face as if he's drunk a litre of vinegar on an empty stomach.'[33] And on the rapid rise to fame of his Defence Minister, Franz Josef Strauss – 'That didn't happen to me; and a good thing too!'[34]

His own, most obvious foibles were punctuality, a passion for fresh air and a feeling that he was being watched.[35] But he was acutely observant of the foibles of others, and knew how to exploit them. Typical of this talent was a birthday present to Winston Churchill. He decided to send him a cigar case. Herbert Blankenhorn was deputed to procure one, and ordered a small, elegant and suitably inscribed case. Adenauer rejected it without hesitation, and had it replaced by one which was heavy, ornate and ten times as expensive. Churchill was delighted. Allegedly he cried out excitedly to his wife, when receiving it from Blankenhorn, 'Look at this Clementine! I believe it'sh, it'sh, 'sholid gold!'[36]

Among the wealth of anecdote about Adenauer there are two stories relating to his advanced age. One was of a conversation which he had, at the age of 81, with his old friend, Robert Pferdemenges, four years his junior. Pferdemenges told him that it was about time for them both to retire. Adenauer was so concerned about this that he paid a special call on Frau Pferdemenges, and asked her: 'Your husband – I'm worried about him. Is he ill?'[37]

30..........*Gar nicht so Pingelig,* Walter Henkels, p. 104.
31..........*Gar nicht so Pingelig,* Walter Henkels, p. 42.
32..........*Gar nicht so Pingelig,* Walter Henkels, p. 121.
33..........*Gar nicht so Pingelig,* Walter Henkels, p. 161.
34..........*Gar nicht so Pingelig,* Walter Henkels, p. 111.
35..........Adenauer had a mild form of persecution-mania about his telephone line being tapped. This was, indeed, done by the British authorities shortly after he became Chancellor. More than once after this, he believed it was happening again, and in 1962 he demanded an inspection of his line by the Federal Post Office. It was carried out and he was told that crackling noises were merely the outcome of 'old age'. Adenauer demanded 'proof', so the Minister of Posts tapped the line, recorded conversations and submitted them to Adenauer. This time, the Chancellor had not noticed anything wrong.

A similar sort of persecution-mania led to him not spending holidays in Switzerland after 1956. He said that he had been spied on, and the carbon-paper used by his secretaries had several times disappeared from the waste-paper baskets without trace!
36..........Dr. Erwin Wickert, in private conversation with the author.
37..........*Gar nicht so Pingelig,* Walter Henkels, p. 138.

The second story was about his garden. Adenauer was becoming bored by the habit of photographers taking pictures of the garden from the road. He had a talk with his gardener, who suggested planting dwarf poplars which were relatively quick-growing. But, he added, even they took time to grow – about 15 years. Adenauer's only comment, aged 83, was 'And what about it?'[38]

Finally, there were two stories about Heinrich von Brentano, his Foreign Minister from 1955 to 1961. In Paris they got into the lift together, with the aim of going two floors higher. Brentano pressed a button and they headed for the basement – 'The first and last time,' as some wag had it, 'that the Chancellor ever let Brentano take the initiative.'[39] Brentano, at least, produced one piece of wit on his own account. He had waited six years before being appointed Foreign Minister and when receiving his post from President Theodor Heuss, remarked: 'Has the Old One had long enough to think it over?'[40]

Adenauer was quite ready to vent his wit on his fellow-countrymen. He told one American journalist: 'A Prussian is a Slav who has forgotten who his grandfather was.'[41] And to the same journalist he said early in 1948 that 'Germans are Belgians, with megalomania'. This remark was published, but officially denied after the 1949 elections. On a later occasion, the American journalist reproached Adenauer about this. The Chancellor countered: 'Of course I said it. But now I'm running a country, and all you have to run is a typewriter.'

One of Adenauer's critics, Rudolf Wolfgang Leonhardt, believed that four midwives assisted at Adenauer's retarded 'birth' as a statesman: the inveterate anti-Communism of the Catholic Rhinelander, the intolerance of the patriarch; the alien feeling towards all things English of a 'Carolingian', – relating to the Catholic Western Europe of the time of Charlemagne – and a highly developed contempt for the 'other man's' point of view.[42] Certainly, Adenauer was not beyond reproach as a statesman. And even at the height of his power, he made mistakes.

In 1953 he made some unfortunate choices of Ministers. Two from the BHE Refugee Party, Waldemar Kraft and Theodor Oberländer, were ex-Nazis. Kraft dropped out fairly soon, but Oberländer was driven into retirement only in 1960 after a violent and embarrassing campaign had been mounted against him by the East German Communists, for alleged

38..........*Gar nicht so Pingelig*, Walter Henkels, p. 20.
39..........Dr. Erwin Wickert, in private conversation with the author.
40..........*Gar nicht so Pingelig*, Walter Henkels, p. 68. A phrase used by one Parliamentarian was, 'When Adenauer sneezes, Brentano blows his nose.'
41..........James O'Donnell, in private conversation with the author.
42..........*This Germany*, Rudolf Wolfgang Leonhardt, p. 135.

war-crimes. Adenauer's Minister of Transport, Hans Seebohm, continued to make, year in, year out, inflammatory speeches about Germany's lost provinces in Czechoslovakia and east of the Oder–Neisse line. Adenauer's contention was that it was time to come to terms with the past. It was; but not by employing Ministers who were historical liabilities.

Adenauer's attempt to impose an undue measure of government control over Press and Radio was a seven-day wonder which began immediately after the 1953 elections. Under the prompting of Otto Lenz, Adenauer proposed creating the 'Super Ministry' which would have had powers which were simply not consonant with democratic practice: powers to fine, censor, imprison and disqualify journalists and others without trial. Lenz openly stated that he would be prepared to remove Press and Radio executives because of their political affiliation with the opposition SPD;[43] his special targets being SPD supporters in the official German news agency, DPA, and in the North-West German Radio Corporation.

For once, Adenauer's advisers were at odds with one another, and the Federal Press Chief, von Eckardt, threatened to resign. Adenauer had not committed himself completely; he was able to draw back in time. But he owed more than he would ever have cared to admit to the original 'breaking' of the story by the weekly, *Der Spiegel*, and to the instant reaction of the foreign press.

Quite suddenly, in May 1956, Adenauer caused a flurry of excitement by intervening in economic matters. At the Gürzenich hall in Cologne he told an amazed audience at a banquet on May 23 that he disapproved of the raising of the bank rate, and had not been consulted beforehand.[44] Bank rate had been raised from $4\frac{1}{2}$ to $5\frac{1}{2}$ per cent on May 22 by the President of the Bank of the German *Länder*, Dr. Hermann Vocke, after consultations with the Ministers of Finance and Economics. At the same time, Adenauer announced his opposition to Professor Erhard's plan to reduce tariffs by 30 per cent, and produced a gibe at his Minister of Finance, Dr. Schäffer, by saying that the tax system was too complex, with 125 regulations for income tax alone, adding that 'People who think as confusedly as this are not often very clever.' Later, Erhard was to reiterate that Adenauer's strictures were 'beyond all reason'.[45] Appropriately, the only person who learned a lesson on this occasion was Adenauer himself; he never intervened in economic questions again.

Erhard and Schäffer were loyal members of the CDU; the solidarity of the party was not seriously shaken by this digression into a world which Adenauer did not understand. But he ran into grave difficulties with his

43..........The *Manchester Guardian*, Terence Prittie, September 25, 1953.
44..........The *Manchester Guardian*, Terence Prittie, May 25, 1956.
45..........Professor Ludwig Erhard, in private conversation with the author.

broadly-based coalition of 1953–7. The troublesome component in it, from his point of view, was the FDP.

In 1956 Adenauer decided that the electoral law might be altered. He himself had a hankering for the Anglo-Saxon system of a direct vote. He proposed only a system of 'bonus seats', the details of which were never clearly laid out, (*Zusatz-Mandate*) for the strongest party. This could have been the end of the FDP, an inadequate 'third force'. But FDP Ministers in the Federal Cabinet were reluctant to oppose the Chancellor. Alteration of the electoral law required the approval of both houses of Parliament. The wariest members of the FDP decided to block constitutional amendment in the *Bundesrat*, or 'Upper' House.

This meant organizing the fall of a CDU-led government, or governments, in the *Länder*. The FDP had the possibility of doing this, because they were 'holding the balance', in North-Rhine–Westphalia, Lower Saxony, Schleswig-Holstein and the Rhineland–Palatinate. To block amendment of the constitution, they needed only to remove the CDU from control in North-Rhine–Westphalia, and this they duly did in February, 1956. It was an unhappy affair, for the man whose political career was ended by this manoeuvre was the upright and enlightened CDU leader, Karl Arnold. It was Arnold who had done most to guide the Ruhr through the dark days of post-war hunger and unemployment. He could have played a major role in Bonn; but Adenauer regarded him as ideologically tainted with Socialist theories, and far too ready to compromise with the SPD in a premature campaign for social justice.

A new government was formed in North-Rhine–Westphalia. Electoral reform was blocked in Bonn. But the FDP suffered too. This party, like all save the SPD, depended on industry for its fighting funds (according to Erich Mende, it received between one third and one quarter of what was contributed at the time to the CDU).[46] Some of these funds were now withdrawn. More important, the FDP leadership split; four Cabinet Ministers took the lead in forming a breakaway 'Free People's Party' and, later, dissolved this party and joined the CDU. The FDP meanwhile dropped out of the Government Coalition. By the end of 1956 it consisted only of the CDU and the German Party; for the BHE also split, with Ministers staying in the Government and the 'rump' of the party drifting into Opposition.

Did Adenauer set out deliberately to split parties which belonged to his Government, and thus build up the strength of the CDU? There was a strong suspicion that this was a piece of Machiavellian tactics on his part. The evidence is operative of Erich Mende, who later became the leader of the FDP and who remained pledged to the maintenance of his independent middle-of-the-road party.

46 ....Dr. Erich Mende, in private conversation with the author.

According to Mende,[47] Adenauer did not set out with the purpose of totally eliminating any third party, and so leaving the field to the CDU and SPD. Adenauer told Mende that Germans must have at least three choices; in this he differed from some of his CDU lieutenants. Whatever troubles there were between CDU and FDP were due to genuine differences of opinion. There was no 'contrived crisis'. Indeed, Adenauer may even have wanted the FDP to reunite in 1956, after the split which resulted in the temporary organization of the Free People's Party. According to Mende, Adenauer was ready to sacrifice two Ministers and put himself, Mende, and Dr. Thomas Dehler, his former Minister of Justice, into the Cabinet. This would, certainly, have represented a big concession on Adenauer's part. He had found Dehler's antics in the *Bundestag* unbearable. The Minister of Justice maddened him with his habit of oblique criticism and his penchant for declamatory, windbag oratory.[48] On balance, one may accept that Adenauer did not try to kill his coalition allies by kindness between 1953 and 1957. The fact remained that the CDU was too big to need them.

During the years of his undisputed supremacy Adenauer became deeply involved in the problem of German reunification. The story of this involvement belongs to the next chapter. It did not directly affect his control of affairs, in spite of the fact that he failed to make the slightest progress towards solving the problem. For the Social Democrats were still suffering from that lack of a coherent programme which had made their dead leader, Schumacher, into what one writer called an 'ideology-substitute'.[49] Apart from the anti-rearmament campaigns which they mounted, the Social Democrats offered no challenge during these years to Adenauer's total control of the Federal Republic. They came up with no new ideas. There was a dearth of ideas, in general. This was the apogee of paternal government; and the great mass of the German electorate liked it. The ructions within the Government Coalition only temporarily obscured this fact.

Any real threat to Adenauer's supremacy would, necessarily, have had to come from outside the limited sphere of orthodox party politics. Between 1953 and 1957, one can pick out only three moments in time, when Adenauer showed uneasiness of mind. The first was in 1954, when his old colleague and superior in the pre-1933 Centre Party, Dr. Heinrich

47..........Dr. Erich Mende, in private conversation with the author.

48..........Dr. Erich Mende, in private conversation with the author. According to Mende, Adenauer asked him if Dehler was 'normal' (*Ist der Mann wirklich gesund?*). Another observer quoted Frau Dehler as saying that she could not understand why her husband's speeches in the *Bundestag* were so fierce – he was 'so nice at home' (*Der Thomas ist so nett, zu Hause*).

49..........*The History of the German Labour Movement*, Helga Grebbing, p. 164.

Brüning, reappeared briefly on the political scene. The second was in 1956, when Sir Winston Churchill, speaking in Aachen, produced ideas which cut diametrically across Adenauer's now established and generally accepted foreign policy guide-lines. The third was later in the same year, when a section of Adenauer's CDU pressed for the banning of the West German Communist Party and Adenauer, with inward reluctance, gave way to this demand.

First, the fugitive 'come-back' of Brüning. The ex-Chancellor returned from the United States to Cologne University in a purely academic capacity. There is no evidence that he had any thought of resuming his political career. But on June 2, 1954, he gave a talk on foreign policy to the 'Rhein-Ruhr Club' in Düsseldorf, which he believed was 'off the record'. It was, however, reported in the German press, and it contained implied criticisms of Adenauer's handling of foreign affairs. In particular, Brüning suggested that Adenauer based his foreign policy on too absolute a dependence on the Western Alliance, giving himself no freedom of diplomatic manoeuvre. Brüning used these words: 'We must be clear that Germany cannot be reunited if the demand is made that this reunited Germany should be fully incorporated in the EDC and a united Europe ... it is understandable that France, as well as the United States, is pressing for Western Germany to be made dependent on the Western World. But no one can maintain that this will necessarily provide greater insurance of peace in Europe and the world.'

The Rhein-Ruhr Club held meetings which were a sort of political seminar; Brüning was merely putting up ideas for discussion. It never entered his head to propose a clear-cut alternative to the existing West German policy of alignment with the Western democracies and abnegation, on understandable grounds of discretion and tact, of some kind of independent 'line', between East and West. As he put it, in Düsseldorf, 'My object was to introduce a more realistic atmosphere into discussions of foreign policy.'[50]

Under Adenauer's instructions the Federal Press Office at once denounced Brüning's 'intervention' in the field of foreign policy. Passages in his speech about the general situation in the United States, and the independence of mind shown by Germany after the First World War, were deliberately misrepresented as attempts to show that the United States was confronting an economic crisis, and that Federal Germany did not need Western allies. This was pure, or impure, propaganda. Brüning had not said, or even implied, anything of the sort.

50..........From Brüning's own text of his speech, supplied by Brüning to the author on June 19, 1954.

Adenauer claimed that the ex-Chancellor had damaged the Federal Republic's 'good name'. It was assumed that he was trying to stage a come-back into political life; in reality, Brüning was perfectly satisfied with the Chair of Political Studies at Cologne University and was keeping himself scrupulously clear of politics. In private,[51] Brüning repeated his criticism of Adenauer's foreign policy; he did not believe that the military and moral union of Western Europe would force the Russians to withdraw from East Germany and so make unification possible, and he urged the use of imaginative diplomacy as an adjunct to building up the Western Alliance. He wanted secret diplomacy in place of propaganda blast and counter-blast, the opening of diplomatic relations with Moscow, and carefully prepared, exploratory Four Power talks with German participation. There was, in these ideas, nothing at all damaging to the Federal Republic's 'good name'.

Adenauer realized that Brüning was still a man of stature, potentially a far more dangerous rival than any member of his own Cabinet. Brüning still enjoyed a political reputation as the last man in the Weimar Era who had made a real effort to stop the Nazis – whereas Adenauer had declined to form a government when given the chance. He was, for that matter, nearly ten years younger than Adenauer. Doubtless Adenauer recalled the lack of sympathy which had existed between him and this austere, humourless man, as well as the petty frustrations caused by his failure to answer letters and his ignorance of the local problems of the Rhineland. Like the proverbial elephant, Adenauer never forgot. His rancorous attacks on Brüning had their effect; the ex-Chancellor withdrew once more to the United States, saying sadly on leaving that it seemed his country did not need him any more, and died fifteen years later in exile. The paradox about the whole 'incident' was that, while Adenauer suspected that Brüning was staging a come-back, Brüning himself had no thought of it, and was plainly amazed by the animosity of his former colleague.

The Brüning episode, as Adenauer saw it, represented a challenge to his authority. Churchill's Aachen speech, on May 10, 1956, was a challenge to his foreign policy. The ex-Prime Minister was being invested with the 'Charlemagne medal', an award instituted in 1950 and given for service to the European cause. In his speech, Churchill proposed taking the Soviet Union and its satellites into NATO and a broadened European alliance – 'I do not see why the new Russia should not join in the spirit of this solemn agreement. We must realize how deep and sincere are Russia's anxieties about the safety of her homeland from foreign invasion. In a

51..........Dr. Heinrich Brüning, in private conversation with the author.

true unity of Europe, Russia must have her part ... It may well be that the great issues which perplex us, of which one of the gravest is the reunification of Germany, could then be solved more readily than they can by rival blocs confronting each other with suspicion and hostility.'

The 'new' Russia was post-Stalin Russia. Churchill's assumption was that it could be induced to make real concessions if something were offered in return. For Adenauer this was alarming; it sailed dangerously close to the concept of a European security system, including the Soviet Union, with which the Social Democrats were hoping to win the 1957 elections. As one account of the occasion had it – 'It was hardly surprising that a pale and preoccupied Adenauer limited himself to generalized pleasantries when answering Sir Winston. There was no consolation to be had in the latter's speech and although Dr. Adenauer knows far more English than he cares to admit, it was not possible for him to make an extemporary reply. His perturbation was indicated by his losing his place in his notes at least three times and complaining testily of the undue proximity of an irrepressible press-photographer.'[52]

There was nothing surprising about Adenauer's unfeigned concern. Already, in the spring of 1953 Churchill had suggested a new 'Locarno Pact', to guarantee the security of the Soviet Union as well as of Germany. That initiative died stillborn as a result of the brutal repression of the East German rising by the Red Army. Churchill's Aachen proposals suffered a similar fate when the Red Army invaded Hungary in the autumn of 1956. In the interval before that happened Adenauer lost no opportunity of preaching his gospel of 'no experiments and no adventures', and of urging that Stalin's death had actually made the European situation more dangerous than before – since it had left a Soviet Union readier to strike out in fear than, as previously, in the certain knowledge of its own strength.

In August, 1956, Adenauer took action which suggested that he regarded compromise over the German Question as less, rather than more, attainable than before. This was the banning of the Communist Party. It was a surprising step to take. In the 1953 elections the Communist vote had dropped by more than half, to a miserable 2·2 per cent of the poll. All fifteen seats in the *Bundestag* were lost. There was no sign of a revival. But police raids were ordered on several Communist offices and material was seized which gave the Federal Constitutional Court in Karlsruhe the chance to declare the Party illegal, on the grounds that it was working to destroy democratic government and the democratic state. There was nothing new about that.

Adenauer's Minister of the Interior, Gerhard Schröder, would have

52..........The *Manchester Guardian*, Terence Prittie, May 11, 1956.

preferred to take legal action against individual Communist leaders when uncovering their subversive activities. The Federal High Court (*Bundesgericht*) advised that legal action, against members of a still legal Party, would have been devious. As Schröder saw it in retrospect, the banning of the Communist Party did at least render its illegal activities on behalf of its masters in Moscow immensely more difficult. Schröder considered that this outweighed the fact that Communist activity now became purely subversive.[53]

Adenauer had one spell of illness in 1956 and there were some signs of restlessness at the thought that a man of over 80 was clearly in no mood to step down from office. Cartoons of the Chancellor multiplied. One showed pictures of him and President Syngman Rhee of South Korea hanging side by side in exactly matching frames, with the caption – 'Here the resemblance ends. For Syngman Rhee did *not* want to stand for a third term, but was elected.'

Adenauer, as it happened, was never in the least degree worried by cartoons of him. They caused him a great deal of amusement, and he was in the habit of saying that it did 'not matter what people say about me, as long as they have something to say'.[54] To provoke, and be provoked was an intrinsic part of his way of life. He was the only leading German politician who never bothered to contradict the sometimes scurrilous and always acid comments of the weekly *Der Spiegel*. But he was feeling his age. In November 1956 there was a report that he had ordered the withdrawal from circulation of all pictures which made him look his age or showed him with a crumpled collar or crooked tie. There was growing criticism, too, of the personal rule which was now popularly known as 'Chancellor democracy', and this criticism was given an additional fillip when Globke, and not one of his Ministers, paid daily attendance at his sick-bed. Two years earlier, at the London Conference of September 1954, Adenauer had been overheard by a *Spiegel* reporter, Lothar Reuel, telling the Belgian and Luxemburg Prime Ministers in Claridge's Hotel that 'when I am gone, it will be too late' and that he did not know what was to become of Germany, unless a United Europe could be created without delay.[55] This conversation with Paul Henri Spaak and Joseph Bech has often been cited as evidence of overweaning egotism. But Adenauer's fears were real; partly on account of them, he was to cling to office for the best part of another decade.

There was trouble, too, over rearmament. The anti-rearmament SPD campaign launched in Frankfurt's St. Paul's Church in 1955 fizzled out

53...........Dr. Gerhard Schröder, in a letter to the author, April 20, 1970.
54...........Will Rasner (CDU), in private conversation with the author.
55...........*Konrad Adenauer*, Rudolf Augstein, pp. 32–5.

fairly quickly. Adenauer's next source of worry was provided by the publication in *Time* Magazine in September 1956 of a plan of the US Chief of Staff, Admiral Arthur Radford, to reduce conventional forces in Europe and concentrate on nuclear weapons.[56] Radford wanted US conventional forces reduced from 2·8 to 2 million by 1960. Adenauer asked both Dulles, and the British Foreign Secretary, Selwyn Lloyd, for reassurances that Allied forces on German soil would be kept at their existing strength. He got them.

On April 5, 1957, Adenauer himself stirred up a hornet's nest by stating at a Press Conference in Bonn that the West German armed forces, the *Bundeswehr*, should be properly armed. He drew a distinction between 'tactical' and 'strategic' nuclear weapons. The first, in his view, were 'basically nothing but an improved form of artillery'. Adenauer went on: 'It is quite obvious that in view of the enormous advances in weapons techniques which have unfortunately occurred, we cannot deny our own troops the newest types, and prevent them from sharing in these latest developments.'

The West German press was wildly excited, and on April 12, 1957, eighteen leading West German scientists sent the Chancellor a telegram of protest, claiming that the Federal Republic must renounce the use of all nuclear weapons. Adenauer invited the scientists to Bonn, where they were given an exhaustive explanation by Generals Adolf Heusinger and Hans Speidel of the military situation in Europe. Adenauer for his part informed them that they were intervening in political matters which they did not understand. The scientists were quelled for the moment, but at the end of April Albert Schweitzer, in distant Lambaréne in West Africa declared that nuclear bombs were a danger to the health of the human race. Adenauer's irritable comment was – 'What Albert Schweitzer said was regarded by a great part of the German people as a kind of gospel.'[57] He was quite right. The SPD put up a huge poster of Schweitzer at their Bonn headquarters and kept it there for the next three years. They used his statement as an election slogan in 1957, coupling it with the motto *Lieber rot als tot* ('Better red than dead'), and launched a new campaign, against 'atom death', in March 1958.

The issue of tactical nuclear weapons turned out to be less adverse for Adenauer than had at first looked probable. Some of the scientists had second thoughts, and Professor Carl von Weizsaecker began to expound the view that it was necessary 'to live with the bomb'. Adenauer's frequently repeated demand for 'equality' for the German soldier gained in

56..........*Time* Magazine, September 3, 1956.
57..........*Memoirs*, Konrad Adenauer, VOL 3, p. 301.

weight. The West Germans, moreover, had become used to the overall idea of rearmament and Gallup polls showed that only one in four opposed it any longer. And one CDU paper published a cartoon showing the German 'Michel' – the apologetic little man, with a woollen nightcap, whom Germans like to regard as 'typical' of the post-1945 era – armed with an umbrella and confronting a menacing Russian bear carrying a bagful of atom bombs. In Berlin, the Social Democratic Mayor Willy Brandt showed a marked disinclination to oppose Adenauer's policy of supporting a militarily strong Western Alliance.

Adenauer received a political shot-in-the-arm in March, 1957, when the Treaty of Rome was signed. This set up the European Economic Community as a Customs-union which was to be completed in three four-year stages. A fully integrated Common Market was to come into being at the end of, at most, fifteen years, with a common external tariff. As special concessions to the Federal Republic, the other members of the Six undertook to re-examine the Treaty in the event of German reunification, and to regulate their trade with East Germany in deference to existing inner German, 'interzonal' trade. Here was a big step forward towards the union of Europe in which Adenauer believed implicitly, backed by a clear majority of the inhabitants of the Federal Republic.

In August, 1957, Adenauer made his first full-length election campaign speech to a crowd of 20,000 in the coal and steel city of Essen. They had braved a high wind, torrents of rain, and thunder and lightning to come to hear him. Blue and white banners proclaimed 'Tot up your facts, vote CDU' and 'At peace, our daily bread'. The crowd was well-fed, contented and prosperous. They found Adenauer at the top of his form.

He told them that CDU rule had brought the end of unemployment and the raising of the labour force by six million. Over four and a half million homes had been built. Consumption of food had shot up, especially the food that mattered, meat, fats, sugar. The cost-of-living index compared immensely favourably with that even of prosperous states like Denmark and Sweden. The German Mark was now the strongest currency in Europe. Every fact and figure was greeted by a storm of cheering, and there were roars of laughter, when Adenauer, mock-cantankerous, made fun of the SPD. With casual arrogance, he commiserated with the SPD for the loss of their leader, Schumacher, and regretted the absence of a more effective Opposition worthy of his mettle. He was setting the tone for the election campaign. This was to be a 'stomach election', and German stomachs were, indeed, well-filled. What time was left over could be devoted to the advance towards European unity, the place of the Federal Republic shoulder-to-shoulder with its Western partners, and the need to go on pursuing a coherent, unexperimental foreign policy.

The German people were in the right mood to be wooed by the government party which had done so much for them. They were given extra inducements. In June and July the Government increased income-tax-free allowances for wives from 250 to 600 Marks a year; raised disability pensions; doubled payments to former Nazi officials who had been drawing drastically downgraded pensions; revised the pensions of government officials upwards; eased the application of the turnover tax. In August it announced its plans to cut import tariffs and cheapen imported food; gave married couples the right to have their incomes taxed jointly or separately; and made a grant of 25 Marks a month to pensioners who had been decorated for valour in the First World War. This feast of bonuses was timed exactly, and unkindly from the Opposition's point of view. Its pathetic counter was the slogan 'Instead of Adenauer, Ollenhauer' – pathetic, because the plump, apologetic but verbose successor to Schumacher cut no figure at all in the popular estimation. What the SPD needed was a programme, and they had none. Efforts to vilify Adenauer boomeranged; they only gave him the extra publicity which he welcomed. The SPD even failed to make adequate use of their strong men in the *Länder*, Max Brauer in Hamburg, Wilhelm Kaisen in Bremen, Hinrich Kopf in Hanover and the much younger, ambitious Willy Brandt in West Berlin.

A CDU victory was always certain. Only the extent of it was a surprise. The CDU vote rose by two and a half million, and from 45 to over 50 per cent. Its seats in the *Bundestag* were up from 244 to 270, giving it an overall majority of 43 over all other parties combined. The SPD vote and representation in the *Bundestag* rose, too, but not enough to matter in the slightest. With 169 seats against a previous 151, it still constituted only a weak Opposition. The electoral law had been revised again; it was now necessary to win three seats by direct election as well as 5 per cent of the overall vote, in order to secure a 'proportional' number of seats on the reserve list. Clearly, this militated against the chances of the smaller parties. Only the FDP and the German Party remained in the *Bundestag*, the latter as a result of an electoral alliance in Lower Saxony with the CDU. As one observer put it, the German Party had to be 'carried into the *Bundestag* in Dr. Adenauer's rucksack'.[58]

Adenauer had made 57 election speeches, and enjoyed every one. He was carried over the length and breadth of the Federal Republic, in transatlantic style, in his own railway train. His party had expended a record sum on this election – according to the SPD, 116 million Marks.[59] Big industry had backed the universal provider, Adenauer, solidly. It financed the full-page advertisements which appeared even in newspapers

58, 59.....*The New Republic*, Terence Prittie, September 30, 1957.

hostile to the Chancellor, *Die Welt*, the *Düsseldorf Mittag*, the *Westdeutsche Allgemeine Zeitung*. To some extent, Adenauer was steam-rollered into power once more. To some extent, a one man cult had been reinforced, even though stable government was assured. There were other worrying features about this undoubted triumph for Adenauer; the SPD were disillusioned, the FDP had failed to create an effective 'third force', and over a million votes were cast for splinter parties on the extreme wings which never had a chance of securing *Bundestag* seats.

The extent of his victory meant that Adenauer could enter into a third four-year term of office believing that he could last out the full term. Prior to the election, he had doubts about this. These doubts were to recur – hardly surprising, in view of the fact that he was already in his 82nd year. But for the moment he was entirely satisfied. He could form a government with the German Party as his only coalition partner, delighted to be rid of his troublesome FDP allies. The return of the Saar had settled the last problem which could have poisoned relations with France. His close personal friendship with Dulles guaranteed a good working relationship with the United States. Western Europe was on the road to union, and the awkward hurdle of rearmament had been surmounted.

If Adenauer continued to warn of the dangers of the world situation, this had become a well-rehearsed part of his technique as a ruler. He believed he was still indispensable. His favourite story at the time was about Pope Leo XIII receiving the *corps diplomatique* on his 90th birthday. The doyen congratulated him, and expressed the hope that he would be just as fit and strong when he reached one hundred. The Pope replied – 'But why, gentlemen, should you set so low a limit on the compassion of God?'

12 Asia begins on the Elbe

In one short passage in his memoirs[1] Adenauer reveals very plainly why, apart from reasons of policy or prejudice, he remained acutely distrustful of Soviet aims in Europe. Facts, as he pointed out, speak for themselves; and, however mortal human memory may be, the Soviet performance in Europe is unforgettable.

As a result of the war, the Soviet Union annexed the three Baltic States of Estonia, Latvia and Lithuania; the eastern half of Poland, Rumanian Bessarabia and the Bukowina, half of the German province of East Prussia, parts of Finland and Czechoslovakia – in all, half a million square kilometres. The Soviet Union tried to seize West Berlin and, later, put down with brutal force popular movements in East Germany and Hungary (much later, in Czechoslovakia, too). Since 1925, Adenauer maintained, the Soviet Union in the course of forty years broke or revoked 45 out of 58 treaties which its Governments signed. In his view, the Soviet Union was the one expansionist and imperialist power in Europe. He would have agreed with the apt definition of Soviet doctrine given by a British politician – 'What's mine is mine, and what's yours is negotiable.'[2]

According to his closest adviser, Hans Globke,[3] Adenauer distrusted the Soviet Union, not (as in the case of his Foreign Minister Heinrich von Brentano), because of emotional feelings but as a result of exact analysis and calculation. He believed that the Soviet philosophy was dynamic and that world domination was its natural final aim. Whereas the Western Powers could become friends and allies of the German people, the Soviet Union regarded Germany simply as a pawn on the European chessboard. So, in face of Soviet pressure which would be persistent and utterly relentless, there was only one policy possible for his Government – to unite with the West, to resist pressure by building up the strength of the West and to hold on to the isolated advance-post of West Berlin. In his heart, Adenauer believed that Soviet aims were designed to make a real solution of the German Question (meaning, essentially, Germany's reunification as a free and independent community) absolutely impossible.

In no major sphere of policy was Adenauer more consistent and, as he

1............*Memoirs*, Konrad Adenauer, VOL 2, p. 18.
2............Desmond Donnelly, MP, at the Koenigswinter Conference, March 22, 1969.
3............Dr. Hans Globke, in private conversation with the author.

saw it, more logical than in the German Question. He was accused of being static, inflexible and the ultimate 'Cold War warrior', but such criticism moved him not at all as long as he was Chancellor. Only after retirement did he begin to have any doubts (see Chapter 14). He believed that there were only two sorts of settlement of the German Question which the Soviet Union could contemplate. The first was the Bolshevization of the whole of Germany; the second was the division of Germany, and the Bolshevization of its eastern zone of Occupation. The second seemed to him the more probable; as one adviser put it, 'Adenauer knew that even the Russians worried about security, and in East Germany they had a bird in the hand.'[4]

There is no place here to enter into a lengthy analysis of Soviet aims. One of the best-informed American observers, George Kennan, has produced a comment which is short and to the point.[5] For the Soviet Union, East Germany was of decisive military importance and there could be no question of it being given up. East Germany was both a bastion of defence and a forward-area of military deployment; its occupation meant 'that the balance of power in Europe and Asia in conventional weapons has been greatly and seriously altered to Russia's advantage'. It gave the Soviet Union advance-posts only seventy miles from the Rhine and a sophisticated communications system leading to them.

In another passage[6] Kennan writes of the abysmal initial failure of the United States to realize what the Russians were doing in Europe. Even in Roosevelt's day there had been a woolly-minded idea that the Russians had been badly treated and that this had 'caused them to be over-sensitive and defensive. A little balm to wounded hearts, a little polite treatment, a little flattery in the form of admission to the counsels of the Allies – this would fix everything.' With little experience in European affairs, leading Americans even forgot Soviet actions at the beginning of the Second World War – the Hitler–Stalin 'Robbers Pact', the attack on Finland, the partition of Poland and the seizure of the unoffending small Baltic States.

The Soviet leaders were well aware of Western ignorance of their motives, and played upon it. In yet another passage, Kennan notes that, 'Of all the hopes in the Soviet breast, the most businesslike and serious ones, the ones most formidable to us, center round this prospect for sowing disunity everywhere in the Western camp, and particularly in every relationship that has anything to do with Western strength.'[7] This, again, was something which Adenauer plainly realized. Western policies were liable at any moment to diverge and the three key Powers – the

4............Dr. Hans Globke, in private conversation with the author.
5, 6, 7.....*Realities of American Foreign Policy*, George Kennan, p. 67.

United States, Britain and France – took it in turns to produce compromise 'solutions' of the German Question which either threatened West German security or were seemingly unworkable. This was why Adenauer felt impelled continually to remind and warn his Western partners of dangers which remained real for a country in the front line of the Cold War.

The fate of West Berlin was an integral part of the German Question, and periodically its focus. Over Berlin, as opposed to the German Question as a whole, both the German people and the three Western Powers showed a fair degree of unanimity. The lesson of the Blockade would not be forgotten in a hurry. The freedom of over two million West Berliners was an intelligible objective, chiefly because it had been so obviously and so viciously threatened.

The story of Four Power negotiation over Germany, and the accompanying story of intermittent Soviet pressure on West Berlin, is long and involved. Only a bare outline can be given here in a series of episodes, when lasting peace or a 'shooting war' seemed momentarily to become more than remote possibilities.

The first such episode was in 1952. The Berlin problem had slumbered after the end of the Blockade in May, 1949. On the broader German Question, however, the Four Powers and the two German States had been busy defining their positions. Thus, the Federal Government appealed on March 22, 1950, for free, universal, direct and democratic elections in the whole of Germany, to be followed by the election of a National Assembly and the drawing up of an all-German constitution. Here was an 'ideal' solution, to which Adenauer reverted whenever under diplomatic pressure from his allies or heavy attack at home. To the Soviet Union it was unacceptable.

The Soviet Block conference in Prague, on October 21, 1950, countered with a demand for a German Peace Treaty, the formation of an all-German 'Council' on a 50–50 basis between East and West, the withdrawal of all Occupying Forces within a year and the total demilitarization of Germany. These opposing Western and Soviet positions were maintained through 1951, when completely inconclusive Four Power talks were held in the Palais Marbre Rose in Paris and an equally futile exchange of Notes took place between Adenauer and the East German Prime Minister, Otto Grotewohl. In January, 1951, Grotewohl suggested the formation of an all-German Council as the first step towards German unity. Adenauer called for the prior establishment of essential liberties in East Germany. In September Grotewohl proposed a Congress to organize elections in the whole country. Adenauer countered by making fourteen conditions, designed to ensure that such elections should be genuinely free and should lead to the creation of a free and democratic society. Grotewohl preferred to maintain tyranny under his Soviet masters. From the Western side came an additional proposal, that there should be a United Nations inquiry into conditions for the holding of free, all-German elections. The United Nations General Assembly approved this proposal by 45 votes to 6. A UN Commission was formed – the *Bundestag* approving – and was due to begin work in March, 1952.

The Federal Government was at this moment negotiating the last stages of the Bonn and Paris agreements (which were to be signed on May 26 and 27). The Soviet Union therefore launched a diplomatic offensive with its Note of March 10, 1952, proposing a Four Power Peace Conference and laying down guide-lines for Germany's future. Germany was to be reunified – and at the same time, democratized, de-militarized, de-nazified, neutralized and evacuated by all Occupying Powers.

Adenauer rejected these proposals out of hand, on the grounds that they would turn Germany into a vacuum and that the Soviet Union would, with the help of dedicated Communist supporters and the armed might of the 300,000-strong People's Police, move into this vacuum. On March 11, he obtained an assurance from the three High Commissioners that they would continue to negotiate the Bonn and Paris agreements 'as if the Soviet Note did not exist'[8] for Adenauer was convinced that the Note was a purely disruptive manoeuvre. On March 25 the Western Powers agreed to insist on free, all-German elections under UN supervision and on the right of a future German Government to choose its friends and allies. Further Soviet and Western Notes, in April and May, merely re-stated these positions.

In years to come Adenauer was often to be bitterly attacked for failing to treat the Soviet Note of March 10, 1952, as a basis for serious negotiation. He was criticized primarily by the Social Democrats, who felt that he could at least have held up the Bonn and Paris agreements while taking a long, hard look at prospects of reunification, and by the neutralists, who went so far as to regard the Soviet proposals as perfectly acceptable. Adenauer's advisers and colleagues saw things much as he did. Thus, Gerhard Schröder, in a television interview given several years later: 'Stalin's Note of March 1952 to the Western Powers was intended to give the impression that the Soviet Union was prepared to agree to reunification and to allow Germany to pursue an independent policy, if she abandoned her alliance with the West. It is my personal conviction that the real aim of the Note was clear just from the date of dispatch, for it was handed to the Western Powers at the very moment when the negotiations on the

8............*Memoirs*, Konrad Adenauer, VOL 2, p. 70.

EDC and the German Treaty were virtually completed.' Schröder thought that Stalin's purpose was to throw Europe into total confusion, and he asked if Germans were expected 'to give up their freedom and enter a prison'.

Felix von Eckardt thought that Adenauer did not lose a chance of bringing reunification nearer – 'There was no common ground with the Soviet Union, ever. They had an ideal strategic position and they had no reason to give it up. The least that they would have accepted was made clear to me years later, by Khrushchev; he said that a united Germany would have to be 'Socialized' and turned into a semi-satellite. That was the minimum Soviet security requirement.'[9] Von Eckardt wrote[10] that the Soviet Union never intended to give Germany unity and freedom – the Russians could not afford to allow free elections. While the Western Powers, for their part, could not leave a helpless, neutralized Germany; nor could they let the US armed forces retire to America, when the Red Army would only go back thirty miles, to the Polish frontier.

Erich Mende agrees with von Eckardt; the Soviet aim in 1952 was to prevent West German rearmament and bring a neutralized all-Germany into the Soviet orbit. Soviet terms were unacceptable to the great bulk of the people of the Federal Republic.[11] Hans Globke went further; in his view, the Russians did not merely want to hold up negotiations between the Western Powers and the Federal Republic, they wanted too to show that the Adenauer Government could be undecided, fickle and more interested in an accommodation with Moscow than with binding agreements with the West.[12] Globke had no slightest doubt that Adenauer was right to reject the Soviet Note. Indeed, there is this to be said for his point of view; if anybody should have been ready to look twice at the Note, it would have been the Western Powers, not the Federal Republic. That the Western Powers did not do so was due partly to a desire not to scare the Federal Government, partly to differences of opinion among themselves and partly to laziness in the field of diplomacy.[13] There was also an element of inferiority complex. One former British Ambassador to Moscow, Sir William Hayter, has written – 'The Russians always negotiate for victory.

9............Felix von Eckardt, in private conversation with the author.
10...........*Ein unordentliches Leben*, Felix von Eckardt, p. 192.
11...........Dr. Erich Mende, in private conversation with the author.
12...........Dr. Hans Globke, in private conversation with the author.
13...........Sir Anthony Eden (later Lord Avon) asked in the British House of Commons: 'Is Germany to be neutral and disarmed? If so, who will keep Germany disarmed? Or is Germany to be neutral and armed? If so, who will keep Germany neutral?' Eden's own view, which he often repeated, was that the Soviet Union's primary objective at the time was to secure the disbanding of NATO.

It never seems to occur to them that the proper object of a negotiation is not to defeat your opposite number but to arrive at an agreement with him which will be mutually beneficial.'[14] Sir William is right; and one can detect that the Western Powers, as a natural reflex to Soviet obstinacy and diplomatic aggressiveness, preferred not to be drawn into negotiation at all.

Mende believed that Adenauer could have done something more to 'test' Soviet motives in March, 1952.[15] So did Ernst Lemmer, a future Federal Minister for All-German Affairs.[16] In a somewhat vaguer way, men like Hermann Ehlers, the Speaker of the *Bundestag*, and Eugen Gerstenmaier, who was to hold that post later, were at the time hinting at the same thing. The Western Powers were still trying to have the UN Commission admitted into East Germany. They regarded this as an acid test of honourable intention on the part of the Soviet Union. The UN Commission was boycotted and banned. The Western Powers decided that there was nothing more to be done. Nor did they react to a further Soviet Note on August 29, 1952, which agreed to the holding of nominally free all-German elections, after a German Peace Treaty had been signed and a German Government formed on a 50–50 East–West basis. One can hardly blame Adenauer for going along with his Allies.

The deadlock over the 1952 Note established the pattern of Four Power exchanges over the German Question. It was followed by a hiatus in which nothing more than casual sparring took place. Adenauer himself claimed that a memorandum which he sent to President Eisenhower on May 29, 1953, represented a serious effort at securing East–West understanding.[17] In it, he asked for free elections under international control; the formation of an independent all-German Government; the right of this Government to associate itself with other nations, and to join in Peace negotiations; the right of every German to his own home (this meant the refugees); no recognition of the existing eastern frontier with Poland along the Oder–Neisse line, but peaceful resolution of territorial questions; finally, German rearmament to be restricted to the EDC, a renunciation of the right to an independent German Army which was a kind of compensatory security guarantee for Germany's neighbours.

One has to admit that this memorandum was nothing more than a

14...........*The Diplomacy of the Great Powers*, Sir William Hayter, p. 28.

15...........Dr. Erich Mende, in private conversation with the author. This was also the view of one of Adenauer's most bitter critics, Rudolf Augstein, of *Der Spiegel*. In his book *Konrad Adenauer*, he argues (p. 75) that the West should have put the Soviet Union 'to the test'.

16...........Ernst Lemmer, in letter to the author October 14, 1969.

17...........*Memoirs*, Konrad Adenauer, VOL 2, p. 243.

strictly rational statement of the West German case for reunification in genuine freedom. Every people, and every statesman representing a people, has the right to ask for what are demonstrably fair terms. But Germany was divided between two world power-blocs. This memorandum ignored this basic fact. One can assume that Adenauer did not want to take account of it. He was playing safe, and playing for time.

On June 17, 1953, the East German rising began. Stalin had died in March. For a moment, Soviet policies faltered. This was the main reason for the rising, although the East Germans had plenty of others. Industry and agriculture were being sequestrated by the Moscow-controlled State; a bad food situation was persisting years after the West Germans had begun to eat well; a Communist campaign against the Christian Churches backfired; and workers' 'production norms' were raised under threat of wage cuts. All this happened when there was talk of concession in the air, with a 'new course' of consultation being proclaimed by a new Soviet High Commissioner, Vladimir Semeonov.

The rising began in East Berlin's Stalinallee, among the building workers. It caught everyone by surprise, for it spread all over East Germany and Soviet troops had to be called in to restore order in every town with more than 50,000 inhabitants save Plauen. In some places, the Red Army opened fire, and after the rising was over, more than 40 death sentences were carried out and more than 25,000 people arrested. A purge of the ruling Socialist Unity Party followed, and three 'national Communist' leaders – men who believed in reunification – were dismissed. Under Soviet directions, the régime made some concessions; work-norms were lowered, old-age and widows' pensions were raised and more consumer goods and foodstuffs made available. The East Germans gained some of their immediate objectives, but the Western Powers and the Federal Government drew no appropriate conclusions from the affair. There should have been an immediate Western diplomatic offensive. Instead, nothing was done, and the Soviet authorities were given a breathing space in which to shore-up the eastern Zone.

The Soviet Union certainly drew one appropriate conclusion from the rising. This was that its Zone of Germany was the very last place in Communist-occupied Europe where experiments and 'new courses' could be tried out. From 1953 onwards the hallmarks of Communist administration there were the carefully phased State take-over of the means of production, the scaling down of reparations and absolutely consistent support for the régime of Walter Ulbricht and his lieutenants. The threat of losing their bastion and advance-post in the heart of Germany was a reminder to the Soviet leaders of its importance to them. Even members of the Communist 'Old Guard' were shocked. The Communist playwright, Bertholt

Brecht, wrote a poem at the time which was discovered only after his death, three years later. One passage read:

> '... you could read that the people
> Had lost the Government's confidence,
> Which it could only regain
> By redoubled efforts. Would it in that case
> Not be simpler if the Government
> Dissolved the people
> And elected another?'

From January 25 to February 18, 1954, the Soviet Union returned to the conference table at the Berlin Four Power Conference. It provided a barren exercise in diplomatic shadow-boxing. The Soviet Union's Foreign Minister, Molotov, again proposed the neutralization of a unified Germany, an all-German Government to be created prior to nominally 'free' elections and this government to be formed after deliberations in which the East and West German states should be equally represented. This time Molotov proposed the withdrawal of all Occupying Forces within six months. Once again, the end result for a reunified Germany was that it would be bound into a European collective security system. By inference, the United States would be excluded from this system.

For the Western Powers the British Foreign Minister, Sir Anthony Eden, called for free all-German elections, the formation of a National Assembly, the drafting of a constitution, the creation of an all-German Government and the negotiation of a Peace Treaty. As Adenauer saw it, there was one particular element of danger in this – the necessarily long interval between the elections and the Peace Treaty. His fear was that the Russians might accept the Eden plan, and would aim to use this long interval to cause internal disorders in West Germany. In his view there was little purpose in offering the Soviet Union terms at a time when its rulers were banking on France going Communist and a Communist-encircled all-Germany following suit. Adenauer may have been well pleased when the Berlin Conference broke up without achieving anything beyond fixing a date, April 24, for another Conference, this time in Geneva.

The Geneva talks, as it happened, concentrated on Indo-China, and agreement was reached among the Four Powers on the termination of France's disastrous struggle to maintain control of this part of her colonial empire. This was in July, and a month later France's rejection of the EDC seemed to eliminate the last main cause of friction between East and West – for the Soviet Union was utterly opposed to any West German contribution to the defence of Western Europe, and at that moment it looked as if no such contribution would be forthcoming. France was turning her attention to Algeria and Tunisia; Britain was preoccupied with the campaign against terrorists in Malaysia – the one place, indeed, where East and West were in active conflict. Adenauer was unimpressed by all this. Writing, admittedly, with the advantage of hindsight, he claimed that it was clear to him at the time that there would be no lasting peace in Indo-China and he realized that the Soviet Union would once more turn its baleful attention to Central Europe.[18] This was what did happen; during the rest of 1954 there was a string of Soviet Notes and oral communications, calling for a European Security Conference in which the German Question, obviously, would be a principal item.

At this point Adenauer – as he saw it – had to fight a battle on three fronts in the overall question of German reunification and a German Peace Treaty. On one front were the Russians, applying intermittent diplomatic pressure against the Western Alliance, relying on disunity among its partners and growing despondence and apathy over Germany, determined to get their way in the end. On the second front were the Western Powers, liable – again, as Adenauer saw it – to make unjustified and even dangerous concessions, or to fall out among themselves. On the third front was West German public opinion. At home, his main adversary was the Social Democratic Party, pleading for the delaying of all plans for Western integration in order to probe Soviet intentions. But there was another, more insidious enemy which could not be routed on the floor of the *Bundestag* – the cult of neutralism. Something must be said here about this enemy.

The first sign of a coherent effort to mobilize neutralist opinion was the formation by a Würzburg professor, Ulrich Noack, of a group calling itself the 'Nauheim Circle'. The Circle attracted the interest of prominent East Germans, some of them Communists, and all sorts of widely different groups in West Germany, right-wing nationalists, Communists and 'parlour Bolsheviks', pacifists and Socialists. In January, 1951, the Circle staged a Congress in Wiesbaden, and attracted to it Pastor Niemöller, the politically non-conforming Evangelical Church leader and tireless critic of any kind of rearmament. Niemöller's principal contention was that the situation should never be allowed to arise in which Germans might have to fight Germans. Although regarded by many as a crank, his word carried much weight. He had opposed the Nazis, been imprisoned by them, but volunteered on the outbreak of war to return to the Navy, in which he had served earlier with distinction as a submarine commander from 1914 to 1918. Thus he could call himself both anti-Nazi and patriot.

Niemöller was a considerable nuisance to Adenauer, for he bombarded

18..........*Memoirs*, Konrad Adenauer, VOL 2, p. 390.

him with letters and made outspoken speeches which attracted more attention than they deserved. More reflective neutralists were marshalled by the ex-Minister of the Interior, Gustav Heinemann, in his 'All-German People's Party', and by Dr. Günther Gereke, also a fall-out from the CDU, in the 'German Social Party'. Both men called for East–West, all-German meetings, as an adjunct to Four Power discussions. Other neutralist groups formed under an ex-Reich Chancellor, Josef Wirth, who tried, unsuccessfully, to win over the remnants of the old Catholic Centre Party; Dr. Hermann Rauschning, the former President of the Danzig Senate when the city was under League of Nations administration; and Rudolf Nadolny, a former Ambassador to Moscow.

Any of these men could have attracted a considerable following. That none did was at least partly due to their personalities. Nadolny and Wirth were senile, Noack was a dilettante and Rauschning a professorial lecturer. Heinemann lacked all popular appeal, while Gereke was frankly untrustworthy and his party was Communist-infiltrated. The groups which formed round them drifted into political backwaters. But their thoughts were picked up again by other, more representative politicians. Free Democrats began talking of a 'third solution' somewhere between total neutralization and total commitment to NATO. So did the CDU Mayor of Hamburg, Dr. Karl Sieveking: and the Speaker of the *Bundestag*, Dr. Eugen Gerstenmaier, threw out the thought that a future all-Germany need not necessarily belong to the Western Alliance. Men like these were deeply impressed when the Austrian State Treaty was signed in 1955, showing that the Russians were really prepared to let a neutral Austria lead its own life free from interference. There were rumours that the United States Government was considering the possibility of a belt of neutral states being created in Central Europe, with the guarantees of the Great Powers to ensure their survival. The Austrian State Treaty prompted a cartoon in *Die Welt*, which showed two small boys – one of them the German 'Michel', the other the Austrian Chancellor Raab – carrying bags of sweets labelled 'freedom' and 'sovereignty'. Michel was shouting, 'Uncle Sam, his bag is bigger than mine.'

West German neutralist feeling was largely a symptom of uncertainty of mind. After 1955 it began to ebb, as Adenauer always believed it would. But the neutralists were always to insist that a great opportunity had been missed of reunifying Germany in 1952. And they would insist, too, that a second, if rather less favourable opportunity was missed three years later.

On January 15, 1955, the official Soviet news agency, Tass, published a statement which was obviously prompted by the Government. It called for German unity to be established through free, all-German elections; stated the Soviet Union's readiness to establish direct relations with the

Federal Republic; and warned that ratification of the Agreements on West German rearmament and sovereignty would force the Soviet Union to 'take measures to safeguard peace and security in Europe'. The Social Democrats at once urged Adenauer to hold up ratification of the Agreements with the Western Powers, pending efforts to reunify Germany. On January 29, 1955, this demand was incorporated in the party's 'German Manifesto' which was proclaimed at a ceremony in the St. Paul's Church in Frankfurt, the 1848 birthplace of German democratic thought. The Manifesto appealed for new Four Power talks aimed at settling the 'German Question' and reunifying Germany, the exclusion of the Federal Republic from the Western Alliance and the binding of a unified Germany in an East–West European Security Pact. Politicians, professors and theologians spoke at the ceremony which earned only a caustic comment from Adenauer, that these were good-hearted men, but, in politics, experience and expertise were of more avail than good intentions.[19]

Adenauer argued that holding up ratification of the agreements with the Western Powers would endanger NATO, rule out the unification of Europe, cause an economic recession and forfeit all faith in the Federal Republic.[20] These arguments were dubious; in reality, Adenauer believed that a policy based on the 'German Manifesto' involved taking very great risks. He was not prepared to do so; it was as simple as that.

He made this plain to Eisenhower and Dulles in June, when he visited Washington, and later during the same month to Eden in London. In Washington he taxed Dulles with planning a reconciliation with the Soviet Union at Germany's expense – an accusation which Dulles fervently denied.[21] His memoirs give a picture of an almost sychophantic Dulles, whereas the debonair and more self-assured Eden talked to him about a new 'package' plan, entailing increased trade, a measure of disarmament and a Five Power Security Pact, in addition to German reunification. Eden was later to assert that Adenauer produced ideas of his own on demilitarization at the time.[22] But when the Four Power Conference met in Geneva from July 18 to 23, the Soviet Union demanded the conclusion of a Security Pact on the basis of a divided Germany. Not all Bulganin's false bonhomie and the sudden optimism of the British press, which came out with headlines on the 'New Spirit of Geneva' and 'The ice melts', could disguise the fact that the Soviet Union was hardening its position rather than the reverse.

The failure of the Geneva Conference strengthened Adenauer's newly

19..........*Memoirs*, Konrad Adenauer, VOL 2, p. 421.
20..........*Memoirs*, Konrad Adenauer, VOL 2, p. 422.
21..........*Full Circle*, Sir Anthony Eden (later Lord Avon), p. 293.
22..........*Memoirs*, Konrad Adenauer, VOL 2, p. 456.

formed resolve to try a little direct diplomacy on his own account. Invited to Moscow, he paid his first and only visit there from September 8 to 14, 1955. It was a unique occasion, for it was the only time that Adenauer ventured into what was politically unknown territory – and enemy territory at that. For once, the Chancellor took a chance. Opinions will always be divided as to whether it paid off, or not.

The first time that Adenauer had said anything in public about the possibility of some kind of reconciliation, or at least 'modus vivendi' with the Soviet Union was in May, 1954. He was then reported by the DPA West German news agency to have said in Hamburg that the establishment of diplomatic relations between the Federal Republic and the Soviet Union was possible in the foreseeable future.[23] A week later the Chancellor took fright, and declared that he had been wrongly reported. His advisers had in the meantime noted the consternation caused in Western capitals, where the old bogey of the 1922 Rapallo Treaty was once again conjured up. That treaty, it may be remembered, entailed a 'de jure' recognition of the Soviet Union – Germany was the first major power to accord it – the cancellation of war claims and pre-war debts, and commercial and clandestine military co-operation. Adenauer's alarm was understandable. The attempt of diplomatic relations with Moscow was dropped as abruptly as it had been broached.

During the rest of 1954 Adenauer was at pains to reassure Western leaders of his government's absolute loyalty.[24] In 1955 Adenauer began to worry about Western deviation from his policy of strength, rather than about Western suspicions of German deviationism. He was particularly concerned by one of Eden's ideas, of creating a 'Zone of limited and equalized armaments' in Germany. What Eden foresaw was a mutual East–West withdrawal of armed forces from the frontier running through the middle of Germany. A zone of limited armaments stretching sixty miles on either side of the interzonal frontier would have caused the Russians grave strategic problems; their military training areas and points of main military concentration would have had to be abandoned. But Adenauer, according to one of his advisers, ruled out this otherwise excellent idea on two grounds: the Western Alliance would have been left with a frighteningly small area of manoeuvre to the west of the partially de-militarized zone, and a large part of the United States forces might have been withdrawn to America – whereas the Russians would go back only to the Polish frontier, fifty miles east of Berlin.[25] Eden himself abandoned his idea; it was to be briefly revived, later, by Harold Macmillan.

23..........The *Manchester Guardian*, May 8, 1954.
24..........*Tides of Fortune*, Harold Macmillan, p. 479.
25..........Dr. Hans Globke, in private conversation with the author.

On June 17, 1955, Macmillan and Adenauer had a meeting in the Waldorf-Astoria Hotel in New York. According to the former, Adenauer told him that the Soviet Union probably wanted a détente and might even abandon its East German satellite in return for solid security guarantees.[26] Adenauer allegedly also suggested that there could be demilitarized zones, with zones of limited armaments to east and west of them, all being integral parts of an overall but misty scheme for general, controlled disarmament. Possibly Adenauer was testing Macmillan's reactions, in order to discover what was in his mind. Otherwise it would seem surprising for Adenauer to have revived the 'Eden plan', even in a modified form. At all events, the Adenauer–Macmillan conversation had no outward result.

That the Soviet Government should have invited Adenauer to Moscow may seem, on the face of it, as surprising as his decision to accept the invitation. But the Soviet leaders had one very good reason for being prepared to establish diplomatic relations with the Federal Republic – after the necessary preliminaries of bogus friendliness and camaraderie. At the Geneva Conference in July, Bulganin put the case for general recognition of two separate German states, and of suspending all steps towards reunification as long as NATO and the Warsaw Pact existed. Russian recognition of the West German State was the natural corollary of this 'two-State' theory; and the Soviet leaders hoped that it would lead to a general loosening-up of East–West relations – which the West might favour – and to mutual recognition of both German States – which the West had so far rigidly opposed. In addition, while a West German diplomatic presence in Moscow would not have the slightest effect on Soviet policies, a Soviet Embassy in Bonn could be used in various ways, some of them questionable.[27]

Adenauer had three reasons for going to Moscow. The first was humanitarian. Negotiations had begun on the return of German prisoners-of-war who had now been more than ten years in captivity. More than 1,150,000 soldiers were still listed as missing. Of 750,000 deported at the end of the war at least half a million were known to have died. By dint of careful questioning of returned prisoners, the German Red Cross had, in the

26...........*Tides of Fortune*, Harold Macmillan, pp. 606–7.

27...........Neutralist opinion could be encouraged, the Social Democrats discreetly wooed, and a close watch kept on Adenauer's Government. The Communist underground would be given a useful postal address in Bonn, and help could be given by the Soviet Embassy to the espionage activities of the singularly inept Soviet Military Mission in Westphalia. Its members spent much of their time patrolling the perimeters of key industrial plants, executing amateurish sketches of them. There were cases of Soviet officers foolishly reporting at the house of the British Liaison Officer, which stood at the gates of the Russian compound at Buende.

summer of 1955, arrived at a figure of around 130,000 prisoners-of-war still held in the Soviet Union. This figure was a terrible indictment of the harshness of captivity in the Soviet Union. Prisoners were not even equated with cattle; they were, in Soviet eyes, far more expendable. The Soviet Government admitted the existence of only 9,000 to 10,000 Germans in their hands, and claimed that they were all war criminals. The negotiations carried out by the German Red Cross were bogged down. Adenauer genuinely wanted to do something about the German prisoners-of-war. It would be unfair to regard his attitude as being dictated by political opportunism.

Adenauer's two other reasons for going to Moscow were less obvious. He hoped to soften the Soviet attitude towards the Federal Republic, as no progress towards a solution of the German Question could be made without Soviet co-operation. And he hoped too that the Soviet Union might be prepared for an accommodation over Germany, in view of pressing domestic problems and the beginnings of trouble with Communist China. At least, it could be worth probing Soviet intentions.

The Moscow visit had all the trappings of high drama. Around seventy members of the huge delegation – it was so large because there was no agenda and the Russians might insist on talking on almost any subject – were sent to Moscow on a special train. Two planes took off from Cologne airfield, with Adenauer in one and his Foreign Minister, von Brentano, in the other. They were met at Moscow airport by the Prime Minister, Bulganin, the Foreign Minister, Molotov, and a guard of honour decked out in new uniforms of Cambridge blue with scarlet facings.[28] Adenauer and his principal advisers were housed in the Hotel Sovietskaya, one of Moscow's biggest and most tasteless 'wedding-cake' buildings. Adenauer's own room contained a grand piano. His 'offices' were in the special train, for which a new siding had been built, flanked with flower-beds and fountains, and surrounded by a high stockade. The negotiations took place in the Spiridonovka Palace, with the principal members of the two 'teams' seated on opposite sides of a long table. Across the table, Adenauer was confronted by the cold, inhuman stare of Bulganin's pale blue eyes, and the mobile peasant features of the rumbustious Khrushchev. They made a formidable combination.

For two days no progress whatever was made. The Russians insisted that there were only 9,628 German prisoners in their hands, all of them war-criminals. They recited long lists of Nazi crimes committed in the Soviet Union. At first they refused to discuss the prisoners at all, unless there were to be a Conference at which the East German State would be

28..........*Ein unordentliches Leben*, Felix von Eckardt, p. 384.

represented. When Adenauer mentioned the fact that some 'terrible things' had happened after the Red Army invaded Germany,[29] Khrushchev nearly burst with rage. He claimed that Adenauer had impugned the honour of the Red Army, which had only carried out its 'sacred duty', and with deliberate brutality he described the fate of Italians who had invaded Russia – they had been 'coffined' (the German word used by the interpreter was *eingesargt*). He fairly yelled the word at the impassive Adenauer. When the latter broached the question of reunification, Khrushchev shook his fist at him. Adenauer rose to his feet and raised both fists clenched.[30]

Later he countered Khrushchev's wilder invective against the Federal Government by asking 'Who in fact signed an Agreement with Hitler? You, or I?', and by indulging in his favourite theme of the decrepit Great Powers who flattered and fawned on Hitler instead of standing up to him.[31] The talks alternated between relatively quiet spells of discussion, and the verbal fireworks of Khrushchev and the coldly bitter denunciations of Bulganin and Molotov. At one stage Khrushchev produced perhaps the most extravagantly absurd remark of the conference, when he said that 'capitalists roast Communists and eat them – what's more without salt!'[32]

On the third day of the talks Adenauer was taken out to a *dacha*, or villa outside Moscow. A long rambling discussion took place there; at least it was on a quieter note. Sunday, September 11, was a 'rest day'. It found Adenauer in a reflective mood, musing on the cheerlessness of the streets and the citizens of Moscow, and the absence of perambulators, which caused him to wonder if the birth-rate was sinking. On the Monday, von Brentano was able to explain quietly to Molotov that diplomatic relations could not be established until progress was made over the prisoners-of-war. But Khrushchev was at his bullying worst. At the end of their meeting Adenauer returned to his hotel and gave instructions that his special 'plane, which had gone back to Frankfurt, should be sent for at once. The astute von Eckardt arranged that the plane should be ordered by an 'open' telephone call. This would ensure that the Soviet leaders knew.[33] The knowledge might soften them up.

It did. That night there was a banquet. Adenauer and his advisers were given their usual doses of olive oil by the tireless Globke beforehand, ensuring that they would stand up to the endless toasts in vodka.[34] At the

29..........*Memoirs*, Konrad Adenauer, VOL 2, p. 509.
30..........*Memoirs*, Konrad Adenauer, VOL 2, p. 512.
31..........*Memoirs*, Konrad Adenauer, VOL 2, p. 515.
32..........*Memoirs*, Konrad Adenauer, VOL 2, p. 519.
33..........*Ein unordentliches Leben*, Felix von Eckardt, p. 396.
34..........*Memoirs*, Konrad Adenauer, VOL 2, p. 530.

banquet, Bulganin took Adenauer aside. He told him that the Soviet Union would return all Germans still held prisoner, if Adenauer would write him an appropriate letter. It was an astonishing volte-face, for only a few minutes earlier Bulganin had been maintaining that virtually all Germans who had been taken to the Soviet Union had been 'buried long ago'.[35] Bulganin's condition was that diplomatic relations should be established. Khrushchev, who had joined them, urged acceptance and said that the Soviet Government pledged its 'word of honour' that the prisoners would be returned.[36] Adenauer asked to be allowed to sleep on this proposal. Toasts began to be drunk, apparently in wine, and Adenauer discovered that the wily Russians were pledging good faith in water. He saw to it that they drank wine too; but it was the sort of minor incident which showed the value of Russian good faith more plainly than anything else could.

On September 13 there were agitated internal German and German–Soviet discussions. Some of Adenauer's advisers were against establishing diplomatic relations. Blankenhorn was afraid of the adverse reactions of Western allies.[37] According to Adenauer, von Brentano and Hallstein were totally opposed.[38] Blankenhorn and Hallstein were men whose advice Adenauer generally weighed, and accepted. This time he took a decision which von Eckardt and Globke, alone among his intimates, seem to have backed. He accepted a verbal assurance on the return of the prisoners-of-war, agreed to write the letter requesting the establishment of diplomatic relations and helped to draft a final joint communiqué. There remained only the leavetaking. It produced a strange vignette, as Adenauer was getting into the car taking him to the airport. An old woman pushed her way through the throng, seized Adenauer's hand and kissed it. Who was she? There is no record. Adenauer, according to von Eckardt, tried gently to stop her act of salutation (he probably realized it could send her to Siberia), then stroked her white hair once and stepped into the waiting car.[39] A small but spontaneous gesture can tell its own story.

There was an immediate tendency to minimize Adenauer's performance in Moscow. One authority considered that he 'was exposed to a roughness of treatment which caught him unawares', that he got a 'shabby deal' and that the 'delayed shock to his ego' caused a bout of pneumonia on his return to Bonn.[40] A British statesman thought Adenauer's visit to Moscow

35..........*Memoirs*, Konrad Adenauer, VOL 2, p. 546.
36..........*Ein unordentliches Leben*, Felix von Eckardt, p. 397.
37..........*Ein unordentliches Leben*, Felix von Eckardt, p. 399.
38..........*Memoirs*, Konrad Adenauer, VOL 2, p. 546.
39..........*Ein unordentliches Leben*, Felix von Eckardt, p. 399.
40..........*Watcher on the Rhine*, Brian Connell, p. 249.

was a 'salutary' experience for him – 'At least it will stop the Germans rebuking us (as they are apt to do) for our weakness towards the Russians.'[41] I myself noted that Adenauer had given two undertakings before he left for Moscow. He would not trade the fate of German prisoners-of-war for concessions in the diplomatic arena, and he would grant the establishment of diplomatic relations only in return for some progress towards German reunification – 'He was unable to fulfil either promise. The lives of 10,000 German prisoners were, as it happened, traded against the establishment of diplomatic relations between Bonn and Moscow. No progress at all was made towards German re-unification.'[42]

These criticisms are still valid. Adenauer's gamble did not come off. In his defence it should be said that he showed all his personal blend of toughness and resilience. He out-stared Molotov, remarking caustically that it must have been an unpleasant experience to find oneself in agreement with Hitler; and he brushed off Khrushchev's clumsy assaults with elegant dexterity, telling him that 'friends' should speak openly, but that rebuke was the only answer to openness of speech which went beyond the limits of civilized intercourse.[43] At the very end of his Moscow visit, he made the agreement reached with the Soviet leaders conditional on acceptance by Cabinet and *Bundestag*, and he expressly stated that opening diplomatic relations with the Soviet Union did not affect the Federal Republic's claim to be the sole legal representative of the German people, or the claim of that German people to homelands which were rightfully theirs.

In a sense, the Moscow Conference was the climax of German–Soviet relations, at least for Adenauer's lifetime. The next years were to bring absolutely no progress towards the German–Soviet understanding for which Adenauer took a gamble and in which the Soviet leaders never took an honest interest. They were difficult years for the Soviet Union and its gradually consolidating East German satellite. For the Federal Republic, and its unenthusiastic Western supporters in its quest of reunification, they were years of total frustration.

At the end of 1955 and during most of 1956 Adenauer was having considerable trouble with his Free Democratic coalition partners. On September 20, 1955, the Soviet Union entrusted the East German Authorities with supervision of all traffic, other than Allied military transport, using the routes through East German territory to Berlin. This led to intermittent friction and to a number of incidents on the Berlin–Helmstedt autobahn, and the Free Democrats – always on the lookout for a chance to assert independent views – began to question the wisdom of the Govern-

41...........*Tides of Fortune*, Harold Macmillan, p. 626.
42...........The *Manchester Guardian*, Terence Prittie, April 10, 1956.
43...........Dr. Hans Globke, in private conversation with the author.

ment's all-German policies. One leading member, Friedrich Middelhauve, called for direct East–West, all-German negotiations. The testy Thomas Dehler began to criticize the establishment of diplomatic relations with Moscow, having formerly been a keen protagonist. Dehler, windily oratorical as ever, had in Adenauer's view become a 'burden' to the coalition.[44] In February, 1956 the 'young Turks' of the FDP engineered the downfall of the CDU-led Government in North-Rhine–Westphalia, and as a result the FDP Parliamentary Party in Bonn split, with four FDP Ministers forming a secessionist 'Free People's Party'. The rump FDP became more vocal in its independent criticism of government policies, and Dehler coined an evocative phrase applying to the subject of reunification, which was to be sought with 'an impatience which is holy'.

These domestic ruptures were less worrying to Adenauer than the attitude of his Western allies. In May, 1956, the US Ambassador in Moscow, George Kennan, produced a memorandum advocating a policy of peaceful co-existence with the Soviet Union. Its contents were leaked to the Press and Adenauer was deeply disturbed.[45] Kennan had been an apostle of 'containment' of the Soviet Union – as against Dulles' frankly chimerical notion of a 'roll-back' of entrenched Soviet power to the pre-war boundaries of the Soviet Union. Now Kennan was arguing that the Communist system had come to stay in Eastern Europe as a whole. The West must learn to live with it, and one way of doing this would be to create a belt of neutral states and gradually extend it. Kennan even questioned the wisdom of rearming West Germany, as a possible impediment to the all-out diplomatic effort to reunify Germany which he urged.

Even more worrying to Adenauer's concept of steadily building up Western strength was the so called 'Radford Plan' published on July 13, 1956. Admiral Arthur Radford, the Chairman of the US Joint Chiefs of Staff Committee, proposed the reduction of US armed forces by 800,000 men to a total of two million, the cutting of military commitments abroad and reliance on nuclear weapons. Then there were rumours that the United States intended to withdraw half of its military contingents in Europe by the next Spring. Leading American Republicans were agog with the prospect of 'bringing the boys home' and scoring a point in the coming election campaign.

Adenauer sent General Heusinger to Washington to find out whether the Radford Plan was likely to be adopted. He himself believed that dependence on the nuclear deterrent meant increasing diplomatic inactivity on the part of the West. When Dulles' brother, Allan Dulles,

44..........*Memoirs*, Konrad Adenauer, VOL 3, p. 88.
45..........*Memoirs*, Konrad Adenauer, VOL 3, p. 143.

called on him in Bonn, the Chancellor told him that NATO was in danger of becoming 'senile' and a 'mere club for Officers', and that the prospects of organizing an effective West German military contribution were jeopardized.[46] He was appalled by the military weakness of France and Britain, and his contempt for their pawky contributions to Europe's defence was reinforced by the sheer ineptitude of the Franco-British attack on Egypt in October, 1956. His spirits were only temporarily revived by the dismissal of Poland's Stalinist leaders and by a fatuously optimistic analysis of the 'Polish spring-time' given to him by his own Foreign Ministry.

Adenauer viewed with deep suspicion the efforts of President Eisenhower at the end of 1956 and in 1957 to sound Soviet intentions, and he was infuriated by the carefully worked-out, if somewhat Utopian blueprint, for European disarmament and a European security pact tabled by the British Labour Party leader, Hugh Gaitskell, in speeches at Harvard University and the Free University of West Berlin early in 1957. Adenauer himself was banging away at the need to strengthen Europe's defences in face of 'nine thousand Russian tanks'.[47] He pointed out that they were confronted by two-and-a-half American and one-and-a-half British divisions, with most of France's unimpressive army in North Africa, and Holland and Belgium only producing token military contributions. Less than ever before was Adenauer prepared to take even a calculated risk in order to bring about a solution of the German Question. He showed not the slightest interest in the plan purveyed at the end of 1956 by the East German leader, Walter Ulbricht, for a 'Confederation' of two equally entitled German states.[48] He believed that impossible conditions would be attached to any such Confederation and that the Soviet purpose would be to bring the Confederation into its own sphere of influence.[49]

At this stage Adenauer was harping on the need to secure general, controlled disarmament. This was not, in spite of SPD claims, incompatible with building up Western military strength. What Adenauer was aiming at was a greater equality of conventional forces between East and West, prior to mutually agreed reductions. In July and August, 1957 the Western Powers put forward promising proposals at the London Disarmament Conference. They included the holding of free elections in the whole of Germany, an All-German Government to be formed with freedom to make its own foreign policy, the four Great Powers to assume responsibility for reunifying Germany and a European Security Pact to be

46..........*Memoirs*, Konrad Adenauer, VOL 3, p. 213.
47..........*Memoirs*, Konrad Adenauer, VOL 3, p. 243.
48..........*Neues Deutschland*, East Berlin newspaper, December 31, 1956.
49..........Dr. Hans Globke, in private conversation with the author.

framed in order to meet Soviet requirements. Adenauer was not over-impressed by these proposals – for one thing their timing was unfortunate, as Federal elections were due to take place in September. He conceded that a probe of Soviet intentions was just worth while, and prophesied its failure. He was right; the London Conference broke up on September 6, 1957, without concrete result. Nor, three months later, did a Soviet initiative for a Summit Conference come to anything; it foundered during the preliminaries of arranging an agenda and deciding on aims.

The Russians had meanwhile launched their first Sputnik, on October 4, 1957. Adenauer's reaction was interesting. He was frankly delighted – 'I regarded this Sputnik almost as a gift from Heaven, for otherwise the free world would have sunk even further into its twilight sleep.'[50] Soviet supremacy in the field of rocketry would, Adenauer believed, force the United States to place greater reliance on the Western Alliance and might even lead to the fulfilment of one of his cherished dreams, to give NATO a political content. The launching of the Sputnik was followed by a long series of intimate talks with the Soviet Ambassador in Bonn, Andrei Smirnov, a man of considerable arrogance and intellectual ability. These talks represented the first intelligible attempt by Adenauer to probe Soviet intentions since his Moscow visit.

They led nowhere. In December, 1957, one finds Smirnov advising Adenauer to emulate the example of Peter the Great and recognize when it was time to 'leave off' – an oblique reference to the Soviet view that West Germany should leave NATO and embrace a creed of neutralism.[51] In February and March, 1958, Smirnov brought Adenauer Soviet Notes urging bilateral talks between the Soviet Union and the Federal Republic, and parallel talks between East and West Germany on a *modus vivendi*. Adenauer's answer was to insist on German unity as a prerequisite to peace in Central Europe – 'Let the seventeen million Germans go free, and you will have rendered an outstandingly great service to the friendly co-operation of our two countries.'[52]

On March 7, 1958, Smirnov called on Adenauer and in hectoring tone demanded why the Federal Republic was opposing both a Summit Conference and bilateral talks with East Germany. Adenauer argued back that the Soviet aim was the signing of separate Peace Treaties with both German states and this would be tantamount to the proclamation of the division of his country. Smirnov retorted that the 'Democratic German Republic' in East Berlin was a sovereign state, had existed as an entity for thirteen years and been 'independent' for eight. He repeated the Soviet

50..........*Memoirs*, Konrad Adenauer, VOL 3, p. 319.
51..........*Memoirs*, Konrad Adenauer, VOL 3, p. 348.
52..........*Memoirs*, Konrad Adenauer, VOL 3, p. 358.

proposal of a 'Confederation' of two equally entitled German states. Twelve days later Smirnov was again in the offices of the Palais Schaumburg, bearing a Soviet Note which, according to Adenauer, 'to put it mildly, was very unfriendly'.[53] This time Adenauer countered unexpectedly by asking Smirnov if the Soviet Union would give the East German state 'the status of Austria'. Smirnov was visibly at a loss. After much mumbling he fell back on the fiction that the East German Republic was 'truly sovereign' and that the Soviet Union could not interfere in its internal affairs. The truth, of course, was very different. Every important East German policy directive emanated from Moscow.

Adenauer was later to tell Smirnov that he had risked 'being stoned by my own people' for making this 'Austrian offer'.[54] His meetings with the Soviet Ambassador ceased for the time being, and the latter turned to the leaders of the SPD Opposition for support for the Soviet aims of West German military neutrality and the two-State Confederation. In an isolated meeting with Smirnov on October 14, 1958, one finds Adenauer appealing vainly to Smirnov to consider the humanitarian aspects of Germany's division. He told the story of the West German woman who applied for an entry permit to East Germany, as her mother was dying there. The official answer of the East German authorities was that her mother would die, whether or not she saw her. Smirnov was not in the least degree interested. His series of conversations with Adenauer had produced no sort of meeting of minds. Nor, one must assume, were they intended to. The Soviet Union was indulging in its favourite practice of shadow-boxing in order to weaken an ageing and exposed enemy. This was the negation of constructive diplomacy. In it, Adenauer could see only dangerous pitfalls. On balance, he was undoubtedly right.

On October 27, 1958, the second major Communist assault on West Berlin began. The first storm signal was a speech by the East German leader, Walter Ulbricht, claiming that the whole of Berlin was within the territory of the 'German Democratic Republic'. In the recent past, under the orders of his masters in Moscow, Ulbricht had been offering West Germany a non-aggression pact, a place in a German Confederation and the prospect, undefined and dim, of closer 'human relations' between the populations of the two German states. Now the direct squeeze on West Berlin was to be substituted for generally aggressive diplomacy which had reaped no rewards. On November 12 Khrushchev declared that all Soviet rights and duties in Berlin would be turned over to the East Germans. The Western Powers rejected this statement as a contravention of the Four

53..........*Memoirs*, Konrad Adenauer, VOL 3, p. 376.
54..........*Memoirs*, Konrad Adenauer, VOL 3, p. 378.

Power status of the city. Then, on November 20, 1958, Smirnov gloatingly read out to Adenauer a message in which his Government declared that the 1945 Potsdam Agreement was null and void, and that the Soviet Union would unilaterally transfer all operative 'functions' in Berlin to the East Germans. On November 27 Khrushchev followed this up with a 44 page Note – a typical example of Soviet saturation tactics – informing the Western Powers that Berlin's Four Power status had ended and that a new status must be worked out in the next six months. Otherwise the Soviet Union would conclude a separate Peace Treaty with the East German State.

The Soviet proposal was that West Berlin should be converted into a demilitarized 'free city', guaranteed by the four Occupying Powers and perhaps by the United Nations. This proposal was sharply opposed by the West Berlin administration under the Governing Mayor, Willy Brandt, and by the Western Powers. On December 14 the Foreign Ministers of the three Western Powers and of the Federal Republic met in Paris and asserted their determination to maintain the existing status of Berlin. The NATO Council confirmed this statement. Firmness paid off; on January 10, 1959, the Soviet Government called for a Summit Conference on Berlin but did not mention the six month deadline for an agreed new status. The Western Powers agreed to a Conference, which opened in Geneva on May 11, 1959. The immediate crisis was, by then, already over. It could have led to catastrophe, had the Soviet Union sensed any hint of weakness on the part of the West and if, as a result, it had been encouraged to apply actual physical pressure on West Berlin. The course of the unproductive Geneva Summit belongs to a later chapter of this book.

In his first ten years in office Adenauer had been unable to make any progress towards a solution of the German Question, meaning essentially German reunification. Was his failure inevitable, or culpable? If the latter, what else could he have done to make reunification a possibility? Or did he commit mistakes which, in fact, helped to make reunification impossible? These are questions which will continue to be asked for generations to come. Here, at least, is an attempt at an answer.

One criticism of Adenauer is that he failed to encourage an 'appropriate climate' for East–West understanding. In a general sense, this is hardly justified. His Social Democratic opponents had no better luck, even when their leader, Erich Ollenhauer, met Khrushchev in East Berlin on March 9, 1959,[55] and their two special delegates, Carlo Schmid and Fritz Erler, went to Moscow a week later.[56] One of Adenauer's closest advisers believed

55..........The *Manchester Guardian*, Terence Prittie, March 10, 1959.
56..........The *Manchester Guardian*, Terence Prittie, March 19, 1959.

that he did what he could to improve the climate of Russo-German relations – he made the 'voyage into the unknown' to Moscow, he listened patiently to the arrogant Andrei Smirnov, he made proposals to him for an interim solution.[57] Admittedly, he may have shown too little imagination. But the criticism of one biographer was surely not justified, that 'the chances of an attempt to preserve national unity, and of delivering East Germany from Ulbricht's loathesome brand of satellite Communism, were not explored because the leading German statesman did not wish it.'[58] Adenauer was never in a position to 'preserve' German unity. He was starkly confronted by the division of Germany when he first came to power.

Equally, one can dismiss what was probably the most violent attack ever made on Adenauer in the *Bundestag*, on January 23, 1958, by Thomas Dehler. In the course of his speech Dehler claimed that Adenauer's sole aim had been to give prosperity and security to 50 million West Germans, that he had induced the Western Powers to turn down an offer of a unified Germany with an army of 300,000, and that he had utterly neglected the interests of the 17 million East Germans. Dehler concluded his speech with the words: 'You, Dr. Adenauer, have proved that you did all that you could to hinder reunification.' All this was pure hyperbole. Adenauer's own speech in this debate proved that he acted with great circumspection and with a distrust of Soviet motives which was amply justified by the post-war Soviet record in Europe and other parts of the world.

There have been more specific criticisms of Adenauer's all-German policy. One was that, by recognizing Germany's eastern frontiers, he could have weakened the Soviet grip on Poland and Czechoslovakia, and might have brought a normalization of the Federal Republic's relations with those countries. Adenauer's chief objection to recognition of the Oder–Neisse line was that it deprived West Germany of a useful bargaining-counter. There was a subsidiary reason; he believed that the Federal Republic would be asked to meet Polish and Czech war-losses, and to recognize the East German state.[59] That far-reaching reparations demands would be made by Poland was actually communicated to Hans Globke by a member of the Polish Parliament, Stanislav Stomma in April, 1958. Under the Potsdam Agreement, Polish occupation of the lost eastern provinces required confirmation in a Peace Treaty. That remained the legal position up to, and after, Adenauer's death.

Adenauer was also taken to task for adopting the so-called 'Hallstein Doctrine', which laid down that the Federal Republic would be entitled to

57..........Dr. Heinrich Krone, in private conversation with the author.
58..........*Konrad Adenauer*, Rudolf Augstein, p. 78.
59..........Dr. Hans Globke, in private conversation with the author.

sever relations with countries recognizing the East German state. Walter Hallstein himself has said that his name was tacked on to this 'doctrine' by 'personal enemies'.[60] The 'doctrine' was applied on October 20, 1957, when relations with Yugoslavia were severed, following that country's opening of diplomatic relations with the East Germans. The 'Hallstein Doctrine' (one must use the phrase for lack of a better one) was intended to be used flexibly. Perhaps it was not always so used. It served at least its purpose of discouraging recognition of the satellite East German state by other powers for as long as could be expected. Certainly, it was not an instrument of East–West understanding, but that was not its purpose.

Another criticism is that Adenauer was unsympathetic towards well-meant efforts to promote East–West détente which would possibly open the way to a solution of the German Question. The epic example of this was rejection of the 'Rapacki Plan' of the Polish Foreign Minister, put forward in October, 1957. The suave, elegant and highly articulate Adam Rapacki proposed the creation of a zone of limited armaments in Central Europe which would include both German states, as well as Poland and Czechoslovakia, and which could later be extended. Adenauer dismissed this plan on the grounds that a zone even 400 miles wide was purposeless in an age of inter-continental rockets, and that it would only divert attention from the need for general, controlled disarmament.[61] In private, Adenauer admitted his fear that the Rapacki Plan would leave the Western Alliance without a 'strategic hinterland'.[62] He distrusted it as an avenue towards the neutralization of Germany and the creation of a 'vacuum' into which Communism would force its way.

Realistic, or unimaginative? One can take one's choice. Statesmen are always blamed, and seldom given the benefit of any doubt. But on the overall question of Adenauer's all-German policy, such benefit of doubt may be justified. His periodic ally but ready critic, Erich Mende, believes that there was never a real chance of German reunification during the 'Adenauer era' – there were only 'formal' chances in 1952, 1955 and 1959.[63] These chances were themselves made dependent on concessions which Adenauer never believed he could afford. Germany would be neutralized, and democratic institutions in West Germany put under Soviet pressure. The United States would be forced out of Europe, NATO disbanded and the whole of Germany brought into the Soviet orbit. In Mende's view, Adenauer could be blamed only for not testing Soviet intentions more openly and readily. But, in his view, they would quickly

60...........Professor Walter Hallstein, in private conversation with the author.
61...........The *Manchester Guardian*, Terence Prittie, December 6, 1958.
62...........Dr. Hans Globke, in private conversation with the author.
63...........Dr. Erich Mende, in private conversation with the author.

have proved – when fully tested – to have been diametrically opposed to the rights and freedoms of the great majority of the German people.

Willy Brandt, governing Mayor of West Berlin (later the first Social Democratic Federal Chancellor), wrote that 'The Geneva Four Power Conferences in 1954 and 1959 foundered on the intransigence of the Soviets.'[64] It may well be that the best chance of making progress towards reunification was not in 1952, 1955 or 1959, but in 1953, when Stalin's death left the Soviet Union temporarily rudderless and Beria was sounding East German 'national Communists' like Zaisser and Schirdewan on the possibility of toppling Ulbricht. But the June, 1953 East German rising ended that interval of Soviet doubt. Thereafter the new Soviet leaders seem to have settled for the reality of 17 million East Germans in the Soviet orbit. The Soviet Union, as one German commentator judged, saw its sphere of influence under periodic threat – the East German rising of 1953, the Hungarian revolution of 1956, the Polish 'Springtime' in the same year, the Roumanian 'deviation' and the gallant Czech effort to find its own synthesis of Communism and democratic freedom.[65] The Soviet Union would therefore always fend off any attempt at a fair solution of the German Question. The only concrete criticism which this commentator had of Adenauer's policies was that he had not built up the economy of the 'boundary areas' along the interzonal frontier through the middle of Germany.[66]

Of Soviet diplomacy Sir William Hayter has written that it 'has great handicaps: a certain clumsiness, amounting on occasion to an alienating brutality; an inability to inspire confidence in anyone, the counterpart of its lack of inhibiting scruples; and above all, an almost total, perhaps incorrigible lack of understanding of the real character, motives and feelings of the foreign countries with whom it has to deal'.[67] In another passage the same author writes of the unshakeable belief of every Soviet negotiator that his 'bourgeois' opposite number is unalterably hostile to the Soviet Union, and that there are no common ideals – not even common denominators – for humanity.[68] This is what the Western Powers, and Adenauer, were up against when trying to achieve progress towards a solution of the German Question. Confronted by the unique combination of Soviet distrust and cunning, brutality and doubt, no statesman in the history of the world would have reached an understanding. The Soviet Union never wanted reunification; it was only prepared to examine such a

64..........*A Peace Policy for Europe*, Willy Brandt, p. 129.
65..........*Rethinking German Policy*, Wilhelm Wolfgang Schuetz, p. 12.
66..........*Rethinking German Policy*, Wilhelm Wolfgang Schuetz, p. 50.
67..........*The Diplomacy of the Great Powers*, Sir William Hayter, p. 32.
68..........*The Diplomacy of the Great Powers*, Sir William Hayter, p. 28.

prospect when it was periodically in despair over the weakness of its East German satellite.

In February, 1959, Adenauer saw John Foster Dulles for the last time. When he arrived in Bonn, the Chancellor was appalled by his appearance. He was dying of cancer, but assured Adenauer that he would need only a minor operation when he returned to Washington. The two men discussed world policies and found themselves, as usual, in complete agreement, especially on the need to maintain a firm front against aggressive Soviet diplomacy. On a grey and wretched day they drove to Cologne airport. A few days later Dulles was dead. His last correspondence with Adenauer was about an oatmeal soup which the Chancellor had discreetly had served to him at a Bonn banquet. His death was a bitter loss to the Chancellor. 'Dulles and I,' he wrote later, 'were agreed on one key principle; no concessions without concessions in return. We were accused of being obstinate and static, and the whole world wrote that we should be more flexible.' Adenauer regarded 'flexibility', where East–West relations were concerned, as an illusion.[69]

69...........*Memoirs*, Konrad Adenauer, VOL 3, p. 479.

13 Ebb-tide

In his last years, Adenauer never made a secret of what he believed his greatest achievement to have been. Already during the First World War he was thinking about the need for Franco-German reconciliation. Immediately after that war was over he was preaching it as a political creed. Adenauer's critics called him a 'Carolingian' and tried to turn his veneration of Charlemagne's Empire into an accusation of outdated sentimentalism. To many of them there was something 'un-German' about his attachment to the ideal of Franco-German understanding. They did not pause to reflect that the bitter hostility which was allowed to grow up between the two nations was wasteful, wrong and periodically disastrous.

When Charles de Gaulle came to power in June, 1958, there was little reason to suppose that this might be the dawn of a new era of reason and light in Franco-German relations. Only one member of Adenauer's Cabinet seems to have believed that it was. The Minister of Defence, Franz Josef Strauss, suggested that he should go at once to Paris to make contact with de Gaulle. Hans Globke advised Adenauer against sending him, on the grounds that the only man who should see de Gaulle was the Chancellor himself.[1] Adenauer, as he so often did, took Globke's advice.

Adenauer had, in any case, grave doubts about de Gaulle. The latter had been a prisoner-of-war in Germany during the First World War, and had little reason to love Germans. In the Second World War he had led the Free French with a single-minded, unflagging determination to defeat Germany. In December, 1944, he had signed the Franco-Soviet Pact of Friendship. He did not appear to be a 'good European', for he had opposed the idea of a European Defence Community – Adenauer's hobby-horse – and was lukewarm towards the burgeoning European Common Market. He had the reputation of being a nationalist, and the two volumes of his memoirs which had already been published were full of references to *la gloire* and *la grande nation*. He proclaimed as his Government's three main aims a settlement of the Algerian problem, the consolidation of the economy and the reform of the constitution. Nothing about Europe. Finally, he had come to power as a result of the threat of military in-

1............Dr. Hans Globke, in personal conversation with the author.

surrection. His Government might be as ephemeral as those of its two dozen short-lived predecessors of the Fourth Republic. One remark of his may have suggested that he thought so himself – 'How can you govern a country which produces 246 different kinds of cheese?'[2]

On June 17, 1958, de Gaulle sent a special emissary, Maurice Picard, to Bonn. Picard told Adenauer that de Gaulle was positively 'the last chance' for France. His failure would mean military dictatorship and the end of French democracy.[3] Picard pointed out that de Gaulle's three ablest lieutenants – Guy Mollet, Maurice Pflimlin and Antoine Pinay – were all convinced 'Europeans'. All 'friends' of both France and Europe should support de Gaulle.

Picard hinted that a meeting between Adenauer and de Gaulle would clear the air. On July 29 the French Ambassador in Bonn, the able, sardonic, Maurice Couve de Murville, called on Adenauer and issued a firm invitation. It was agreed that Adenauer, who was about to start on a holiday in North Italy, should 'look in' at de Gaulle's home at Colombey les Deux Églises, on his way home to Bonn, on September 14. The ground for this meeting was further prepared when Pinay called on Adenauer at Cadenabbia on August 16. Pinay assured him that de Gaulle's talk of *grandeur* and *gloire* could be discounted, and that de Gaulle was a good European and a realist.

Adenauer's own account of the September 14 meeting at Colombey was a rosy one.[4] De Gaulle and his wife were friendly and informal. The General was alert and debonair – Adenauer used the word *frisch* of him – and, more important, well-informed and obviously interested in the subject of Franco-German relations. The two men sought common ground and found it, in such issues as disarmament, East–West détente in the economic field, common arms production, support of the Common Market and the Middle East. They both liked talking history. Their scepticism about Britain was shared, and Adenauer remarked that 'England is like a rich man, who has lost all his property but does not realise it'.[5] According to his own memoirs, de Gaulle made it plain that Britain should not enter the Common Market, as long as she 'remained politically and economically as she was'. Adenauer had no comment to make about this. De Gaulle stressed his interest in a united Europe although he added, significantly, that it must cease to be 'the tool of America'. He told Adenauer with great seriousness: 'In Germany they said, when I was in political life, that my policy towards Germany was one of might and

2............*De Gaulle*, Aidan Crawley, p. 385.
3............*Erinnerungen*, Konrad Adenauer, VOL 3, p. 418.
4............*Erinnerungen*, Konrad Adenauer, VOL 3, pp. 426–34.
5............*Erinnerungen*, Konrad Adenauer, VOL 3, p. 428.

vengeance. I can prove the contrary to *you.*'[6] There was a heavy emphasis on the last pronoun.

Difficult questions were skated over delicately. Thus Adenauer promised that there would be no 'Prussian policy against Poland' – without alluding to de Gaulle's known belief that the Oder–Neisse line eastern frontier had come to stay. And de Gaulle admitted casually that he did not favour supra-national European institutions, but urged that the consolidation of the Europe of the Six (Belgium, The Netherlands, Luxembourg, West Germany, France and Italy) should not be side-tracked by British proposals for a broader European 'Free Trade Zone'. Barefaced flattery was used to great effect; de Gaulle said that Adenauer was in reality younger than him 'in spirit' and Adenauer, enchanted, replied that the General would regain youth in office 'as has been the case with myself'.[7]

All this sounded highly satisfactory, and in his memoirs, Adenauer capped the episode by praising de Gaulle's grasp of the 'big' problems. He added 'I was glad to have met a totally different person from what I had expected. I was convinced that de Gaulle and I would have a good and mutually trusting relationship.'

Was this first meeting such a brilliant success? One of de Gaulle's biographers believes it was[8] – 'Adenauer was captivated by de Gaulle's charm and even found Colombey congenial.' That exact observer, Hans Globke, agrees. Adenauer, according to his recollection, at once liked de Gaulle's 'personal aura' – he was so clearly upright, correct, moral.[9] He liked his concept of a truly united Europe, in which no single power would dominate but in which France and Germany would stand united, and where there was no place, at least for the present, for Britain. According to one member of Adenauer's family, Frau Reiners, the Colombey meeting was indeed 'a pleasant surprise'. Her father had viewed it with apprehension and had remarked that de Gaulle thought he was 'a second Joan of Arc'. But when he returned to Rhöndorf, he was 'full of excitement and enthusiasm'.[10]

But there were different views of the Colombey meeting. One of Adenauer's biographers believed that he found de Gaulle 'very strange', with his military aura, his mystical sense of mission, his over-polished diction and over-dramatized, pompous gestures.[11] One close confidant of

6............*Erinnerungen*, Konrad Adenauer, VOL 3, p. 429.
7............*Erinnerungen*, Konrad Adenauer, VOL 3, p. 434.
8............*De Gaulle*, Aidan Crawley, p. 402.
9............Dr. Hans Globke, in personal conversation with the author.
10..........Frau Ria Reiners, in personal conversation with the author.
11..........*Adenauer und die Folgen*, Burghard Freudenfeld, edited by Hans-Joachin Netzer.

the Chancellor maintained that Adenauer returned from Colombey dubious and uneasy, in spite of the trouble de Gaulle had taken over his guest – he had made a point of greeting him with some carefully chosen sentences in German.[12] In his view, Adenauer 'never conquered a certain reserve' in his relations with de Gaulle. The British Ambassador in Bonn, Sir Christopher Steel, confirms this view; Adenauer talked to him, if somewhat obliquely, about the 'militaristic' and even the 'fascist' tendencies of France's new leader.[13]

What at least is sure is that the second meeting between the two was an unmitigated success. It took place on November 26 at Adenauer's invitation, at the Kurhaus in Bad Kreuznach, a small watering-place in the Palatinate, selected because it was almost equidistant from the two statesmen's homes at Colombey and Rhöndorf. The Kurhaus, situated in its own park, had been the military headquarters of Kaiser Wilhelm II and Field Marshal Paul von Hindenburg in the First World War.

At Bad Kreuznach Adenauer repaid the compliment by greeting de Gaulle in French – not altogether to the latter's comprehension, for the Chancellor's French was appalling.[14] The talks were kept strictly confidential, and a short communiqué referred only to solidarity on the maintenance of the freedom of West Berlin and on the need to move on to the next stage of the consolidation of the Common Market. But one observer believed that de Gaulle won Adenauer's total support in opposing the 'Maudling Plan' of the British Government for a Free Trade Zone, and, at the same time, sowed seeds of distrust in Adenauer's mind over Britain's position on the Berlin question.[15] Be that as it may, the brief appearance of the two men before the press on the steps of the Kurhaus was revealing. De Gaulle called his host 'a great man, a great statesman, a great European and a great German'.[16] The author remembers de Gaulle's follow-up gesture. He turned to Adenauer, clasping him by both shoulders, leaving him for once at a slight loss, but looking absurdly pleased and somehow like a favourite pupil who has been commended by his revered teacher.

The Bad Kreuznach meeting was the starting point for the formation of a Paris–Bonn axis. It was followed up by visits by Adenauer to Rambouillet and Marly le Roi as de Gaulle's guest, and much later by a triumphal tour of West Germany by de Gaulle, during which the General

12..........Felix von Eckardt, in personal conversation with the author.
13..........Sir Christopher Steel, in personal conversation with the author.
14..........His interpreter, Herr Weber, is probably the best judge of this.
15..........Sir Christopher Steel, in personal conversation with the author.
16..........The *Manchester Guardian*, from a Special Correspondent, November 27, 1958.

descended from his official car and shook hands with hundreds of enthusiastic Germans. With two men at the helm as purposeful as Adenauer and de Gaulle, the Paris–Bonn axis should have been an outstanding success. It was, indeed, to be crowned by the Franco-German Treaty of Friendship and Co-operation of January 22, 1963. But this lay far in the future, and in the meantime there were plenty of signs that the axis would come under considerable strain.

Thus, in January, 1959, the French Premier, Michel Debré, used the phrase *Europe des patries* in the National Assembly, a phrase which de Gaulle would employ as his own later in the year and which was a warning that France might never accept Adenauer's own grandiose aim of a politically-integrated, united Europe. In March, 1959, de Gaulle scandalized the Federal Republic's right-wingers, and many of Adenauer's Christian Democrats, by telling a press Conference in Paris that Germany could only ever be reunified within her existing frontiers, including the Oder–Neisse line. These are, in fact, the 'de facto' frontiers which have existed since 1945 and which were recognized by Herr Willy Brandt's SPD-led government in 1970. His statement was especially embarrassing in view of the fact that Adenauer had only just been to Paris.[17] In December, 1959, one finds Adenauer, once again in Paris, being badgered by de Gaulle and Debré about the alleged undependability of the United States and the readiness of its Government to withdraw all troops from Europe. Couve de Murville, always a willing and cold-blooded Devil's advocate, actually claimed this withdrawal was imminent; according to Adenauer, 'His statements were horrifying.'[18]

This attempt to make Adenauer's flesh creep was followed up by an unsatisfactory Paris Conference of the Western Powers from December 19 to 21. Adenauer was worried by the complacent atmosphere. His comment was, 'the gentlemen had absolutely no notion what a dangerous situation we were in'.[19] President Eisenhower and the British Prime Minister, Mr. Harold Macmillan, indulged in some loose talk about a German Peace Treaty which, in Adenauer's view, would have left the status of Berlin undefined and the position of the city exposed. But the Chancellor was becoming even more worried by France's ambivalent attitude towards NATO. During the course of 1960 France withdrew her Mediterranean fleet from NATO; refused to allow US aircraft, equipped to carry nuclear weapons, to be stationed in France; siphoned-off French troops for service in Algeria, while failing to reinforce absurdly under-strength contingents in Ger-

17..........The *Manchester Guardian*, from its Own Correspondent, Bonn, March 28, 1959.

18..........*Erinnerungen*, Konrad Adenauer, VOL 4, p. 16.

19..........*Erinnerungen*, Konrad Adenauer, VOL 4, p. 27.

many; and proposed that NATO forces in Europe should be commanded by a Frenchman, not an American.

On October 8, 1960, Debré came to Bonn with a blueprint for European reorganization, containing the following demands: NATO should be directed by a 'triumvirate of the USA, France and Britain; France should have a veto on the use of the nuclear deterrent in Europe; and the de Gaulle design of a *Europe des patries* should be formally substituted for plans for a European political community. This 'Europe des Patries' would be a confederation of fully co-operating but fully sovereign states, as against the closely-knit, supra-national European political Community envisaged by the Treaty of Rome.' Adenauer could have fended off Debré easily enough, but he was deeply disturbed because precisely while his talks with Debré were going on, de Gaulle made a series of speeches at Grenoble, St. Julien-en-Genevois and Chambèry demanding a French veto on the use of the nuclear deterrent. These speeches were clearly designed to force Adenauer's hand.

At this, the Chancellor's patience cracked. On the evening of October 9 he showed Debré a letter which he had received from Eisenhower, expressing the view that the Western Alliance should be strengthened politically and militarily. At the same time, he rejected the French blueprint and nothing more was heard of it. The joint communiqué issued in Bonn could not speak of agreement on any basic question. In Paris ex-ambassador François-Poncet uttered a dire warning; the Franco-German entente, he said, was the biggest accomplishment in Europe since 1945, and 'Woe to them who may be responsible for nullifying this achievement!' François-Poncet evidently believed that an Anglo-German flirtation might supersede the Franco-German '*mariage de convenance*'. However, this did not happen. The German partner had mutinied, and the initial period of honeymoon was over.

At least there had been a honeymoon, and there was the Franco-German Treaty to come. Where Britain was concerned there would never be anything to show, not even a coherent attempt on Adenauer's part to develop Anglo-German relations. This may well have been deliberate on his part, and in that event it can scarcely be termed a failure. But Adenauer's omission merits at least some explanation.

Adenauer, one may suppose, never forgave the British for dismissing him from his post of Mayor of Cologne. One British writer, Richard Loewenthal, quotes him as saying, not long after the event, that his three chief dislikes were 'the Russians, the Prussians and the British'.[20] That the British were inimical to him is quite certain, and in this respect he was only

20..........Richard Loewenthal, *This is Germany*, edited by Arthur Settel, p. 60.

typical of a great many German Catholics, who tend to seek friends in Latin Europe. Adenauer's instinctive distrust of the British might have been considerably modified, had he met a British statesman with whom he could have formed a personal friendship. It never happened. There was not time for Churchill to become a friend, while Eden did not care for Germans. Yet there seemed, at last, the chance that he might find a kindred spirit in Mr. Harold Macmillan, who succeeded Eden as Prime Minister at the end of 1956, following the fiasco of Anglo-French military intervention at Suez. Adenauer and Macmillan had much in common – elegance, restraint, shrewd wit and enjoyment of good conversation.

Macmillan had his reservations about Adenauer. He had his first personal talk with him in Bonn in June, 1954. Macmillan describes it: 'After a dinner in my honour he took me aside for a talk. He delivered a long and fascinating discourse, covering not merely the immediate problems but the whole history of the German peoples from Roman times until the present day. I found this monologue deeply interesting.'[21] So far, so good; but Macmillan went on: 'During the next nine years I was destined to listen to it on every occasion when we met.'

Macmillan believed that Germans, Adenauer included, were sadly ignorant about the Soviet Union. We have already noted how Macmillan thought that Adenauer's Moscow visit in September 1955 had been a salutary experience for him: 'At least it will stop the Germans rebuking us for our weakness towards the Russians.'[22] It was Macmillan's view that Germans were needlessly opaque; of Russian feelings, he once said: 'The really genuine thing was fear of Germany. Fear and hatred of Germany. Hatred of Germany because of the terrible treatment which Hitler's people had done in occupied Russia, and fear of a country who they believed to be fundamentally more intelligent, more developed and who, in the final analysis, could be more powerful.'[23]

For his part, Adenauer was convinced that Macmillan was inclined to make concessions to the Soviet Union for electoral purposes, and was too ready to suggest German concessions in Britain's interest. In his last years, Adenauer more than once described Britain as the exploiter of 'us poor dumb Continentals', and Britain's European policy as *ein einziges Feilchen* – literally, 'one long fiddle'.[24] The biggest shock Macmillan caused Adenauer was in February, 1959, when he decided, at short notice, to go to Moscow. Adenauer was obsessed by the thought that his British ally might deal with

21..........*Tides of Fortune* 1945–1955, Harold Macmillan, p. 479.
22..........*Tides of Fortune*, Harold Macmillan, p. 626.
23..........Harold Macmillan, BBC Television Interview, September 8, 1969.
24..........Hans-Werner, Graf Finck von Finchenstein, in personal conversation with the author.

the Kremlin behind his back. As it happened, Adenauer that week sent Hilmar van Scherpenberg, a State Secretary of the Foreign Ministry, over to London for consultations with the British Foreign Office. He spent two days in London, was told nothing about the Moscow visit and arrived back in Bonn the day before Macmillan announced it in the House of Commons. Adenauer was very angry, believing this to be a piece of calculated deception. In fact it was bureaucratic ineptitude on the part of the Foreign Office.

In March, Macmillan was in Bonn, but nothing would go right in his relations with Adenauer. Macmillan brought with him a plan for a 'thinning out' of military forces on either side of the Iron Curtain, without 'discrimination' against either NATO or the Warsaw Pact Powers. The so-called Macmillan Plan was held to offer three potential benefits. By limiting and controlling armed strength in Europe, it would increase the chance of progress in the field of general, controlled disarmament. Since the strictly military and strictly political reasons for Soviet distrust were closely interwoven, it offered the hope of parallel progress in the field of political coexistence. Finally, a fair agreement on military forces could produce relaxation of tension within Germany itself. The Macmillan Plan, in fact, offered positive advantages, but Adenauer would have nothing to do with it, even if it were to lead to an inspection of armed forces in East Germany. Of his personal advisers only two were sufficiently courageous to argue with him, his Press Chief, Felix von Eckardt, and the President of the *Bundestag*, Eugen Gerstenmaier.

Adenauer remained determinedly within his self-imposed diplomatic strait-jacket. He was as much opposed to flexible diplomacy as ever, believing that NATO's armed strength should be gradually built up and that nothing else could be done in the meantime. In August, he invited Macmillan and his Foreign Secretary, Sir Alec Douglas-Home, to Bonn. The meeting did nothing to help Anglo-German relations. Macmillan had no clear idea why he had been invited – the real reason being that Adenauer was in a disillusioned mood about de Gaulle. Talk about reviving the idea of a broadly-based European Free Trade Zone petered out aimlessly.

In November, 1959, Adenauer gave an interview to the correspondent of the *Manchester Guardian* which represented one of his very rare efforts to improve Anglo-German relations.[25] In it, he said that he regarded Mr. Macmillan as 'a most successful Prime Minister' and 'my friend', and he complimented him and the Conservative Party on their positive attitude towards Europe, their interest in joining the Common Market and their

25..........The *Manchester Guardian*, from its Own Correspondent, Bonn, November 16, 1959.

firm policy on Berlin. But an undertone of uneasiness crept in; he urged the dropping of all talk about 'Disengagement', whether it meant a thinning out of NATO and Communist forces or any other kind of East–West agreement on arms reduction in defined zones in central Europe, and he castigated a part of the British Press for ignorance and ill-will.

Two days after this interview Adenauer arrived in London, but this meeting with Macmillan, too, was a failure. On the evening of November 18, after two working sessions, Macmillan took Adenauer with him to Chequers for the night. That evening, the conversation turned again to reductions of armed strength in Europe. Adenauer remained totally unreceptive, and Macmillan pointed out that Britain might feel inclined to withdraw her Rhine Army. Adenauer remarked testily that he did not suppose that British troops were stationed in the Federal Republic 'just to please the Germans'. After that passage of arms, the conversation ebbed away to nothing. Von Eckardt went to Adenauer's room the next morning to tell the Chancellor that he would prepare a statement 'of a routine nature' for the Press Conference which the Chancellor was to give that afternoon in London. Adenauer only said, 'Write whatever you want to write.'[26]

Adenauer had been additionally depressed on November 17, when he paid a courtesy call on Sir Winston Churchill at his home in Hyde Park Gate, and that veteran statesman, who was his own contemporary, could not muster up the energy to brush off a budgerigar which had been let out of its cage and had landed on his balding head. This made Adenauer feel his age.[27]

The chance of a real improvement in Anglo-German relations was missed in 1959, and the chance did not recur. A year later the question of Britain joining the Common Market was becoming acute, and Adenauer was – in spite of protestations of support in public – setting his face against it in private. Throughout 1961 the negotiations between Britain and the Six were moving towards a climax which few people foresaw. Adenauer may have been one of them, for there is every reason to suspect that he and de Gaulle reached prior agreement on the need to keep Britain out. But this belongs to a later chapter. The year 1959 was to be a crucial year for Adenauer in a quite different respect. It was the year of the so-called 'Presidential crisis', and this affair has generally been regarded as marking the point at which his fortunes definitely took a downward turn.

The 'Presidential crisis' first loomed above the horizon in December, 1958, when the Federal President, Professor Theodor Heuss, wrote to

26...........*Ein unordentliches Leben*, Felix von Eckardt, p. 495.
27...........Dr. Erwin Wickert, in personal conversation with the author.

Adenauer about his impending retirement. Heuss, that soft-spoken, philosophical and mildly sarcastic Swabian, would, by September, 1959, complete his second five-year term in office. The Federal Constitution did not provide for a President serving for a third term and Heuss pointed out in his letter that there was no case for constitutional amendment in order to make this possible. He felt only that it might be reasonable to amend the constitution, in order to extend the five-year term of office to seven years. But this, he insisted, could only be done after his retirement.

Heuss had been a successful Federal President. He had a gift for finding the right word for the appropriate occasion. He kept himself scrupulously clear of party politics. He gave his duties intellectual content. There was a general feeling that he would be very hard to replace, but a successor would have to be chosen by the 995 members of the *Bundesversammlung*, or Federal Assembly, on July 1. In this assembly the Christian Democrats did not have a clear majority, and the Social Democrats nominated a strong candidate, Professor Carlo Schmid, their portly, witty spokesman on foreign affairs.

Adenauer, as his memoirs show, regarded Carlo Schmid as a most unsuitable man to become President. He had opposed German entry into the Council of Europe and NATO, and had agitated against nuclear arms being kept on German soil. The Chancellor organized a CDU Committee of 17 members to select a candidate. Its first meeting was on February 24, 1959, and at it Adenauer proposed Professor Ludwig Erhard and secured the committee's approval.

Adenauer's account of the subsequent developments was as follows:[28]

He himself telephoned Erhard, who was taking a short rest at the small watering place of Glotterbad, and Erhard said he was 'agreeable'. On February 28 Erhard called on Adenauer, who was ill with a short bout of influenza, at Rhöndorf. According to Adenauer, Erhard said he was being assailed with appeals that he should stay in active politics, and he asked the Chancellor what he ought to do. Adenauer replied – 'If you are wise, go back to the Glotter valley and don't say a thing.' Adenauer returned to work on March 2 and learned the next day that Erhard was not prepared to run for the Presidency. Erhard informed him of this personally the same evening.

Erhard's own account of what happened is very different.[29] Adenauer, he told the author, did indeed telephone him on February 24, and told him, 'We have decided unanimously that you are the right man for the job.' Erhard said at once that it was strange that he should be chosen as

28..........*Erinnerungen*, Konrad Adenauer, VOL 3, pp. 494–5.
29..........Professor Ludwig Erhard, in personal conversation with the author.

the CDU candidate without being consulted, but that it would be stranger still if he were expected to give an immediate answer. His immediate reaction was to refuse, but he did not do so at once, out of deference to Professor Heuss's feelings. He telephoned his refusal on the next day, and called on Heuss when he returned to Bonn, to explain his reasons. Erhard said categorically: 'I never showed any interest in becoming President. The truth was that Adenauer wanted to kick me upstairs.'

Even allowing for the vagaries of long-distance telephone-calls, it is impossible to square these accounts. What then transpired was a month of internal Party discussions, during which it became plain that the CDU Parliamentary Party wanted Erhard to stay in active politics, for as President he would take no part in them and would be politically neutral, and regarded him as Adenauer's natural successor as Chancellor. Various names were bandied about as possible candidates for the Presidency including Heinrich Krone, Franz Etzel and Eugen Gerstenmaier. Nothing was decided.

Then, on April 2, Hans Globke told Adenauer that some prominent members of the CDU wanted him, the Chancellor, to run for the Presidency. The two men were taking their usual walk in the gardens of the Palais Schaumburg and Adenauer, according to his own account, was astonished.[30] But he pricked up his ears when Globke suggested that the idea could make sense, if the President's office – like that of de Gaulle in France – carried more authority and political power. The Chancellor was even more intrigued when he met a small group of personal advisers on April 6, and they told him that the continuity of CDU rule might be best served if he became President and Franz Etzel succeeded him as Chancellor. Adenauer believed that Etzel – Minister of Finance since 1957 and a convinced European integrationist – was a man whom he could trust implicitly. What had at first appeared as fantasy now began to appear feasible.

On April 7, Adenauer met the CDU Selection Committee and sounded it out. He had learned in the meantime that his own family was in favour of him becoming President. They reminded him that he was 83, that he was overworked, that he was never shot of his everlasting callers and commitments and that he had actually considered being President ten years earlier.[31] They did not need to point out to him that the office of President was mainly representational in character, that it was completely divorced from the hurly-burly of party politics and that the President only had the right to be consulted on Government policies but played no part whatever in framing them. These considerations were the bases of President Heuss'

30..........*Erinnerungen*, Konrad Adenauer, VOL 3, p. 497.

31..........Dr. Paul Adenauer and Frau Ria Reiners, in personal conversation with the author.

interpretation of his role, but Adenauer had very different ideas. To the Committee, he argued that the President had the right to propose the new Chancellor, to be kept fully informed of all policy decisions, to attend Cabinet meetings and even to take the chair at them.[32] He added, rather more tentatively, that the President nominated Ministers on the 'proposal' of the Chancellor but might not be bound to accept the Chancellor's proposals. Ingeniously, he suggested that no awkward problems had arisen since 1949 because he and Heuss worked things out on a 'friendly' basis and listened to each other's arguments. He gave no examples of what Heuss's arguments could have been.

In his memoirs[33] Adenauer suggested, too, that the President need not follow 'advice' over foreign policy 'blindly', that he could demand re-examination of laws before signing them, and that he had 'special' rights in matters of peace and war. Moreover, he was not in any way committed to keep politics out of his speeches! It is still not clear how directly these latter points were put to the CDU Selection Committee. But the upshot of the April 7 meeting was that Gerstenmaier, on behalf of the Committee, asked Adenauer to run for the Presidency, and he accepted. He supplied his own footnote of comedy by remarking that he would have to 'change myself in many respects', which included 'being fair to the SPD!'

Was Adenauer temporarily dazzled by the prospect of initiating a 'Presidential democracy' of the type already instituted by de Gaulle in France? It seems highly probable. On April 8, he appeared on television and, with a somewhat arch seriousness, declared that his decision to run for the Presidency had been very carefully weighed-up. Of course, he had only just told the CDU Selection Committee that the decision had been a sudden one, and he had had virtually no time to consider it. But on television Adenauer had something more relevant to add. He said he intended 'to safeguard the continuity of our policy for years to come'. This sentence betrayed the close communion which Adenauer enjoyed at that time with Heinrich Krone, a man who sank all personal interest in trying to serve his Chancellor and his country. It was Krone who had spelt out to him the potential meaning of the word 'continuity' – ten years of total supremacy as Chancellor could be matched by ten years of purposeful Presidency.[34] Adenauer succumbed to the allure of this magnificent mirage.

On April 8, after his television interview, the Chancellor left at once for a four-week holiday in Cadenabbia. That evening the four most obvious candidates for the Chancellorship – Erhard, Etzel, Strauss and Schröder, Ministers respectively of Economics, Finance, Defence and the Interior –

32..........*Erinnerungen*, Konrad Adenauer, VOL 3, pp. 501–3.
33..........*Erinnerungen*, Konrad Adenauer, VOL 3, pp. 504–5.
34..........Dr. Heinrich Krone, in personal conversation with the author.

met at Strauss's home and reached a gentleman's agreement, not to campaign against each other. Thus the CDU could reach its own decision, without influence or favour. Politically speaking, this was a remarkably adult performance. It gave the lie to those critics of 'Chancellor democracy' who maintained that, under it, politicians had ceased to have minds of their own.

In Cadenabbia, Adenauer worked out the guide-lines of his future Presidency in his usual cool, precise way. What they were became crystal-clear subsequently. Without reforming the constitution, he would exercise the powers of the President in a manner which Theodor Heuss had never dreamt of. He would nominate his successor as Chancellor, who would be Franz Etzel. And his decisions would be above criticism and debate. As he had told Gerhard Schröder, when the latter visited him months before in Cadenabbia, he was tired of party indiscipline and political fracas.[35]

In the first days at Cadenabbia, Adenauer was well contented, both with his decision and with the sensation which it had caused. The people of the Federal Republic were thunderstruck – they had come to regard Adenauer as a permanent fixture and they found it next to impossible to visualize anybody else as Chancellor. But the press, radio and television commentators were lavish with praise. But there were shocks to come. On April 15 Robert Pferdemenges arrived at Cadenabbia, bearing a personal message from Erhard. The latter declared his loyalty to Adenauer, superfluously, but claimed that there could be no objection to himself becoming Chancellor. What was more, Pferdemenges, Adenauer's most trusted friend, agreed!

On May 2 Heinrich Krone and Hans Globke arrived. They told Adenauer that a substantial majority among the CDU Parliamentary members wanted Erhard as Chancellor. Adenauer was intensely irritated by being brought the 'wrong' news. On May 4 he returned to Bonn. At Baden-Baden, Hermann Hoecherl, after Strauss the most influential member of the CSU Bavarian branch of the party, joined Adenauer and Krone. His information was that the CSU favoured Erhard's candidature.

On May 13 Adenauer had an hour and a half's talk with Erhard, in an effort to convince him not to run for the Chancellorship. But Erhard, conventionally depicted as a *Gummi-löwe* ('paper tiger'), was stubborn even if mainly silent. He even had the courage to tell Adenauer that, as Chancellor, he would retain the Ministry of Economics as well, which he could 'manage on ten per cent of his working time'.[36]

The next three weeks were confusing and stormy. On May 14 Adenauer

35..........Dr. Gerhard Schröder, in personal conversation with the author.
36..........*Erinnerungen*, Konrad Adenauer, VOL 3, p. 525.

told the Cabinet that the 'international situation' might force him to reconsider his decision to stand down as Chancellor. His Ministers remained intractable. Then came an interview with Pferdemenges. Adenauer had talked his old friend round in Cadenabbia, but he found now that Pferdemenges had been won over for the second time by Erhard. As a 'tour de force' Adenauer told his party that, if Etzel were not chosen as Chancellor, he would resign the Presidency – an office which he had not yet taken! On May 19 he gave Krone a letter outlining his objections to Erhard's candidature, and telling him to use it as he saw fit. His objections were that Erhard knew too little about foreign affairs, that he was not a sufficiently convinced European 'integrationist', that he was unacceptable to France and Italy, and that he could not be 'spared' from the Ministry of Economics.[37] He reminded Krone of the latter's emphasis on 'continuity', and claimed that the continuity of his own policies could not be guaranteed with Erhard as Chancellor.

Krone was expected to hawk the letter around and talk sense into the CDU leaders. Instead, he called on Adenauer and urged him to change his mind about Erhard. This was nearly the last straw. On May 20, Adenauer penned two letters. The first, to Krone, proclaimed his intention of remaining Chancellor, if Erhard became the CDU's candidate. The chief reason which he gave was that, under Erhard, the CDU would lose the 1961 elections. The second letter, to Erhard, urged him to remain Minister of Economics. With transparent guile, he appealed to Erhard to consider the national interest and not his personal interest. Erhard's answer was to call on Adenauer on May 22 and reaffirm his wish to become Chancellor, and then to induce Gerstenmaier to ask Adenauer to maintain the latter's candidature for the Presidency.

On May 25, John Foster Dulles died, and Adenauer had a useful pretext for claiming that experienced statesmen should stay at the helm in the Western World. He asked Karl Blessing, the President of the Federal Bank, to intercede with Erhard and on the same day presided over a stormy meeting of the CDU Parliamentary members. There, Gerstenmaier – bursting with self-importance – demanded a declaration from Adenauer that he would be ready 'under all circumstances' to run for the Presidency. Adenauer replied 'certainly not' and flew the next day to Washington for Dulles's funeral.[38]

The last act of the drama of the 'Presidential crisis' was now about to be played. In Washington, Adenauer finally made up his mind. Back in Bonn on May 30, he relapsed into a silence which his advisers found unnerving.

37..........*Erinnerungen*, Konrad Adenauer, VOL 3, p. 528.
38..........*Erinnerungen*, Konrad Adenauer, VOL 3, p. 540.

Then, on June 4, he withdrew his candidature for the Presidency, just 58 days after accepting it. With admirable aplomb, he wrote in a letter to Krone that he deplored the controversy being conducted in public and doing 'grave damage to our party and our cause'. He ordered a CDU Parliamentary Party meeting for June 11, when the decision would have to be taken on a candidate for the Presidency. He had left this as late as possible; the Presidential election would then be just three weeks away.

Having at last reached a decision, Adenauer could be relied upon to see it through with a combination of steely determination and studied elegance. The next day he confirmed his instructions to Krone at a Cabinet meeting. Afterwards, the official Government spokesman said that Dr. Adenauer had simply announced that he would remain Chancellor – 'Naturally there was no discussion,' he added.

The meeting of the CDU Parliamentary members was more eventful. Gerstenmaier had already told the Press that the whole CDU executive, with the exception of Gerhard Schröder, disapproved of Adenauer's action. Gerstenmaier now decided to outface the Chancellor in the *Fraktionszimmer* or chamber of the Parliamentary members. He stationed himself directly in front of the door, and so directly confronted Adenauer when the Chancellor, studiedly late and at his ease, entered.[39]

Gerstenmaier, a very short man, struck a bellicose attitude, staring Adenauer aggressively in the face but saying nothing. With detached calm, the Chancellor, looking down at him, remarked: 'It's a curious thing that you can tell, just from a man's eyes, the hate in his heart.' With a face like a turkey-cock, Gerstenmaier stumped past Adenauer and flounced out of the room. The CDU revolt against Adenauer died stillborn.

There was a mainly comical postscript. Erhard was in Washington when Adenauer fired his final bombshell. On June 7, Erhard told reporters there that Adenauer's decision to remain Chancellor was a blow to West German democracy. On June 9, he arrived by plane at Düsseldorf, still unaware how utterly his CDU friends had deserted him, and gave a Press Conference at the airport. Showing unusual animation, he declared that democracy was in danger and that 'the last word has not been spoken'. On June 10 he saw Adenauer and demanded 'satisfaction'. Afterwards he told the press that 'the atmosphere was not very friendly'. He had, in fact, been fobbed off with the promise of a CDU vote of confidence in him. But, long after the event, Erhard's sense of injustice remained. 'Adenauer mistrusted me, because everyone else trusted me,' was his explanation.[40] He denied that he would have radically changed Adenauer's foreign policy,

39..........Lance Pope, of the British Embassy and a close friend of Gerstenmaier, in personal conversation with the author.

40..........Professor Ludwig Erhard, in personal conversation with the author.

then or later – 'Of course, I was known to be an Atlanticist but that did not mean I was anti-French. I wanted a more practical, a less sentimental relationship with France.' In a more mellow moment, Erhard said the difference between Adenauer and him was 'structural. He was Gothic, and I was Baroque.'

There were two further postscripts to the whole affair. The first was provided by the *Bundestag* debate of June 11. The leader of the SPD, Erich Ollenhauer, launched a vigorous assault. He accused Adenauer of treating the Presidency as a 'Party office' and so demeaning it, of trampling on his own Party, and of showing 'a profound contempt for his fellow beings' and for German democracy. Adenauer did not trouble to answer these charges, but adopted an ironically quipping tone. 'I would have missed you all so much,' was one of his witticisms. Another was, 'As President I should have been unable to make a single fighting election speech.' He made a slip when he said that he had reached his decision only after consulting his conscience and after 'very mature reflection'. For he had used the same phrase on April 7 when announcing an exactly opposite decision, to resign the Chancellorship and run for President. The Opposition's laughter was both raucous and spontaneous.

There was only one mildly dramatic moment. This was when Adenauer claimed that he told his Cabinet on May 14, that his resolve to become President had '90 per cent disappeared'. Erhard, sitting silent and embarrassed, made a surprised movement of his head. There were shouts of '*Liar*!' from the SPD benches, and Adenauer added pointedly, 'Erhard was present, too'. Erhard was seen to shake his head at this point, but this was not because he denied being present but because he believed then – and has believed ever since – that Adenauer failed to make clear to the Cabinet on May 14 that he had changed his mind about becoming President. After the debate was over the official spokesman of the Ministry of Economics, Dr. Karl Hohmann, told the press that 'Professor Erhard left for America in the knowledge of the fact that the Chancellor would abide by his decision to become President'. Ten days later Adenauer made some amends, but only under pressure from Krone and Pferdemenges, by writing Erhard a letter in which he expressed his appreciation for his service and his understanding for his feeling that he had been wronged.

There remained, finally, the question of who should be the CDU candidate for the Presidency. Adenauer had already been annoyed by the *Bundestag* decision to hold the Presidential election in Berlin – he had tried to avert this decision by informing the *Bundestag*, untruthfully, that the Western Powers had formally objected to the choice of Berlin. Now the Chancellor seemed to lose all interest in who should be President, and went along with the proposal that the Party candidate should be Heinrich

Lübke, a comparative nonentity who had been Minister of Agriculture since 1953. His own view of Lübke can be judged by a remark made at the dinner-table to a Western diplomat – 'Do you know who that is, two along from you? It's my new Minister of Agriculture, and he is even stupider than the last one.'[41] Lübke, an honest but undistinguished President, has subsequently been bitterly lampooned in a collection of his inappositely naïve sayings, published under the title *Der grüne Heinrich* – 'Simple Henry'.

The cloudburst of criticism which descended on Adenauer's head as a result of the 'Presidential crisis' was predictable. Even his favourite for the Chancellorship, Franz Etzel, remarked whimsically that he might well be considered now as a candidate for the Papacy. One anonymous letter to Adenauer contained only the words: *Du alter jauner* – 'You old rogue', in Cologne dialect.[42] The American public, which had heard Erhard's side of the case while he was in Washington, was especially disenchanted and the advice of a New York public relations firm was sought on means to restore the Chancellor's image. But at least one leading German intellectual, Professor Theodor Eschenburg, defended Adenauer's actions on the grounds that his objections to Erhard were 'genuine' and the result of 'patriarchal concern' for his people.[43] And a key member of the CDU, Will Rasner, put the eminently practical point that Adenauer would have been a disaster as President – 'There would have been a chronic conflict over the constitution.' Yet Rasner agreed, too, that Adenauer made a major blunder in ever accepting the candidature of the CDU for the Presidency. He ranked this as the biggest political mistake of his career, fundamentally because Adenauer was a man who was incapable of becoming politically neutral and of totally forsaking the arena of party politics.[44]

Certainly, it was a turning-point. From the middle of 1959 onwards, Adenauer's cares multiplied and his successes, at home and abroad, became few and far between. In 1959 his only consolation prizes were a successful visit to Japan, and the award of three honorary doctorates, of the universities of Princeton, UCLA, and California at Berkeley. Honorary doctorates, and the ceremonial and trappings that went with them, were very dear to Adenauer's heart.

The year of 1959 was to end on a thoroughly unhappy note. On Christmas Day two introverted and oafish young men daubed swastikas on the walls of the Roonstrasse synagogue in Cologne and on the memorial to the men of the German Resistance to Hitler. The two, Arnold Strunk,

41..........For reasons of tact, this Western diplomat cannot be named.
42..........*Adenauer. Democratic Dictator*, Charles Wighton, p. 298.
43..........*Zur politischen Praxis in der Bundesrepublik*, Theodor Eschenburg, p. 105.
44..........Will Rasner, in personal conversation with the author.

a baker's assistant, and Paul Schönen, a clerk, were both 25 years old and had been aged only 10 at the time of Hitler's death and the dissolution of the Nazi Party. Their motives were hopelessly confused. Strunk said he was an anti-Semite, because 'the Jews mix with us, and then we go under'; while Schönen felt he must 'protest' because he 'besmirched' himself by allowing the German people to be associated with Nazi crimes. The slogan which they chalked up was: 'Germans! We demand that the Jews get out!' It was not at all clear, when the court proceedings took place, whether the two men had ever knowingly seen a Jew. The once thriving Jewish community in Cologne was reduced by Nazi persecution to a few hundred.

There had been plenty of post-war rumblings of anti-Semitism. Only a year previously the Düsseldorf synagogue had been desecrated and a number of cases had been reported of discrimination against individual Jews, and even threats of physical violence. One of the most usual manifestations of anti-Semitism was the writing of poison-pen letters, usually anonymously. There were a number of neo-Nazi book-clubs, and ex-Nazis were well-entrenched in the publishing trade. A number of volumes of memoirs of prominent ex-Nazis, or of their widows and friends, had been published. Paul Schönen was an avid reader of them. Anti-Semitism, as the Minister of the Interior pointed out,[45] was frowned on by the great mass of the German people. But it seemed impossible to eradicate, not just in Germany but in any democratic Western country. This judgement was borne out by a public opinion survey conducted by the *Institut für Sozialforschung* (Institute of Social Research) in Frankfurt early in 1960. This showed 19 per cent strongly disapproved of racial prejudice, and 41 per cent mildly so. But 10 per cent had 'anti Semitic tendencies' and 24 per cent no discernible opinion at all.[46]

Adenauer was infuriated that the latest, most spectacular anti-Semitic smearings should have taken place in his native Cologne. A few days after the event he broadcast to the nation, telling it to react in what he called a 'healthy' way, by giving racialists 'a good hiding' (he used the phrase *eine Tracht Prügel*). This was not the language of diplomacy, but it did not merit the criticism showered on the Chancellor for encouraging German citizens to do bodily violence to each other. A fortnight later Adenauer denounced anti-Semitism in more measured terms, when he accompanied the President of the World Jewish Congress, Dr. Nahum Goldmann, to Belsen and laid a wreath at the memorial to the victims of Nazism in the former concentration-camp. In March, Adenauer met the Israeli Prime

45..........The *Manchester Guardian*, January 15, 1960. Interview by Terence Prittie of Dr. Gerhard Schröder.

46..........*The Politics of Post-War Germany*, Hendrik van Dam, edited by Walter Stahl, p. 310.

Minister, Mr. David Ben-Gurion at the Waldorf-Astoria Hotel in New York, and discussed the possibilities of future co-operation between the Federal Republic and his country.

The shadow of the Nazi past had an uncomfortable way of falling on the Federal Republic, and in the early months of 1960 the Government was much vexed by the accusations being brought against Theodor Oberländer, the Minister for Refugees. Charges had first been brought against Oberländer in 1959 by the Association of Victims of Nazism for war-crimes allegedly committed in Southern Poland in 1941. The East German authorities built up these charges into a violent propaganda campaign in early 1960. Its purpose was far less to do with the cause of justice than with finding pretexts for labelling the Bonn Government 'fascist' and 'militarist'. Oberländer did not show much perspicacity in defending himself. He first pleaded ignorance of massacres committed by Ukrainian militia units in Lemberg under German command, and then maintained that the massacres were the work of the retreating Red Army. A part of the West German Press joined in the campaign against him. Matters reached a head in April, 1960 and Oberländer resigned in May. A subsequent judicial inquiry revealed that he had taken no part in the massacres in Lemberg, although he was certainly there when some of them were perpetrated.

Adenauer came under heavy fire for clinging on to his Minister for Refugees for so long. It was not his way to surrender to outside pressure. He had refused to dispense with the services of Hans Globke, and he paid no attention at all to spasmodic complaints against other government servants, like Herbert Blankenhorn and Gerhard Schröder, who had at some time been members of the Nazi Party. Oberländer was a highly efficient Minister. On the whole, Adenauer's loyalty to him, once he had decided to employ him, was commendable. Whether he should have been given Cabinet office in the first place was another matter.

The shadow of the Nazi past would obtrude again, in the following year, when Adolf Eichmann, one of the perpetrators of the 'final solution' of the Jewish question, was brought to trial in Jerusalem. The hideous story of genocide was unrolled once more, in greater and more gruesome detail than ever before. A keen sense of shame afflicted a great part of the East German people, and the East German Communist regime took the opportunity of whipping up feeling afresh about 'Nazi generals' in the *Bundeswehr* and 'Nazi judges' in the West German law-courts. Adenauer in a newspaper interview said that the 'poison' of anti-Semitism had already been dissipated; he asked only that the trial would bring the 'full truth' to light, and that justice would be done.[47]

47..........The *New York Times*, April 17, 1961.

One must return, for a moment, to that one central problem on which no progress had been made since 1945, that of German reunification. A public opinion survey in 1957 showed that 52 per cent of those questioned thought that reunification in the foreseeable future was unlikely. By the end of 1958 this figure had risen to 74 per cent. The West German people had already by then surrendered to a mood of settled pessimism, and voices among the minority interested in such matters were being increasingly raised in favour of disengagement in Central Europe – implying acceptance of the division of Germany into two separate states as well as a scaling down of the East–West armed confrontation on German soil – and the formulation of a policy to secure minor relaxations in the lives of the 17 million East Germans. A debate was just beginning in West Germany as to whether the time had not come for Germans themselves to develop new ideas for a solution of the German problem – rather than waiting for mildly sympathetic but mainly uninterested Western allies to do something about it. It was to be nearly another decade before Willy Brandt and a Social Democratic Government began to try seriously to implement a policy of 'small steps' to improve all-German relations and the lot of the East Germans.

In January, 1959, the Soviet Government firmly rejected the granting of priority to the holding of all-German elections, and urged instead a step-by-step progress towards the solution of the German Question. Khruschev demanded the military neutralization of the Federal Republic and the demilitarization of West Berlin. The final objective should be the formation of a Confederation of two equally entitled German states. The Soviet Union stuck to these proposals at the Foreign Ministers Conference in Geneva, which sat intermittently from May to August. A four-stage Western plan – for the reunification of Berlin, the formation of an all-German Committee, all-German elections within two and a half years, and a Peace Treaty – was never given any consideration. Soviet threats against West Berlin were uttered, then withdrawn. Geneva provided the longest round yet of diplomatic shadow-boxing. Cynics were saying that the only two people who were pleased were Adenauer and the East German ruler, Walter Ulbricht. They were not obliged to make concessions to anybody, and the division of Germany remained as absolute as before.

Adenauer's all-German concepts were bound up with his insistence on the unity and strength of the Western Alliance. He had no views to express on the subject of diplomatic moves to break the East–West deadlock. A visit to Washington in March, 1960, produced no new ideas, beyond a misty proposal for a plebescite among the West Berliners on Berlin's future status. In May, 1960, there was a Summit Conference in Paris, and Adenauer was temporarily obsessed once more with his most recurrent nightmare – that of a Big Four compromise at Germany's expense and the revival of the Potsdam Agreement. But the Paris Conference was torpedoed by Khruschev, who used the shooting down over Russian territory of the American U2 reconnaissance-plane as his pretext for wild denunciations of the West. He called the Western Powers 'Adenauer's valets' and the Western press 'Adenauer's riff-raff'. He left the conference predicting the signing of a separate peace treaty with the East German state and demanding that West Berlin should become a 'free city'.

In September the East Germans instituted a 'little blockade' of West Berlin. The *Bundestag* had refrained from holding its usual post-summer holiday session in Berlin, but a refugee 'Day of the Homeland' was being staged there. Visits by West Germans to the city were prohibited for a five day period, from August 31 to September 4. Fresh restrictions were imposed on September 9. The 'little blockade' ended as abruptly as it had begun. It was a sharp reminder of the geographical vulnerability of West Berlin.

These were worrying days for Adenauer. There were minor frustrations too. In December, 1960, and January, 1961, Adenauer was ill with bronchial trouble, more ill than he liked to admit. On January 19 he had his usual small group of specially selected German newspapermen in to tea, and Georg Schröder of *Die Welt* noted the considerable effects of his illness.[48] His face was much thinner, and there were new lines on it, particularly on the forehead. The Chancellor spoke slowly and very softly. But his mind seemed as keen as ever.

Erhard was again causing him annoyance, not just because he was still accepted by the majority of the CDU as the natural successor to the Chancellorship. He had been appealing for greater European unity, and Adenauer suspected him of sniping at his Common Market policy. A report by Erhard was published in a number of German newspapers under the heading '6 + 7 + 5 = 1'. The thought behind this was that there should be a new degree of economic union between the six countries of the Common Market (Belgium, Luxembourg, France, West Germany, The Netherlands and Italy), the seven of the European Free Trade Association (Austria, Denmark, Great Britain, Norway, Portugal, Sweden and Switzerland) and the five others belonging to NATO (US, Turkey, Greece, Canada and Iceland). Adenauer regarded this as a lot of nonsense, and he was not at all pleased when Erhard was given the credit for the efficient and painless revaluation of the D.Mark in March, 1961. To his interpreter, he remarked: 'I'm told I ought to nail Erhard down. How do you nail down a pudding?'[49]

48..........Georg Schröder, in a private memorandum given to the author.
49..........Herr Weber, in personal conversation with the author.

He had fallen out, finally, with his Press Chief, Felix von Eckardt. The latter worked out a memorandum on reunification and showed it to members of the Foreign Ministry before he took it to Adenauer. Next, Eckardt went to Washington and on his return came into a meeting between Adenauer and German journalists. With asperity the Chancellor told him, 'You can report now on what happened in Washington. But this happens to be my group, not yours.'[50] On another occasion he told von Eckardt that he would do better to go the rounds of the newspaper-offices in the *Länder*, rather than play at politics in Bonn. He and his Press Chief had come to the parting of their ways. It was a foretaste of the loneliness that was to come.

Another parting was of a more momentous kind. Eisenhower, for whom Adenauer retained a real regard, stepped down from the American Presidency. Franz-Josef Strauss, on his own initiative, ordered his Defence Ministry staff to make an appreciation of the consequences, as related to foreign policy, of the Democratic candidate, John F. Kennedy, becoming President. A copy of the adverse report was leaked to the *Baltimore Sun*, which wrote an article under the headline, 'Nixon more acceptable to Germans.' It was perfectly true, as far as Adenauer and the CDU were concerned, and Kennedy's victory was a real shock – even though the personally inimical Adlai Stevenson did not become Vice-President.

According to Kennedy's speech-writer in the election campaign, no sympathy was lost between Kennedy and Adenauer. The President remarked that, 'The real trouble is that he is too old and I am too young for us to understand each other.'[51] Adenauer, less generously, called Kennedy 'a cross between a junior naval person and a Roman Catholic boy-scout'.[52] The difference in age had something to do with it, but Adenauer was highly suspicious of Kennedy's political methods, operating on a basis of flair and instinct and with the help of his band of brilliant 'whiz-kids'. As for many Americans, Kennedy seemed too exotic for Adenauer's taste. His own predilection was for order, experience and much careful reflection. He told de Gaulle in February, 1961, in Paris that Kennedy had 'many prima-donnas around him' – an odd way of describing young technocrats.[53] Both he and de Gaulle were gloomy, without reason, about Kennedy's foreign policy and supposed that he would make unwelcome concessions to the Soviet Union.

In fact, Kennedy made it plain when Adenauer visited Washington in April that there would be no change in the German policy of the United States. He declared full support for NATO, the Common Market and the

50..........Georg Schröder, in personal conversation with the author.
51, 52.....James O'Donnell, in a private memorandum on Adenauer.
53..........*Erinnerungen*, Konrad Adenauer, VOL 4, p. 80.

West German aims of seeking reunification in freedom and maintaining the status of West Berlin in the meantime. Nor did Kennedy give ground at the 'Super-Power Summit' with Khrushchev in Vienna on June 3 and 4. There was no response to Khrushchev's demand for a separate Berlin settlement and his threat of a separate Peace Treaty between the Soviet Union and East Germany. Yet the election of Kennedy as President did mean that the Washington–Bonn axis no longer existed in its old form. Adenauer would not have time to adjust himself to the new style of American administration.

By the time the Kennedy–Khrushchev meeting took place, campaigning was well under way for the 1961 Federal elections. In them, Adenauer faced a stronger challenge than at any time since 1949. There were two reasons for this. At their Bad Godesberg Party Conference in 1959 the SPD dropped their programmes for state planning of the economy and nationalization of heavy industries, their concept of class warfare and their opposition to rearmament within NATO. In deference to the existence of an 'affluent society' and to the German people's need of security, the SPD jettisoned economic and political ideology and sought to become a middle-of-the-road party. It was a thoroughly wise move, for West German prosperity was such that a purely left-wing party could no longer hope to come to power on the so called working-class vote.

The second reason for the strengthened SPD challenge was the selection at the party conference at Hanover in November, 1960 of Willy Brandt as candidate for the Chancellorship. Brandt had three advantages over his predecessor as SPD candidate, the dumpy, dutiful but uninspired Ollenhauer. He was young, only 47. He had gained a big reputation as the staunch and successful Governing Mayor of Berlin. Finally, he was a man of ideas, vigorous, enterprising and vital. Here, at last, was a formidable rival for an Adenauer already well past the peak of his power.

14 Bowing out, unwillingly

The 1961 Federal election campaign was proceeding rather more placidly than had been expected when, in the early hours of August 13, 1961, units of the East German People's Police and armed forces began building what became known as the 'Berlin Wall'. Roads all along the sector boundaries between East and West Berlin, and along West Berlin's 'outer' perimeter with the East German Republic, were sealed-off and barricaded. Deep trenches were dug across all but a dozen of them, and then the building of the Wall itself began with thousands of tons of bricks and concrete slabs which had been rushed into the city in the first hours of darkness. The Wall was at first a modest four to five feet high but it was to become in course of time a twelve to fifteen feet high barrier surmounted by barbed wire and 'protected' on its eastern side by a whole system of minor obstacles, trenches and cleared 'death-strips' giving a perfect field of fire to trigger-happy 'People's Police'.

Two months earlier the East German dictator, Walter Ulbricht, let drop the remark that 'no one has any intention of erecting a wall'. It was precisely what he did intend doing. The exodus of Refugees from East Germany increased rapidly in June and July. Nearly three million had 'voted with their feet' since 1945 by seeking refuge in the Federal Republic. Now the flow increased to well over 1,000 a day. There had always been a high proportion of people of working age; the old preferred to stay in their homes and die there, whatever the conditions. The East German labour-force was being continually denuded, and the planned expansion of the East German economy was rendered impossible. For this situation the Ulbricht regime had only itself to blame. It was based on a system of political repression and material austerity. The 1953 rising had shown what the vast majority of the East German population – especially the workers – thought of it. Early in August 1961, Ulbricht – himself a Soviet citizen and the faithful servant of the Kremlin – paid a two-day visit to Moscow. It was then that Khrushchev gave him permission to build the Wall. It was the alternative to the vain Soviet attempt to force the Western Powers to 'neutralize' and abandon their sectors of the city; and its essential purpose was to cut off the flow of refugees and so enable the East German economy to be first stabilized and then expanded. Khrushchev intended the East German Republic to become the 'workshop' of the Soviet Bloc.

The building of the Berlin Wall caught the Western Powers, and the West Germans, completely by surprise. Their intelligence services had no inkling of what was happening, in spite of the massive movement of police, troops and building materials into the city. Adenauer was telephoned at 4.30 in the morning in his home at Rhöndorf by Globke, two hours before he was due to be called for Mass. It was a Sunday, and the Chancellor went to Mass as usual. Indeed, a kind of paralysis seemed to have afflicted him, for he did absolutely nothing for twenty-four hours, in spite of an urgent appeal from his Minister for All-German Affairs, Ernst Lemmer, to come to Berlin at once. On August 14 all that the Chancellor did was to appear on television, telling the German people that there was no cause for alarm. Lemmer's explanation was that the three Western Powers, anxious to play down this new crisis, may have discouraged Adenauer from going to Berlin, for fear of 'incidents'.[1]

The building of the Wall was to affect the 1961 election campaign. For whereas Willy Brandt flew at once to Berlin, demanded an immediate protest from the Western Powers and wrote to President Kennedy urging a vigorous follow-up at the highest level, Adenauer was found wanting. Less than forty-eight hours after the Wall went up, he resumed electioneering as if nothing had happened, and at Regensburg uttered the most damaging sentence of his career – 'If ever anyone has been treated with the greatest consideration by his political opponents, it is Herr Brandt, alias Frahm.' Willy Brandt had, in fact, been born the illegitimate son of a shop-girl, and he was known as Herbert Frahm until, having emigrated from Nazi Germany, he joined the Norwegian resistance against Hitler and gave himself a new name. Brandt showed astonishing restraint and chivalry by ignoring this wounding assault.

Only on August 16 did Adenauer, back in Bonn, make a statement to the *Bundestag*. He called the Wall 'a declaration of bankruptcy on the part of the sixteen year tyranny', and he called for Four Power negotiations to restore a sane and civilized situation in Berlin. Not until August 22, did he, at long last, visit Berlin, where he met with a chilly reception. And in an election speech at Hagen, in Westphalia, he told an amazed audience that Khrushchev organized the building of the Wall in order to help the SPD in the election. Brandt, stung to a retort, countered by advising Adenauer to 'seek a peaceful evening to his life', and added that 'the old gentleman really cannot grasp what's going on any more'.

The West German Press was bitterly critical of Adenauer's antics. The *Stuttgarter Zeitung* complimented Brandt on showing so much greater common-sense than 'the election orator, alias Federal Chancellor'. The

1............Ernst Lemmer, in personal conversation with the author.

weekly *Spiegel* wrote that 'this 85-year-old is incapable of being at the head of a modern industrial State'. On Adenauer's side it must be said that he was given a bad example by the Western Powers who were, after all, primarily responsible for West Berlin. The three Western Commandants took two days to draft a formal protest, and their Governments only handed Notes to the Soviet Union on August 17. Two days later Vice-President Lyndon Johnson arrived in Berlin, and pledged the lives, possessions and honour of the people of the United States in maintaining the freedom of the Berliners. The United States did at least take some action on the ground, too; troop reinforcements rolled up the autobahn to Berlin, American tanks were moved to 'Check-point Charlie' on the Friedrichstrasse, (which had become the only crossing-place for foreigners between East and West Berlin), and General Lucius Clay was sent back, after twelve years out of Germany, as a kind of 'Special Commissioner' of the President's – unfortunately, with ill-defined powers which were to cause considerable trouble, leading to his recall.

But all this happened too late. By the time that Vice-President Johnson arrived in Berlin, the Wall was already a formidable obstacle. The damage was already done. Adenauer, admittedly, could not have stopped it. As one of his Ministers pointed out, he could have done little in a physical sense, 'beyond casting a sad look through the Brandenburg Gate', although it 'would have no doubt been wiser, in a political sense, for him to have flown to Berlin at once'.[2] For the sake of national morale, he was needed there.

Only a footnote is necessary here on the subsequent story of the Wall. In spite of immense courage shown in escaping over, through or under it, the Wall effectively cut down the flow of refugees from East Germany to the merest trickle. Its fortifications were continually extended, until it became as nearly as possible impermeable. The inaction and helplessness of the Western Powers enabled Ulbricht to proclaim a strategic victory, when his régime had in reality suffered its worst moral defeat. On December 31, 1961, Ulbricht at last confessed, appropriately in the Soviet paper *Pravda*, that the 'Wall of Peace' had been built to succour the ailing East German economy. The exodus of East German refugees had, he wrote, cost the economy around 30,000 million Marks, had encouraged opposition to his régime's policies, and had caused a mood of chronic unrest and uncertainty of mind.[3]

The Wall killed the Four Power Statute for Berlin stone-dead, by creating a 'state frontier' through the middle of the city, and cemented

2............Dr. Gerhard Schröder, in personal conversation with the author.
3............The *Pravda* article was analysed in the *Manchester Guardian* of January 1, 1962.

the division of Germany. One cannot rule out, writing nearly ten years after the event, that its building – which achieved its immediate objective of stabilizing the East German economy and the East German State – may still turn out to have been the 'beginning of the end' of West Berlin's independent existence. For East Germans, it was crucial. Before August, 1961, they knew that they could always, at a pinch, pack up and leave. After the Wall was built, they simply had to settle down and make the best of things.

In that it was a blow to the West, the building of the Berlin Wall was a setback to the Bonn Government. This, coupled with Adenauer's poor performance, undoubtedly affected the results of the 1961 elections, held on September 17. Up to August, the odds were on a sweeping CDU victory. The economy was in excellent shape. West Germany's place in the Western Alliance was assured, and the electorate was well satisfied with Adenauer's foreign policies. Brandt had recognized this in a speech made on April 8, when he said: 'Anyone who tries to give the impression that the Social Democrats want experiments would be laughed out of court. Any such attempt is unbelievable. That is the big difference from the situation of four years ago.'[4] It certainly was; the SPD was, in fact, borrowing the well-tried CDU slogan of 'No experiments', along with the CDU's cloak of bourgeois respectability. The CDU's own slogans remained as acceptable as ever – 'Don't play around with Germany', 'Live tomorrow too in security', and 'Germany needs a strong Government'.

Adenauer appeared to have been given additional help by an angry Note of Khrushchev's on August 31, attacking the Federal Government and announcing the resumption of Soviet nuclear bomb tests. The CDU produced an imposing advertisement, published in almost every non-Socialist newspaper, which showed an irascible Khrushchev, with mouth wide open and fist upraised, and the caption: 'Now we all know – Khrushchev demands Adenauer's downfall.' There followed a summary of the August 31 Note, and then again: 'In this threatening hour the German people stands solidly behind Konrad Adenauer. The German people will give Khrushchev the right answer on September 17!'

In the event, the election results were a disappointment for the CDU and something of a personal shock for Adenauer. In a larger electorate than before, the CDU vote dropped by over 700,000 and its seats in the *Bundestag* from 277 to 241. The SPD increased its vote by over one and a half million and its seats from 181 to 198. The Free Democrats, led with panache by Dr. Erich Mende, did even better. Their seats increased from

4............*Die Welt*, April 9, 1961.

43 to 66, and their share of the poll from under 8 to over 12 per cent. For the moment, the FDP were very much a 'third force' in West German politics, and Mende was to exploit this situation with real skill. Prior to the election he had said very plainly that he would not serve under Adenauer in a future Government, and had publicly proposed Erhard as Adenauer's successor. The operative result of the 1961 election was that the CDU had lost its absolute majority in the *Bundestag*. The CDU, as had been the case in 1949 and 1953, had now to seek coalition partners, rather than choose them. This meant that Adenauer, who was determined even at the age of 85 to lead the next government, was put in a most delicate position. In face of Mende's belief that he was too old to remain Chancellor, he had to bargain for his survival.

The inter-Party discussions which now began were bound to be protracted. It is hard not to admire the manner in which Adenauer played his part in them. In a way, it was reminiscent of Napoleon's nearly miraculous campaign of 1814 on French soil. In that campaign the Emperor was faced with overwhelmingly powerful enemy armies, which he skilfully forced apart and prevented, right up to the point of defeat, from combining in his destruction. Adenauer, like Napoleon, wanted to remain in power. His adversaries may not have been so formidable. But they had the strength to destroy him, if they could bring themselves to gather and use it.

Brandt had talked openly of the need for an all-Party Government of 'national emergency'. Such a government would, in fact, be formed six years later. Brandt's proposal was honest but possibly ill-advised. It was of real consolation for Adenauer to know that the SPD might be prepared to serve in a coalition led by him – for Brandt, unlike Mende, had not ruled this out. At the same time, Mende had indicated that an SPD/FDP coalition was impracticable. The reason, which Mende did not publicly explain, was essentially financial. The FDP secured its financial backing from the same source as the CDU – the *Bundesverband der deutschen Industrie* the Confederation of German Industry'. The BDI was not prepared to go on financing an FDP which was no more than a junior partner in a coalition led by Brandt. The SPD's conversion to bourgeois philosophy was altogether too recent, and the BDI required time to assess its validity. As a struggling third force, the Free Democrats needed all the financial help they could get. Adenauer, one may be sure, was fully aware of this.

Although his twelve year era of constructive political thinking was over, Adenauer retained an innate instinct for political bargaining. He had understood, automatically, how to form a government in 1949, in a multi-Party setting. Now he had to survive by playing off the SPD against the Free Democrats. He took the most operative step four days after the election, on September 21, when he invited the SPD to negotiate with him. During those four days, Mende had stood out for a CDU/FDP coalition under Erhard. Adenauer confronted the SPD with the future frustration of remaining, after a sojourn of 12 years, in the political wilderness. One observer wrote that day that 'Adenauer is a master tactician and his real object may be to spur the Free Democrats into accepting him as Chancellor.'[5]

This was what happened. But Mende fought his own, most individualistic rearguard action. He wanted a CDU/FDP coalition under Erhard. He realized, very quickly, that he would not get it. The CDU/SPD negotiations seemed, even up to the morning of September 28, to have a good chance of succeeding. The Free Democrats, with 66 seats only, could not have organized a viable opposition (they were to have actual experience of this problem from 1967 to 1969), in the face of a 'big' coalition of the two main parties. On September 28, Mende decided to seek a coalition with the CDU, with the question of the Chancellorship left open.

Mende has explained his reasoning to the author of this book. He would have gone on backing Erhard for the Chancellorship, but he found that Erhard was not prepared to fight for his own candidature. It took four weeks of jockeying to establish this for sure, but by September 28 Mende realized that he could not force Erhard into the Chancellor's seat unaided. His subsequent negotiations with the CDU took another fortnight. They hinged on talks between him and Adenauer. The Chancellor warned him of the danger of trouble between the United States and the Soviet Union over Cuba. This showed remarkable prescience; the climax of the confrontation over Cuba was still a year distant. Adenauer, according to Mende, had his information from Averell Harriman.[6] The case put by Adenauer was that he was still needed as Chancellor, and that he should hold this post for at least two years more.

Mende, again according to his own account, agreed that there was a good case for Adenauer remaining Chancellor. He asked Adenauer to give him a letter, setting down in black and white that he would resign in around two years time – or, at least, well before the 1965 elections. Mende and Heinrich Krone were the only people to receive copies of this letter.[7] The letter was, for the time being, a State secret; not even the Cabinet as a whole would be informed, although the Ministers of Defence and Foreign Affairs were told of the letter's existence. Mende undertook to stay silent for the next year, anyway. He kept his promise; even members of the FDP executive were informed only of the gist of the agreement and not of the exact terms laid down in the letter.[8]

5............Terence Prittie, in the *Manchester Guardian*, September 22, 1961.
6 7, 8.....Dr. Erich Mende, in personal conversation with the author.

Mende did not overplay his hand. He might well have been able to force Adenauer's retirement in 1961. Two of Adenauer's closest confidants agree that the CDU/SPD coalition talks were a bluff.[9] One of them admitted that the idea of a 'big' coalition did lodge in Adenauer's brain, and that he was only positively interested in it four years later.[10] But Mende was concerned with the national interest. He stayed out of Adenauer's fourth and last Cabinet himself in order to underline this, but he made one condition: the 'quid pro quo' was that Heinrich von Brentano should cease to be Foreign Minister. This was perfectly fair. Brentano was loyal to a fault; he appeared no longer to have a mind of his own. Clearly he was not the right man to hold the Foreign Ministry under a Chancellor due to resign in two years time.

Brentano made a most dignified exit. He sent his letter of resignation to Adenauer on October 28. He forebore to mention the fact that he was being sacrificed so that Adenauer might survive, save in one oblique reference – 'Public opinion might be led to feel, wrongly, that the obstacle to the formation of a new Government was the demand of the present Foreign Minister that he should be a member of a future Cabinet.' Inarticulate and somewhat obsequious, a nervous chain-smoker and a loyal lieutenant who automatically accepted Adenauer's directions, Brentano departed to relative obscurity and early death. Adenauer would miss him.

On November 7 Adenauer reaped the reward for the concessions which he had made under duress. He was elected Chancellor for the fourth time, but he received only 259 votes out of a total of 499. There were seven members of the *Bundestag* absent, and 26 others abstained. The 188 Social Democrats present could be assumed to have voted against Adenauer, and this meant that 17 members of the CDU/FDP coalition voted against him too, while another 26 abstained. The new Cabinet, with five Free Democratic Ministers in it, was sworn in on November 14. Brentano was succeeded as Foreign Minister by the immensely more resourceful and positive Gerhard Schröder. Once again, Adenauer had won through, but only just. This time it had required a mingling of Jesuitical guile with something of the ruthlessness of a Renaissance Prince. And he was under two years notice to quit.

During these two years he was, more than ever before, to concentrate his attention on foreign affairs. In the past he had been criticized for neglecting social affairs, education, welfare and labour relations. Now he really had no time, as he saw it, for such matters. He was no sooner installed as

9............Felix von Eckardt and Dr. Gerhard Schröder, in personal conversation with the author.

10..........Felix von Eckardt, in personal conversation with the author.

Chancellor again in the Palais Schaumberg than he was off to Washington. His talks there with Kennedy were inconclusive; Adenauer was won over with difficulty to the idea of a Foreign Minister's conference in Paris in mid-December. Before it began he was once more in Paris himself, but his talks with de Gaulle were even less satisfying. De Gaulle scotched his idea that a Soviet–Chinese confrontation was imminent, and that the Soviet Union might become 'the bastion of the white world' against China.[11] De Gaulle, one imagines, preferred to produce such geo-political concepts on his own. When the General later launched into a soliloquy about the weaknesses of British policy, Adenauer interrupted him to ask that France should not 'stand aside' over the Berlin question. This drew a sharp retort from the aggrieved de Gaulle and Adenauer noted, in his memoirs, that he had been 'most dissatisfied with this talk; I was in fact very angry'.[12]

On one question, at least, the two statesmen were in agreement. This was the British application to join the Common Market. Negotiations between Britain and the Six had begun in Paris on October 10, and the Lord Privy Seal and leader of the British delegation, Mr. Edward Heath, declared his Government's readiness to abide by the principles and rules of the European Economic Community. The ruling Conservative Party pledged its support on November 14, although the Labour Opposition continued to insist on adequate safeguards, without giving any clear definition of what they should be.

Now, on December 8 in Paris, de Gaulle reported a conversation which he had just had with the British Prime Minister, Harold Macmillan. The latter had told him that Britain wanted to join the Common Market more for political than economic reasons, and wanted to bring the Commonwealth in too. De Gaulle had replied that if the Commonwealth joined, the United States would be next in line. The Common Market would be turned into a world organization, and all prospect of political unity would be forfeited. De Gaulle added that Britain's economic situation was shaky.

This conversation was highly significant, for it led to others, and the theme was always the same – Britain was not a suitable partner for the Six and was not really keen on joining them. A co-ordinated Franco-German pattern of behaviour began to emerge. France would oppose, or at least seek to postpone a British entry into the Common Market. West Germany would express readiness to consider the British application, but would do nothing to further it.

It was not therefore surprising that Macmillan made no headway during

11..........*Erinnerungen*, Konrad Adenauer, VOL 4, p. 122.
12..........*Erinnerungen*, Konrad Adenauer, VOL 4, p. 125.

a visit to Bonn on January 8 and 9, 1962; nor in Paris on June 2 and 3. Meanwhile there had been a whole series of discussions about steps by the Six to promote political union. These discussions got nowhere; nor were they intended to, for de Gaulle was utterly determined to preserve the national identity of France. Vastly more important were the Adenauer–de Gaulle talks which took place when the Chancellor paid a six-day official visit to France from July 2 to July 8. De Gaulle said that Macmillan had been beside himself at their recent meeting; talking about a Continental blockade and a tariff war against Britain, and of the danger of Europe repulsing Britain's advances, the Conservative Party losing the next election and all Europe suffering as a result.[13] Macmillan had insisted on agricultural arrangements favourable to Canada, Australia and New Zealand.

Adenauer – and this is, after all, his own account[14] – made not the slightest effort to explain Britain's case. Quite the reverse; he volunteered the information that Macmillan had offered economic union to the United States and had been turned down by President Kennedy. This sounded like tittle-tattle, probably emanating from the highly unreliable West German Ambassador in Washington. Adenauer, apparently intent on ingratiating himself with de Gaulle, went on to suggest that Britain's entry into the Common Market should be considered on two basic considerations – that it benefited the EEC economically, and that it did not render the EEC administrative apparatus in Brussels impotent. In addition, he pointed out that the £ sterling was shaky, and concluded: 'No three cheers for a British entry.' It is significant that all the arguments advanced by Adenauer were avidly accepted by the French Government, and used against Britain both in the negotiations which lay immediately ahead and four years later, when Britain reapplied for membership.

Two days later Adenauer came up with two further, damaging considerations. The EEC apparatus was not sufficiently developed to absorb Britain and other applicants (he meant Norway, Denmark and the Irish Republic); and Britain's underlying purpose in seeking entry might be to undermine the existing Franco-German unity of action.[15] Certain of West German backing, the French attitude in the Common Market negotiations with Britain hardened and the negotiations were broken off on August 5.

The next act in the drama which, for Britain, was developing into tragedy, took place in the following month. In Bonn on September 5 Adenauer had a long talk with de Gaulle. Once again it was the Federal

13..........*Erinnerungen*, Konrad Adenauer, VOL 4, p. 163.
14..........*Erinnerungen*, Konrad Adenauer, VOL 4, pp. 164–5.
15..........*Erinnerungen*, Konrad Adenauer, VOL 4, p. 173.

Chancellor who led the way. He told de Gaulle that his doubts about a British entry were more grave than ever.[16] The British Labour Party was against it, and might soon come to power. The British people had not abandoned their 'insular concepts'. Above all, if Britain wanted to join the Six, then she must make concessions – and not the other way round.

At the same time, Adenauer pressed for fresh steps to be taken in order to secure a Franco-German treaty, which would be complemented by a 'gentlemen's agreement' between himself and de Gaulle. French and German policies should be brought increasingly into line over Berlin, defence, East–West relations, Africa and the developing countries – as well as the Common Market. Adenauer proposed the setting-up of a joint Committee, so that something could be drawn up 'in black upon white'. The trend of Adenauer's thoughts was obvious; he would support France in keeping Britain out of Europe, in return for the Franco-German Treaty which he believed would be his crowning achievement. It is remarkable that he later committed these thoughts to paper with such bold, almost brazen honesty.

The British negotiators remained in the dark about Adenauer's attitude, fondly imagining that France's objections would be overcome with the help of the 'Friendly Five', Belgium, Italy, Luxembourg, The Netherlands and West Germany. The Federal Vice-Chancellor, Ludwig Erhard, had already warmly welcomed the British application for entry. Adenauer on more than one occasion publicly paid lip service to the idea of an expanded Common Market. Now, on September 24, the Foreign Minister, Gerhard Schröder, told the Council of Europe in Strasbourg that the negotiations between Britain and the Six were of 'historic importance'. They constituted 'almost the biggest venture of all' for Europe at that time. Three days later, Schröder told the Foreign Policy Committee of the *Bundestag* that Britain's entry into the Common Market was a primary factor for the Six, who should defer steps towards political union until Britain joined them. Schröder, it would seem, was being kept as much in the dark by Adenauer as was the British delegation in Brussels.

Suspicions of the Chancellor's real intentions were growing. In the *Bundestag*, on October 11, he was accused of deliberate ambiguity by the Chairman of the SPD, Erich Ollenhauer. Adenauer answered with unconcealed and unusual irritation. He said that the negotiations with Britain in Brussels were both complex and tough. Mr. Heath had admitted to him when they had last met that some difficult problems had not yet even been broached. Britain was not applying for membership 'out of feelings of human kindness'; and his own task was to represent Germany's

16..........*Erinnerungen*, Konrad Adenauer, VOL 4, p. 178.

interests, not Britain's. The ambiguity, however, remained; and Adenauer was calculatedly evasive when he met Kennedy on November 14 and 15 in Washington. To one German journalist, at least, he was more explicit; Britain, he said, would never belong to a European political union and should only be accepted into the Common Market if this were 'absolutely unavoidable'.[17] He added that Labour would win the next General Election in Britain, and 'one doesn't want those people in Europe'.

October and November were months of Government crisis in Bonn; the situation was so acute that the Common Market negotiations vanished completely from the newspaper headlines. The Christmas holiday intervened. The talks with Britain were due to be resumed early in the New Year and the general expectation still was that they would be brought to an early and successful conclusion. Meanwhile a date had been fixed, January 22, 1963, for the signing of the Franco-German Treaty of Friendship and Co-operation. The French draft had been completed by September 19; German additions were incorporated into it at the end of November and the final text was approved at a meeting of experts in Paris on December 17.

On January 14, 1963, de Gaulle dropped his diplomatic nuclear bomb. At a press conference in Paris he declared that France would veto Britain's entry into the Common Market, come what may. Britain's economic interests and political system were, he said, incompatible with membership. For two days the West German Press and public waited in vain for Adenauer to react, while the Governments of Italy, Belgium, Holland and Luxembourg were expressing their anger and dismay at de Gaulle's high-handed and unilateral action. But the Chancellor maintained a tight-lipped silence. He had no intention of endangering his cherished Franco-German Treaty. Moreover, de Gaulle's action had really not conflicted with his own views at all. To Schröder he made the significant remark that Britain had waited until the Common Market had proved a success and only then wanted to climb on to the band-wagon.[18] On a more political plane, Adenauer indicated that Britain's entry would hold up progress towards political union. This, however, was a palpable smoke-screen; no real progress had been made with the two so-called 'Fouchet Plans' for political union and this had been recognized by de Gaulle and Adenauer when they met in Paris in September, 1962.

On January 20, Adenauer left for Paris for the ceremonial signing of the Franco-German Treaty, with a chorus of dissent echoing in his ears. In a broadcast Schröder said that differences of opinion over a British entry

17..........Georg Schröder, of *Die Welt*, in personal conversation with the author.
18..........Dr. Gerhard Schröder, in a personal letter to the author.

into the Common Market should be eliminated and everything possible done to help Britain's candidature. Von Brentano, who had never dared to differ publicly with the Chancellor, said that Franco-German friendship should be used as a weapon to forge a fresh understanding with Britain. One FDP Minister, Walter Scheel, warned France that she would find herself in total isolation and accused de Gaulle of seeking a position of hegemony in Europe.[19] (Adenauer was subsequently to classify Scheel as a 'mere light-weight'). Erhard would certainly have added his voice to the clamour, but he was ill at the time. His deputy in the Ministry of Economics, Dr. Müller-Armack, said bitterly that there was no point in maintaining a 'diplomatic keep-smiling' posture; Britain had negotiated sensibly and objectively, and had been grievously let down.

In the circumstances, the ceremonial signing of the Franco-German Treaty in Paris was bound to be something of an anti-climax. De Gaulle was not pleased by German insistence that the Treaty had to be ratified by the *Bundestag*, and by the addition of a preamble, which laid down that the Treaty would not militate against German commitments to the Western Alliance as a whole. This latter point was one on which the totally compliant Adenauer, had for once, failed to get his way with his own Cabinet.[20] The Treaty was overshadowed by the breakdown of the Common Market talks. Moreover, it did not significantly change the political scene. It provided for regular consultations between heads of governments, increased youth and cultural exchanges, and harmonization of foreign and defence policies. De Gaulle was later to remark that 'Treaties are like maidens and roses. They each have their day.' The Franco-German Treaty changed nothing, and added – as later became clear – only an expression of intentions. The *Bundestag* ratified it on May 16, 1963.

Adenauer was provokingly evasive when he returned from Paris. He claimed to have spoken to de Gaulle 'in the same terms as my Minister', meaning the pro-British Schröder, a statement which was to say the least dubious. He suggested that the fact that the breakdown of the Brussels negotiations and the signing of the Treaty had been roughly co-terminous, was purely fortuitous. In reality, the link between the two events was obvious; Adenauer's heartfelt desire for the Treaty had sustained de Gaulle in his determination to keep Britain out of Europe. So deep had been this desire that, 'When, after signing the Franco-German Treaty of Friendship, de Gaulle suddenly stepped forward and kissed the German Chancellor on both cheeks, tears came into the old man's eyes.'[21]

19..........Terence Prittie, in the *Manchester Guardian*, January 21, 1963.
20..........Dr. Erich Mende, in personal conversation with the author.
21..........*De Gaulle*, Aidan Crawley, p. 402.

Konrad Adenauer in his study.

The Chancellor surrounded by younger members of his family.

Erich Mende's view was that, in the Treaty, Adenauer saw a symbol and a 'great and auspicious date in history'.[22] De Gaulle, on the contrary, had severely practical aims in view when he signed it – 'To isolate West Germany from both the United States and Britain, and eventually to draw us out of the Western Alliance.' To Adenauer, de Gaulle made the revealing admission that he had broken off the Common Market negotiations because the Nassau Agreement – signed between Macmillan and Kennedy on December 21, 1962, and giving Britain Polaris nuclear missiles – had 'not been fair play'.[23] Macmillan had previously turned down de Gaulle's proposal for an integrated European system of defence, in which France and Britain would be the two main pillars.

The lure of a grandiose act of reconciliation with France was certainly one factor which prompted Adenauer's decision to back de Gaulle, albeit surreptitiously, in keeping Britain out of the Common Market. As one of his close advisors put it – 'He was over-sanguine about the Treaty and about the direction that de Gaulle's policies would take. He may have been blinded by the supposed affinity with de Gaulle; old age, too, was a factor.'[24] Certainly, the powerful personality of the General had its effect. One bitter opponent of Adenauer's described this effect in flowery language: 'By the side of this man from Lorraine, who promptly cut off European integration in its prime and remained its irreconcilable enemy, the German Chancellor appeared like a princeling of the Rhine Confederation overcome with admiration of the *Roi Soleil*.'[25] Perhaps the real explanation of Adenauer's actions in January lay in his own mind. Where the Treaty was concerned, Schröder appositely quoted from Milton – 'The desire for posthumous fame is the last infirmity of noble minds.'[26] As for Britain and the Common Market, Lord Robertson put it most simply of all – 'England did not form part of Europe, as Adenauer saw it.'[27]

One must return to the events of October and November, 1962, and to the Government crisis which derived from them. Earlier in the month the Chancellor had delivered a Government statement in the *Bundestag* which was full of confidence and satisfaction, especially where the economic situation was concerned.[28] Since 1949 the national income had multiplied three times, exports had risen from a trickle to 51,000 million

22..........Dr. Erich Mende, in personal conversation with the author.
23..........*Erinnerungen*, Konrad Adenauer, VOL 4, p. 208.
24..........Professor Walter Hallstein, in personal conversation with the author.
25..........*Konrad Adenauer*, Rudolf Augstein, p. 99.
26..........Dr. Gerhard Schröder, in personal conversation with the author.
27..........General Lord Robertson, in personal conversation with the author.
28..........*Bundestag* Debate, October 9, 1962.

Marks, 6·5 million new homes had been built. West Germany was now producing 70 per cent of her own food, 380,000 soldiers were under arms as a contribution to the defence of the West, and the country had moved from a period of dynamic growth to one of more modest but impressively steady expansion. De Gaulle had just concluded a spectacularly successful visit to the Federal Republic; negotiation on the Common Market and the Franco-German Treaty were proceeding; the Western Alliance was, in face of the Soviet Communist threat which Adenauer never underrated, strong and enduring.

The picture which Adenauer painted was rosier than was really justified, but it earned him an ovation from the Government benches. Here was a man of almost 90, still alert and commanding, retailing the successes of thirteen years of successful husbandry with the air of a spruce and spry headmaster announcing the school's prize-winning achievements. The rearing of the sinister Berlin Wall, the diminished CDU vote in the 1961 elections, even perhaps the undertaking to change Chancellors two years from then – these frustrations were, for the moment, forgotten. This *Bundestag* speech looked like another landmark; and the Chancellor was visibly delighted with his mastery of this mass of economic facts. The economy was generally, to him, an uncharted jungle.

But, at the moment when Adenauer was speaking, a storm was brewing. A member of the staff of the weekly paper, *Der Spiegel*, Conrad Ahlers, was penning an article on West German military strategy which was published on October 10. In this article, Ahlers claimed that the 1962 late summer NATO manoeuvres in West Germany had convinced the Ministry of Defence that the size of the *Bundeswehr* should be increased – to ensure a 'forward strategy of defence' on the Elbe – and that the *Bundeswehr* should be given medium-range rockets. This would give the Federal Republic greater political as well as military influence in NATO.

Ahlers, a highly competent journalist who later became the official spokesman of the Federal Press Office, was believed to have received his information from a member of the *Bundeswehr*'s Headquarters Staff, Colonel Alfred Martin. He was later to admit that information was given to him by Martin from March, 1962, onwards, and that contact with Martin was established through Josef Augstein, brother of Rudolf Augstein, the publisher of *Der Spiegel*. There was, in reality, nothing sinister about all this, and nothing sensational about Ahlers article, but the *Spiegel* (often called a 'substitute opposition', because it was such a trenchant and fearless critic of government policies)[29] was a violent opponent of the ebullient Minister of Defence, Franz-Josef Strauss. It had

29..........Jürgen Seiffert, in *Die Spiegel Affäre*, edited by him, p. 48.

accused him two years earlier of personal favouritism in allocating government contracts, and by 1962 it had extended what had become a regular campaign against Strauss to include his friends and political associates. It should be noted, in passing, that the *Spiegel* found criticism profitable and this encouraged its readiness to 'take a bang' at all established authority.[30] The traditions of 'Grub Street', the earlier sensationalist English Press style, still flourish. In the case of the *Spiegel* they were perpetuated with a combination of energy, snap, ferocity and undoubted journalistic 'know-how'.

On Friday, October 26, the West German police swooped on the head office of the paper in Hamburg and its branch office in Bonn. The Hamburg office was sealed and searched by thirty policemen and no member of the paper's staff was allowed in. The Bonn office was likewise searched, but only briefly – whereas the head office was still under 'police occupation' three days later. The private homes of four leading members of the paper's staff were searched, too, and the police confiscated, among other things, a school essay written in 1939 by the publisher Rudolf Augstein. At the home of his Assistant Editor, two small children had to get out of bed in the middle of the night to have their mattresses taken apart.

Various members of the paper's staff, including Rudolf Augstein, were put under arrest. Meanwhile Conrad Ahlers, the author of the offending article, was arrested by the Spanish police in Malaga, in southern Spain, where he was on holiday. His arrest was the work of Strauss, the Minister of Defence, who gave orders to that effect to his Under Secretary of State, Volkmar Hopf. The latter established that Ahlers was in Spain and told Strauss. The Minister rang up the German Military Attaché in Madrid, Colonel Achim Oster, at 1.25 a.m. on the morning of October 27. At 3 a.m. Oster reported back that the necessary action was under way. Ahlers was duly 'detained' by the Spanish police, put on a plane to Frankfurt and arrested there. Here was a ghostly reminder of the Hitler-Franco understanding during the Spanish Civil War.

The Ministry of Defence denied, on October 29, that Strauss was taking 'revanchist' action against the *Spiegel*.[31] The Minister of the Interior, Herr Höcherl, denied a day later that he had any knowledge of the way in which events had been carried out by police under his control. On November 8, in the *Bundestag*, Hoecherl was to admit that the arrest of Ahlers in Spain was 'somewhat outside legality' – *etwas ausserhalb der Legalität*. Strauss issued various denials of personal complicity, and on November 9 explained that he had been no more than the judiciary's

30...........Alfred Grosser, in *Die Spiegel Affäre*, p. 30.
31...........Terence Prittie, in the *Manchester Guardian*, October 30, 1962.

agent on the telephone, and had merely 'repeated' to Colonel Oster in Madrid what had to be done about Ahlers. Strauss clung to office until November 30, when he resigned and withdrew, for the time being, to *Land* politics in Bavaria. The Minister had earlier on November 8, given an astonishingly bland account of the incident to the *Bundestag*, in which he treated the arrest of a German subject, by German orders, in a foreign country as the most normal thing in the world and justified it on the grounds that Ahlers had committed 'treason' and 'might try to escape'.[32]

Adenauer remained silent during the first wild flurry of denials, accusations and counter-accusations. On November 7, he denounced Rudolf Augstein in the *Bundestag* for 'systematically betraying the state in order to make money'.[33] At the same time he did his best to play down an increasingly serious situation, by suggesting that no one should 'get worked up' about where Ahlers had been arrested – 'There had even been talk of Tangier, and just how would one collect a German citizen in Tangier?'[34] The *Bundestag* was at its worst during this session, with wild cat-calls from the SPD alternating with obviously forced and half-hearted applause from the CDU benches. The only worthwhile speech came from one of the younger members of the FDP, Wolfgang Döring, who stood up boldly for his friend Augstein and admonished Adenauer for assuming guilt in a case which was *sub judice*.

The '*Spiegel* Affair' was to drag on for many weary months until legal proceedings were finally dropped. As late as November 29 and December 4, indeed, two more people connected with the paper were arrested, Paul Conrad and Josef Augstein. Twenty-nine University professors sent an open letter to Kurt-Georg Kiesinger, the President of the Federal Second or *Länder* Chamber, complaining of breaches against the rule of law. Petitions were sent in by 63 professors of Bonn University, 54 of Tübingen and 29 of Cologne. Adenauer cared not a rap for the views of intellectuals, but worse was to come. On November 19 the five Free Democrat Ministers resigned, mainly as a protest against the flouting of the authority of one of them, the Minister of Justice, Dr. Stammberger. Strauss lingered on only until November 30 before resigning, and it was surprising that Hoecherl, who had come out of the affair nearly as badly, did not go too. There was talk of a CDU 'palace revolution', and the Minister of Posts, Herr Paul Lücke, actually did begin talks with the SPD leaders on the possibility of forming a 'big' coalition. It was Adenauer's idea and he let the SPD leaders know that he was ready to introduce electoral reform if they wanted it. The bait was not swallowed; Adenauer began to realize

32..........Terence Prittie, in the *Manchester Guardian*, November 8, 1962.
33..........*Konrad Adenauer*, Rudolf Augstein, p. 61.
34..........*Die Spiegel Affäre*, p. 115.

that a 'big' coalition would mean his own retirement. He decided to soldier on.

When he held one of his 'intimate' tea-parties in December for a few chosen German journalists, they noticed how desperately tired he looked.[35] His face was even more deeply lined than before and he had deep black shadows beneath his eyes. He cheered up a little when they began to ask him questions, and 'warmed' to his own themes. But he had no cheering news for them. The Cuban crisis was much on his mind, as well as the fact that there had been no progress in the field of disarmament. Khrushchev was again making bellicose statements about West Berlin. He was to threaten a separate Peace Treaty with the East Germans once again, on December 24. But, as before, he did not follow this threat up. As far as home affairs were concerned, Adenauer had only a few words to say about the new Cabinet, formed on December 11.

The home front, when the New Year opened, could hardly have been bleaker. The once solid ranks of the CDU were in a state of extraordinary disarray. The last, long battle with that most unwilling adversary, Vice-Chancellor Erhard, was just beginning. The Chancellor had fallen out with Gerhard Schröder, who continued to talk about the necessity of bringing Britain into the Common Market. Gone was his glum paladin, von Brentano, who he had thrown to the FDP wolves with such indecent haste. There had been no real reconciliation with Gerstenmaier. Yet something of Adenauer's old mischievousness remained; the short, dumpy Gerstenmaier had a block of wood which he pushed into position when mounting the rostrum in the *Bundestag*. Adenauer, from just within reach, took to pushing it round the corner, just out of Gerstenmaier's sight.

Blankenhorn was now an Ambassador and out of the country, while von Eckardt had long since fallen out of favour. Of the Chancellor's former circle of close advisers only the ubiquitous Krone and the self-effacing Globke remained. Among the younger members of the CDU there were mutterings of revolt. The 'Old One' was not only being deserted by followers who previously frowned on him; he did not seem to care any more. Less and less often was he ready to intervene in *Bundestag* debates, but when he did, that false, 'yellow' note crept quickly into his voice. For the most part he sat silent and brooding in the *Bundestag*, brooding most probably on the long list of recent CDU reverses in *Land* elections – in Berlin, Hesse, the Rhineland-Palatinate. His decline in power and authority was clear to see; yet he did not seem to grasp what was happening to him.

Adenauer once told a Party colleague that he would have to learn to

35..........Georg Schröder, of *Die Welt*, in a personal note, December 20, 1962.

despise humanity.[36] It was this contempt for others, allied to an old man's increasing petulance, which inaugurated the last important episode of his career as Chancellor – the renewal of his bitter personal quarrel with Vice-Chancellor Erhard. He was waiting for a suitable pretext. On February 5, 1963, he was given one. Erhard gave two interviews to newspapers, the Düsseldorf *Mittag* and the *Sueddeutsche Zeitung* of Munich. In the first, he criticized France for not honouring agreements with the Federal Republic and urged careful consideration before the Franco-German Treaty were ratified.[37] In the second, he said that he was prepared to shoulder the burdens of the Chancellorship, whenever his Party asked him to do so; and repeated his belief that negotiations on a British entry into the Common Market should be resumed.[38]

On February 6, in the *Bundestag*, Adenauer ostentatiously turned his back on Erhard, as they sat next to each other on the Cabinet bench. After his speech, in which he made an unusual slip by referring to 'Federal Chancellor Erhard', Adenauer buried himself in his notes and ignored his neighbour. When the *Bundestag* adjourned, Erhard stole away surreptitiously. The two men had not exchanged a single word.

The breach between them, after this deliberate cold-shouldering of Erhard before the full gaze of the *Bundestag*, was complete. From that moment on, Adenauer complained ceaselessly about his Vice-Chancellor, voicing faults that had become part of a familiar litany over the years. He was a man lacking 'political qualities' (Adenauer used the word *Eigenschaften*). He was not a good European, and he knew too little about foreign affairs. He was too fat, too soft, and lacking the fibre needed by a Chancellor. Pernickety in small things, Adenauer thought he ate too much and smoked too much. His feud with Erhard threatened to undermine the the unity of the CDU, and in March the Party appointed a special Commission to examine the question of the succession to Adenauer and restore Party solidarity.

On April 22, Adenauer made what turned out to be his last effort to bar Erhard from the succession. That morning, before the Executive of the Parliamentary Party of the CDU had convened, the Chancellor gathered a small band of advisers at the Palais Schaumburg – the ever-faithful Krone, and the Ministers of Posts, Labour and Länder Affairs, Paul Lücke, Theodor Blank and Alois Niederalt. How little, how pitifully little was left of his 'Old Guard'! Adenauer asked these men to help him oppose Erhard's candidature; his vain hope was that Krone would talk round the members of the Party Executive, Blank would bring the support

36..........*Zwischen Stabilität und Krise*, Fritz René Allemann, p. 68.
37..........*Düsseldorf Mittag*, February 5, 1963.
38..........*Sueddeutsche Zeitung*, February 5, 1963.

of the Christian Trade Unionists and Niederalt that of the Bavarians. Blank and Lücke were unhelpful, and the little-known Niederalt was even reported to have said, 'Don't make me laugh.'[39] Adenauer made even less headway at the Party Executive committee meeting which followed. He said that there were excellent alternatives to Erhard, and hinted that either Schröder or Krone would make a good Chancellor. Both men promptly indicated that they were not prepared to run against Erhard.

The game was up. Erhard was nominated as Adenauer's successor and the Chancellor was asked to reaffirm his intention of retiring in October. He did so with an ill-grace. With a long summer holiday at Cadenabbia in prospect, a politically almost empty interval lay ahead. There was a tumultuous welcome for President Kennedy in May, when he visited Berlin and Bonn, with a preternaturally silent Adenauer appearing at his side. Kennedy, admittedly, did his best to be friendly. He told Adenauer that he was one of the only three great statesmen of 'this era'.[40] De Gaulle, inevitably, was another, but Adenauer may not have been so pleased at the inclusion of homespun Harry Truman.

Nor may de Gaulle have been happy either, when he visited Bonn on June 4 and 5, and Adenauer gave him a long – perhaps too long – account of his talks with Kennedy and the tremendous ovation given to the American President wherever he went. There was talk of the overtures which Khrushchev had been making to the United States, Britain and West Germany, and de Gaulle warned his host against accepting an invitation to go to Moscow. Then the General had his usual strictures to make about NATO, which Adenauer found less disturbing than before.[41] He would, after all, be bowing out soon, and this would no longer be essentially his concern. He got in at least one dig at Erhard; the man, he told de Gaulle, would not be strong enough to take the risks required if the German Question were ever to be solved. And the Chancellor must have agreed wholeheartedly with de Gaulle's remark that, with Erhard in the saddle, German foreign policy would become 'a question-mark'.[42]

Almost the last action of Adenauer in office was to pay a farewell visit to de Gaulle at Rambouillet. Then, in October, he said goodbye as Chancellor, first to Berlin and then to the Federal Parliament. There were moments of irony at both ceremonies, on October 10 and October 15 respectively. Speaking on Berlin's behalf, Willy Brandt recalled that 'Berliners would have liked to have seen Adenauer more often in their city', and added in pointed reference to August 13, 1961, when the Wall

39..........Terence Prittie, in the *New Republic*, May 11, 1963.
40..........*Erinnerungen*, Konrad Adenauer, VOL 4, pp. 222–3.
41..........*Erinnerungen*, Konrad Adenauer, VOL 4, pp. 228–9.
42..........*Erinnerungen*, Konrad Adenauer, VOL 4, p. 230.

went up, 'At one particular moment we really did miss the Federal Chancellor.' But Adenauer had no intention of making an *amende honorable* and expressing regret, even this late in the day. In his answer he claimed, with a touch of genius, that the notes taken during Brandt's speech were illegible. So he made no reference to the content of the speech whatever!

In the *Bundestag*, the Chancellor was more at home. He paid a handsome tribute to the fortitude and good sense of the German people, thanked God that the Germans had found good friends again, and called for the continuity of post-war policies. He made no reference to Erhard, his successor, and he must have writhed inwardly when Eugen Gerstenmaier, in his address, congratulated him on being the first German Chancellor in a hundred years to withdraw of his own free will. Nothing could have been further from the truth. But withdraw he did, by leaving his seat on the Cabinet bench and going down to his numbered desk in the front row on the floor of the chamber. It was, on the surface, a dignified and worthy departure.

15 The End

The valedictions, with a thin layer of sentiment, could not conceal the fact that Adenauer's resignation of the Chancellorship had been a singularly untidy affair. He had bitterly opposed his party's virtually unanimous choice of a successor, and had refused to accept defeat gracefully over this. He had deserted his political principles by angling – unsuccessfully at that – for alliance with the SPD, and the thought behind this Machiavellian manoeuvre may well have been to renege on his agreement with Mende and the Free Democrats to retire in 1963. He had grievously shaken his own Party's self-confidence; in the final period of his stewardship, as one observer put it – the CDU 'acquired too much fat, and lost its muscle'.[1] His part in the '*Spiegel* Affair' had been, at the very least, highly ambiguous. Certainly, he had utterly failed to give a lead in clearing it up. Even the trusty Krone later admitted that: 'He would perhaps have done better to have retired in 1961.'[2]

For the moment, at least, the signs were that retirement would be graceful. The ex-Chancellor announced his intention of writing his memoirs. There was going to be a great deal to write; and his study at Rhöndorf was cleared for the task, with his personal secretary, Fräulein Poppinga, in constant attendance. There was a form of reconciliation with Erhard; Adenauer told him that he would help in any way possible and Erhard, immediately and typically responsive to a friendly gesture, assured him that he would 'come to him'.[3] Indeed, he did so on several occasions and on others sent along Dr. Lüdger Westrick, for many years his State Secretary in the Ministry of Economics and now promoted, along with his master, to the Palais Schaumburg. As far as Erhard was concerned, a reconciliation was not just desirable but eminently necessary; for Adenauer had been re-elected Chairman of the CDU in June, 1962, and by an only slightly reduced vote. He was to cling to this post like a limpet until March, 1966.

But there were several reasons why his retirement was to be the reverse of peaceful. His memoirs were not a labour of love. According to Leo Schwering he referred to them as *meine scheuszliche Arbeit* – 'my *frightful*

1............*Das Erbe Adenauer's*, Rüdiger Altmann, p. 97.
2, 3.........Heinrich Krone, in personal conversation with the author.

task'.[4] Von Eckardt called them his 'duty-exercise' (*Pflichtübung*), which gave him no pleasure at all.[5] His son, Paul, who was living with him at Rhöndorf during his last years, qualified this: 'He was very disciplined about writing his memoirs and he did get some satisfaction out of them. They represented an achievement. And he never ceased to want to achieve something. He was the last man in the world to rest on his laurels.'[6] Adenauer wrote the first volume of his memoirs with scrupulous care – he managed, with a certain inverted artistry, to avoid virtually all mention of Erhard, the principal architect of the German economic miracle. The second volume betrayed signs of haste and impatience, and the third had to be 'doctored' before being published, after his death. The fourth volume was no more than a bundle of notes, although some of them were revealing.

He took great pleasure in his family, and in the doings and sheer number of his grandchildren – there were 23 of them before he died and his first great-grandchild would shortly be on the way. To them he was an interesting and individual figure, but inevitably remote.[7] He spent more time than before admiring the sunsets, his roses and his pictures – he had assembled a considerable collection over the years but a sale of them, organized long after his death, in 1970, was a flop. He continued to play *boccia* – the Italian version of bowls – usually with his son Paul. He read more than before; conservative in his tastes, Joseph Conrad and Agatha Christie remained his favourites. And he listened to music often – his old favourites, Brahms, Mozart and, most of all, Schubert. He went to Mass each Sunday and at least once a week walked up the road to the small cemetery in the Löwenbürger Strasse, where both his wives were buried. But there was, even though he was nearing 90, just not enough for him to do.

He was given a small office in the Parliament building, close to the room used by the Second Chamber, the *Bundesrat*. Next to it was an even smaller room with a couch, where he took an after-lunch siesta. There was a kitchenette and he took to having a light lunch there, prepared by Fräulein Poppinga. There was nothing to remind him of the spacious elegance of the Palais Schaumburg, save his desk which he brought with him, and a picture of the Acropolis, painted by Winston Churchill. His rooms were significantly far removed from the offices of the Parliamentary Party of the CDU.

4............Dr. Leo Schwering, in personal conversation with the author.
5............Felix von Eckardt, in personal conversation with the author.
6............Dr. Paul Adenauer, in personal conversation with the author.
7............The children of Frau Libeth Werhahn, in personal conversation with the author.

Few people came to visit him there, and Adenauer probably felt this keenly. One German journalist who made a point of looking in to see him, recalls how, on the very first day after his resignation, he saw the Chancellor making his way entirely alone to the *Plenarsaal* where *Bundestag* debates took place.[8] Nobody stopped to speak to him. How different it had been for the fourteen years preceding! Adulation, spontaneous or sychophantic, had been showered on him, and his path to the *Plenarsaal* has resembled a royal progress. Now all was changed. Adenauer was often credited with the hide of a rhinoceros. The truth was that hiding his feelings was a part of his iron self-discipline, and that beneath an impassive exterior he was a great deal more sensitive than he allowed anyone to suspect. He was a stoic and he did not complain, but he must have felt the relative isolation of his small room in the *Bundeshaus* very keenly.

Then there was the question of Chancellor Erhard. That comfortable fat man, with his gentian-blue eyes and look of primal innocence, with his habit of making remarks of almost childlike ingenuousness,[9] seemed to Adenauer to be fatally unsuited to be Chancellor. He took to making quips about Erhard to all and sundry. To a young German journalist, he produced: 'Shall we discuss serious politics, or Chancellor Erhard?'[10] And when someone remarked to him that, under Erhard, there was 'no government', he answered; 'That is quite wrong. There are at least three governments, and he's not in charge of any of them.'[11] Such pleasantries were relatively harmless, but Adenauer soon began sniping much more dangerously at Erhard, in interviews with the press, in statements to the CDU and, most damaging of all, in conversations with foreign statesmen. He was perfectly ready to slight Erhard publicly or privately. Thus, when de Gaulle came to Bonn for talks with Erhard in July, 1964, he called first on Adenauer and the latter kept him until he was already twenty minutes late for the Chancellor. It could of course be argued that the main 'credit' for this gesture of sly effrontery should go to de Gaulle.

It would be tedious to give a detailed list of Adenauer's attacks on Erhard. One or two examples suffice. There was Adenauer's interview with the weekly *Bild am Sountag* published on November 1, 1964. In it he said that the Erhard Government was responsible for the worsening of relations with France, that de Gaulle had been treated with obvious 'cool-

8............Hans-Werner, Graf Finck von Finckenstein, in personal conversation with the author.

9............One quoted by Graf Finckenstein was, after visiting Cape Kennedy with President Johnson, 'Ich liebe der Präsident Johnson, und er liebt mich auch.' ('I love President Johnson, and he loves me too.')

10..........James O'Donnell, in a personal memorandum on Adenauer.

11..........Hubertus, Prinz zu Löwenstein, in personal conversation with the author.

ness' when he came to Bonn in July and that a future French Government might turn to the Soviet Union as an ally. At the same time, Adenauer aimed a below-the-belt blow at the Foreign Minister, Gerhard Schröder, who was ill, saying that it was a pity he was not well enough to be at his post. Schröder was later to comment, sadly; 'He took to attacking me latterly, when his attacks were really intended for someone else.'[12] – in fact, for Erhard.

There was the occasion of the CDU celebration of Adenauer's 89th birthday. The ex-Chancellor used it to speak of the alleged decline of West German foreign policy. With cutting sarcasm, he said he had no wish to do anything which could bring down the present Government, with elections coming that year. But since it was going to fall in any event, then the sooner the better. In March, 1965, he was at it again at the 13th CDU Party Rally in Düsseldorf, criticizing both the Bonn and Paris Governments for failing to get on with one another and ostentatiously avoiding Erhard. Some painful photographs were taken of them for the occasion, sitting side by side and looking in opposite directions.

Erhard, understandably, felt a lasting resentment over Adenauer's treatment of him. 'For my own part, I did my best to get on with him. I tried to give him the feeling that I valued his advice. I telephoned him often, and I went to see him before going to Paris to meet de Gaulle. He only reacted occasionally in a truly human manner. I believe that, by his attitude to me, he did great harm to his party and his country. One obvious consequence is the present decline of the CDU.'[13] And in answer to the question what was Adenauer's salient characteristic as a person, he answered briefly: 'Contempt for humanity' (*Menschenverachtung*).

In 1965 there were Federal elections. Adenauer's vendetta against Erhard might have been expected to have seriously weakened the CDU's chances. But the Chancellor's outwardly placid and confident appearance, his brilliant record as the country's economic director and the overall trend towards a two-party system, actually enabled the CDU to increase its share of the poll from 45·3 per cent to 47·6 per cent. The SPD's share went up too, from 36 to 39 per cent, but this did not bring it within striking distance. A neck-and-neck race had been predicted by the public opinion pollsters. Adenauer had been gloomily predicting a defeat caused by lack of leadership. Now, for the first time, it became apparent that the 1961 setback at the polls had been a personal failure for him. It was the unkindest cut of all.

A few politicians and journalists continued to pay court to him. One of

12..........Dr. Gerhard Schröder, in personal conversation with the author.

13..........Professor Dr. Ludwig Erhard, in personal conversation with the author. He was speaking in November, 1969.

them remembered clearly his last conversation with him.[14] He was still acutely interested in the world of politics, but he was downcast and, uncharacteristically, there was an air of total resignation about him. He was bitter about the Kennedy Administration, and there was more than a trace of resentment even against de Gaulle. National rivalries were, he thought, wrecking his dream of a truly united Europe. He had begun to doubt the wisdom of his own policy of holding the Russians at arm's length; perhaps there should, even at this late stage, be a more coherent effort to talk to them, and to talk sense into them. Heinrich Brüning had suggested just this, more than a decade earlier, and Adenauer had driven him out of the country.

In public the ex-Chancellor remained a 'Cold War warrior'. His last notable public speech was in the Ateneo in Madrid on February 16, 1967. Its subject was the world of 1900 and the world of 1960; and Adenauer appealed, for the last time, for a unified Europe which should on no account include the Soviet Union. Were it to do so, Europe would be 'submerged' by the sheer weight of Soviet power. Adenauer urged a European 'Third Force', to counter the American and Soviet monopoly of nuclear weaponry – 'the greatest danger to the nations of the rest of the world'.[15] Spain, too, should take her place in a uniting Europe.

Back in Rhöndorf, Adenauer went on making notes for his last volume of memoirs. He was pleased with the financial success of the first volume – Adenauer always enjoyed the feeling of affluence which money gave him – but worried over the amount of tax which had to be paid on the proceeds of the French edition.[16] His brain remained active until the last, mercifully short illness, and he read the newspapers religiously; when he became too weak to do so, the faithful Fräulein Poppinga read him carefully selected extracts.[17]

The last 'business interview' which he had was with Kurt-Georg Kiesinger, now Chancellor in Erhard's place, on April 3. By then he had taken to his bed; he only had another sixteen days to live. During these sixteen days he saw, apart from one or two members of his staff, only his family; for the last week he was unconscious.[18] Understandably, his family do not talk much about this last illness and, very rightly, they brought nobody into the house during the final struggle for life. According to his son, Paul, 'He worried a lot at the end, but never about himself. He was

14...........Hans-Werner, Graf Finck von Finckenstein. In *Die Welt*, April 20, 1967. Obituary Notice.
15...........*Erinnerungen*, Konrad Adenauer, VOL 4, p. 240.
16...........Felix von Eckardt, in personal conversation with the author.
17...........Frau Ria Reiners, in personal conversation with the author.
18...........Dr. Max Adenauer, in personal conversation with the author.

worrying about Europe's disunity and impotence, about the dangers of nuclear war, about people becoming the victims of their illusions. He wanted to go on fighting.'[19] Certainly, he had no fear at all of death;[20] and the last coherent thought which he put into words was that members of his family should stick together and see as much as possible of one another. Konrad Adenauer remained a stoic to the very end, and to the very end he knew that the family was the vital unit in the form of ordered society (*Etablierte Ordnung*) in which he believed implicitly.

He died on April 19, 1967. On April 22 the official obsequies began. His body was taken by boat to Bad Godesberg and from there to the Cabinet room in the Palais Schaumburg in Bonn. He lay there in state for one night, and the next night in the Cathedral in Cologne. Here the funeral service was conducted by his old friend, Cardinal Frings, before his body was brought back, by boat, to Rhöndorf and the 'Waldfriedhof' cemetery where others of his family were buried. There were valedictory speeches at each stage of the long drawn-out ceremonial; and all the great of the Western world came to pay him honour, de Gaulle and President Johnson in the van and David Ben-Gurion, who had helped him close a dreadful chapter of German–Jewish relations, travelling all the way from Israel.

Beyond lay the 'Waldfriedhof', the abyss of the unknown; but one can guess that Adenauer journeyed into it with the manly self-confidence which marked his religious convictions. Nearly sixty years earlier, his father-in-law had expressed slightly pained surprise that Adenauer had never been to Rome, and he had replied: 'And do you suppose, because I have never stood in St. Peter's, I might lose my Christian faith?'[21]

There is a convention that it is not possible to assess what a statesman has achieved, until many years after his death. In one sense this is true; much becomes plain only in the course of time. But much, too, is plain even before a man is dead. Some analysis of Adenauer's achievement is, therefore, justified and necessary.

First, there has been a tendency to compare him with Bismarck, possibly because of Winston Churchill's remark that Adenauer was the greatest German statesman since Bismarck's day, or perhaps because there was no German Chancellor of real stature – with the possible exception of Heinrich Brüning – in the sixty year interval between Bismarck's departure from, and Adenauer's accession to, the Chancellorship. Bismarck unified the German nation; Adenauer failed to reunify it, and because of

19...........Dr. Paul Adenauer, in personal conversation with the author.
20...........Dr. Max Adenauer and Frau Libeth Werhahn, in personal conversation with the author.
21...........Frau Libeth Werhahn, in personal conversation with the author.

this the comparisons which have been drawn have mostly been in Bismarck's favour. Thus one British historian – 'Compared with that supreme diplomatic juggler (Bismarck), Adenauer was a man who plodded along carefully with a single basketful of eggs. He never re-insured, he devised no alternative schemes to those he was concerned to carry out, he was above all anxious to avoid a situation where Germany might be tempted to play off the East against the West.'[22]

A serious attempt was made to compare the work of the two men by Thomas Mann's son, the historian Golo Mann.[23] Golo Mann saw in Adenauer the citizen, or *Bürger*, who thought in social terms, as compared to Bismarck the *Junker* and member of the landed aristocracy, who was concerned with Germany's position of power and influence in the Concert of Europe. Adenauer was an ultra-careful chess-player in the field of diplomacy; Bismarck a sometimes showy and reckless, but generally effective gambler. Bismarck 'led a hectic, undisciplined life'; Adenauer's was 'the epitome of order and conduct, a model of physical and mental equilibrium'. Both had strength of character, a pragmatic approach to their problems and an innate distrust of the German people, and both were capable of candour, consistency and honesty yet, at the same time, of acting in an exactly contrary spirit. But while Bismarck left a united Germany in a position of power and apparent independence of her neighbours, Adenauer placed the truncated Federal Republic firmly in a Western Alliance which was nominally one of interdependent democracies but was in practice dominated by the United States.

It may be that the situations which they inherited were at least as relevant as the situations which they left behind them. Bismarck led a Prussia with a great military tradition behind it, fully accepted as a member of the Concert of Europe, and with a heterogeneous and decaying Austrian Empire as the only rival for the leadership of the German nation. How different was Adenauer's situation when he became Chancellor! Germany had lost two World Wars, millions of soldiers and civilians and a huge slice of what was her territory from 1870 to 1918. The country was in the front line of the Cold War between the Free World and the Communist bloc, and physically divided between East and West. Its people had been left by the traumatic experience of the Nazi Era in a state of acute mental turmoil; and were regarded, and at first treated, as pariahs by virtually the whole world. Before even thinking of embarking on the great task of uniting the German people which had confronted Bismarck, Adenauer had to restore Germany's honour, reputation and credibility. And in the

22..........*German Reunification*, Philip Windsor, p. 47.
23..........Golo Mann, in *Encounter*, April, 1964.

course of doing that he had to preside over the rebuilding of Germany's shattered cities, the absorption of 13 million refugees (or roughly a quarter of the Federal Republic's population) and the inception of democratic government among a people which had never fully accepted it in the past.

The magnitude of Adenauer's task has to be taken into account in any comparison between him and Bismarck, or between him and statesmen like Metternich and Talleyrand. Metternich sought only to shore up an *ancien régime*, while Talleyrand was given plenty of outside assistance in restoring the prestige and position of a France which had never become a total outlaw in the eyes of the civilized world. Neither Metternich nor Talleyrand had to mould political thinking in their countries. Yet Adenauer had time left over to propagate the 'European idea' and become, indeed, its leading exponent. Here, then, is the briefest possible summary of his achievements:

He won back full sovereignty for the West German State, in stages which involved shrewd planning and immense pertinacity in negotiation. He bound the Federal Republic indissolubly into the fabric of Western Europe, by bringing it into the Schuman Plan Coal and Steel Community, the Council of Europe, NATO and the Common Market. He ended the two centuries-old bitter and fratricidal strife with France, both in a practical sense and in a formal one, by the 1963 Treaty of Friendship. He gave the Federal Republic, containing the great majority of the German people, firm friends and allies – the first, with the possible exception of Austria-Hungary, since the days of Bismarck. He helped his Vice-Chancellor to secure an economic prosperity more dynamic and also more enduring than that achieved by any other European country. Most important of all, he helped to restore the self-respect of over 50 million Germans after an era of unparalleled self-deception and degradation, culminating in total defeat.

Of course, he had his failings and his failures. He had a complex about Prussia, and no feeling for the people of Eastern Germany. Thus his saying that: 'Once the night-train from Cologne to Berlin crossed the Elbe, I got no more sleep.'[24] And the more frequently quoted story of how he first saw the portrait done of him in 1963 by Professor Kallmann of Munich. Adenauer remarked: 'Here I look just like a Hun.' Then, as an afterthought – 'Now I come to think of it, some of my ancestors on my mother's side did in fact come from the Harz Mountains.' His critics maintained that Adenauer's obsessive dislike of all things Prussian coloured his thinking on the subject of German reunification, and made him supremely unwilling to take risks on account of it.

24..........James O'Donnell, in a personal memorandum on Adenauer.

Certainly, he failed to make any progress towards reunification. Was that his fault? This question could be argued indefinitely. There is the unbiased opinion of Professor Theodor Eschenburg, a ready critic of the Chancellor's – 'The Soviet Union has not for a single moment been prepared to allow reunification in freedom – not even under the condition that a reunified Germany accepted neutrality between the blocs.'[25] One of Adenauer's ablest, if most unpredictable Ministers, Franz-Josef Strauss, felt that Adenauer could in his day only consolidate the Federal Republic and that his achievements offered a base for a 'second phase' of all-German policy in which the Soviet Union must be won over to the idea of a united but friendly Germany, as an integral part of a united but friendly Europe.[26] But that 'united but friendly Europe' still does not exist, in spite of Adenauer's own considerable contribution towards the first stages in its creation. And the first signs that Khrushchev might be considering accommodation with West Germany occurred only in 1964, hastening Khrushchev's fall.

A more valid criticism is that Adenauer expected too much from his policy of Western strength, and underrated the inevitable Soviet reaction, which was to tighten its control of the satellites when feeling threatened, particularly control of the East German puppet state. The co-efficient of this policy of strength was the application of an active, imaginative diplomacy in the field of East–West relations. Adenauer was only becoming aware of this in his last years. But his two immediate successors as Chancellor, Erhard and Kiesinger, did little in this respect, and it has been left to Willy Brandt to make a start late in 1969, with his modest policy of 'small steps' to normalize East–West relations and to bring closer contact between the two German states.[27]

Was Adenauer an obsessive anti-Communist? I think not. His central reason for deep distrust of the Soviet Union was that Soviet leaders – Stalin, Khrushchev or Kosygin – have never for one moment wavered from a policy built on brute force and diplomatic deception. Had Adenauer lived a few years longer he would have considered that his distrust of the Soviet Union was amply justified by the ruthless suppression of civil liberties in Czechoslovakia and by the starkly imperialistic Soviet incursion into the Middle East. There has been only one yardstick for measuring Soviet intentions, and that has been provided by Soviet actions. As long as the Soviet régime represses its Jews and commits its critics to lunatic asylums, it is the enemy of civilized society. Adenauer's view of Soviet régimes was based on cool realism, ultimately on sanity.

25...........*Zur politischen Praxis in der Bundesrepublik*, Theodor Eschenburg, p. 89.
26...........*The Grand Design*, Franz-Josef Strauss, p. 21 and p. 65.
27...........*A Peace Policy for Europe*, Willy Brandt, p. 24.

Adenauer may, or may not, have been wrong to support de Gaulle in keeping Britain out of the Common Market in 1963. On balance, one must assume that he genuinely believed that Britain was not ready to come into Europe. His supporters can legitimately argue that he was proved right by the victory at the polls so soon afterwards of a Labour Party pledged at that stage to oppose Britain's entry into the Common Market. Adenauer's distaste for the Labour Party was heightened by his personal distrust of the incoming Prime Minister, Mr. Harold Wilson. This distrust was shared by a large section of informed opinion in the Federal Republic. Once again, it may have been more fundamental that Adenauer had an ingrained aversion to Britain and the British people as a whole. To him, Britain could never be a 'neighbour' or 'partner' in the same way as, say, France or Italy. To Heinrich Krone he used to say – 'England is a sea-power. She has her colonies, and she has to think about them. She has her way of life; it's not ours.'[28]

Adenauer may have lacked charity. He was impatient over stupidity, and easily moved to contempt. One of his sayings: 'If God had made men cleverer, they could have ruled themselves better. If he had made them stupider, I could rule them more easily.' He was asked: 'How would you have liked them to be?' The answer – 'Stupider, of course.'[29] Another of his sayings – 'More fools go to Heaven than clever people.' His lack of charity was at the root of his feud with Erhard, his slighting of his former standby, Gerhard Schröder, his casual disinterest in human rights during the '*Spiegel* Affair'. Statesmen, of course, must have a streak of ruthlessness. But it should never degenerate into mere stubborn resentment. This is what happened when Adenauer first refused to retire gracefully, and then failed to play the natural role of elder statesman.

There were other criticisms of Adenauer which had some validity. He did, to some extent, demean the office of President by his wayward behaviour in 1959. Probably this did, indeed, mark the end of his effective, sovereign rule. He did, very willingly, absorb the Ministers of other parties into the CDU – Kraft and Oberländer of the BHE Refugee Party; Seebohm, Hellwege and von Merkatz of the German Party; Blücher, Neumayer, Preusker and Schäfer of the FDP. He did, periodically, bypass the *Bundestag* and govern through his own Chancellery Staff. This was one of the reasons for the accusation so frequently levelled against him, that he instituted a kind of 'Chancellor democracy' and retarded the growth of fully-functioning Parliamentary institutions. It was the origin of Augstein's complaint that he was 'a good European but a bad German'.[30] One

28, 29.....Dr. Heinrich Krone, in personal conversation with the author.
30..........*Konrad Adenauer*, Rudolf Augstein, p. 94.

can only repeat that the Germans, after the shocks and horrors of a Nazi Era and a lost war, probably needed the patriarchal authority which Adenauer was able to supply. They needed a breathing space, an interval in which the rule of law could be instituted, and with it, something like an integrated and democratic society. Looking round Europe, one must remark that, in the so called 'Adenauer Era', the Federal Republic made greater progress towards a free but ordered way of life than any other major Continental power.

The 'Adenauer Era' has been blamed for a measure of spiritual frustration, unrest among youth, growth of materialism, anarchist deviationism and dearth of constructive ideas. Adenauer would have had little sympathy for the juvenile *Jacquerie* of Red Rudi Dutschke, or the off-beat philosophic despair of Herbert Marcuse. Nor would he have felt any responsibility for such developments. The same sort of thing was happening in every other European democracy. It is not just England which, in the words of the American statesman Dean Acheson, 'has lost an Empire but failed to find a new role'. Europe has become no more than a fringe along the shores of the Atlantic. This is the principal reason for European loss of sense of purpose, self-confidence and faith. Adenauer was one of the few post-1945 statesmen who sought to give this morally, as well as physically, shrunken Europe a new role. 'Fathers,' one is told, 'can teach, but never father-figures.'[31] Very good; but even if widely regarded as a father-figure, Adenauer had views which were both enlightened and his own.

Bismarck, it was said, considered politics to be not a science, but an art.[32] Adenauer saw politics, rather, as a vehicle for the exercise and implementation of the guiding principles in which he believed. In 1946 he told an American journalist: 'Any fool, Nazi or Communist maybe, can be a man of conviction. In fact, fanatics are sincere, all too sincere. What I am interested in are values, permanent values. And if you have values, you may have a prejudice here and there.'[33] Speaking like this, Adenauer was the living testimony that the Rhineland was once a Roman province. Not for him the Teutonic creed of dynamism, the primitive mythology of the great Northern forests or the berserk rage of the followers of Thor and his mighty hammer. The Roman virtues were clarity of thought and expression, the ordered life and the supremacy of the law. These were virtues in which Adenauer implicitly believed. He broke away from the long-established traditions of hysteria and hate, of gods and demons dominating the German scene. He gave the German people a long overdue

31..........*Zwanzig Jahre Danach*, Helmut Lindemann, p. 145. Edited Helmut Hammerschmidt.

32..........*From Bismarck to Adenauer*, Gordon A. Craig, p. 23.

33..........James O'Donnell, in a personal memorandum on Adenauer.

dose of commonsense, as well as *das kleine Habe* – a decent competence in material well-being.

Like the skilful investor, Adenauer did not aim at too many targets or dissipate his purposes in too many ideas. He operated within his own capacities and with due regard for his own shortcomings. Like the best kind of craftsman, he did not let his thoughts and his plans rove too far into the future. He kept his eye and his hand on the immediate task, and he discharged it with unfailing patience and tenacity. It was primarily due to him that the makeshift Federal Republic developed into a consolidated democracy.

He dedicated his memoirs 'to my Fatherland' – '*an meinem Vaterland*'. This would have done well enough as his own epitaph. Or one may prefer George Bernanos' aphorism – '*La plus haute forme de l'espérance, c'est le désespoir surmonté.*' – 'The noblest form of hope is the triumph over despair.' Adenauer conquered the despair of the Nazi Era and of the criminal war which he knew his country had to lose. His place in German and European history is assured, irrespective of what is happening now or may happen in the future. History continues to advance. The old Germany may never be restored; but Adenauer was the principal architect of the new.

Bibliography

ABSHAGEN, Karl-Heinz, *Schuld und Verhängnis*, Stuttgart, Union Verlag, 1961
ADENAUER, Konrad, *Memoirs*, VOL 1, London, Weidenfeld and Nicolson, 1966
VOL 2, Stuttgart, Deutsche Verlagsanstalt, 1966
VOL 3, Stuttgart, Deutsche Verlagsanstalt, 1967
VOL 4, Stuttgart, Deutsche Verlagsanstalt, 1968
ALEXANDER, Edgar, *Adenauer and the New Germany*, New York, Farrar, Straus and Cudahy, 1957
ALLEMANN, Fritz Rene, *Bonn ist nicht Weimar*, Cologne, Kiepenhauer and Witsch, 1956
ALLEMANN, Fritz René, *Zwischen Stabilität und Krise*, Munich, Piper Verlag, 1963
ALTMANN, Rüdiger, *Das Erbe Adenauers*, Munich, Kindler Verlag, 1963
ARNTZ, Helmut (Editor), *Regierung Adenauer 1949–63*, Wiesbaden, Franz Steiner Verlag, 1963
AUGSTEIN, Rudolf, *Konrad Adenauer*, London, Secker and Warburg, 1964
BALFOUR, Michael and MAIR, John, *Four Power Control in Germany and Austria*, London, Oxford University Press, 1956
BARING, Arnulf, *Aussenpolitik in Adenauer's Kanzler Demokratie*, Munich, Oldenbourg Verlag, 1969
BETHGE, Eberhard, *Dietrich Bonhöffer*, London, Collins, 1970
BLUM, Hans (Editor), *Aus kölnischer und rheinischer Geschichte*, Cologne, Wamper Verlag, 1969
BONHÖFFER, Dietrich, *Letters and Papers from Prison*, London, Fontana, 1959
BRANDT, Willy, *A Peace Policy for Europe*, London, Weidenfeld and Nicolson, 1969
BRANT, Stefan, *The East German Rising*, London, Thames and Hudson, 1955
BRENTANO, Heinrich von, *Germany and Europe*, London, André Deutsch, 1964
CHALMER, Douglas A., *The Social Democratic Party of Germany*, New Haven, Yale University Press, 1964
CHAMBERLIN, William Henry, *The German Phoenix*, London, Robert Hale, 1964
CHRIST, George E., *The Myth of Munich*, London, E. D. O'Brien, 1969
CLAY, General Lucius, *Decision in Germany*, New York, Doubleday
COBLENZ, Gaston, *Duel at the Brink*, Weidenfeld and Nicolson
CONANT, James Bryant, *Germany and Freedom*, Baltimore, Johns Hopkins, 1958
CONNELL, Brian, *Watcher on the Rhine*, London, Weidenfeld and Nicolson, 1957
CONZE, Werner, *Die Zeit Wilhelm II und die Weimarer Republik*, Tübingen, Verlag Hermann Leins, 1964
CRAIG, Gordon A., *From Bismarck to Adenauer*, Baltimore, Johns Hopkins, 1958
CRAWLEY, Aidan, *De Gaulle*, London, Literary Guild, 1969
DAVIDSON, Basil, *Germany. What Now?*, London, Frederick Muller, 1950
DILL, Marshal jnr, *Germany*, Ann Arbor, University of Michigan Press, 1961
ECKARDT, Felix von, *Ein Unordentliches Leben*, Düsseldorf, Econ Verlag, 1967
EDEN, Sir Anthony, *Full Circle*, London, Cassell, 1960
EDINGER, Lewis J., *Kurt Schumacher*, Stanford, University Press, 1965

EINSIEDEL, Heinrich von, *The Shadow of Stalingrad*, London, Allan Wingate, 1953
EMMET, Christopher and MUHLON, Norbert, *The Vanishing Swastika*, Chicago, Henry Regnery Co., 1961
ERDMANN, Karl Dieter, *Adenauer in der Rheinlandpolitik nach dem ersten Weltkrieg*, Stuttgart, Ernst Klett Verlag, 1966
ERHARD, Ludwig, *The Economics of Success*, London, Thames & Hudson, 1963
ESCHENBURG, Theodor, *Zur politischen Praxis in der Bundesrepublik*, Munich, Piper Verlag, 1963
FEST, Joachim, *The Face of the Third Reich*, London, Weidenfeld and Nicolson, 1970
FRISCHAUER, Willi, *The Man who Came Back*, London, Frederick Muller, 1958
GATZKE, Hans W., *Stresemann and the Rearmament of Germany*, Baltimore, Johns Hopkins, 1954
GERARD, James W., *My Four Years in Germany*, London, Hodder & Stoughton, 1917
GOLDMANN, Nahum, *Memories*, London, Weidenfeld and Nicolson, 1970
GRASS, Günter, *Speak Out!*, New York, Harcourt Brace, 1969
GREBBING, Helga, *The History of the German Labour Movement*, London, Oswald Wolff, 1969
GROSSER, Alfred, *Western Germany from Defeat to Rearmament*, London, Allen & Unwin, 1955
GROSSER, Alfred, *Der Bundesrepublik Deutschland*, Tübingen, Rainer Wunderlich Verlag, 1967
HAMMERSCHMIDT, Helmut (Editor), *Zwanzig Jahre Danach*, Munich, Verlag Kurt Desch, 1965
HAYTER, Sir William, *The Diplomacy of the Great Powers*, London, Hamish Hamilton, 1960
HEIDELMEYER, Wolfgang (Editor), *Documents on Berlin*, Munich, Oldenbourg Verlag, 1963
HEIDENHEIMER, Arnold J., *Adenauer and the CDU*, The Hague, Martinus Nighoff, 1960
HEIDENHEIMER, Arnold J., *The Governments of Germany*, New York, Thomas Y. Crowell, 1964
HENDERSON, Sir Nevile, *Failure of a Mission*, London, Hodder & Stoughton, 1940
HENKELS, Walter, *Gar nicht so Pingelig*, Düsseldorf, Econ Verlag, 1965
HEUSS, Theodor, *Bilder meines Lebens*, Tübingen, Rainer Wunderlich Verlag, 1964
HEUSS, Theodor, *Würdigungen*, Tübingen, Rainer Wunderlich Verlag, 1955
HISCOCKS, Richard, *Democracy in Western Germany*, London, Oxford University Press, 1957
HOEHNE, Heinz, *The Order of the Death's Head*, London, Secker & Warburg, 1969
HORNE, Alistair, *The Price of Glory*, London, Macmillan, 1962
HUBATSCH, Walther (Editor), *The German Question*, New York, Herder Book Center, 1967
KENNAN, George F., *Realities of American Foreign Policy*, London, Oxford University Press, 1954
KING-HALL, Sir Stephen, *German Parliaments*, London, Hansard Society, 1954
KIRKPATRICK, Sir Ivone, *The Inner Circle*, London, Macmillan, 1959
KITZINGER, Uwe, *German Electoral Politics*, Oxford, Clarendon Press, 1960
KNICKERBOCKER, H. R., *Germany. Fascist or Soviet?*, London, Bodley Head, 1932
KOHN, Hans (Editor), *German History. Some new German Views*, London, Allen & Unwin, 1954
KOHN, Hans, *The Mind of Germany*, London, Macmillan, 1961

LEMMER, Ernst, *Manches war doch Anderes*, Frankfurt, Verlag Heinrich Scheffler, 1968
LEONHARDT, Wolfgang, *This Germany*, Greenwich, New York Graphic Society, 1955
MACMILLAN, Harold, *Tides of Fortune 1945–55*, London, Macmillan, 1969
MAIER, Reinhold, *Ein Grundstein wird gelegt*, Tübingen, Rainer Wunderlich Verlag, 1964
MARRIOTT, J. A. R., *The Evolution of Prussia*, Oxford, University Press, 1917
MCBRIDE, Will and FINCKENSTEIN, Hans Werner Graf von, *Adenauer, Ein Porträt*, Starnberg, Joseph Keller Verlag, 1965
MCCORMICK, Donald, *Mr France*, New York, Jarrolds, 1955
MCDERMOTT, Geoffrey, *Berlin. Success of a Mission*, London, André Deutsch, 1962
MEINHARDT, Günther, *Adenauer und der rheinische Separatismus*, Recklinghausen, Kommunal Verlag, 1962
MOMMSEN, Wilhelm, *Deutsche Parteiprogramme*, Munich, Isar Verlag, 1951
MOWAT, R. C., *Ruin and Resurgence*, London, Blandford Press, 1966
MÜLLER, Hans Dieter, *Press Power. A Study of Axel Springer*, London, Macdonald, 1969
MUMM, Reinhard, *Der Christlich-Soziale Gedanke*, Berlin, Mittler, 1933
NAMIER, Sir Lewis, *In the Nazi Era*, London, Macmillan, 1952
NAUMANN, Friedrich, *Die Politischen Parteien*, Berlin, Georg Remer Verlag, 1913
NELSON, Walter Henry, *The Berliners*, New York, David Mackay, 1969
NELSON, Walter Henry, *The Soldier Kings*, New York, Putnam, 1970
NETZER, Hans-Joachim (Editor), *Adenauer und die Folgen*, Munich, Verlag Beck, 1965
NEVEN-DUMONT, Jürgen, *After Hitler*, London, Penguin Press, 1970
OPPEN, Beate von (Editor), *Documents on Germany 1945–55*, London, Oxford University Press, 1955
OSTERROTH, Franz, *Chronik der Sozialistischen Bewegung Deutschlands*, Bonn, SPD Press, 1957
PAKENHAM, Lord, *Born to Believe*, London, Jonathan Cape, 1953
PECK, Joachim, *Dr Konrad Adenauer 1917–1952*, Berlin, Verlag der Nation, 1952
PRITTIE, Terence, *Germany Divided*, London, Hutchinson, 1961
PRITTIE, Terence, *Germans Against Hitler*, Boston, Little Brown, 1964
REICHARDT, Fritz, *Andreas Hermes*, Neuwied, Raffeisendrueckerei, 1953
REUTHER, Helmut, *Adenauer. Bildnis und Deutung*, Bonn–Beuel, Komm mit Verlag, 1963
ROWSE, A. L., *All Souls and Appeasement*, London, Macmillan, 1961
RUGE, Friedrich, *Politik, Militaer, Buendnis*, Stuttgart, Deutsche Verlagsanstalt, 1963
SCHÄFER, Emil, *Von Potsdam bis Bonn*, Lahr, Verlag Schauenburg, 1950
SCHLABRENDORFF, Fabian von, *The Secret War against Hitler*, New York, Putnam, 1965
SCHRÖDER, Georg (Editor), *Konrad Adenauer, Eine Bilddokumentation*, Guetersloh, Bertelsmann Verlag, 1966
SCHRÖDER, Gerhard, *Decision for Europe*, London, Thames & Hudson, 1964
SCHULZ, Gerhard, *Die CDU: Merkmale ihres Aufbaues*, Stuttgart, Ring Verlag, 1955
SCHUMACHER, Fritz, *Stufen des Lebens*, Stuttgart, Deutsche Verlagsanstalt, 1935
SCHUETZ, Wilhelm Wolfgang, *Rethinking German Policy*, New York, Praeger, 1967
SCHWERING, Leo, *Frühgeschichte der Christlich-Demokratische Union*, Recklinghausen, Kommunal Verlag, 1963

SEALE, Patrick and MCCONVILLE, Maureen, *French Revolution 1968*, London, Penguin, 1968
SEIFERT, Jürgen (Editor), *Die Spiegel Affäre*, Olten, Walter Verlag, 1966
SETTEL, Arthur (Editor), *This is Germany*, New York, William Sloane, 1950
SHIRER, William L., *The Rise and Fall of the Third Reich*, New York, Simon & Schuster, 1960
SMITH, Jean Edward, *Germany Beyond the Wall*, Boston, Little Brown, 1969
STAHL, Walter (Editor), *The Politics of Post-War Germany*, New York, Praeger, 1963
STEGERWALD, Adam, *Deutsche Lebensfragen*, Berlin, Verlag fuer Politik und Wirtschaft, 1921
STEINERT, Marlis, *Capitulation, 1945*, London, Constable, 1969
STERN, Carola, *Ulbricht*, Cologne, Kiepenhauer & Witsch, 1963
STERNBERGER, Dolf, *Lebende Verfassung*, Miesenheim, Hain Verlag, 1956
STRAUSS, Franz Josef, *The Grand Design*, London, Weidenfeld and Nicolson, 1965
THAYER, Charles, *The Unquiet Germans*, London, Michael Joseph, 1958
TREVOR-ROPER, H. R., *The Last Days of Hitler*, London, Macmillan, 1946
VANSITTART, Lord, *The Mist Procession*, London, Hutchinson, 1958
VARIOUS AUTHORS, *Sind die Deutschen wirklich so?*, Herrenalb, Horst Erdmann Verlag, 1965
Die Universität Köln 1919–24, Cologne, Oskar Mueller, 1925
Die Universität Köln 1919–29, Cologne, Dumont Schauberg, 1930
Deutsche und Juden, Frankfurt, Suhrkamp, 1967
Adenauer, Würdigung und Dank, Bonn, Bundespressamt, 1964
Russia and the West, 1945–63, London, COI, 1963
Background of Heads of Government Conference 1960, Washington, Dept of State, 1960
VOGEL, Rolf (Editor), *The German Path to Israel*, London, Oswald Wolff, 1969
WALSER, Martin (Editor), *Die Alternative*, Hamburg, Rowohlt, 1961
WELTERS, Hans and LOBECK, Helmut, *Kleine Illustrierte Geschicht des Stadt Köln*, Cologne, Bachem Verlag, 1958
WEYMAR, Paul, *Konrad Adenauer*, London, André Deutsch, 1957
WHEELER-BENNETT, Sir John, *The Nemesis of Power*, New York, Macmillan, 1953
WHITE, Theodore H., *Fire in the Ashes*, New York, William Sloane, 1953
WIECK, H. G., *Die Entstehung der CDU und die Wiedergrundung des Zentrums im Jahre 1945*, Düsseldorf, Droste Verlag, 1953
WIECK, H. G., *Christliche und freie Demokraten in Hessen, Rheinland-Pfalz, Baden und Württemberg*, Düsseldorf, Droste Verlag, 1958
WIGHTON, Charles, *Adenauer. Democratic Dictator*, London, Frederick Muller, 1963
WILLIS, F. Roy, *France, Germany and the New Europe*, Stanford, University Press, 1965
WINDSOR, Philip, *City on Leave*, London, Chatto & Windus, 1963
WINDSOR, Philip, *German reunification*, London, Paul Elek, 1969
WISKEMANN, Elizabeth, *Germany's Eastern Neighbours*, London, Oxford University Press, 1956
ZINK, Harold, *The United States in Germany 1945–55*, Princeton, Van Nostrand, 1957

Index